GREECE, EUROPEAN POLITICAL COOPERATION AND
THE MACEDONIAN QUESTION

# Greece, European Political Cooperation and the Macedonian Question

ARISTOTLE TZIAMPIRIS

LONDON AND NEW YORK

First published 2000 by Ashgate Publishing

Reissued 2018 by Routledge
2 Park Square, Milton Park, Abingdon, Oxon OX14 4RN
711 Third Avenue, New York, NY 10017, USA

*Routledge is an imprint of the Taylor & Francis Group, an informa business*

Copyright © Aristotle Tziampiris 2000

All rights reserved. No part of this book may be reprinted or reproduced or utilised in any form or by any electronic, mechanical, or other means, now known or hereafter invented, including photocopying and recording, or in any information storage or retrieval system, without permission in writing from the publishers.

Notice:
Product or corporate names may be trademarks or registered trademarks, and are used only for identification and explanation without intent to infringe.

Publisher's Note
The publisher has gone to great lengths to ensure the quality of this reprint but points out that some imperfections in the original copies may be apparent.

Disclaimer
The publisher has made every effort to trace copyright holders and welcomes correspondence from those they have been unable to contact.

A Library of Congress record exists under LC control number: 00134474

ISBN 13: 978-1-138-73705-1 (hbk)
ISBN 13: 978-1-138-73704-4 (pbk)
ISBN 13: 978-1-315-18558-3 (ebk)

# Contents

| | |
|---|---|
| List of Tables | vii |
| List of Maps | ix |
| List of Appendices | xi |
| Preface | xiii |
| Acknowledgements | xv |
| List of Abbreviations | xvii |
| Introduction | xix |

1    The Theory of Institutionalism     1
     A.    Defining International Regimes     1
     B.    The Functional Approach to International Regimes     4
     C.    Institutionalist Theory     10

2    EPC as an International Regime     21
     A.    The Road to EPC     21
     B.    Principles     23
     C.    Norms     25
     D.    Rules     28
     E.    Decision-Making Procedures     30
     F.    Scope     32
     G    Organisational Form     33

3    'One of the Most Explosive Topics in the Universe'     39
     A.    The Importance and Origins of the Macedonian Question     39
     B.    Armed Struggle in Macedonia     42
     C.    The Communist Factor     44
     D.    The Contentious Emergence of FYROM     48
     E.    Greece and FYROM: An Account of Common Interests     50

4    The Politics of Greek Cooperation, June 1991-January 1992     63
     A.    Yugoslavia Disintegrates, EPC Mediates and Greece Cooperates     63

|   |    |                                                                        |     |
|---|----|------------------------------------------------------------------------|-----|
|   | B. | The Intensification of Greek Cooperation                               | 67  |
|   | C. | The Issue of Recognition                                               | 70  |
| 5 |    | The Politics of Greek Cooperation: Explanation and Decline             | 85  |
|   | A. | The Problematic Nature of the Politics of Greek Cooperation            | 85  |
|   | B. | Greek Foreign Policy Objectives                                        | 89  |
|   | C. | Institutionalist Relevance                                             | 92  |
|   | D. | The Decline of the Politics of Greek Cooperation                       | 96  |
| 6 |    | The Challenge of Samaras, February-April 1992                          | 109 |
|   | A. | The Political Parties Respond to Popular Discontent                    | 109 |
|   | B. | Samaras Attacks His Government                                         | 114 |
|   | C. | The 'Pinheiro Package' and the Break with Samaras                      | 117 |
|   | D. | The Point of No Return: 13 April 1992                                  | 122 |
|   | E. | The Beginning of Institutionalist Breakdown                            | 125 |
| 7 |    | The Politics of Limited Greek Cooperation and Confrontation, April-December 1992 | 137 |
|   | A. | Limited Greek Cooperation: The Road to Lisbon                          | 137 |
|   | B. | Greek Confrontation                                                    | 144 |
|   | C. | The Continuation of Institutionalist Breakdown                         | 154 |
| 8 |    | Conclusions                                                            | 167 |
|   | A. | The Theory of Institutionalism Reconsidered                            | 167 |
|   | B. | EPC as an International Regime: An Evaluation                          | 172 |
|   | C. | Lessons on the Conduct of Greek Foreign Policy                         | 177 |

*Tables* 187
*Maps* 191
*Appendices* 201
*Bibliography* 265
*Index* 293

# List of Tables

TABLE I The Prisoner's Dilemma                                189

TABLE II FYROM's imports and exports with Greece              190

# List of Maps

MAP I                                                                                      193
Post-War Yugoslavia (1945-1991)

MAP II                                                                                     194
Territorial settlements at the Treaties of San Stephano (1878) and
Berlin (1878)

MAP III                                                                                    195
Territorial agreements of the March 1912 alliance between
Bulgaria and Serbia

MAP IV                                                                                     196
Territorial settlements of the May 1913 London Conference and the
August 1913 Treaty of Bucharest

MAP V                                                                                      197
Bulgaria's conquests during the First World War

MAP VI                                                                                     198
The Balkan States after the First World War and the Treaty of Neuilly

MAP VII                                                                                    199
Bulgarian conquests during the Second World War

# List of Appendices

**APPENDIX I**      203
Examples of propaganda practised by FYROM against Greece.

**APPENDIX II**      207
Letter that Greece's Foreign Minister Antonis Samaras sent to his EPC counterparts on 17 January 1992. The official English translation of this letter is published here for the first time.

**APPENDIX III**      214
Founding declaration of the Macedonian Committee that was issued on 17 January 1992.

**APPENDIX IV**      218
Previously unpublished Address that was delivered by Greece's Foreign Minister Antonis Samaras to his EPC counterparts in Lisbon on 17 January 1992.

**APPENDIX V**      233
Letter that US Secretary of State James Baker sent to Greek Foreign Minister Antonis Samaras on 5 March 1992. It is published here in its entirety for the first time.

**APPENDIX VI**      237
Previously unpublished list by Greece's Ministry of Foreign Affairs containing projects aimed at developing economic relations between Greece and FYROM.

**APPENDIX VII**      238
Previously unpublished telegram that Greece's Prime Minister Konstantinos Mitsotakis sent to various Greek Embassies on 15 May 1992.

XII    GREECE, EUROPEAN POLITICAL COOPERATION AND THE MACEDONIAN QUESTION

APPENDIX VIII                                                                 241
The flag that FYROM's Parliament adopted on 11 August 1992 and an
ancient representation of the Vergina Star.

APPENDIX IX                                                                   242
Previously unpublished letter that Greece's Foreign Minister Michalis
Papaconstantinou sent to his EPC counterparts on 12 October 1992.

APPENDIX X                                                                    243
Previously unpublished speech that Greek Foreign Minister Michalis
Papaconstantinou gave during the crucial meeting of New Democracy's
Parliamentary Group on 21 October 1992.

APPENDIX XI                                                                   247
Previously unpublished excerpts from Antonis Samaras' speech and
supporting documents that the former Greek Foreign Minister presented
at the 21 October 1992 meeting of New Democracy's Parliamentary
Group.

APPENDIX XII                                                                  259
Previously unpublished letter that Greek Foreign Minister Michalis
Papaconstantinou sent to his EPC counterparts on 3 November 1992.

APPENDIX XIII                                                                 261
Previously unpublished letter that FYROM's President Kiro Gligorov
sent to Greek Prime Minister Konstantinos Mitsotakis on 2 December
1992.

APPENDIX XIV                                                                  263
Letter that Antonis Samaras sent to Konstantinos Mitsotakis on 15
March 1993. It is published here in its entirety for the first time.

# Preface

The purpose of this study is to present and explain Greece's foreign policy towards former Yugoslavia within the context of European Political Cooperation (EPC) during the period of June 1991-December 1992. This aspect of Greece's foreign policy was primarily defined by the dispute with the Former Yugoslav Republic of Macedonia (FYROM), and essentially constituted the more recent manifestation of the Macedonian Question.

The analysis of Greek foreign policy within EPC will be based on the theory of institutionalism, which claims that international regimes can influence state behavior towards cooperative actions. The application of institutionalism requires the existence of common interests and the presence of at least one regime. This book shows the significant interests shared by Greece and FYROM, as well as how EPC can be viewed as a regime. Crucially, EPC was primarily responsible for dealing with issues arising from the disintegration of Yugoslavia during the months covered in this study. It will be demonstrated that until mid-January 1992, the Greek government pursued politics of cooperation and flexibility, often contrary to perceived national interests. These politics were primarily regime-produced and related, and hence explained by the theory of institutionalism.

After 17 January 1991 however, Greece practised politics of limited cooperation within EPC and confrontation against FYROM. The issue of the new republic's exact name gradually became of paramount importance, provoking popular passions and subordinating all other issues and concerns connected to former Yugoslavia. Such developments were ultimately the result of domestic and partisan politics that were entirely unrelated to EPC, thus causing the decline of institutionalism's explanatory power.

Given this record, this study will argue that the specific expansion of the conditions required for the application of institutionalism would allow the theory to retain its explanatory and predictive relevance. Finally, specific lessons on the conduct of Greek foreign policy will be discussed.

Throughout this book I have strived not to be influenced by personal feelings and opinions, which are rather strong on the Macedonian Question. My ancestors fought with Greece's national hero Pavlos Melas during the

Greek struggle in Ottoman Macedonia in the early 20th century, while I personally participated in a huge demonstration that took place in Thessaloniki in 1994. I have laboured to remain objective, and I regard it as a high compliment that a very careful and critical reader of this study (as well as a famous Professor of International Relations who is not particularly sympathetic to Greek concerns), concluded that he could detect some national bias in only two footnotes.

I must also stress that this book does not constitute a partisan undertaking aiming to vilify certain politicians while verging on the territory of hagiography when relating the actions of others. Nevertheless, although the primary purpose of this academic study has been to explain and not to judge, the attentive reader will inevitably reach conclusions about both the events and protagonists that are presented in the subsequent chapters.

# Acknowledgements

The writing of this book which is dedicated to my family, is based on my PhD thesis at the London School of Economics and Political Science, and would hence have been impossible without the guidance, encouragement and wisdom of my supervisors, Dr Howard Machin and Dr Spyros Economides. My debt to them is enormous. Dr Elias Mossialos also deserves particular recognition for being my mentor and close friend for all the years that I spent studying in London. Moreover, I would like to thank several people whom I also regard as my friends. They have been a source of help, encouragement, inspiration, wisdom and admiration. Thus, special thanks to Niki Kalogiratou, Maria Ammari, Nicolas Bakatselos, Brianna Becker, Sarah Cameron, Penelope Emmanouelidou, Yiannis Evrigenis, Maria Kangelidou, Yiorgos Papadopoulos, Dimitris Pavlakis, Natasa Pazaiti, Hilary Rose, Lisa Sotiriadou, Mirto Tachia, Nicholas Trimmatis and Chiara Vascotto. The constant kindness and support of Diana and Jack Clymer, Paola and Konstantinos Tsakiris, and Tania and Thanasis Vildiridis also deserve particular acknowledgement. Finally, I would like to thank Greece's former Prime Minister Konstantinos Mitsotakis and former Foreign Ministers Michalis Papaconstantinou and Antonis Samaras, for sharing so much with a student of politics. Of course, I am solely responsible for the arguments and conclusions presented in this book.

# List of Abbreviations

| | |
|---|---|
| AC | Arbitration Commission. |
| ASNOM | Anti-Fascist Assembly of the National Liberation of Macedonia. |
| COREPER | Committee of Permanent Representatives. |
| CFSP | Common Foreign and Security Policy. |
| CSCE | Conference on Security and Cooperation in Europe. |
| CSO | Committee of Senior Officials. |
| DSE | Democratic Army of Greece. |
| EAGGF | European Agricultural Guidance and Guarantee Fund. |
| EAM | National Liberation Front. |
| EC | European Community. |
| ECJ | European Court of Justice. |
| ECU | European Currency Unit. |
| EDC | European Defence Community. |
| EDES | National Democratic Greek League. |
| EIB | European Investment Bank. |
| ELAS | National Popular Liberation Army. |
| EMU | Economic and Monetary Union. |
| EP | European Parliament. |
| EPC | European Political Cooperation. |
| ERDF | European Regional Development Fund. |
| ESF | European Social Fund. |
| EU | European Union. |
| FYROM | Former Yugoslav Republic of Macedonia. |
| GATT | General Agreement on Tariffs and Trade. |
| GDP | Gross Domestic Product. |
| ICJ | International Court of Justice. |
| IMF | International Monetary Fund. |
| IMRO | Internal Macedonian Revolutionary Organisation. |
| ITO | International Trade Organisation. |

| | |
|---|---|
| JNA | Yugoslav National Army. |
| KEDKE | Central Committee of Municipalities and Communities of Greece. |
| KKE | Greek Communist Party. |
| OAKKE | Organisation for the Reconstruction of the Greek Communist Party. |
| MEP | Member of the European Parliament. |
| MP | Member of Parliament. |
| NATO | North Atlantic Treaty Organisation. |
| ND | New Democracy. |
| NOF | Popular Liberation Front. |
| PASOK | Panhellenic Socialist Movement. |
| PD | Prisoner's Dilemma. |
| PHARE | Poland and Hungary: Aid for Economic Reconstruction. |
| SEA | Single European Act. |
| SNOF | Slav Macedonian Popular Liberation Front. |
| TEU | Treaty on European Union. |
| UN | United Nations. |
| VMRO-DPNE | Internal Macedonian Revolutionary Organisation-Democratic Party of Macedonian National Unity. |
| WEU | Western European Union. |

# Introduction

Macedonia has evidently lost none of its power to excite.

-Mark Mazower, *Introduction to the Study of Macedonia*, 1996.

The disintegration of Yugoslavia has been the most violent event in Europe since the conclusion of the Greek Civil War in 1949.[1] The dissolution and destruction of a country resulting in the death of more than 300,000 people '68,000 wounded [and] 3 million refugees,' the practice of 'ethnic cleansing,' the establishment of concentration camps and numerous instances of unimaginable brutality, constitute central aspects of a conflict that shocked world opinion.[2]

Its resolution eventually required the active involvement of several states, organisations and institutions. However, beginning in the summer of 1991 and for a significant period of time, it was European Political Cooperation (EPC) that was primarily responsible for addressing the many problems emanating from the war. As an EPC member that actually neighboured Yugoslavia, Greece had undisputed and significant security and foreign policy interests in the region, as well as the power to veto all EPC decisions.

Despite the seriousness of the Yugoslav crisis and its importance to Greece, the actions of the country's government have been portrayed as extremely non-cooperative and counter-productive, ultimately endangering the efforts to contain and end the Yugoslav War.[3] Most criticisms revolve around the dispute with the Former Yugoslav Republic of Macedonia (FYROM).[4] At issue were the new republic's name, actions, certain constitutional provisions, various propaganda claims and ultimately its identity and survival. This dispute constitutes the most recent development in the more than century-old Macedonian Question, which (as will be explained in the relevant chapter) has played a crucial and often fateful role in the international politics of the Balkans since at least 1870. The geographic region of Macedonia has been the apple of discord among many states and in order to gain eventually its larger part, the Greek people have fought a number of costly and traumatic wars. This historical record partly explains their sensitivity and reactions that will be presented in this book.

Despite the widespread perception to the contrary, a closer examination of Greece's behaviour will actually reveal that the country's government also pursued substantial politics of cooperation, moderation and flexibility towards former Yugoslavia and FYROM, especially between June 1991 and 17 January 1992. For instance, the possibility of a compromise on the new republic's name was maintained, bilateral talks sponsored, and decisions of a confrontational nature against FYROM were avoided almost entirely. Further instances of cooperation included agreement to EPC's recognition of Croatia and Bosnia, the imposition of an arms embargo and a trade embargo on all Yugoslav republics, as well as the eventual maintenance of the latter only against Serbia and Montenegro.

Significantly, Greece's foreign-policy record incorporates the endorsement of decisions that were regarded by key decision-makers as negative for the region and contrary to at least some national interests. Hence, it will be shown that EPC was allowed to establish an Arbitration Commission with responsibility to advise on whether any Yugoslav republics merited recognition, thus allowing the possibility of a favourable ruling concerning FYROM. Furthermore, the decisions to recognise Croatia and particularly Bosnia (both signed by Greece), were seen as serious EPC mistakes that would contribute to the escalation of the war in Yugoslavia. Also, the Greek government endorsed unfailingly EPC's singling out, condemnation and penalisation of Serbia as the state primarily responsible for the war in Yugoslavia, despite the existence (as will be analysed), of a special Greco-Serbian relationship.

The process of the decline of the politics of cooperation began on 17 January 1992, when a restrictive but negotiable position was adopted according to which the word Macedonia had to be excluded from FYROM's name. In order to comprehend and trace this process, it will be necessary to make a 'boundary change' and 'plunge' into an account of Greek domestic and partisan politics.[5] Crucial events such as the huge Thessaloniki demonstration of 14 February 1992, and the high-stakes campaign of Foreign Minister Antonis Samaras against his government will be discussed. It will be shown that the ultimate result was the pursuit of a non-negotiable restrictive policy concerning the new republic's name, and the subordination of all other decisions regarding former Yugoslavia to this name-issue. Subsequently, limited cooperation was practised within EPC, while confrontational politics were pursued against FYROM. This strategy found expression in decisions such as the imposition of an oil embargo on the new republic, the 'story of the labels,' the rather creative dual name formula, as well as the rejection of some major EPC mediative efforts. Greece's foreign policy record towards former Yugoslavia and FYROM will hence prove to be rather 'mixed,' exhibiting serious cooperative efforts, as well as confrontation and discord. It will be the purpose of this book to present and explain precisely this record.[6]

The period that will be analysed in detail begins with EPC's early efforts towards a Yugoslavia that was sliding towards war, and ends with the December 1992 Edinburgh European Council meeting. There is consensus among experts and decision-makers that the latter date signals the end of EPC being the most significant and influential actor dealing with Greek foreign policy towards Yugoslavia and FYROM.[7] After December 1992, the UN and the US become far more important, while EPC recedes to the background. Hence, the examination of this period provides the opportunity to analyse the effect of EPC on Greek state action, when there was the minimum possible influence and interference by other actors.

The attempt to explain Greece's foreign policy, and especially its cooperative aspects will be based on the insights of the theory of institutionalism. The theory's core arguments are provided by the 'functional' approach to international regimes.[8] After defining international regimes, it will be explained that according to the functional logic, regimes can promote cooperation by helping create economies of scale, institutionalise reciprocity, link the present with the future, increase reputational concerns, reduce transaction costs, provide reliable information, and facilitate bargaining by creating linkages and increasing issue density.

By accepting this analysis, the theory proclaims that institutions can influence state behaviour. Thus, an institutionalist explanation of Greek foreign policy would concentrate on the effects of EPC, viewed as an international regime. In other words, the theory would ultimately attribute instances of Greek cooperation to the influence of the relevant international regime.

As will be shown, the application of institutionalism requires the prior satisfaction of certain conditions. Most importantly, the theory claims relevance only when some mutual interests exist among actors. This condition will be satisfied by the book's' case-study, since the desire that the war in Yugoslavia be contained and not spread to the new republic was shared by Greece, FYROM, as well as all EPC member states. Although this constituted the most important common interest, others also existed. For example, a resolution of the dispute would have allowed FYROM's international recognition and the securing of much needed aid. On the other hand, Greece would have avoided serious reputational costs, and gained an opportunity to exploit its larger economy and comparative advantages by penetrating FYROM's market.

Any fruitful and meaningful application of the theory of institutionalism also requires the active presence of at least one regime. Hence, the demonstration of how EPC can be viewed as an international regime becomes necessary. This will be undertaken in the relevant chapter, which will contain an analysis of EPC's principles, norms, rules, decision-making procedures, organisational form and scope.[9]

In assessing the explanatory power of institutionalism, it should be stressed that

> The proper test of a functional theory is not the mere existence of a regime, but the demonstration that actors' behaviour was motivated by benefits provided uniquely, or at least more efficiently, through the regime, or by reputational concerns connected to the existence of rules.[10]

Proving the theory's relevance requires an attempt

> To identify issues on which regime rules conflicted with the perceptions of self-interest held by governments...We could then ask whether the reputational and other incentives to abide by regime rules outweighed the incentives to break those rules. How much impact did the regime rules have? Only by examining internal debates on such issues could the analyst go beyond the self-justificatory rhetoric of governments.[11]

While following such an approach, the danger of counter-factual arguing must be both appreciated and avoided. This was missed by Keohane and Nye who argued that empirical studies, in order

> To ascertain the impact of the regime...must trace internal decision-making processes to discover what strategies *would have been* followed in the absence of regime rules.[12]

It is however impossible to know with any sufficient or satisfactory degree of certainty what *might* have happened, though it can be investigated *why* and *how* certain events did take place. Thus, this book will attempt to explain the *actual* influence that an international regime had on Greece's foreign policy within the context of EPC.

The proposed case-study may be considered a difficult one for institutionalism, since many scholars have claimed that it has greater explanatory power when applied to issues of the environment or of political economy.[13] Nevertheless, studies have also claimed that institutionalism is relevant and applicable to foreign affairs and security issues.[14] What is essential for its application is not the issue area examined, but that the theory's conditional nature is satisfied; and this will clearly be accomplished in this book.

Furthermore, there is considerable virtue in presenting a 'difficult' case-study.[15] To quote Kenneth Waltz,

> We should [try to] make tests even more difficult. If we observe outcomes that the theory leads us to expect even though strong forces work against them, the theory will command belief.[16]

On the basis of its empirical research, this book will eventually 'dissect,' and analyse Greek foreign policy towards former Yugoslavia within the context of EPC during the period of June 1991-December 1992. The final sections will present an assessment of the relevance of the theory of institutionalism to this study. Significantly, certain specific amendments expanding the theory's conditional nature will be proposed. Such an expansion will allow the theory of institutionalism to retain its explanatory relevance and power by avoiding application to issues in which it almost certainly exhibit 'poor' theoretical results, regardless of the existence of common interests.

This book's conclusions will also include a discussion of EPC as an international regime. More specifically, it will be shown that on the basis of the case-study examined, EPC performed as a regime, thus allowing the application of institutionalism, and hence gaining the theory's insights. Further conclusions will be reached concerning this approach, and especially on the breakdown of EPC in its various principles, norms, rules, decision-making procedures, and scope. Finally, the study will end with a series of lessons concerning the conduct of Greek foreign policy.

**Notes**

1 "The total loss of population, by death or long-term exile, resulting from [the Greek] Civil War seems to...have been over 200,000" (Close, 1993a, p. 10).
2 *Time*, 26 July 1993, p. 22. The numbers concerning wounded and refugees refer only to the war in Bosnia-Hercegovina. The estimate of 300,000 dead is taken from *Newsweek*, 20 April 1998, p. 53, and refers to fatalities of the 'wars of the Yugoslav succession' during the period of 1991-1995. This estimate is generally accepted. See for example, Holbrooke, 1998, p. xv. To these deaths, the number of killed during the 1999 Kosovo

conflict ought to be added. However, at this point substantial controversy and uncertainty surrounds their precise number. Particularly good accounts of the Yugoslav War are Cohen, 1993; Crnobrnja, 1994; Glenny, 1992 and Woodward, 1995. An important analysis of the international response to the conflict can be found in Gow, 1997.

3 For example, see *The New York Times*, 5 April 1992, p. E16; Gow, 1997, p. 78 fn 32; *The Guardian*, 5 May 1992, p. 8; *The Economist*, 9 May 1992, p. 41; *Time*, 1 June 1992, p. 72; *International Herald Tribune*, 24 November 1992, p. 8 and *Financial Times*, 9 December 1992, p. 3.

4 For the purposes of this book, the term FYROM will be utilised. It must be admitted that the use of any term concerning the new republic is susceptible to attacks of bias. However, this approach has the advantage of conforming to the 1993 UN Security Council Resolution 813, according to which 'this state [will be] referred to for all purposes within the United Nations "the former Yugoslav Republic of Macedonia" pending settlement of the difference that has arisen over the name of the state.' Resolution 813 can be found (in English) in Valinakis and Dales, 1994, p. 147.

5 See Clark and White, 1989, p. 7-8.

6 Admittedly, other states also pursued policies towards former Yugoslavia. However, it must be stressed that it is not the goal of this study to explain the decision-making record of states such as FYROM or Germany. Nevertheless, attention will be paid to other actors and countries when they became important in eliciting Greek reactions.

7 See for example Kofos, 1994c, p. 18 and Tarkas, 1995. Furthermore, this argument was never disputed during any of the interviews that were conducted for this book.

8 In this book '"functional" [will] refer to a particular form of explanations, and should be distinguished from earlier functional and neofunctional theories of international organization' (Haggard and Simmons, 1987, p. 506 fn 55). Of course, other approaches to international regimes also exist. For the best and most succinct overview of the major ones, see Hasenclever et al, 1997. Various applications of these approaches to specific case-studies can be found in Krasner, 1983.

9 It should be explained that an account of the formation of the regime EPC is not pertinent to this study, and will not be attempted.

10 Haggard and Simmons, 1987, p. 508.

11 Keohane and Nye, 1989, p. 259.

12 Ibid.; emphasis added.

13 See Axelrod and Keohane, 1993, p. 92-3; Lipson, 1993 and Mearsheimer, 1995, p. 345-6 and fn 54.

14 See for example Keohane et al, 1993 and Keohane and Martin, 1995, p. 43-4.

15 See Eckstein, 1975, p. 113-32.

16 Waltz, 1979, p. 125. See also ibid., p. 123.

# 1 The Theory of Institutionalism

Do regimes have independent influence on state behavior, and, if so, how?

-Stephen Haggard and Beth A. Simmons, *Theories of International Regimes*, 1987.

## A. Defining International Regimes

Institutionalism has emerged as one of the major theories aimed at explaining state behaviour and cooperation in world politics.[1] The purpose of this chapter will be to present the theory's basic assumptions, arguments and conditions, as well as some of the more important criticisms that have been levelled against it. At the centre of institutionalist theory lies the argument that institutions may have important effects on state behaviour. In order to understand its development and various aspects, an analysis of the functional approach to international regimes theory is necessary. However, regimes will first be defined.[2]

The term international regimes was coined by John Gerard Ruggie in his 1975 essay *International Responses to Technology: Concepts and Trends*.[3] He noted the problems that had been created by recent scientific and technological developments and argued that their solution required collective response.[4] Collective response 'refer[s] to the international institutionalization of certain aspects of national behavior.'[5] Ruggie argued that international regimes comprise a form of collective response, and called for both the creation and fuller theoretical understanding of them. In doing so, he managed to set the tone and agenda for the subsequent meteoric rise of academic interest in the study of regimes.[6]

The most influential and important examination of international regimes can be found in the volume *International Regimes*, which was edited by Stephen Krasner.[7] It is noteworthy that all the contributors to the volume accepted a common definition.[8] Concerning definitions, it might actually be the case that they

Can...be refined, but only up to a point...Ultimately...the concept of regimes, like the concept of "power," or "state," or "revolution," will remain a contestable concept.[9]

Nevertheless, and despite this pessimistic warning, an attempt will be made to define international regimes, based on the discussion and evaluation of various other definitions provided by theorists who primarily follow the functional approach to international regimes.

In their study *Power and Interdependence*, Keohane and Nye define regimes as 'sets of governing arrangements that affect relationships of interdependence.'[10] Interdependence is defined as 'mutual dependence.'[11] This is a rather unsatisfactory and confusing definition, mainly because it fails to specify the nature of these arrangements: the degree of their formality, or the importance of principles and norms are simply not addressed.[12]

The most widely used and influential definition of regimes is Stephen Krasner's, according to which international regimes are

> Sets of implicit or explicit principles, norms, rules, and decision-making procedures around which actors' expectations converge in a given area of international relations. Principles are beliefs of fact, causation, and rectitude. Norms are standards of behavior defined in terms of rights and obligations. Rules are specific prescriptions or proscriptions for action. Decision-making procedures are prevailing practices for making and implementing collective choice.[13]

This definition has received a number of criticisms. Oran Young cautions that

> Part of the problem with the definition that Krasner sets forth is that...we must cope with another set of ambiguous terms in the form of beliefs, standards, prescriptions, and practices, in addition to the original set consisting of principles, norms, rules, and procedures.[14]

Vinod Aggarwal attempts to overcome this confusion 'by distinguishing between rules and procedures, on the one hand, and norms and principles, on the other, and terming 'the principles and norms underlying the development of regimes [as]..."meta-regime.""[15] It should be clear though, that the definition of regimes as 'multilateral system[s] of rules and procedures to *regulate* national actions' to which 'meta-regimes' are added, does not depart from Krasner's in any significant way.[16] Furthermore, Aggarwal fails to indicate at which point and in what ways norms and principles are to be examined and incorporated into the analysis of international regimes. Ultimately, his definition fails to overcome confusion, and it is not surprising that it has won no adherents.[17]

More recently, Keohane has defined international regimes as 'institutions with explicit rules, agreed upon by governments, that pertain to particular sets of issues in international relations.'[18] Institutions are 'persistent and connected sets of rules (formal and informal) that prescribe behavioral roles, constrain activity, and shape expectations.'[19] Possibly, 'this definition of an institution is a somewhat simplified and less demanding edition of that of a regime.'[20] Furthermore, in this definition principles and norms (as well as decision-making procedures), have been abandoned. This has taken place, despite Keohane's earlier assertion that

> What is important [about a definition] is not whether [it is]..."correct," but that principles and norms are integral parts of many, if not all, of the arrangements that we regard as international regimes.[21]

'Rules may in fact be the most important element of international regimes or institutions.'[22] However, a definition concentrating on explicit rules 'risks the charge of formalism—a charge which has plagued the study of international law.'[23] This emphasis on rules also excludes the possibility that principles, norms and decision-making procedures, explicit or implicit, may be of importance in defining and explaining international regimes. Hence, although Keohane's most recent definition reduces the scope for confusion, this simplification is purchased at the price of considerable explanatory and theoretical poverty.

Given the problematic nature of the alternatives, Krasner's definition will be utilised for the purposes of this book. It is certainly the most comprehensive and perhaps the most sophisticated one as well. In following it, warnings that it may lead to some confusion or vagueness are not avoided or ignored. The quest to define and examine terms such as norms and principles though must not be abandoned *a priori*. It is not necessarily beyond our human faculty to observe and analyse them in a precise and satisfactory way.

A more comprehensive and accurate description of regimes also requires that a number of additional concepts be introduced. These will be of assistance in the subsequent chapter, when the definition of international regimes will be applied to European Political Cooperation, which will subsequently be viewed as one. Thus, regimes may incorporate some kind of '*organizational form.*'[24] At this point, it is crucial to distinguish organisations from institutions and international regimes. More specifically, organizations are

Material entities possessing physical locations (or seats), offices, personnel, equipment, and budgets. Equally important, organizations generally possess legal personality in the sense that they are authorised to enter into contracts, own property, sue and be sued, and so forth[25]

Finally, regimes may vary in *scope*, which 'refers to the range of issues [that a regime]...covers.'[26]

## B. The Functional Approach to International Regimes

The functional, 'modified-structural,' or 'contractualist' approach to international regimes provides the central insights and arguments of the theory of institutionalism.[27] This approach seeks to 'account for causes in terms of their effects,' and argues that cooperation is possible even under conditions of anarchy, egoism and lack of hegemony.[28] For contractualist theorists, cooperation occurs 'when actors adjust their behavior to the actual or anticipated preferences of others, through a process of policy coordination.'[29] In order to reach and substantiate its arguments, modified-structuralism borrows but also supplements and synthesises insights from game-theory, the problem of collective action and microeconomic theory.

According to functionalism, international regimes 'have an impact when Pareto-optimal outcomes could not be achieved through uncoordinated individual calculations of self-interest. The Prisoner's Dilemma [PD] is the classic game-theoretic example,' and the most relevant to the functional approach.[30] The extent, value and limits of the important connection between the functional and game theoretic approaches, will be examined first.[31]

PD 'becomes a much better model of international relations when viewed not as a single event, but rather as an extended series of encounters.'[32] In order to illustrate this point, a well-known game tournament that considered the possibility of cooperation emerging in an environment lacking central authority and governed by iterated PD logic will be utilised.[33] The surprise winner of the tournament was TIT FOR TAT, 'the policy of cooperating on the first move and then doing whatever the other player did on the previous move.'[34]

Further analysis of the success of TIT FOR TAT and of the tournament results, led to the conclusion that cooperation in an anarchic world which lacks a hegemonic power can both emerge and thrive given the existence of 'two key requisites...that cooperation be based on *reciprocity* and that the *shadow of the future* is important enough to make this reciprocity stable.'[35]

The 'shadow of the future' becomes important when 'it requires that the players have a large enough chance of meeting again and that they do not discount the significance of their next meeting too greatly.'[36] Reciprocity

> Refers to exchanges of roughly equivalent values in which the actions of each party are contingent on the prior actions of the others in such a way that good is returned for good and bad for bad.[37]

It becomes of great consequence for the fostering of stable cooperation, 'if the interaction will last long enough to make the threat [that is implicit in the concept of reciprocity] effective.'[38]

However, any attempt to explain international regime dynamics that is exclusively based on PD related game theory would be flawed. The reason is related to some of the major problems and shortcomings of this approach. For example, Robert Axelrod admits that a list of 'examples of what is left out by [the PD] formal abstraction...could be extended indefinitely.'[39] Some of these omissions are particularly important, since PD as well as game theory in general,

> Cannot always adequately incorporate other important available information— including relevant historical details about the context of the interaction, insights into the personalities and behavior of decision makers, and understandings of the diplomatic or foreign policy process.[40]

PD has also been criticised for failing to consider the possible importance of relative gains. It is noteworthy that TIT FOR TAT 'can't possibly score more than the other player in a game.'[41] Rather, it won the tournaments by accumulating a sufficiently high number of points on every single game. It is not impossible though, to conceive of 'occasions when defeating the opponent is more important than maximizing one's own payoff.'[42]

The functional approach to international regimes learns from game-theory that under certain circumstances, cooperation may take place in an environment of anarchy by rational egoists. Modified-structuralism also incorporates and utilises the PD game-theoretic conclusions concerning the importance of reciprocity and of the 'shadow of the future.' However, as will be shown, by arguing that international regimes may help enlarge the 'shadow of the future,' identify the nature and extent of responses and promote reciprocity, modified structuralism 'provides a useful supplement' if not solution to some of the game-theoretic problems outlined above.[43]

The functional approach to international regimes also derives important lessons from Mancur Olson's analysis of the problem of collective action.[44] The problem both assumes and stresses the rational selfishness of individuals, and is essentially a PD-like problem.[45] According to Olson, it occurs when selfish but rational individuals, despite their obvious interest, fail to participate in collective action aimed at obtaining certain public goods.[46]

For Olson, the size of the group that seeks to obtain certain public goods is of central importance.[47] He argues that in small groups

> Each of the members, or at least one of them, will find that his personal gain from having the collective good exceeds the total cost of providing some amount of the collective good...[Thus] the good is provided, even if he has to pay all of the cost himself.[48]

Olson calls these groups 'privileged.'[49] Given the incentives that such groups have to cooperate, cooperation among them is both possible and likely, even in the absence of hegemony.

Exactly the opposite logic applies to very large groups, which Olson calls 'latent.'[50] They have substantial organisational problems and their members are apathetic to whether any member does, or does not attempt to provide the collective good.[51] Olson argues that cooperation is possible even among latent groups. What is required is 'an incentive that operates...rather *selectively* toward the individuals in the group.'[52] Such an incentive could be the result of coercion, in which case the analysis is rather simple, in the sense that in essence the option of not cooperating is denied or incurs an extreme cost. Perhaps more significantly, it may also be the result of organisations offering important by-products of a private (i.e. non-collective), nature.[53]

Olson also presents a third category of groups, called intermediate in which no one has an incentive to provide the public good by herself, but 'which does not have so many members that no one member will notice whether any other member is or is not helping to provide the collective good.'[54] Although there is uncertainty about whether intermediate groups will be conducive to collective action, clearly Olson considers them to be closer to the privileged ones.[55]

The functional approach to international regimes learns from the logic of collective action that when small or intermediate groups are involved, cooperation among rational egoists is possible and likely even in the absence of hegemony. Furthermore, in the case of latent groups, important incentives to cooperate may be created through the provision of private goods. Adherents of the functional approach point out that 'international regimes frequently do the same thing.'⁵⁶ In order to explain how this conclusion is reached, the important connection of the functional approach with microeconomic theory must be examined.

Economists have contemplated about the likely effects of institutional arrangements on economic efficiency. They have first of all pointed out that such arrangements may range from being voluntary to being entirely imposed, usually by governments.⁵⁷ Following these distinctions, functionalist theorists have applied the language of supply and demand to international regimes. They accept the contention of hegemonic stability theory that a hegemon may play an instrumental role in the establishment or imposition of various international regimes.⁵⁸ To quote Vinod Aggarwal: 'the *supply* of regimes is affected by the presence or absence of a hegemonic state.'⁵⁹ The functional approach though, emphasises that 'fluctuations in *demand* for international regimes are not taken into account by the theory [of hegemonic stability]; thus it is necessarily incomplete.'⁶⁰

In order to demonstrate the reasons that may lead to the demand for international regimes, the concept of externalities and the Coase theorem must be examined. Externalities refer to

> Some costs or revenues [that] are external to the decision-making unit. Whenever these external costs and revenues exist it is possible that unaided the market will not yield the most efficient result.⁶¹

Government intervention has often been advocated on the basis of being able to confront and alleviate the negative impact of externalities. In a celebrated article, Ronald Coase argued that 'direct governmental regulation will not necessarily give better results from leaving the problem [of externalities] to be solved by the market or the firm.'⁶²

Coase demonstrated that efficient cooperation is possible in the absence of government intervention, despite the problems caused by externalities. Importantly,

> Coase specified three crucial conditions for his conclusions to hold. These were: a legal framework establishing liability for actions, presumably supported by governmental authority; perfect information; and zero transaction costs (including organization costs and the costs of making side-payments). It is clear that none of these conditions is met in world politics...Thus, an *inversion* of the Coase theorem would seem more appropriate to our subject.⁶³

Functional regime theorists argue that the conditions that are assumed by Coase and that are absent from world politics can be provided, with various degrees of success and efficiency, by international regimes. Subsequently, a demand is created for both their creation and maintenance.[64] Modified structuralists admit that regimes are rather weak in establishing clear and enforceable frameworks of legal liability. Nevertheless, regimes may still create 'bits and pieces of law,' thus having at least some positive effect.[65]

International regimes may also affect transaction costs by creating economies of scale: 'once a regime has been established, the marginal cost of dealing with each additional issue will be lower than it would be without a regime.'[66] Transaction costs would be significantly reduced when the issue density in a regime, which 'refer[s] to the number and importance of issues arising within a given policy area,' is high.[67]

The fact that various agreements tend to be 'nested' within regimes may also affect transaction costs.[68] This can occur

> By making it easier or more difficult to link particular issues and to arrange side-payments, giving someone something on one issue in return for help in another. Clustering of issues under a regime facilitates side-payments among these issues: more potential *quids* are available for the *quo*.[69]

As regards the functions and value of information, economists have explained that it is often costly and subject to increasing returns.[70] They have also pointed out that

> The lower the cost of information...the better the markets will operate..[and that] it is likely that substantial profits are to be earned from increasing information flows that reduce uncertainty.[71]

The argument of the functional approach is that international regimes can provide information at a lower cost, given the existence of economies of scale. Furthermore, regimes may provide information concerning the reliability and reputation of governments or actors

> By providing standards of behavior against which performance can be measured, by linking these standards to specific issues, and by providing forums, often through international organizations, in which these evaluations can be made.[72]

Hence, regimes will 'effect the ability of governments to monitor others' compliance and to implement their own commitments—hence their ability to make credible commitments in the first place.'[73] Finally, institutionalist theory 'anticipates [that] the rules of institutions constrain the bargaining strategies of states and therefore make their actions more predictable.'[74]

To summarise, according to the modified-structural approach, international regimes may foster cooperation by performing certain important functions. Functional regimes provide reliable information, monitor behavior and reputation, increase the costs of violating agreements and help create an (admittedly imperfect), legal liability framework. They also help enlarge the 'shadow of the future,' since their

> Principles and rules...make governments concerned about precedents, increasing the likelihood that they will attempt to punish defectors. In this way, international regimes help to link the future with the present.[75]

Although regimes 'do not substitute for reciprocity...they reinforce and institutionalise it' by identifying defection and by often 'incorporating the norm of reciprocity' in their rules.[76] Also, by reducing transaction costs, producing economies of scale and providing information, regimes may provide the kind of by-products that foster cooperation among latent groups.

Turning very briefly to some of the more important criticisms of the functional approach, James Rosenau has claimed that 'if states accede to [regimes], their compliance derives from autonomous acts and not from responses to control effects.'[77] This criticism may perhaps apply to a state's accession to a regime. However, it certainly fails to predict, or provide any sophisticated or useful analysis as to why states may act in a specific way within a regime, following their accession.

O'Meara's has accused modified-structuralists for failing to transcend the 'traditional, state-centric, power-politics paradigm.'[78] Despite the various other problems of his criticisms, this observation is correct to the extent that both the functional approach and the theory of institutionalism do not deny the central importance of states in world politics.[79]

The functionalist approach has also been criticised for the 'strong liberal bias [that] operates in [it].'[80] The extent and nature of the connection with liberalism will be analysed in detail in the subsequent section examining institutionalist theory. Finally, it must be stressed that the functional approach to international regimes neglects the importance of domestic politics. This is somewhat surprising, given their significance in the account of events provided by modified-structural theorists.[81] Helen Milner suggests that this neglect is explained by

Two reasons...the centrality of anarchy as *the* condition for differentiating between domestic and international politics...[and] the use of game theory with its assumption of unitary, rational actors.[82]

The empirical testing that will be undertaken in this book will provide an evaluation of the effects that the neglect of domestic politics has on of institutionalist theory.

## C. Institutionalist Theory

The central argument of the theory of institutionalism is that 'variations in the institutionalisation of world politics exert significant impacts on the behavior of governments.'[83] In making this claim, the theory comes close to identifying institutions as an independent variable that helps explain the dependent variable of state action. In order to substantiate this claim, institutionalism accepts and incorporates into its analysis the previously presented modified-structural arguments concerning the importance and functions of international regimes. They are applied to institutions in general, which in addition to regimes may also include 'formal intergovernmental or cross-national nongovernmental organizations [and]...conventions.'[84] These distinctions are 'not as clear in actuality as this stylization might seem to imply.'[85] This observation ought to be kept in mind, since the subsequent chapter will view EPC as an international regime, albeit one with important intergovernmental aspects.

Institutionalist theory is often called neoliberal because of its connection with classical liberal theories. This connection will prove to be rather weak, since institutionalism rejects or ignores some important liberal assumptions and variants. As regards liberalism,

> There is no canonical description...What we tend to call *liberal* resembles a family portrait of principles and institutions, recognizable by certain characteristics—for example, individual freedom, political participation, private property and equality of opportunity—that most liberal states share, although none has perfected them all.[86]

The analysis and classification of the various political and economic liberal characteristics has allowed the theoretical development of three closely related variants of liberalism: commercial, republican and regulatory.[87] Republican liberalism is based on Kant's argument that republics (defined as polities in which the legislative and executive branches of government are separate), are prone to peace.[88] Institutionalism does not concentrate on republican liberalism, as this variant of liberalism is essentially a 'second image' theory, which concentrates on domestic politics.[89] As will be analysed next, institutionalism is a 'third image' theory.

Commercial liberalism argues that the spread of capitalism and free trade is conducive to peace and cooperation among nations. To quote Montesquieu:

> The natural effect of commerce is to lead to peace. Two nations that trade with each other become reciprocally dependent; if one has an interest in buying, the other has an interest in selling, and all unions are founded on mutual needs.[90]

Regulatory liberalism emphasises the importance of rules and regulations in promoting and fostering cooperation. It 'argues that we have to specify the institutional features of world politics before inferring expected patterns of behavior.'[91]

Institutionalism learns from liberal theories the importance of 'tak[ing] political processes seriously.'[92] It accepts the liberal belief that progress in human affairs is possible and indeed often desirable, and takes notice of the potential beneficial impact on cooperation and peace among nations of institutions, rules, and the spread of capitalism. Ultimately, it creates a 'sophisticated' or neo-version of liberalism, which consists of

> A synthesis of commercial and regulatory liberalism...[which] does not posit that expanding commerce leads directly to peace but rather...[argues] that conditions of economic openness can provide incentives for peaceful rather than aggressive expansion. This is only likely to happen however, within the framework of rules and institutions that promote and guarantee openness.[93]

This version of liberalism emphatically rejects liberal utopianism and unmitigated optimism, according to which a harmony of interests exists between states.[94] Finally, institutionalism is not concerned with individual liberty. Institutionalist liberalism is

> An emasculated liberalism, shorn of its normative concerns with the liberty and well-being of individuals, focusing on economic variables, using the utilitarian discourses and theories of liberal economics, and making states the agents in international relations...Liberalism's goals of individual emancipation and personal development, the ethical values that are central to liberalism, disappear.[95]

It can be concluded that the connection of institutionalism with some of the major assumptions and variants of liberalism is weak, and in some cases non-existent. Institutionalism ignores republican liberalism and concerns about individual liberty. It rejects the existence of a harmony of interests, and unlike classical liberalism, is only guardedly optimistic. Nevertheless, a connection between liberalism and institutionalism does exist, given the latter's acceptance of a synthesis of commercial and regulatory liberalism. Subsequently, the theory of institutionalism can be referred to as neoliberal.[96]

Turning to another aspect of institutionalism, it must be pointed out that it presumes 'that states are the principal actors in world politics and that they behave on the basis of their conceptions of their own self-interest.'[97] The existence of anarchy is also accepted, though institutionalism cautions that 'while anarchy is an important condition in world politics it is not the only one...An exclusive focus on anarchy may be overly reductionist.'[98] Not surprisingly, the effects of anarchy are mitigated by the effects of institutions: 'to understand world politics, we need to know about institutions, not merely about the existence of 'anarchy' defined as the lack of common government.'[99]

Institutionalism is a systemic theory, in which

> The actors' characteristics are given by assumption, rather than treated as variables; changes in outcomes are explained not on the basis of variations in these actor characteristics, but on the basis of changes in the attributes of the system itself.[100]

Finally the *conditional* nature of institutionalism must be stressed. In order to claim relevance, it demands that two conditions be satisfied. First, that 'actors...have some mutual interests;'[101] and secondly that 'institutionalisation [be] a variable rather than a constant in world politics.'[102] The latter condition is important in order to make any meaningful comparisons and evaluations. It also implies (as would had been logically expected), that the presence of at least one institution is essential for the application of institutionalist theory.

Despite its explicit conditionality, critics have claimed that institutionalism overestimates the role played by institutions, and ultimately fails to present an accurate understanding and explanation of the process of cooperation in international relations.[103] The reason is primarily related to what is considered to be the erroneous and misleading institutionalist assumption that 'the preferences of actors in world politics are based on their assessments of their own welfare, not that of others.'[104] Critics charge that states are actually constantly preoccupied with concerns over the relative distribution of gains. According to such an understanding, anarchy means more than just the absence of common government. It also means that states operate in an environment that can never offer permanent reassurance or security.[105]

The ultimate result of anarchy is that 'relative gain is more important than absolute gain.'[106] Hence 'the fundamental goal of states is to prevent others from achieving advances in their relative capabilities.'[107] Failure to do so may lead to the curtailment of a state's independence, or even to its enslavement or destruction. Awareness of such a possibility

> Generate[s] a relative-gains problem for cooperation: a state will decline to join, will leave, or will sharply limit its commitment to a cooperative arrangement if it believes that gaps in otherwise mutually positive gains favor partners.[108]

Stephen Krasner in addition has highlighted the importance of distributional gains. In an essay examining global communications, he explains that the establishment of international regimes in this issue area would be Pareto optimal for all participants.[109] In this case, the problem would be one of coordination and not collaboration, and the Battle of the Sexes a more relevant theoretical game. Thus, Krasner concludes that

> There are...many points along the Pareto frontier: the nature of institutional arrangements is better explained by the distribution of national power capabilities than by efforts to solve problems of market failure.[110]

Keohane concedes that he made 'a major mistake by underemphasizing distributive issues and the complexities they create for international cooperation.'[111] Nevertheless, the criticisms concerning the institutionalist neglect of the importance of relative gains are hotly contested. Keohane maintains that whether relative gains are important is not a matter of dogma, but is conditional on the opportunity and incentive to use them against others.'[112] The validity of these opposing claims concerning the significance of relative gains will be evaluated in subsequent chapters.

To conclude, the theory of institutionalism follows the logic of the functional approach to international regimes, and argues that institutions may have an important impact on state behavior. It neglects domestic politics, considers rational egoistic states to be the most important actors in world politics and accepts the existence of anarchy. The theory has a somewhat benign view of the consequences of anarchy, and claims that concerns about the relative distribution of gains are conditional.

Institutionalism has an affinity with liberalism, since it appreciates the potential importance of processes, rules, institutions and free trade. The connection though is rather weak, since the theory rejects liberalism's optimism, as well as the existence of any harmony of interests among states. It also ignores republican liberalism and concerns about individual liberties.

Finally, institutionalism is a conditional theory which (most importantly), requires the existence of some mutual interests among actors When its conditionality is satisfied, it claims to have considerable theoretical relevance. This claim will be evaluated on the basis of this book's case-study. However, before any empirical testing is undertaken, Chapter 2 will present EPC as an international regime, according to the definition that was adopted.

## Notes

1   The theory of institutionalism has been tremendously influential in most social sciences. For a discussion of its influence, see Young, 1994, p. 1-7.
2   This will be attempted despite warnings that 'arguments about definitions are often tedious' (Keohane, 1983, p. 158).
3   Ruggie, 1975.
4   See ibid., p. 557.
5   Ibid., p. 568.
6   It seems that Ruggie is aware of both the importance and limits of his essay. For his interesting comments, see Ruggie, 1992, p. 565 fn 17.
7   See Krasner, 1983. The volume is composed of articles that had appeared in previous issues of the journal *International Organization*. Discussion, quotations and page numbers from these articles will refer to the edited volume. The same method will be applied to articles that are contained in Baldwin 1993; Brown et al, 1995; Kegley 1995; Keohane, 1986 and Keohane, 1989.
8   This appears as a remarkable achievement for academia. However, during a conversation on 2 September 1995, Mr Krasner explained that he considers the use of a single definition as a mistake. For him, the definition of an international regime must be dependent on the theoretical approach that someone is adopting. In other words, a theoretical orientation must be chosen first. This is the strategy that will be adopted in this book, as regards the functional approach to international regimes. Perhaps Krasner's new position is a result of the fact that despite the use of a common definition, the adoption of various theoretical perspectives resulted to authors having essentially different understandings of what regimes actually are. This was noticed in the same volume by Susan Strange, who attacked the concept of international regimes as being 'woolly' (Strange, 1983, p. 342) and pointed out that despite Krasner's 'consensus' definition, it was still being used in either very restricted or too general ways. Thus, she complained about 'a concerted effort to stretch the elasticity of meaning [of international regimes] to...extremes' (Ibid., p. 343) and concluded that 'there is no fundamental consensus about the answer to Krasner's...question "What is a regime?"' (Ibid.). For an excellent

discussion of definition-related issues and arguments that are central to non-functionalist approaches to international regimes theory, see Hasenclever et al, 1997, p. 14-21.
9   Kratochwil and Ruggie, 1986, p. 763-4.
10  Keohane and Nye, 1977, p. 19.
11  Ibid., p. 8.
12  For further criticisms of this definition, see Aggarwal, 1985, p. 17.
13  Krasner, 1983a, p. 2. This is also the definition that Robert Keohane uses in *After Hegemony*. See Keohane, 1984, p. 57.
14  Young, 1989, p. 195.
15  Aggarwal, 1985, p. 18.
16  Ibid.; emphasis in the original.
17  For Aggarwal's rather confusing framework of analysis, see Aggarwal, 1985, p. 20.
18  Keohane, 1989a, p. 4.
19  Ibid., p. 3.
20  Suhr, 1997, p. 103.
21  Keohane, 1983, p. 158.
22  Grieco, 1990, p. 23. It is noteworthy that Grieco is supportive of Keohane's recent emphasis on rules. See ibid., p. 23-5.
23  Haggard and Simmons, 1987, p. 495. Keohane is aware of this criticism: 'Defining regimes simply in terms of explicit rules and procedures risks slipping into the formalism of some traditions of international law' (Keohane, 1993a, p. 27). For the reasons that he ultimately opts for such an approach, see ibid., p. 26-8.
24  Ibid., p. 496.
25  Young, 1989, p. 32. As examples of organisations, Young provides 'the United States Steel Corporation (now USX), the Red Cross, the New York State Highway Department, and the corner grocery store' (Young, 1994, p. 4).
26  Haggard and Simmons, 1987, p. 497.
27  Krasner, 1983, p. 7 and Keohane, 1993a, p. 36 fn 6. These terms will be used interchangeably in this chapter.
28  Keohane, 1984, p. 80. On anarchy see the subsequent brief discussion in this chapter.
29  Keohane, 1984, p. 51. This definition 'is now [the] consensus...definition of cooperation' (Milner, 1992, p. 467) and will be used throughout this thesis. It is important to note that 'cooperation should not be viewed as the absence of conflict, but rather as a reaction to conflict or potential conflict. Without the spectre of conflict there is no need to cooperate' (Keohane, 1984, p. 54). Furthermore, 'it is also worth stressing that it is not interests...that are adjusted when states cooperate, but policies' (Hasenclever et al, 1997, p. 32). As regards policy coordination, it is defined as follows: 'a set of decisions is coordinated if adjustments have been made in them, such that the adverse consequences of any one decision for other decisions are to a degree and in some frequency avoided, reduced, or counterbalanced or outweighed' (Lindblom, 1965, p. 227; cited in Keohane, 1984, p. 51). It is also important to distinguish cooperation from harmony. 'Harmony refers to a situation in which actor's policies (pursued in their own self-interest without regard for others) *automatically* facilitate the attainment of other's goals' (ibid., p. 51; emphasis in the original).
30  Krasner, 1983a, p. 7. A situation is defined as Pareto optimal, when 'in any given situation, it is found to be impossible to make *any* change without making some individual in the group worse off' (Buchanan and Tullock, 1962, p. 172; emphasis in the original). For an excellent and more detailed discussion of Pareto optimality, see ibid.: chapter 12. PD presents a case 'in which narrow self-maximazation behavior leads to a

poor outcome for all...Hence the dilemma. Individual rationality leads to a worse outcome for both than is possible.' (Axelrod, 1981, p. 306). On PD, see also Table I.
31  References to the game-theoretic approach and to the PD game will be used interchangeably in this chapter.
32  Behr, 1981, p. 290.
33  For a presentation of the rules, entries and results of both rounds of the tournament, see Axelrod, 1980a and Axelrod, 1980b.
34  Axelrod, 1984, p. 13. Interestingly enough, TIT FOR TAT was also the simplest among all the rules that were submitted. See ibid., p. 31. In explaining the success of this rule, its clarity must be pointed out, since it allowed the other player to easily understand its intentions and strategy. Furthermore, TIT FOR TAT 'was nice [i.e. it cooperated first], provocable into retaliation by a defection of the other, and yet forgiving after it took its one retaliation' (Axelrod, 1981, p. 310).
35  Axelrod, 1984, p. 73; emphasis added.
36  Ibid., p. 174.
37  Keohane, 1986a, p. 8; emphasis in original.
38  Axelrod, 1984, p. 126.
39  Axelrod, 1980a, p. 5.
40  Snidal, 1985b, p. 26. For a discussion of some recent (albeit somewhat inconclusive), game-theoretic efforts to incorporate to an extent in their analysis some of these factors, see Kydd and Snidal, 1993. Other problems of the game-theoretic approach are related to the fact that it assumes the existence of two clear choices, p. cooperation and defection. In reality though, 'we should [perhaps] think not of a dichotomy, but of a continuum' (Jervis, 1988, p. 329). Also, 'states often co-operate in part and defect in part' (Kydd and Snidal, 1993, p. 117). Furthermore, the issue of accurately detecting behavior is of extreme importance, since 'if defection cannot be reliably detected, the effect of present cooperation on possible future reprisals will erode' (Oye, 1985, p. 16). Additional criticisms of the PD game-theoretic approach exist, though inclusion of all of them would simply be impossible within the confines of this chapter. See however Cohen, 1990, p. 276-78; Gowa, 1986; Jervis, 1988, p. 321, 324, 329 and 340; Snidal, 1985b, p. 50 and 53 and Wagner, 1983, p. 344. For a brief but excellent discussion of various other games utilised by theorists within the functional approach to international regimes, see Hasenclever et al, 1997, p. 44-53. Nevertheless, PD remains of central importance to functional logic and theory.
41  Axelrod, 1984, p. 137.
42  Behr, 1981, p. 299.
43  Haggard and Simmons, 1987, p. 506.
44  See Olson, 1965/1971.
45  See Hardin, 1982, p. chapter 2, especially pages 25-30.
46  See Olson, 1965/1971, p. 2. 'Public goods are defined by two properties: *jointness of supply and impossibility of exclusion*' (Hardin, 1988, p. 17; emphasis in the original). See also Kindleberger, 1981, p. 243; Olson, 1965/1971, p. 14-6 and Snidal, 1985, p. 590-5.
47  For a critique of the importance that Olson places on the size of groups see Hardin, 1982: chapter 3. However, Hardin's criticisms are not entirely persuasive. For example, his illustration of an enormous privileged group involves the case of billionaire Howard Hughes buying a TV station, in order to enjoy late night western and aviation movies. Hardin points out that almost 250,000 people benefited from this move, and hence all of them constitute a privileged group. See ibid., p. 42. Leaving aside the extreme rarity of

such an instance, it can be pointed out that this privileged group is clearly not consistent with Olson's definition of groups, namely 'the kinds of organizations that are *expected* to further the interests of their members' (Olson, 1965/1971, p. 6; emphasis in the original). Clearly, a potential television audience that has not attempted to organise in any way, and almost certainly does not even care about 3:00 A.M. movies, does not fall under the definition of the groups that Olson examines in his study.

48  Olson, 1965/1971, p. 33-4.
49  See ibid., p. 49-50.
50  Ibid., p. 50.
51  See ibid.
52  Ibid., p. 51; emphasis in the original.
53  See ibid., p. 139-41.
54  Ibid., p. 50.
55  See ibid., p. 57 and 134.
56  Keohane, 1984, p. 77.
57  See Davis and North, 1971, p. 10-11.
58  According to hegemonic stability theory, 'cooperation and a well-functioning world economy are dependent on a certain kind of political structure, a structure characteristic by the dominance of a single actor' (Grunberg, 1990, p. 431). This single actor has been called a hegemon, a 'stabilizer' (Kindleberger, 1973, p. 305) or a 'leader' (Kindleberger, 1976, p. 32). Proponents of hegemonic stability theory disagree on who stands to gain the most in a hegemonic system. For the 'malign' version of the theory, see Haggard and Simmons, 1987, p. 502; Gilpin, 1975, p. 150-3; Gilpin, 1977, p. 55; Gilpin, 1981, p. 144; Kindleberger, 1976, p. 32 and Krasner, 1976, p. 322. For the 'benign' version of the theory, see Kindleberger, 1976, p. 34; Snidal, 1985a, p. 582 and Stein, 1984, p. 358. For some empirical tests of the claims of hegemonic stability theory, see Cowhey and Long, 1983; Gowa, 1984; Keohane, 1989c, p. 94; Krasner, 1976, p. 335 and McKeown, 1983.
59  Aggarwal, 1985, p. 21; emphasis added. See also Keohane, 1984, p. 49-51.
60  Keohane, 1983, p. 142; emphasis added.
61  Davis and North, 1971, p. 15.
62  Coase, 1960, p. 18. In doing so, Coase attacked the predominant pro-government intervention school that was primarily influenced by the work of economist A. C. Pigou. For Coase's discussion of Pigou's arguments see Coase, 1960, p. 28-39. These pages also include a fascinating argument on the possible existence and effects of a Pigovian oral tradition.
63  Keohane, 1984, p. 87; emphasis in the original.
64  The following discussion is primarily based on Keohane 1983 and Keohane, 1984: chapter 6.
65  Keohane, 1984, p. 88.
66  Keohane, 1984, p. 90. For a brief discussion concerning the concept of economies of scale, see Davis and North, 1970, p. 12-4.
67  Keohane, 1983, p. 155.
68  The concept of nesting was originally coined by Vinod Aggarwal. For an explanation and examples see Aggarwal, 1985, p. 27 and Keohane, 1984, p. 90.
69  Keohane, 1984, p. 91. See also the discussion of 'contextual issue-linkage' in Axelrod and Keohane, 1993, p. 101.
70  See Davis and North, 1971, p. 20-3.
71  Ibid., p. 21.
72  Keohane, 1984, p. 94.

73　Keohane, 1989a, p. 2.
74　Keohane and Nye, 1993, p. 15. See also Keohane and Hoffmann, 1993, p. 397 and 399.
75　Axelrod and Keohane, 1983, p. 94.
76　Ibid., p. 110.
77　Rosenau, 1986, p. 881.
78　O'Meara, 1984, p. 256.
79　O'Meara has the tendency to use strong words in attacking modified-structural theorists. For example, he regards Keohane's 'analogy with microeconomics analysis' (ibid., p. 255) as 'dubious' (ibid.), though he fails to explain precisely why. Furthermore, he derides 'the ease with which a "straw man" Realist position can be systematically constructed and subsequently destroyed' (ibid., p. 251), and then proceeds to do exactly that in the following pages. See ibid., p. 251-3. For example, he criticises the realist 'belief that states are the *only* actors in world politics' (ibid., p. 251; emphasis added). However, any sophisticated realist would argue that states are the most important actors and not the only ones. O'Meara's mistreatment of realism is important, because the crux of his criticism of the functional approach is that it fails to establish a radical and clear break with realist concepts and assumptions. It should also be pointed out that Keohane eventually relaxes the unitary state-centric assumption, through the introduction of concepts such as 'bounded rationality' and 'myopic' and 'farsighted' self-interest. See Keohane, 1984, p. 67, 99 and 110-16.
80　Haggard and Simmons, 1987, p. 508. See also Keohane, 1984, p. 10-11 and Rosenau, 1986, p. 891-3.
81　For example, in discussing the failure of the US Senate to ratify the International Trade Organization (ITO), Keohane asserts that '*domestic politics constituted a crucial factor* affecting this outcome' (ibid., p. 140; emphasis added). See also ibid., p. 144, 147 and 150; Keohane, 1993a, p. 35 and Milner, 1992, 481-95. More recently, Keohane has noted that 'domestic politics is neglected by much game-theoretic strategic analysis and by structural explanations of international regime change' (Keohane, 1989d, p. 173), and called for the 'use [of] game theory [in a heuristic way] to analyze the "two-level games" linking domestic and international politics, as Robert Putnam [in Putnam, 1988] has done' (ibid.). He has also admitted that 'in seeking to account for the increase in the number of international regimes, the contractual theorist will not ignore the structure of world power or domestic politics' (Keohane, 1993a, p. 37). However, the fact remains that domestic politics are not, and in a sense can not be incorporated in any significant, clear or sophisticated way into the functional analysis of international regimes, since the theory focuses 'on states as unified rational actors (Martin and Simmons, 1999, p. 98) whose preferences and options are exogenously given and thus taken for granted.
82　Milner, 1992, p. 489; emphasis in the original.
83　Keohane, 1989a, p. 2.
84　Ibid., p. 3-4; emphasis in the original.
85　Ibid., p. 5.
86　Doyle, 1986, p. 1152; emphasis in the original. For a somewhat more assertive statement concerning the principles, rights and institutions of liberalism, see Doyle, 1993, p. 173-4.
87　See Keohane, 1990, p. 175-82.
88　See Kant, 1795/1983, p. 113. Given the many wars that democracies have fought (including colonial wars), the argument of republican liberalism has now been qualified to one that asserts that democracies do not fight with each other. For a justification of this argument, see Doyle, 1986, p. 1156 and Appendix 2 and Russett, 1993. For excellent

critiques of this qualified argument, see Gowa, 1995; Laynard, 1994 and Weede 1984. Kant's 1795 essay *To Perpetual Peace: A Philosophical Sketch*, is crucial to all variants of liberalism. For an early examination of Kant's importance to international relations, see Waltz, 1962. For an excellent discussion of Kant's seminal essay, see Doyle, 1986, p. 1155-63; Doyle 1993, p. 186-93 and Doyle, 1995, p. 94-100. For a more expansive reading of Kant that claims to differ from Doyle's analysis, see MacMillan, 1995.

89  See Keohane, 1990, p. 177. Theories usually tend to look for explanations 'within man, within the structure of the separate states, [and] within the system...These three estimates of cause...[are] referred to as images of international relations, numbered in the order given, with each image defined according to where one locates the nexus of important causes' (Waltz, 1959, p. 12). See also Powell, 1994, p. 315.

90  Montesquieu, 1748/1989, p. 338. For an incisive analysis of the importance of commerce in the political philosophy of Montesquieu, see Pangle, 1973: chapter 7. For further elaboration of the argument connecting commerce and peace, see Schumpeter 1959, p. 69; cited in Fukuyama, 1992, p. 260.

91  Keohane, 1990, p. 181.

92  Ibid., p. 175.

93  Ibid., p. 183.

94  See Carr, 1939/1964, p. 24-5.

95  Long, 1995, p. 496.

96  Subsequently, the theory of institutionalism can perhaps be referred to as neoliberal. 'Keohane [however,]...has [recently—see Keohane and Martin, 1995] withdrawn the term neoliberal from the self-description of his theory and now prefers merely "institutionalism"' (Long, 1995, p. 494). This approach will be followed in this thesis. It is also interesting to note that Moravcsick, 1997 approves of such an approach, bur argues that institutionalism can not be termed neoliberal because 'it has little in common with liberal theory...[since] most of the analytic assumptions and basic causal variables by institutionalist theory are more realist than liberal' (ibid., p. 536). This is a correct assessment, but the fact that institutionalist theory has an (admittedly weak) connection with liberalism remains; and although institutionalism is not a clear-cut fully fledged liberal theory, to ignore this connection allows the risk of diminishing the scope and potential explanatory power of the theory of institutionalism.

97  Keohane, 1993b, p. 271. See also Keohane, 1984, p. 29 and 63.

98  Milnrer, 1993, p. 167.

99  Keohane, 1989a, p. 11.

100 Keohane, 1983, p. 143. See also Keohane, 1984, p. 29 and Keohane, 1989b, p. 40-1. Subsequently, it comes as no surprise that the neorealist emphasis on the importance of the constraints imposed by the structure of the international system is appreciated. See Keohane, 1984, p. 25.

101 Ibid., p. 2. See also Keohane, 1984, p. 6, 9 and 79; Keohane 1993b, p. 275 and Krasner, 1983a, p. 8.

102 Keohane, 1989a, p. 3.

103 See Grieco, 1990; Grieco 1993a; Grieco 1993b; Krasner 1993 and Mearsheimer, 1995.

104 Keohane, 1984, p. 66.

105 On anarchy, see also Rousseau 1917, p. 78-9; cited in Waltz, 1959, p. 180. Anarchy should not be confused 'with complete disorder' (Wight, 1979/1986, p. 105).

106 Waltz, 1959, p. 198; cited in Powell, 1993, p. 209. See also Gilpin, 1975, p. 35.

107 Grieco, 1993a, p. 127; original in emphasis. For an excellent analysis of Grieco's approach to international regimes, see Hasenclever et al, 1997, p. 113-25.

108 Grieco, 1990, p. 10.
109 Krasner, 1993.
110 Ibid., p. 235. On collaboration and coordination, see Hasenclever et al, 1997, p. 48, Martin and Simmons, 1999, p. 104 and Snidal, 1985c. On the Battle of the Sexes, see Krasner, 1993, p. 237-9. For an analysis of Krasner's approach to regimes theory, see Hasenclever et al, 1997, p. 104-13.
111 Keohane, 1993b, p. 292. For an interesting argument, attempting to explain that Keohane's and Krasner's analyses complement each other, see Powell, 1994, p. 340.
112 Keohane, 1993b, p. 283. Some empirical studies on the importance of relative gains have been conducted. For example, Keohane cites as evidence for his position an examination of US actions towards Japanese industrial policy. See Mastanduno, 1993. The study concluded that 'relative gains do matter significantly, but not unconditionally' (ibid., p. 251; cited in Keohane, 1993b, p. 281). In addition to concerns about relative gains, Mastanduno identifies as important factors ideology, the institutional setting and the ability to mobilise members of the US Congress. See Mastanduno, 1993, p. 261-3. For a different reading of Mastanduno's study, see Grieco, 1993b, p. 315-6.

# 2 EPC as an International Regime

The European Community is condemned to be, at best a success in the economic realm, but a fiasco in "high politics."

-Stanley Hoffmann, *Obstinate or Obsolete? The Fate of the Nation State and the Case of Western Europe*, 1968.

## A. The Road to EPC

Attempts for European cooperation in the field of 'high politics' have a long and interesting history. In the early 1950's,

> Because of the outbreak of the Korean War, the American government feared that its military resources might become overstrained, and it demanded that Germany be permitted to rearm in order to strengthen the western military posture in Europe...Unable to resist the request of their powerful ally, the French suggested an integrated army.[1]

The army was to be controlled by a European Ministry of Defence, in order to keep fears of a rearmed Germany to a minimum.[2] This plan culminated with the signing of the European Defence Community (EDC) Treaty in May 1952. However, it was never implemented, since it failed to win ratification by the French Parliament. General de Gaulle and his supporters abhorred its supranational elements, while French communists denounced it as being anti-Soviet. Thus, a remarkable Gaullist and Stalinist alliance halted in late August 1954 the effort to create integrated European defence policies, and also fatally weakened the ambitious attempt to create a European Political Community.[3] Pursued during the years of 1952-54, the latter was intended 'to embrace such highly sensitive areas of national sovereignty as foreign policy, defence and the establishment of a common market.[4]

The failure of these European integrative efforts was mitigated to an extent, by a British proposal for the creation of a Western European Union

(WEU) which would allow for the discussion of security issues. The WEU was intended to operate among strict intergovernmental lines, since unanimity was to be required for the taking of any decision. Until the 1980's though, the WEU did not play any particularly important role, since security affairs were almost exclusively discussed within the North Atlantic Treaty Organisation (NATO).[5]

The next major effort for a common European foreign policy was carried out by France between 1960 and 1962. What became known as the Fouchet Plan proposed procedures and institutions that would lead to the coordination of the foreign policies of the EC member states.[6] The plan was consistent with de Gaulle's aim to create "'a European Europe," less bound to the United States...[and] able to defend its own interests.'[7] However, fear that this initiative would undermine NATO and the drive towards a closer and more integrated Europe, as well as de Gaulle's hardening stance during the final stages of negotiations, led to the ultimate failure of the Fouchet Plan.

These failures generated considerable pessimism. Nevertheless, the members of the European Community (EC) managed to successfully launch a new foreign policy cooperative effort. This was achieved with the 1970 Luxembourg Report that established European Political Cooperation.[8] EPC was further developed by the 1973 Copenhagen Report, the 1981 London Report, and the 1986 Single European Act (SEA). More recently, the Treaty on European Union (TEU) transformed EPC not least by changing its name: it declared (almost certainly too optimistically), that 'a common foreign and security policy [CFSP] is hereby established.'[9] This chapter though will not include any discussion of the TEU's CFSP provisions, or of the subsequent developments, since the events that will be covered in this book took place before they came into effect.[10]

During its existence, EPC made numerous contributions (with different degrees of importance), to various international events and issues.[11] It also developed an elaborate structure, which was 'less than supranational, but more than intergovernmental.'[12] It will be the purpose of this chapter to demonstrate how EPC can be viewed as an international regime on the basis of the definition that was adopted in Chapter 1. In order to achieve this, EPC's principles, norms, rules and decision-making procedures will be presented. Furthermore, its scope and organisational form will be discussed, thus allowing for EPC's more comprehensive understanding.

It is also important to clarify that there will be no explicit or implicit argument that the concept of international regimes should be applied to the EC as a whole. Such an application would almost certainly

Underestimate the significance and influence of the EC's legal framework and the normally high rate of national compliance with frequently detailed Community legislation, especially when political attention is concentrated on an area like monetary policy where the degree of commitment to common policy-making is variable.[13]

The Community is probably 'even more than [a regime], owing to the historical circumstances in which it was created, the particularity [and complexity] of its structures and its evolutionary character.'[14] However, the application of the concept of international regimes to the 'sectoral level' of foreign policy cooperation will prove to have certain important advantages.[15]

## B. Principles

Principles, defined as 'beliefs of fact, causation and rectitude' play a crucial role in the operation of EPC.[16] Perhaps the most basic principle is that of 'parallelism between accession to the Communities and participation in [EPC.]'[17] Full participation in EPC requires first that a state be admitted to the European Community. EPC also operates on the principle that no military confrontation of any kind is conceivable among member states. As a result, it can be argued that EPC members constitute a pluralistic security community. According to Karl Deutsch, such a community is one 'within which the expectation of warfare has been abolished, together with all specific preparations for it.'[18]

Another important principle is connected to the realisation that the international role of Europe is not commensurate to its capabilities.[19] To quote the Preamble of the London Report:

> [The Foreign Ministers of the Member States of the European Community] note that, in spite of what has been achieved, the Ten are still far from playing a role in the world appropriate to their combined influence. It is their conviction that the Ten should seek increasingly to shape events and not merely to react to them.[20]

The role of Europe would be substantially strengthened if politics of scale could be achieved:

> Politics of scale refers to the benefits of collective over unilateral action in the conduct of civilian foreign policy. Politics of scale enables members to conduct

joint foreign policy actions at lower costs and risks than when they act on their own. Members generally perceive that they carry more weight in certain areas when they act together as a bloc than when they act separately.[21]

For such politics of scale to be utilised, EPC members must manage to act on the principle of solidarity, which would guarantee cooperation.[22] If solidarity in all instances was achieved, a more important role in world affairs would almost certainly ensue.

The importance of the principle of solidarity is recognised in the Luxembourg Report, which calls for member states 'to increase their solidarity by working for a harmonisation of views, concertation of attitudes and joint action when it appears feasible and desirable.'[23] Similar calls are also made in the Copenhagen Report, the London Report as well as in the SEA.[24]

EPC also operates on the principle of consultation, which is mentioned in all of the documents that have led to EPC's development. According to the Copenhagen Report:

> Governments will consult each other on all important foreign policy questions and will work out priorities, observing the following criteria:
> (i) the purpose of consultation is to seek common policies on practical problems;
> (ii) the subjects dealt with must concern European interests whether in Europe itself or elsewhere where the adoption of a common position is necessary or desirable.
> On these questions each state undertakes as a general rule not to take up final positions without prior consultation with its partners within the framework of the political cooperation machinery.[25]

The SEA further states that 'The High Contracting Parties undertake to inform and consult each other on any foreign policy matters of general interest.'[26]

It has been claimed that the principle of consultation, aided by the development of a telex system (COREU), has led to the creation of a *'communaute d'information.'*[27] EPC members provide to each other reliable and constant information on the positions that they are adopting on various issues. 'Surprises' are [thus] minimised, and it is quite possible that a socialisation effect on all participants has been created.[28] The success of the consultation principle though, does not necessarily mean that common positions are actually adopted.

In the operation of EPC importance is also placed on the principle of confidentiality. This is clearly expressed in the London Report:

> The success of the process of Political Cooperation depends to a large degree on its confidentiality; certain particularly delicate matters need to be handled in a way which guarantees that the required level of confidentiality is maintained. In such cases, papers will be transmitted to the Foreign Ministries via Embassies, and distributed within Foreign Ministries by the European Correspondent.[29]

Certain problems arise from the enforcement of this principle, given the right of the European Parliament (EP) to submit questions pertaining to EPC matters.

## C. Norms

Norms 'are standards of behaviour defined in [relatively general] terms of rights and obligations.'[30] EPC's fundamental and defining norm is that of 'diluted' intergovernmentalism, which is sustained by the fact that states are the most important actors, having reserved for themselves crucial rights and privileges. However, states have also accepted certain obligations towards the Commission and the European Parliament. As a result, EPC's intergovernmentalism is 'diluted' and not as strict as some had envisioned originally. This section will present in general terms this norm, while the specific ways in which it operates will be demonstrated in the section devoted to EPC's rules. This analysis will also permit the fuller understanding of the actions of EPC's intergovernmental bodies, as well as of the EP and the Commission, that will be witnessed in the following chapters.

The central role and important rights exercised by the member states is evident in all EPC documents. The 1970 Luxembourg Report assigns the major responsibility for seeking cooperation to the intergovernmental Council of Foreign Ministers, which since then has constantly played a significant role in EPC affairs.[31] The Report also created the intergovernmental Political Committee, with responsibilities for preparing Ministerial meetings.

The Luxembourg Report did not impose any stringent requirements on EPC members. For example, they had to 'ensure greater mutual understanding with regard to the major issues of international politics' or 'increase their solidarity *by working for* a harmonisation of views.'[32] Ifestos correctly observes that the Report contains no 'definite obligation [or] commitment to agree or to comply with any issue where views appear to converge.'[33] The same applies to the subsequent Copenhagen Report, which also upgraded the role of the intergovernmental Presidency.[34] Assumed every six months by one of the member states, the Presidency was made responsible for initiating and coordinating EPC actions.[35]

During the Paris Summit meeting of 1974, the European Council was established. An additional intergovernmental body comprised by the Heads of Government of the member states, it stands at the apex of EPC. The rationale behind its creation is stated in the Paris communique:

> Recognising the need for an overall approach to the internal problems involved in achieving European unity and the external problems facing Europe, the Heads of Government consider it essential to ensure progress and overall consistency in the activities of the Communities and in the work on political cooperation.[36]

The 1981 London Report created the intergovernmental Troika, consisting of the previous, current and subsequent holders of the Presidency, and also retained to a large extent the rights enjoyed by member states.[37] In the same spirit, the 1986 SEA revealingly states that: 'The High Contracting Parties, being members of the European Communities, shall *endeavour* jointly to formulate and implement a European foreign policy.'[38] It also

> Makes it abundantly clear that the member states have not renounced the sovereign right of determining their own foreign policy—which is exactly the difference between merely cooperating and, on the other hand, building an effective common policy.[39]

Thus, it can safely be concluded that in accordance with EPC's norm of 'diluted' intergovernmentalism, member states have important rights. They are entitled to hold the Presidency and participate in the European Council, the Council of Ministers and the Troika. In addition, the operation of EPC is based on the rule of consensus: states have the right to veto any decision that they oppose. Subsequently, it is not surprising that they have accepted no obligation to actually reach common positions or participate in common actions.[40]

Nevertheless, member states have accepted some obligations. Their acceptance is partly related to the failed attempts to maintain an absolute form of intergovernmentalism for EPC. An interesting episode reveals the flawed logic behind such attempts.[41] On 23 July 1973, the Foreign Ministers met in Copenhagen for EPC business, and then flew to Brussels in order to discuss EC matters on the very same day. This took place because of the French desire to emphasise the distinction between the somewhat supranational Community and the strictly intergovernmental EPC. The French action backfired, and made evident that some degree of reform was necessary. It primarily took the form of member states granting responsibilities and assuming obligations towards the European Parliament and the Commission. The subsequent brief discussion of their powers will not only allow a comprehensive understanding of EPC's norm of 'diluted' intergovernmentalism, but also explain the reasons that permitted their actions that will be presented and analysed in this book.

Significantly, since 1979 the European Parliament has been the only democratically directly elected Community body. Possibly recognising the importance of this fact, EPC's members have accepted the obligation to provide the EP with information concerning EPC affairs. The occasions and ways in which such information is provided, have both increased and improved since the Luxembourg Report. The SEA expressly recognised the obligation that the EP be informed, stated that the EP 'is *closely associated* with European Political Cooperation,' and noted that it's 'views...are duly taken into consideration.'[42]

In practice, the EP's role in EPC affairs has been rather limited. It has consistently complained about the vague and poor quality of information that it has received. To an extent, this is the result of the fact that foreign policy actions often require a degree of confidentiality. The accurate provision of information has also been hampered by the fear that it could show 'the divergences among member states [thus embarrassing them and] prevent[ing] the adoption of more substantial positions.'[43] Ultimately though, it has probably been the EP's relative lack of any substantial powers over foreign policy matters that has allowed member states to limit the quality and extent of obligations towards it.[44]

Unlike the EP, the Commission has succeeded in obtaining more important rights in EPC affairs. Having 'always been more than an observer in political cooperation but less than a full participant,' the Commission lacks any voting rights but participates in all EPC proceedings, is generally consulted, and helps ensure consistency between Community and EPC actions.[45] The Commission though was not granted this enhanced role immediately. The Luxembourg Report devoted merely one sentence to it, noting that it 'will be consulted *if* the activities of the European Communities are affected by the work of the Ministers;'[46] and it would be the latter who would decide when such instances arose. Furthermore, it should be added that the limited right of consultation did not necessarily guarantee for the Commission any substantial influence in EPC affairs.

The Copenhagen Report expressed the desire that consultation with the Commission should continue.[47] Interestingly, the annex of the report specifically mentioned examples of consultation that were related with the Commission's participation in Ministerial meetings, as well as in discussions of economic issues related to the Conference for Security and Cooperation in Europe (CSCE). The latter reference reflected its important contribution to the process in which it had proved that it could offer valuable assistance based on its substantial technical expertise on economic affairs.[48] The same proved to be the case with the Euro-Arab dialogue of the early 1970's.[49]

The successful involvement of the Commission in these instances was acknowledged and in a sense rewarded in the 1981 London Report, which stated that 'within the framework of the established rules and procedures the Ten attach importance to the Commission of the European Communities being *fully associated* with political cooperation, at all levels.'[50] The full participation of the Commission in EPC proceedings was retained in the SEA, though it did not grant it 'any of the powers of initiative, execution, and control which it possessed on Community issues.'[51]

As a Treaty, the SEA probably created legally binding obligations for the member states, and thus decreased the extent of their rights.[52] Also, the Commission's and the EP's rights were given a legal basis for the first time. However, the legal obligations and implications of the SEA should not be overestimated, since it was specifically mentioned that the European Court of Justice (ECJ) would not have any jurisdiction over EPC proceedings; and no enforcement mechanisms were provided, in cases of member state non-compliance.[53]

## D. Rules

Rules in international regimes 'are difficult to distinguish from...norms; at the margin they merge into one another. Rules are however, more *specific*.'[54] Hence, this section will concentrate on the 'specific prescriptions or proscriptions for action' that allow and determine the operation of EPC's defining norm of 'diluted' intergovernmentalism.[55]

The important rights in EPC that are enjoyed by member states ultimately depend on specific rules that govern the operation of the European Council, the Presidency, the Troika and the Council of Ministers. The most important rule is that of consensus: member states have the right to veto any EPC decision. This obviously affects the efficiency of EPC, although it has been argued that 'EPC policies [manage to] follow the median line, not the lowest common denominator.'⁵⁶ Whether this is actually the case will be discussed in the final chapter.

In addition to the fundamental rule of consensus, there are rules that govern the frequency of meetings for the Council of Ministers and the European Council. The latter, according to the 1974 Paris communique meets 'three times a year, and, whenever necessary, in the Council of the Communities and in the context of political cooperation.⁵⁷ As regards the Council of Foreign Ministers, the Luxembourg Report specified that it would meet twice annually.⁵⁸ This was increased to four times a year in the Copenhagen Report, while the SEA realistically stated that the body should convene 'at least four times a year within the framework of European Political Cooperation.'⁵⁹

Rules governing the operation of the Presidency are somewhat more complicated. The major rule arranges the holding of the Presidency by a member state every six months. Further rules ensure that the holder of the Presidency is in a position to exercise considerable influence in EPC proceedings. Importantly, 'each step in the development of political cooperation has been marked by an increase in powers and responsibilities for the Presidency.'⁶⁰ The Luxembourg Report included rules that gave it the power to convene meetings of the Foreign Ministers and the political committee, organise consultations for crisis meetings, inform the EP, and provide information to possible applicant states.⁶¹

The Copenhagen Report enhanced the role of the Presidency by adding the rule that it would also be in charge of the implementation 'on a collegiate basis' of 'conclusions adopted at meetings of Ministers and of the Political Committee,' while the London Report inserted rules that made the Presidency responsible for informing the press and coordinating activities with the Community.⁶² The SEA gave the Presidency the right to initiate EPC actions, and made it responsible for 'the management of Political Cooperation, and in particular for drawing up the timetable of meetings and for convening and organising meetings.'⁶³ Thus, it becomes clear that through rules that greatly allow the setting of EPC's agenda, the initiation of actions, the convening of meetings, as well as responsibility for the implementation of EPC decisions, the periodic holding of the Presidency substantially increases the rights of EPC member states.

Specific rules also determine the extent and nature of the obligation of the member states to provide the EP with information concerning EPC affairs. In the Luxembourg Report it was agreed to inform the EP in bi-annual informal sessions.⁶⁴ The subsequent Copenhagen Report increased somewhat these obligations, deciding that four colloquies were to be held each year, 'at which the Ministers would meet with Members of the Political Committee of the

European Parliament.'[65] Furthermore, the Foreign Minister holding the Presidency would submit an annual report dealing with EPC affairs.[66] The London Report acknowledged the democratic legitimacy of the directly elected EP, and stated that 'the Ten *envisage the possibility* of more frequent reference to resolutions adopted by Parliament.'[67] It is obvious though, that no such specific commitment was undertaken. More significantly though, the member states did decide to introduce informal meetings between the Council of Ministers and the EP. In the 1983 Solemn Declaration on European Union, EPC's members also 'undertook to respond to oral or written questions...but also to "resolutions concerning matters of major importance and general concern."'[68] Finally, the SEA obliged the Presidency to 'regularly inform the European Parliament' and the member states to take under consideration the positions of the EP.[69]

As regards the Commission, certain rules guarantee its role as an important EPC participant, which is also responsible for ensuring consistency with Community actions. Perhaps the most significant rules are the ones that allow the presence and participation of Commission representatives in all EPC meetings. When the European Council is convened, the Commission is represented by its President. The Commission also receives all COREUs and can send its own. Its presence in the Troika is of particular importance, since given the Troika's rotating system 'the Commission is the only permanent dialogue partner on the European side.'[70] Consultation of member states with the Commission also extends to their foreign representations and international organisations.[71]

The Commission's importance and mission to ensure consistency are also enhanced by rules that allow it to draft the preliminary version of the Community Budget. In addition, it is the Commission that is 'solely responsible for the execution of the Budget.'[72] Furthermore, its competence over the Community's commercial policy, based on Article 113 of the Treaty of Rome, allows it to be involved in the administration of sanctions and aid. However, these economic instruments of policy belong to EPC's decision-making procedures, which will be discussed next.

### E. Decision-Making Procedures

Decision-making procedures have been defined as 'prevailing practices for making and implementing collective choice.'[73] EPC's decision-making procedures include the imposition of sanctions or the granting of aid, conference diplomacy, as well as a crisis management procedure. The most frequently employed decision-making procedure involves the issuing of declarations. Not surprisingly, the publication of such statements often fails to make an impact or achieve any important goals in international relations. However,

> A common declaration of intent, although [it can not often be implemented] immediately, may very well have long run effects. Such a declaration may, for instance, lay the foundation for the tacit co-ordination of the policies of the [member states] in relation to some other international actor.[74]

Potentially more effective procedures involve the imposition of economic sanctions, or the granting of aid, both of which will appear in the case-study of this book. The latter is often based on political, as well as on humanitarian considerations. For example, aid has been directed towards various countries including South Africa during apartheid, or Nicaragua during the Cold War.[75] As regards sanctions, they were originally applied on a strictly national level. 'The leap forward was made in February 1982, when they were applied [on a Community level] to the Soviet Union following the imposition of martial law in Poland.'[76] Since then, sanctions have been collectively applied on several occasions, and always on a Community level, though they have not always proved decisive in achieving their goals.[77] 'Nonetheless [they] do have a useful symbolic function; they can signal to third parties...the sincerity of the common European stance beyond the purely declaratory level;'[78] and at any rate, punitive economic measures make at least some specific and concrete contribution towards the implementation of EPC's collective choice.

Turning to another decision-making procedure, it is noteworthy that EPC lacked any specific arrangement to quickly confront an important international crisis. This became painfully apparent during the 26 December 1979 Soviet invasion of Afghanistan, when it took EPC members more than two weeks to arrange for a meeting in order to discuss the issue and try to agree on a common reaction. In the words of the British Foreign Secretary Lord Carrington, the situation was 'frankly...a bit of a mess.'[79]

Having learned from this rather spectacular and public failure to hold a meeting promptly, EPC members agreed to introduce a crisis management procedure. Thus, the 1981 London Report stated that

> The Political Committee or, if necessary, a ministerial meeting will convene within forty-eight hours at the request of three Member States. The same procedure will apply at the level of Heads of Mission.[80]

This procedure actually failed to operate properly during the subsequent (December 1981) imposition of martial law in Poland. Since then though, it has operated smoothly, at least as regards the holding of meetings under the provisions of the London Report. However, 'the main difficulty is not the lack of procedure, but rather the lack of commonality of view and of confidence among the member states themselves.'[81]

In order to implement its collective choice, EPC has also utilised a decision-making procedure that evolves around the organisation of conference diplomacy. Such diplomacy may bestow certain important advantages to EPC, since it 'prevents the marginalization of individual member countries and reduces the possibility of international bargaining process...producing outcomes that adversely affect Western Europe.'[82]

## F. Scope

The scope of an international regime 'refers to the range of issues [that]...it covers.'[83] EPC's scope has expanded significantly throughout the years, to the extent that it was possible to deal with the issues that arose from the disintegration of Yugoslavia that are covered in this book. More specifically, the Luxembourg Report stated that EPC would deal with 'the major issues of international politics.'[84] An attempt for expansion was made in the Copenhagen Report, which in accordance with the spirit of the previous Report noted that 'Governments will consult each other on all important foreign policy questions.'[85] It also specified that 'the subjects dealt with must concern *European interests* whether in Europe itself or elsewhere where the adoption of a common provision is necessary or desirable.'[86]

The 1981 London Report expanded the scope of EPC in a somewhat conservative way, by including the first reference to security issues:[87]

> As regards the scope of European political cooperation, and having regard to the different situations of the Member States, the Foreign Ministers agree to maintain the flexible and pragmatic approach which has made it possible to discuss in political cooperation certain important foreign policy questions bearing on the *political aspects of security*.[88]

The subsequent SEA solidified the security connection by stating that the member states were 'ready to coordinate their positions more closely on the political and economic aspects of security.'[89]

Thus, it becomes clear that EPC's scope is broad, flexible and somewhat ambiguous, although it does not incorporate defence matters and includes only certain aspects of security issues.[90] These limitations are of particular importance, since in the words of Christopher Hill:

> If a state's security consists in its ability to preserve from threat its core elements and interests, and foreign policy is the sum of a state's official actions towards a potentially dangerous outside world, we can see that the two concepts are inherently related. Security concerns will be at the heart of foreign policy, even if the latter also encourages a much wider range of issues.[91]

## G. Organisational Form

The organisational form of EPC is rather limited. It took some 17 years for EPC to acquire a poorly staffed and under funded Secretariat. The reason for this substantial delay is related to the debate concerning the nature of EPC. Proponents of a more supranational approach viewed with considerable suspicion and ultimately opposed the creation of a strong and intergovernmental Secretariat. On the other hand, advocates of a strictly intergovernmental EPC opposed any plans for what could have been perceived as a pro-integrationist Secretariat.[92] However, the need for some organisational form, especially to assist the President-in-Office was evident. Thus, the Copenhagen Report stressed the considerable duties bestowed upon the Presidency, and called for at least some administrative assistance from other member states.[93] The London Report attempted to remedy the problem by assigning to the Presidency 'a small team of officials seconded from preceding and succeeding presidencies.'[94]

A Secretariat was eventually created by the SEA. Located in Brussels, it was to 'assist the Presidency in preparing and implementing the activities of European Political Cooperation, and in administrative matters.'[95] A subsequent meeting of the Council of Foreign Ministers held on 28 February 1986, further specified its duties. They included:

- assisting the Presidency in the organization of political cooperation meetings, including the preparation and circulation of documents and the drawing up of minutes;...
- assisting the Presidency in the preparation of texts to be published on behalf of the member states, including replies to parliamentary questions;
- maintaining the European Political Cooperation archives;

- preserving the rules according to which political cooperation is used;
- assisting the Presidency in its contacts with third countries.[96]

The Secretariat was assigned a staff of only seventeen and no budget of its own.[97] Clearly, it lacked autonomy and, according to the SEA, had to 'carry out its duties under the authority of the Presidency.'[98] Wisely 'it concentrated on making itself useful and threatening no one.'[99]

On the basis of all of the above, it can be concluded that EPC is a particularly complex international regime that operates on the principles of confidentiality and consultation. No warfare among members states is expected and it is understood that EPC membership parallels EC membership. Concerning the potentially consequential principle of solidarity, in the following chapters it will be viewed in action and its importance and impact evaluated.

As will also be shown, EPC is defined to a great extent by the norm of 'diluted' intergovernmentalism. This norm allows member states to enjoy important rights, such as holding the Presidency and participating in the European Council, the Council of Ministers and the Troika. However, member states have also accepted the obligation to inform the EP, consult with the Commission, and allow it to participate in all EPC proceedings, as well as help ensure (together with the holder of the Presidency), consistency between Community and EPC actions. Furthermore, it should be noted that as a Treaty, the SEA created legally binding obligations for member states, though enforcement mechanisms are absent and the ECJ has no jurisdiction over EPC.

The important role enjoyed by member states in EPC is solidified by the rule of consensus, which allows them to veto any undesirable EPC decision. Other rules determine the significance and character of EPC's intergovernmental bodies, and especially of the Presidency that sets EPC's agenda. Specific rules also guarantee the full participation of the Commission in all EPC meetings. The Commission is assisted in its role of ensuring consistency by rules that allow it to make the initial budgetary proposals, and be the sole executor of the Community budget. Specific rules also oblige member states to inform the EP, though the quality of the information provided is often poor.

The scope of issues covered by EPC has considerably expanded throughout the years to include all foreign policy issues, as well as the political and economic aspects of security, though defence matters (and hence a military option), are excluded. However, EPC can utilise a variety of other decision-making procedures in order to implement its collective choice. They include the issuing of declarations, conference diplomacy, a crisis procedure, the imposition of sanctions, and the granting of aid. Most of these procedures, as well as certain innovations, will be discussed subsequently in this book. Finally, as previously explained, EPC's organisational structure includes a small, and understaffed Secretariat.

Based on the case-study that will be presented in the following chapters, it will be shown that EPC operated as an international regime, and the theoretical implications of this finding will be presented and evaluated. Furthermore, conclusions will be reached concerning the nature and importance of EPC's principles, norms, rules, decision-making procedures and organisational form. However, before plunging into an in-depth examination of Greek foreign policy towards former Yugoslavia within the context of EPC, the next chapter will provide a brief but necessary account of the controversial and complicated Macedonian Question. An analysis of the often neglected but crucially important interests that were shared by Greece and FYROM, will also be included.

## Notes

1   Gilbert, 1970/1984, p. 415. See also Cardozo, 1987, p. 50-1 and Jopp, 1997, p. 153.
2   See Urwin, 1991, p. 63.
3   See Cardozo, 1987, p. 71. 'The European Political Community was...to be...nothing less than the beginning of a comprehensive federation to which the [European Coal and Steel Community] and EDC would be subordinated. The draft Treaty of the Political Community, with 117 articles, was presented on 10 March 1953' (Urwin, 1991, p. 64). For an excellent and comprehensive account of the European Political Community project, see Cardozo, 1987.
4   Ibid., p. 49.
5   The existence of NATO and of a separate European security organisation, partly explains why all aspects of security issues were completely absent from EPC's scope for a significant period of time.
6   For a detailed account of the proposals and negotiations of the Fouchet Plan, see Gerbet, 1987.
7   Ibid., p. 108.
8   The Luxembourg Report is also referred as the Davignon Report, after the name of its author.
9   Title V. Article J. The TEU is commonly referred to as the Maastricht Treaty.
10  The TEU came into force on 1 November 1993. For an excellent account of its ratification problems, see Duff 1994.
11  This chapter will not include an analysis of EPC's record on major international events. For the best general account of this record, see Nuttall 1992a. For other excellent, though less extensive and comprehensive accounts, see Hill 1992; Nuttall 1988 and Wallace, 1983. For an analysis of EPC's actions towards the Yugoslav War, see Salmon 1992 and Tziampiris 1992. For EPC and the Middle East, see Ifestos, 1987. An excellent account of EPC actions towards South Africa is contained in Holland, 1995. Martin, 1995 and Stavridis and Hill, 1997 cover EPC's responses to the Falklands War, while Salmon, 1992 covers EPC's reactions to the Gulf War.

12  Wessels, 1982, p. 15; cited in Ifestos, 1987, p. 209. Hence, it is perhaps not surprising that EPC has caused considerable theoretical confusion and controversy. For the plethora of theoretical approaches that have been applied to EPC, see Holland, 1991 and Wessels, 1988.
13  Webb, 1983, p. 36.
14  Ifestos, 1987, p. 58. See also Ginsberg, 1989, p. 12; Wallace, 1983, p. 409-10 and Wessels, 1991, p. 73-4. For attempts to view the European Community as a regime, see Hoffmann, 1982 and especially Moravcsik, 1994.
15  Webb, 1983, p. 36.
16  Krasner, 1983a, p. 2.
17  Nuttall, 1992a, p. 43. See also Dehousse and Weiler, 1991, p. 136 and Nuttall, 1992a, p. 260.
18  Deutsch, 1979, p. 180. See also Deutsch, 1968/1978, p. 244-5.
19  References to 'Europe' will refer to the states constituting the European Community.
20  See also the Preamble of the SEA and Ifestos, 1987, p. 125 and 150.
21  Ginsberg, 1989, p. 3.
22  The connection between politics of scale and the principle of solidarity is also made by Christopher Hill (see Hill, 1992, p. 122). Hill states that 'the Twelve are concerned to exploit the *economy of scale* available to them' (ibid.; emphasis added). Although he does not use Ginsberg's term of politics of scale, the meaning is essentially the same.
23  Part Two. I. b.
24  See Part I. ii of the Copenhagen Report, the Preamble of the London Report and the Preamble of the SEA.
25  Part II. 11; cited in Holland, 1995, p. 21.
26  Title III. Article 30. 2. a.
27  Regelsberger, 1988, p. 34. The number of COREUs sent during the years 1985-6 and 1990-4 can be found in Regelsberger, 1997, p. 68. More specifically, in 1991 10,184 COREUs were sent, while for the year 1992, the number was 11,394. See ibid.
28  See Nuttall, 1992a, p. 312. See also Ohrgaard, 1997, p. 18-20.
29  Article 6; cited in Ifestos, 1987, p. 239.
30  Krasner, 1983a, p. 2. The point that concerns the generality of norms is taken from Keohane, 1984, p. 58.
31  Part Two. II. The Council of Foreign Ministers is also referred to as the General Council.
32  Part Two. I. a. and Part Two. I. b; emphasis added.
33  Ifestos, 1987, p. 154.
34  The Presidency is only briefly mentioned in the Luxembourg Report that limits its responsibilities to consultation and information. See Part Two. II. c; Part Two. III. 1 and Part Three. 4.
35  Part II. 8. The rotation of the Presidency takes place according to the alphabetical order of the names of the member states. For an example of how this operates, see Hill, 1992, p. 115.
36  Cited in Nugent, 1989/1991, p. 194.
37  See Article 10.
38  Title III. Article 30. 1; emphasis added. The use of the words 'High Contracting Parties' implies the intergovernmental nature of the SEA's EPC provisions.
39  Terme, 1992, p. 276.

40  However, member states clearly recognise that common positions and actions would confer benefits to them. On this point, see the discussion of the principle of solidarity in this chapter.
41  For additional accounts of this episode, see Ifestos, 1987, p. 172 and Nuttall, 1992a, p. 75.
42  Title III. Article 30. 4; emphasis added.
43  Nuttall, 1992b, p. 59. For further discussion of the problems that arise the process of informing the European Parliament, see de Schoutheete, 1988, p. 81.
44  It is noteworthy that the SEA required the assent of the Parliament for the accession of new members, and the conclusion of association agreements.
45  Nuttall, 1988, p. 104.
46  Part Two. V; emphasis added.
47  Part II. 12. i.
48  For an excellent account of the Commission's involvement with CSCE, see Nuttall, 1992a, p. 58, 110-11 and Nuttall, 1994a, p. 289-91.
49  See Nuttall, 1992a, p. 97-100.
50  Article 12; emphasis added.
51  Ohrgaard, 1997, p. 11. The Commission was also given (together with the Presidency), the right and responsibility of ensuring consistency in EPC and Community affairs. See Title III. Article 30. 5. The relevant article in the SEA also stated that the Presidency and the Commission were to act 'within [their] own sphere of competence' (ibid.). 'This proviso was introduced at the request of Denmark to make it clear that the Commission did not hereby acquire any new powers in EPC' (Nuttall, 1994a, p. 293). For further analysis of consistency as it appears in the SEA, see Lak, 1992, p. 48-51 and Wessels, 1991, p. 153-4.
52  For a persuasive argument of why the SEA created legally binding obligations for the member states, see Dehouse and Weiler, 1991, p. 128-31.
53  See Title IV. Article 31.
54  Keohane, 1984, p. 58; emphasis added.
55  Krasner, 1983a, p. 2.
56  Nuttall, 1992a, p. 314.
57  Cited in Nugent, 1989/1991, p. 194.
58  See Part Two. II. 1. a.
59  See Part II. 1 of the Copenhagen Report and Title III. Article 30. 3.a of the SEA.
60  De Schoutheete, 1988, p. 75.
61  See the following sections of the Luxembourg Report, p. Part Two. II. 1 a; Part Two. II. 1. c; Part Two. III. 1; Part Three. 4, Part Four a.
62  Part II. 8. i of the Copenhagen Report and Articles 1 and 12 of the London Report.
63  Title III. Article 30. b.
64  See Part 2. VI.
65  Part II. 10.
66  Ibid.
67  Article 11; emphasis added.
68  Nuttall, 1992a, p. 190.
69  Title III. Article 30. 4.
70  Nuttall, 1992b, p. 64.
71  See SEA. Title III. Article 30. 9. The Commission has more than 100 diplomatic representations around the world. See Regelsberger, 1991, p. 171.
72  Nuttall, 1994a, p. 292.

73  Krasner, 1983a, p. 2.
74  Sjostedt, 1977, p. 48; cited in Ifestos, 1987, p. 234.
75  See Nuttall, 1992b, p. 72.
76  Nuttall, 1992a, p. 262.
77  For a summary of cases between 1967 and 1990 in which EPC applied sanctions or granted aid, see Rhein, 1992, p. 33-4. See also Nuttall, 1992a, p. 260-65 and Nuttall, 1992b, p. 69-73.
78  Pijpers, 1988, p. 156.
79  Cited in Ifestos, 1987, p. 230.
80  Article 13.
81  Rummel, 1988, p. 123. For some further comments on EPC's emergency procedure, see Regelsberger, 1997, p. 69.
82  Ibid., p. 121.
83  Haggard and Simmons, 1987, p. 497.
84  Part Two. I. b.
85  Part II. 11.
86  Part II. 11. ii; emphasis added.
87  The London Report also states correctly in its preamble that EPC's scope has 'continually broadened' since its beginning.
88  Preamble; emphasis added. For comments on the diplomacy behind the adoption of this reference to security issues, see Nuttall, 1992a, p. 178.
89  Title III. Article 30. 6. a.
90  The London Report, as well as the SEA, deliberately did not contain any references to the coordination of defence policies. See Wessels, 1991, p. 157.
91  Hill, 1992, p. 136.
92  For some useful comments on the debate concerning the creation of an EPC Secretariat, see Bonvicini, 1988, p. 58 and especially Nuttall, 1992a, p. 19.
93  See Part II. 8.
94  Article 10.
95  Title III. Article 30. 10. g.
96  EC Bull. 2/1986; cited in da Costa, 1988, p. 93.
97  For an account of the interesting and revealing process by which the first head of the Secretariat, Mr Giovanni Januzzi was selected, see da Costa, 1988, p. 87.
98  Title III. Article 30. 8. g.
99  Nuttall, 1992a, p. 20.

# 3 'One of the Most Explosive Topics in the Universe'[1]

That nothing changes in the East is a commonplace which threatens to become tyrannical. Assuredly there is something in the spirit of the East which is singularly kindly to survivals and anachronisms. The centuries do not follow one another. They coexist. There is no lopping of withered customs, no burial of dead ideas.

-H. N. Brailsford, *Macedonia: Its Races and Their Future*, 1906.

### A. The Importance and Origins of the Macedonian Question

The Macedonia Question has played a central and often defining role in the international politics of South-Eastern Europe. Any attempt to discuss it, is greatly complicated by the fact that it

> presents...a medley of jarring races, long standing animosities, and ever-recurring atrocities [as well as]...a jumble of ethnographical uncertainties, unreliable statistics, assertions and counter-assertions flatly contradictory on every point.[2]

Nevertheless, the fact remains that there was an almost continuous struggle among most of the states of the Balkan Peninsula for control of Ottoman Macedonia, during the period of 1870-1949. As this chapter will demonstrate, the Greeks contested developments in this region through educational and guerrilla activities during 1895-1912, and fought for parts of Macedonia in two Balkan Wars, two World Wars, as well as in the Greek Civil War. Macedonian territories were lost to Bulgaria as a result of the 1878 San Stephano Treaty, and in the First and Second World Wars; and they were almost lost again because of the policies pursued by the KKE during the Civil War. Furthermore, brutal occupations were suffered during the two World Wars. After

1949, contentious arguments over the falsification of history, minority issues and the practice of propaganda replaced considerations of warfare.

The appreciation of this long-standing, turbulent, controversial and traumatic historical record is essential, in order to understand the dispute between Greece and FYROM, and the reactions of the Greek people and government that will be described in the following chapters of this book and which essentially constitute the most recent developments of the Macedonian Question. As will be shown, Greek reactions included demonstrations with more than one million participants, passionate feelings and arguments concerning the new republic's exact name, and even a spontaneous popular boycott of products originating from countries whose foreign policy was judged unfriendly to Greek positions. This chapter will also present a discussion of the common interests between Greece and FYROM, thus partly satisfying institutionalism's conditional nature, but also offering an often neglected perspective to subsequent developments.

As with every aspect of the Macedonian Question, any argument concerning its precise origins would almost certainly be controversial and disputed. Nevertheless, it is probable that the beginning of the modern phase of the Macedonian Question is connected with the establishment of the autocephalous Bulgarian Orthodox Church (Exarchate) in 1870.[3] In order to comprehend the significance of this event, it must be kept in mind that the peoples residing within the borders of the Ottoman Empire were organised in various *millets*, according to their faith.[4] The *millet* comprising the Empire's Orthodox Christian population was under the supervision of the Ecumenical Patriarchate, located in Constantinople.[5] Thus, the Orthodox Christian Church was a kind of supranational organisation, responsible for the religious (and also educational) requirements of all Christians, regardless of race or language.

The 'ecumenical community of Balkan Orthodoxy' was seriously weakened with the 10 March 1870 *firman* (decree) that established the Exarchate.[6] Although the Ottoman government was pressured by Russia, this decision also included an important element of a 'divide and rule' strategy.[7] Article X of the *firman* stated that territories would fall under the control of the Exarchate, given the request of at least two thirds of the population.[8] This stipulation initiated the struggle for Macedonia by religious, educational and eventually military means, between Bulgarians, Greeks and to a much lesser extent, Serbs. The *firman's* strategy proved short-sighted, since as will be explained, it allowed the unleashing of competing forces that ultimately overthrew the Ottoman yoke from the Balkan Peninsula.

After the establishment of the Exarchate, Bulgarians proved particularly troublesome for the Sublime Porte. In April 1876, they rose in a rebellion that was brutally crushed.[9] The atrocities committed against the Bulgarian population made an impression in Europe. Gladstone's condemnation was characteristic:

> There is not a cannibal in the South Sea Islands, whose indignation would not arise and overboil at the recital of that which has been done, which has too late been examined, but which remains unavenged.[10]

Following this outrage, a conference was held in Constantinople in 1876, in which Europe's Great Powers proposed the creation of two Bulgarian provinces within the Ottoman Empire, governed by Christians.[11] The Ottoman refusal to accept such a plan led to the Russian-Turkish War of 1877-8. The victorious Russian troops reached the outskirts of Constantinople, and thus made possible the 1878 San Stefano Treaty which effectively created Great Bulgaria, encompassing an enormous territory.[12]

The Treaty of San Stephano provoked an armed but unsuccessful Greek uprising in Macedonia.[13] It also threatened to upset the European balance of powers, primarily because it was perceived as a 'unilateral Russian settlement of the "Eastern Question."'[14] A 'correction' subsequently took place in the 13 June-13 July 1878 Congress of Berlin, and the Bulgarian state was limited to almost half its original size.[15]

Despite this setback, Bulgarians continued to entertain national goals in Ottoman Macedonia, which were originally pursued through educational means with the founding of many Bulgarian schools in the last quarter of the nineteenth century.[16] The ultimate aim of these educational efforts (and rivalries) was to inculcate a specific national identity to students.[17]

On 3 October 1893, the Macedonian Revolutionary Organisation (IMRO) was founded in Thessaloniki, aiming at 'furthering Bulgarian plans in Macedonia.'[18] During the following years, IMRO exhibited a preference for violence, and played a crucial role in preparing a rebellion in Ottoman Macedonia.[19] It must be noted however, that IMRO's goals were never clearly defined, since it 'was...divided...between protagonists of Macedonia for Bulgaria, and of a separate Macedonian state, existing either within some form of federation, or independently.'[20]

## B. Armed Struggle in Macedonia

After 1895, armed Bulgarian guerrilla groups (*comitadjis*) began to operate in Macedonia. Following increased guerrilla activities in 1902, IMRO decided to organise an uprising, which was declared on 2 August 1903 on Saint Elijah's day (Ilinden).[21] The initially successful Bulgarians captured the town of Krusevo and proclaimed the short-lived 'Krusevo Republic.'[22] Eventually, faced against superior Ottoman forces, it became impossible to maintain military momentum and the uprising began to falter after just three weeks. It ended officially on 3 November at a significant cost: villages and crops lay damaged or destroyed, some four thousand people were killed, and many more were left homeless.[23]

IMRO's leaders were aware that it was impossible to overthrow by militarily means the Ottoman rule in Macedonia. Rather, the brutal strategy behind the failed Ilinden uprising was based on the expectation that it would provoke Turkish atrocities, and thus produce a European public outcry and a direct Great Power intervention in the region.[24]

Ilinden represented the culmination of Bulgarian efforts in Macedonia, and demonstrated their vitality and strength. In this sense, it provoked Hellenism's ultimately successful counterattack.[25]

> Hellenism, in the widest sense of the term [was] a force which in Macedonia was not to be identified solely with the Greek language or race. Hellenism derived largely from the Patriarchal Church; from the flourishing Greek schools; and from a class which enjoyed in some measure an economic superiority, a class which was conservative, which had everything to lose...Hellenism was a way of life, of which the outward manifestation was the acceptance of the Greek Orthodox Church.[26]

The struggle of Hellenism was carried out by small armed bands, which essentially received no aid from the Greek government, and only limited from private sources.[27] This situation began to change after the death of Pavlos Melas, an army officer, prominent citizen and organiser of guerrilla activities in Ottoman Macedonia.[28] News of his fate had a profound effect on public opinion.[29] In the words of the patriot Ion Dragoumis: 'Pavlos Melas died...and the Greeks woke up.'[30] The result was a more determined, organised and better funded Hellenic effort in Macedonia, aimed at weakening Bulgarian military activities.[31] The Greeks also attempted to persuade (or force), villages to abandon the Exarchate, as well as 'protect and support Greeks who were not afraid to claim a Greek *national* identity and to inculcate it into those who felt only a Greek *Orthodox* identity.'[32] By 1908 these activities had succeeded, at least to the extent that they had 'prevented what later became Greek Macedonia from being lost.'[33]

In July 1908, the Young Turk revolution took place. Carried out by army officers in Thessaloniki, it achieved the securing of a constitution for the Empire, and this produced a wave of optimism and much rejoicing in Macedonia. Significantly, the various guerrilla groups ceased their activities, though hopes were soon met with disappointment. The Young Turk revolution turned out to be essentially nationalist in character, since its ultimate goals were not only to modernise the Empire, but also to 'Ottomanise' it 'through the complete abolition of the rights and privileges of the different ethnic groups.'[34] Soon after, guerrilla activities resumed.

The Young Turk 'revolution, far from arresting the disintegration of the Empire...at once accelerated it.'[35] Eventually, the Balkan states embarked upon the signing of bilateral alliances.[36] Serbia and Bulgaria signed one in March 1912, while Greece and Bulgaria followed in May.[37] Finally, Montenegro joined in alliances with Serbia and Bulgaria in October.[38] Montenegro also started the First Balkan War by initiating armed hostilities in Macedonia in which Ottoman forces were outnumbered and eventually almost completely thrown out from the Peninsula. Greece managed to capture Thessaloniki, and Bulgaria was consoled with Adrianople.[39] The May 1913 London Conference formalised the new *status quo*.[40]

The victorious Balkan alliances were made possible because a unifying common goal did exist: the overthrow of the Ottomans from the Peninsula. Nevertheless, there was considerable uncertainty and vagueness as regards the ways in which the newly liberated territories were to be divided among the victors. George F. Kennan has astutely observed that 'never...did any coalition of powers launch a war on the basis of flimsier understandings among them about what it was they were fighting for.'[41]

Thus, despite the military victory in the First Balkan War and subsequent negotiations, 'the great problem of the division of Macedonia remained.'[42] Desiring a favourable resolution of this contentious issue, Bulgaria decided to attack its former allies, and thus initiated the 1913 Second Balkan War. Without the support of any Great Power and facing a variety of problems, Bulgaria had actually committed one of the greatest political and military blunders in modern history, and was thus soundly defeated.[43] The August 1913 Treaty of Bucharest gave Greece and Serbia 51,5 and 38,4 per cent of Macedonia respectively; Bulgaria received a paltry 10,1 per cent.[44] This was undoubtedly disappointing for a state that had once encompassed a huge part of Macedonia, and had actively contested developments in the region for more than four decades.

> The treaty of Bucharest created a revanchist mentality amongst Bulgarians...for those in the territories now alienated who showed any sign of affiliation with Bulgaria or Bulgarian culture were dealt with harshly. This naturally complicated relations with Bulgaria's immediate neighbours and exposed the Greek communities in Bulgaria itself.[45]

Bulgaria's revisionism almost certainly influenced its siding with the Central and Axis Powers in the two World Wars.

During the First World War, Bulgaria succeeded in regaining parts of Greek and Serbian Macedonia, as well as Western Thrace.[46]

> The Bulgarian occupation authorities in Greek eastern Macedonia...behaved towards the Greek population with brutality singularly inappropriate in supposed liberators...30,000 people...died of hunger, blows, and disease during the occupation...42,000 [were] deported to Bulgaria, and...16,000...fled to Greece.[47]

After the defeat of the Central Powers, Bulgaria was once again forced to abandon its Macedonian conquests, a development confirmed by the November 1919 Treaty of Neuilly.[48] A Greek-Bulgarian Convention was also signed, which allowed for the voluntary exchange of populations between Greece and Bulgaria. As a result, by 1926 only some 77,000 Bulgarians were left residing in Greek Macedonia.[49]

### C. The Communist Factor

The interwar years saw the rise in importance of communist forces, who quickly moved to exploit national antagonisms and tensions in Macedonia.[50] In March 1924 the Balkan Communist Federation passed a resolution declaring that 'a united and autonomous Macedonia is now the slogan of the Macedonians in all corners of their Fatherland, which is covered in ruins.'[51] This resolution was approved after the exercise of heavy Bulgarian pressure, and despite the misgivings of the Greek and Serbian communist parties.

The Balkan Communist Federation's position on Macedonia was endorsed at the May-June 1924 Fifth Comintern Congress, and was praised as 'wholly correct and truly revolutionary.'[52] Furthermore, the policy implications were clarified:

> The Communist Parties and the Balkan Federation must support to the utmost the national-revolutionary movement of the oppressed nationalities of Macedonia and Thrace *for the creation of independent republics.*[53]

In other words, the territorial settlements reached in the Treaty of Bucharest were directly challenged, which in turn helps to explain the Bulgarian attempt to persuade the Comintern to accept such a revisionist (and of course revolutionary) policy.[54]

The KKE's agreement to the Comintern's policy on Macedonia amounted to calling for the loss of Greek territory, and caused a major split within the party's ranks.[55] It also reduced its popular appeal and prompted the intensification of state anti-communist persecution.[56] The plight of Greece's communists was only alleviated in 1935, when the Comintern was almost exclusively preoccupied with the rise and dangers of Europe's Nazi and Fascist regimes. Thus, as regards Macedonia, the KKE 'introduced the slogan of "complete equality for the minorities"' which would remain the party's policy until the final and dramatic stages of the Greek Civil War.[57]

The Civil War was preceded by the Greek-Italian war, and the 6 April 1941 Nazi invasion and subsequent occupation of Greece.[58] Although the origins and history of the Greek involvement in the Second World War are well-known and documented, of relevance to this study is that following the Nazi conquest, Bulgaria (which had joined the Axis Powers), was awarded parts of Greek Macedonia and Thrace.[59] Bulgaria's King Boris III declared triumphantly:

> Thanks to this cooperation [with the Germans and the Italians] Macedonia and Thrace, these lands which have been so loyal to Bulgaria, which have been unjustly detached from her, and for which Bulgaria has been compelled to make innumerable sacrifices in the span of three generations, have now returned to the fold of the Bulgarian Motherland.[60]

Importantly, Bulgaria's occupation forces exhibited again tremendous brutality. 'A German report of the time described the Bulgarian occupation as "a regime of terror which can only be described as Balkan."'[61]

In occupied Greece, a resistance movement was soon organised. Some groups were right-wing (most notably the National Democratic Greek League-EDES), though it was the KKE that became the major resistance force. The party took advantage of the political vacuum, utilised its experience from operating in a clandestine way and succeeded in setting up EAM (National Liberation Front), and its military wing ELAS (National Popular Liberation

Army).[62] Although not everyone associated with EAM was a communist, the organisation was ultimately controlled by the KKE.[63]

Within EAM/ELAS, as Evangelos Kofos has analysed, there were also

> Slavophones, not only of the Greek faction, but also persons who distanced themselves both from the Greek and the Bulgarian factions...[Thus] the traditional dichotomy of Slavophones [pro-Greek and pro-Bulgarian] gradually grew into a trichotomy.[64]

In order to exploit this situation, the KKE established the Slav Macedonian Popular Liberation Front (SNOF) in November 1943.[65] There were important reasons why SNOF's creation was considered advantageous for ELAS' armed struggle. First of all, it allowed the recruitment of additional forces, particularly from Western Greek Macedonia. Recruitment was also increased by the fact that SNOF operated as a way of 'rebaptisement.'[66] Compromised individuals who had fought or collaborated with the Bulgarians, were given a chance to enter the communist struggle via SNOF, and thus save themselves from retributions.[67] Furthermore, SNOF's creation was in accordance with the wishes of the leadership of Yugoslavia's communist partisans, who under the guidance of Josip Broz (*nom de guerre* Tito), had at that point become the most powerful communist force in the Balkans.[68]

As regards Macedonia, Tito aimed at the very least to maintain the part that belonged to Yugoslavia. He also entertained thoughts of uniting parts of Bulgarian and Greek Macedonia 'under his own aegis,' a fact that once again demonstrates the importance that Macedonia has played in the international politics of the Balkans.[69] Tito's intentions were partly expressed in the 2 August 1943 creation of the Anti-Fascist Assembly of the National Liberation of Macedonia (ASNOM).[70] On that day, ASNOM declared: 'Macedonians under Bulgaria and Greece! The unification of the entire Macedonian people depends on your participation in the gigantic anti-Fascist front.'[71]

ASNOM's declarations form part of the basis on which the Socialist Republic of Macedonia (and subsequently FYROM), was founded. Significantly, they clearly reveal ASNOM's irredentist character and goals. For example, on 4 August 1944 ASNOM proclaimed the following:

> People of Macedonia!
> In the course of three years of combat you have achieved your unity...With the participation of the entire Macedonian nation against the Fascist occupiers of Yugoslavia, Bulgaria and Greece you will achieve unification of all parts of Macedonia, divided in 1915 and 1918 by Balkan imperialists.[72]

These irredentist goals eventually came to represent a significant aspect of the dispute between Greece and FYROM. Suspected adherence to these goals also caused friction between ELAS and SNOF during the final stages of the Second World War. As liberation approached, the KKE felt that SNOF forces had adopted a secessionist policy on Greek Macedonia that was not consistent with the party's position. SNOF was also suspected for being more loyal to Tito than to the KKE. As a result, ELAS and SNOF clashed militarily, and the latter's forces were expelled from Greece in October 1944.[73] By November, the Germans had also left the country.

In December, there were bloody clashes in Athens between communist and government supporters.[74] The KKE was defeated, primarily because of the intervention of British forces. The February 1945 Varkiza agreement provided for the demobilisation of all armed units.[75] Despite it however, the country did not manage to avoid the descent into civil war.[76]

As was the case with the two Balkan and World Wars, the Macedonian Question also proved of central significance to the Greek Civil War.[77] Its importance was initially related to the creation by Tito in April 1945 of the National Liberation Front (NOF).[78] It was comprised primarily by former SNOF members, and 'acted as the instrument of the Yugoslav plans in Greek Macedonia.'[79] NOF did not honour the Varkiza agreement and engaged in periodic guerrilla activities in Greek Macedonia. In November 1946, NOF's forces were integrated with those of the KKE's military wing, the Democratic Army of Greece (DSE).[80]

During the Civil War, the DSE managed to control various villages and mountainous regions, though almost all cities and towns remained under constant government control. Despite Tito's backing of the KKE, government forces received substantially more aid from the US.[81] Eventually, during the 1948/9 winter, communist activities were essentially limited to parts of Western Greek Macedonia.

Facing an acute recruitment problem, the DSE was forced to rely heavily upon Slav-Macedonians. It has been estimated that they represented some 14,000 out of the DSE's total of 20,000 soldiers.[82] Given their important role, the KKE's General Secretary Nikos Zachariades proceeded to change his party's policy on Greek Macedonia. At the KKE's Fifth Plenum on 31 January 1949, the following resolution was passed:

> The Macedonian people are distinguishing themselves, and there must be no doubt that after the liberation, they will find their national restoration as they wish it. Various elements which are trying to break the unity between the Slav-

Macedonia and Greek peoples should be guarded against. This unity should be presented as 'the pupil of the eye' and should be reinforced and strengthened firmly and continuously.[83]

Any ambiguity was clarified in a statement that was broadcast by the KKE's radio station 'Free Greece':

The Second Conference of the NOF...will declare the union of Macedonia into a complete, independent, and equal Macedonian nation within the Popular Democratic Federation of the Balkan peoples.[84]

This policy advocated the secession of national Greek territory, and was thus viewed by government forces as treasonous.[85] However, it was never implemented, since in August 1949 the DSE was soundly defeated in the mountainous battlefields of Grammos and Vitsi.

## D. The Contentious Emergence of FYROM

The People's (subsequently Socialist) Republic of Macedonia became a part of the Yugoslav Federation in 1944. In the years after the end of the Greek Civil War, a passionate and sensitive debate emerged between Greece and Yugoslavia (and later FYROM), concerning human rights, propaganda and irredentist claims. Evaluating the validity of all the various charges is beyond the scope and intentions of this book. The aim of this section will simply be to present (at their proper dimension), some of the most contentious issues that help explain the dispute between FYROM and Greece that will be covered in the following chapters.

One of the greatest issues of contention has centred on the numbers, treatment and national identity of Slavophones residing in Greek Macedonia. Some have ridiculously claimed that a minority of one million 'Macedonians' [i.e. people with a FYROM national identity] reside in Greece, though other reports reduce this number substantially and refer to an only linguistic minority.[86]

At this point, it should be stressed that it is generally accepted that

The nation-state building process [in Greek Macedonia] has been enormously successful. Most of the inhabitants today, regardless of their ethnic background and how they or their ancestors might have defined themselves one hundred or even fifty years ago, conceive themselves now as nothing less than Greek.[87]

There are important reasons why this is the case. First of all, many Slavophones lacking a Greek national identity abandoned Greece after the end of the Second Balkan War. Secondly, during the Metaxas dictatorship (1936-41) a series of repressive measures aiming at forced assimilation were taken, and there was further repression during the Colonel's dictatorship (1967-74), though all Greek citizens suffered from it.[88]

The consequences of the Greek Civil War must also be analysed. As previously stated, many Slavophones had been associated with the KKE and the NOF. Following their defeat, and fearing retributions, some 35,000 left Greece.[89] Thus, the 1951 Greek census indicated that 'Slavophones had diminished from 86,086 [in 1940] to 41,017.'[90] Finally, the practice of intermarriage has also contributed to the Greek national identity of the country's Slavophones.[91]

The exact number of Slavophones residing in Greece today and having a pro-FYROM national identity is almost impossible to estimate.[92] In the 1993 elections for the European Parliament, the Rainbow Party (with a heavy emphasis on human rights issues) that was close to representing such a viewpoint received 7,263 votes, representing an insignificant 0.1 per cent of the total vote.[93] In the 1996 general election, the Rainbow Party fielded common candidates with a party called the Organisation for the Reconstruction of the KKE (OAKKE), and received 3,485 votes (0.05 per cent of the total), 2,000 of which in Greek Macedonia.[94] It is possible that these voters 'constitute the "hard" electoral core of [their party].'[95] In the June 1999 elections for the European Parliament, both the Rainbow Party and the OAKKE were represented, gaining 4,983 and 4,622 votes respectively (0.078 per cent and 0.072 per cent of the total).[96]

In addition to numerical disagreements, the Greek government has been consistently accused of human rights violations.[97] One of the most frequent accusations refers to a law passed in 1982 allowing the return of 'all Greeks by genus [origin] who during the Civil War of 1946-1949 and because of it had fled abroad as political refugees.'[98] This stipulation forbids the return of people who declare a non-Greek nationality.[99]

The Greek government has also been accused for not permitting special minority educational arrangements, as well as for rejecting an application to create a 'Centre for Macedonian Culture.'[100] Furthermore, there have been some four cases of human right activists who have been brought to trial on various charges.[101] However, with one exception, charges have either been dropped, or the courts have issued acquittals.[102]

While denying accusations of human rights violations, the Greek government has charged Yugoslavia (and then FYROM), for falsifying ancient Greek history, conducting hostile propaganda and making irredentist claims.[103] As regards the Greeks, probably the most infuriating practice involves what is considered to be the unjust appropriation of the history of the ancient Macedonians. In numerous FYROM publications, maps and school textbooks, the claim has been made that they were not Greek.[104] This issue is not merely of historical significance, since the seriousness of the Greek reaction which will be described in this book, possibly intends 'to proclaim that the name [and history] of Macedonia is an integral part of Greek identity and that no one can claim to be a Macedonian without being Greek.'[105]

FYROM has further been accused for irredentist propaganda (usually taking the form of maps depicting a Macedonian state that includes parts of Greece), that have appeared in schoolbooks, calendars, and even labels on alcoholic drinks.[106] The Greek government also considered as containing possible irredentist claims several articles of FYROM's constitution that was adopted on 20 November 1991.[107] More specifically, the constitution's Preamble was contentious because it claimed to rest (among various events), 'upon the statehood-legal traditions of the Krusevo Republic and the historical decisions of the Antifascist Assembly of the People's Liberation of Macedonia [ASNOM].'[108] The Krusevo Republic was related to the Ilinden uprising that partly took place in territories that comprise contemporary Greek Macedonia. As regards ASNOM, its irredentist character was analysed previously.

Greece also objected to Article 3 because it implied that 'the only changes that can take place in the territory of [FYROM] are changes of annexation of new territories.'[109] In other words, it was presumed that Article 3 provided legal sanctioning to any future annexations. Finally, there was Greek disagreement to Article 49, which stated that 'the republic takes care of the status and rights of the members of the Macedonian people in neighbouring countries.'[110] This was perceived as a call to interfere with Greek domestic politics, and was considered even more provocative given the fact that the government and all major political parties do not recognise the existence of such a minority in their country. Eventually, as will be shown in the next chapter, Greek pressure and criticisms resulted to both Articles 3 and 49 being amended by FYROM's Parliament.[111]

### E. Greece and FYROM: An Account of Common Interests

Despite the controversies and contentious issues between Greece and FYROM, it is crucial to present also the common interests that are shared by both countries. More specifically and for obvious reasons, FYROM's government did not want the war that had broken out in Croatia and later in Bosnia to spread within their republic's borders.[112] It is of extreme importance that the Greek, as well as all EPC governments, shared precisely the same desire.[113] This probably constitutes the most important common interest between the two states.

Thus, Greece's President Konstantinos Karamanlis explained in a letter to EC leaders on 24 November 1992 that his country 'has an interest in the maintenance of [FYROM's] independence and territorial integrity.'[114] In an interview, the then Prime Minister Konstantinos Mitsotakis noted that his country had absolutely nothing to gain from FYROM's dissolution, especially since Greece had 'no [geopolitical and economic] conflict of interests' with the young republic.[115] Former Foreign Minister Michalis Papaconstantinou in agreement with this analysis, pointed out that had there been a war in FYROM, the results would have been disastrous for Greece.[116] Similarly, former Deputy Minister of Foreign Affairs Ioannis Tzounis declared that 'if this state did not exist, we should have invented it;'[117] and in a previously unpublished address to his EPC counterparts on 17 February 1992, former Foreign Minister Antonis Samaras stated that

> It is in our interest to have a small, but truly independent state as a neighbour, than a big and powerful one. Such a state would serve our concern, and the concerns of the Community, for stability in the region.[118]

There are several reasons that explain this unusual level of agreement between Greek politicians.[119] Perhaps most importantly, they feared that a war in FYROM could have eventually escalated into a Third Balkan War.[120] Apparently, the then leader of the Opposition Andreas Papandreou was also fully aware of this potential scenario. He later succinctly summarised its implications by stating that the 'irony of this [dispute] is that we have every interest that [FYROM] does not disintegrate because this will mean a Balkan War.'[121]

Misha Glenny has pointed out that Greeks were particularly apprehensive about the consequences of such a war, fearing that

> The eventual outcome (after fighting more bloody than in Bosnia) would probably be the consolidation of a Greater Albania and a Greater Bulgaria on Greece's northern border and a concomitant increase in Turkish influence (via Albania) in the region.[122]

The possibility of a war taking place within FYROM's borders (with all its potential results), was not considered by the Greek government a mere theoretical possibility. In an interview, Papaconstantinou revealed that contingency plans had been prepared, in order to deal with what was expected to be a wave of refugees from FYROM and possibly Albania.[123]

Another area of common interests between FYROM and Greece involves the realm of economics. The resolution of the dispute with Greece would have produced substantial financial benefits for FYROM, since as a recognised republic it would have been allowed to receive much needed assistance from various international organisations such as the International Monetary Fund (IMF) and the World Bank. This is proved by the fact that after the dispute with Greece was partially resolved with the signing on 13 September 1995 of an Interim Agreement, FYROM managed to secure 55 million US dollars from the IMF and 99 million US dollars from the World Bank.[124]

Being a land-locked country, FYROM would have also been able to use the strategically located port of Thessaloniki.[125] In the words of FYROM's former Vice President of the government Mr Risteski: 'we have no access to the sea...Close economic relations with Greece are a must...Greece is an ideal area for trade.'[126] FYROM could have benefited from Greek investment and perhaps even used its neighbour as a market for surplus labour. Furthermore, given the resolution of the dispute, the costs associated with the various trade restrictions and the oil embargo that were imposed by Greece (and will be analysed in subsequent chapters), would have ceased to exist.

Normalised relations between the two states would have also produced economic benefits for Greece—a fact that was recognised by most major Greek decision-makers.[127] It has even been argued by Papaconstantinou that his state's economic penetration could potentially be of such a magnitude, that FYROM could 'fall within [its] sphere of interest.'[128] It must be explained that trade with FYROM has a particular significance for the economy of Northern Greece.[129] Furthermore, Greek products have a comparative advantage, as a result of factors such as

> Geographic location and reduced transportation costs. This advantage is further strengthened from the considerable recognition and acceptance that Greek products have from [FYROM's] consumers.[130]

Greece's relatively large and consistent trade surpluses with FYROM can perhaps be submitted as further evidence of its comparative advantage over FYROM.[131] Greek companies have also exhibited important economic activity in the new republic. It has been estimated that since September 1995, their investments have been worth 250 million US dollars.[132] As a result, Greece has become 'the largest direct investor in FYROM.'[133]

More specifically, Greek companies have bought one of FYROM's biggest tobacco companies, are attempting to buy FYROM's biggest bank, and have begun establishing a supermarket chain.[134] Furthermore, they have invested in the fields of mining, meat processing, beer brewing and cement production.[135] More recently, there have been negotiations and discussions concerning the construction of an oil pipeline connecting Skopje with Thessaloniki, cooperation in the production of electricity, as well as the expansion of certain railway lines between the two countries.[136]

On the basis of the above analysis, it can be concluded that important economic interests were shared between the two neighbouring states. Furthermore, both Greece and FYROM (as well as all EPC member states), shared the desire to avoid the war from spreading to the new republic. The existence of these common interests satisfies institutionalism's most crucial condition and hence allows the theory to be applied to the events that will be analysed next. These common interests also add an interesting perspective to what eventually became a particularly contentious dispute.

## Notes

1. The phrase refers to the Macedonian Question, and is taken from Robert Legvold's brief review of Danforth, 1995. See Legvold. (1996), *Foreign Affairs*, vol. 75, no.2, p. 161.
2. Palmer and King, 1971, p. vii; cited in Economides, 1990, p. 131.
3. In agreement with this starting point for the modern phase of the Macedonian Question are Barker, 1950, p. 7; Mazarakis-Ainian, 1992, p. 30 and Karakasidou, 1997b, p. 78.
4. For further analysis of the *millet* system, see Poulton, 1995, p. 35-7.
5. For the role and power of the Ecumenical Patriarchate within the Ottoman Empire, see Daikin, 1972, p. 11-2.
6. Kitromilides, 1989, p. 156. For the text of the *firman*, see Vacalopoulos, 1989, p. 53-6. As expected, the Patriarchate in Constantinople declared the Exarchate schismatic.
7. See Mertzos, 1992, p. 49-50.
8. However, some territories were explicitly named in the *firman* as being under the control of the Exarchate. For Article X, see Vacalopoulos, 1989, p. 55-6.
9. See Crampton, 1987, p. 19.
10. Jenkins, 1995, p. 403.
11. See Kofos, 1964, p. 16. It must not be assumed that mere moral outrage produced this conference. Russian pressure on behalf of a potentially important and fellow Slav ally was also significant.
12. See Map II for the San Stephano territorial settlements.
13. See Kofos, 1969 and Mertzos, 1992, p. 52-60.
14. Kofos, 1964, p. 17.
15. See Map II for the Treaty of Berlin territorial settlements. Bulgaria was somewhat compensated with the 1885 annexation of Eastern Rumelia. See Kofos, 1964, p. 18-9.

16 They eventually rivalled the numbers and quality of Greek schools. For an excellent study of educational rivalries and policies in North-Western Macedonia during the period of 1870-1904, see Vouri, 1992. See also Vacalopoulos, 1989, p. 134, for an interesting table showing the number of Bulgarian and Greek schools in the Thessaloniki *vilayet* (administrative unit), in 1885. See also ibid., p. 131-47. The numbers of Bulgarian, Greek, Romanian and Serbian schools, pupils and teachers in the *vilayets* of Thessaloniki and Monastir in 1900 can be found in Mazarakis-Aenian, 1992, p. 31.

17 See Perry, 1988, p. 28 and Vouri, 1992, p. 182-3. According to Anthony D. Smith, the 'fundamental features of national identity [are], p. 1. an historic territory, or homeland. 2. common myths and historical memories. 3. a common, mass public culture. 4. common legal rights and duties for all members. 5. a common economy with territorial mobility for members' (Smith, 1991, p. 14). On the other hand, ethnic communities (on which ethnic identities are based), have the following 'main attributes...1. a collective proper name. 2. a myth of common ancestry. 3. shared historical memories. 4. one or more differentiating elements of common culture. 5. an association with a specific 'homeland'. 6. a sense of solidarity for significant sectors of the population' (ibid., p. 21). These are the definitions that will be mostly in mind when referring to national and ethnic identities in this book. Admittedly though, a separate study could have been written contesting or validating these definitions. The interested reader could begin an investigation with Connor, 1994.

18 Vlasidis, 1997, p. 65-6.

19 IMRO's subsequent history and mutations are of unusual complexity. See Perry 1988 and especially Vlasidis, 1997. For an account of some of IMRO's more spectacular terrorist acts, see Kofos, 1964, p. 31-3.

20 Poulton, p. 1995, p. 53-4. See also Barker, 1950, p. 16-7 and Jelavich, 1983, p. 93.

21 The decision to organise the Ilinden uprising was taken on 17 January 1903. See Perry, 1988, p. 121-4 for a discussion of this fateful meeting. The brief account of the Ilinden uprising is based on Brailsford 1903 and Brailsford, 1906, p. 111-71; Council for Research into South-Eastern Europe, 1993, p. 50-2; Daikin, 1966, p. 92-107; Kofos, 1964, p. 33-6 and Perry, 1988, p. 127-40. See also the fascinating collection of diplomatic documents in Gounaris et al, 1993.

22 Whether the Ilinden uprising was the work of Bulgarians or Slavs with a national 'Macedonian' consciousness has been disputed. For an important publication arguing for the latter interpretation, see Council for Research into South-Eastern Europe, 1993. Significantly however, H. N. Brailsford who eyewitnessed the events, devoted a chapter in his book *Macedonia Its Races and Their Future* to the Ilinden uprising, that was titled 'The Bulgarian Movement.' See Brailsford, 1906, p. 111.

23 For the destructive results of the Ilinden uprising, see ibid., p. 158-65; Daikin, 1966, p. 104; Gounaris et al, 1993, p. 185-97 and Perry, 1988, p. 140.

24 See Dragoumis, 1907/1992, p. 22 and Perry, 1988, p. 124-5 and 138.

25 Far-sighted Greeks were able to understand that the Bulgarians represented their most serious and long-term adversaries in Macedonia. Hence, the fact that Greeks aided the Turks in their struggle to quell the Ilinden uprising becomes understandable. For accounts of Greek actions against Bulgarians during Ilinden, see Brailsford, 1906, p. 129-30 and Perry, 1988, p. 137-8. See also Karavangelis, n.d., p. 189-92 for examples of Greek cooperation with the Ottoman authorities. Karavangelis was the Patriarchical bishop of Kastoria during the 1900-7 period. Fearless and something of an organisational genius, he was primarily responsible for the Hellenic effort in the region. Karavangelis'

memoirs of this period are strikingly straightforward and make fascinating reading. For Brailsford's account of his interview with Karavangelis, see Brailsford, 1906, p. 191-3.
26 Daikin, 1966, p. 117-8.
27 In a letter that Pavlos Melas sent to Germanos Karavangelis, he poignantly asserted while referring to the Greek Ministry of Foreign Affairs that 'they are asleep.' This passage is cited in Karavangelis, n.d., p. 42. Concerning the Greek struggle in Macedonia, the best account is probably Daikin, 1966. For an excellent analysis of the various studies of this topic, see Gounaris, 1997a.
28 It was Melas' direct involvement in such activities that caused his violent death. An important and at times moving biography of Melas was written by his wife, which is primarily based on a series of letters that her husband had sent to her. See Mela, 1964. It should also be noted that Melas is considered a national hero. His name is often given to streets, and his statue can be found in many cities. Patricia Storace has correctly noted that Melas' 'image is as famous in Greece as Davy Crockett's is in the United States' (Storace, 1996, p. 350).
29 In Athens, 'all work stopped...everyone walked about mournfully in the streets and squares; and the church bells tolled the passing of a national hero' (Daikin, p. 1966, p. 191). For an account of Melas' death and funeral, see Karavangelis, n.d., p. 60-71.
30 Dragoumis, 1907/1992, p. 9. For an exceptionally perceptive analysis of the life, character and ultimately soul of Ion Dragoumis, see Evrigenis, 1961. See also Karakasidou, 1997b, p. 90-2.
31 See ibid., p. 103. For an important and illuminating collection of diplomatic documents from Greece's Ministry of Foreign Affairs that refer to Greece's counterattack in Ottoman Macedonia during the years of 1905-6, see Mouseio Makedonikou Agona, 1997.
32 Koliopoulos, 1989, p. 209; emphasis in the original.
33 Daikin, 1966, p. 475.
34 Carnegie Foundation, 1914/1993, p. 35.
35 Kinross, 1964, p. 31.
36 For an account of events in Macedonia between the Young Turk Revolution and the First Balkan War, see Daikin, 1966, p. 382-421.
37 See Map III for the territorial agreements included in the alliance between Serbia and Bulgaria. Significantly, the agreement between Greece and Bulgaria did not cover post-victory territorial settlements.
38 For an account of these alliances, see Jelavich, 1983, p. 97 and Vacalopoulos, 1992, p. 347.
39 In 1919 Adrianople was occupied by Greece. Since the 1923 Treaty of Lausanne, the city has belonged to Turkey. See Pettifer, 1997, p. 182.
40 See Map IV for the London Conference territorial settlements.
41 Carnegie Foundation, 1914/1992, p. 5.
42 Jelavich, 1983, p. 99. It should be noted that 'by the end of May [1913] the Greeks and Serbs had signed a secret agreement to divide Macedonia west of the Vardar and to allow the fate of the areas east of that river to be determined by the principle of effective occupation' (Crampton, p. 1987, p. 61).
43 See Crampton, 1987, p.61-2 and Jelavich, 1983, p. 99. It is also noteworthy that 'the Second Balkan war...cost more [Bulgarian] lives than the campaign against the Ottoman empire' (Ibid., p. 62).
44 These figures are taken from Kofos, 1964, p. 44. See Map IV for the Bucharest Treaty territorial settlements.
45 Crampton, 1987, p. 63.

46 See Map V for Bulgaria's conquests during the First World War. For an account of the events and consequences of the First World War in the Balkans, see Jelavich, 1983, p. 106-33. For an excellent analysis of Bulgaria's foreign policy concerning Western Thrace during the years 1919-23, see Stavrinou-Paximadopoulou, 1997.
47 Barker, 1950, p. 29-30; cited in Kofos, 1964, p. 41.
48 See Map VI for the boundaries of the Balkan states after the Treaty of Neuilly territorial settlements, as well as after the end of the First World War.
49 This number was provided by the League of Nations. According to the same source, there were 119,000 Bulgarians (the national classification belongs to the League of Nations), residing in Greece in 1912. See Kofos, 1964, p. 47. Other accounts put the number to 200,000 (Close and Veremis, 1993, p. 98), or even 240,000 (see Rossos, 1991, p. 285). However, Kofos probably concludes correctly that 'Greece [was] the most homogeneous state in the Balkans, if not of the entire Eastern Europe' (Kofos, 1964, p. 47). This was aided by the fact that more than one million Greeks had left their ancestral homes in Asia Minor, following the conclusion of the 1922 Greek-Turkish War, and the signing of the 1923 Treaty of Lausanne. Almost half a million refugees relocated in Greek Macedonia. See Karakasidou, 1997b, p. 145; Koliopoulos, 1997, p. 51 and Voutira, 1997, p. 119.
50 The interwar years also witnessed IMRO's decline. The reasons for its decline are succinctly and expertly summarised in Barker, 1950, p. 45.
51 Cited in ibid., p. 52. On the Balkan Communist Federation, see Kofos, 1964, p. 69.
52 Cited in Barker, 1950, p. 58.
53 Ibid.; emphasis added.
54 Apparently, Bulgarian communists utilised several arguments in order to persuade the Comintern. See Kofos, 1964, p. 76.
55 A protracted debate and power struggle took place within the KKE, before the Comintern's policy on Macedonia was accepted. A comprehensive and definitive account of this struggle can be found in Dangas and Leontiades, 1997, p. 11-91.
56 See Kofos, 1964., p. 78-84.
57 Cited in ibid., p. 91.
58 Some parts of Greece were occupied by Italy.
59 See Map VII for Bulgaria's territorial conquests during the Second World War. For Mussolini's decision to conquer Greece, see Averof-Tositsa, 1996, p. 52 and Jelavich, 1983, p. 227-8. For an analysis of Metaxas' statesmanship during this period that culminated with the rejection of an Italian ultimatum on 28 October 1940, see ibid., p. 228-9 and especially Koliopoulos, 1994, p. 137-245. The latter study, based primarily on British sources, corrects many misperceptions and myths. Concerning the resistance of Greek forces to the Nazi *Blitzkrieg*, it must be stressed that they exhibited tremendous valour. Thus, the Germans, 'in token of respect to the enemy had insisted that the Greek officers should keep their swords. That was to be almost the last gesture of chivalry between warriors in a war imminently fated to descend into barbarism' (Keegan, 1989, p. 158). For an excellent study of occupied Greece, see Mazower 1993. The damages caused to Greece's economy and infrastructure as a result of the Nazi occupation are succinctly summarised in *E Kathimerini*, 14 December 1997, p. 24.
60 Cited in Kofos, 1964, p. 100.
61 Poulton, 1991/1993, p. 177.
62 King George II, as well as many leading politicians had left Greece.

63  See Averof-Tositsa, 1996, p. 168 and Koliopoulos, 1995a, p. 102-3. EAM did not openly espouse or promote a Marxist revolutionary agenda. See Smith, 1993, p. 59-60. Significantly, none of the words contained in EAM suggested Marxist goals or ideology.
64  Kofos, 1989b, p. 7.
65  On the SNOF, see Barker, 110-2; Kofos, 1964, p. 123-27 and Koliopoulos, 1995a, p. 113-38.
66  Koliopoulos, 1995a, p. 127.
67  An interesting example of 'rebaptisement' at work is given in a 1944 report of a British officer. He refers to a *komitadji* who had brutally murdered at least one Greek civilian, and then essentially received immunity by joining ELAS. In this particular case however, it is probable that some sort of 'justice' was eventually enforced. See Rossos, 1991, p. 301.
68  See Barker, 1950, p. 110. Apparently, Tito's emissary Tempo was instrumental in the creation of the SNOF. As regards Tito, numerous books and articles have been published. Of the more recent ones, the interested reader should consult Pavlowitch, 1992 who offers a brief and highly critical appraisal of Tito's career. West, 1994 is written in an engaging style and is particularly good in covering Tito's Second World War years. For a somewhat conventional though comprehensive and well-written biography, see Ridley, 1994.
69  Barker, 1950, p. 83.
70  The date was significant, since 2 August is Ilinden. ASNOM was created by 'the "Central Committee of the Communist Party of Macedonia" (promoted from the former "Regional Committee for Macedonia of the Yugoslav Communist Part"' (ibid., p. 93).
71  Cited in Poulton, 1995, p. 105-6.
72  Cited in ibid., p. 106. See also ASNOM's 29 November 1949 declaration at the Jajce Conference. The crucial passages can be found in Kofos, 1964, p. 117.
73  See Close, 1995, p. 75. Some limited clashes between EAM and SNOF also took place in November 1944.
74  These events are known as the *Dekemvriana* (the December events). For an account, see Baerentzen and Close, 1993, p. 84-92; Close, 1995, p. 137-49, as well as the somewhat idiosyncratic and certainly controversial analysis in Mazower, 1993, p. 340-54. See also Winston S. Churchill's intriguing remarks on Stalin's stance during the December events that can be found in Churchill, 1953, p. 369.
75  See Jelavich, 1983, p. 283.
76  Numerous books have been written on the Greek Civil War. Of particular merit are Close, 1993; Iatrides, 1981 and Woodhouse, 1976.
77  See Kofos, 1989b, p. 3.
78  On the NOF see Barker, 1950, p. 118-8; Kofos, 1989b, p. 17-21 and Koliopoulos, 1995b, p. 25, 31 and 146-69.
79  Kofos, 1964, p. 107.
80  For the text of the agreement that integrated NOF with the DSE, see Sfetas, 1996, p. 220-1.
81  See Close and Veremis, 1993, p. 108.
82  See Woodhouse, 1976, p. 262. In agreement with this estimate are Close and Veremis, 1993, p. 120; Koliopoulos, 1995b, p. 221 and Rossos, 1991, p. 307 fn 54. Richard Clogg however, states that 'by 1949 as much as 40 per cent of the [DSE] was composed of Slav Macedonians' (Clogg, 1992, p. 141). Sfetas estimates the by the end of 1948, half of the DSE fighters were Slav-Macedonians. See Sfetas, 1996, p. 228. Despite these

different estimates by various scholars, there is essentially consensus that a substantial and crucial percentage of the KKE's fighting force was comprised by Slav-Macedonians.
83  Cited in Barker, 1950, p. 119. Important passages from Zachariades' speech at the KKE's Fifth Plenum that both preceded and provided the guidelines for the passage of this resolution can be found in Sfetas, 1996, p. 231-2. For Zachariades' explanation of this decision after the conclusion of the Civil War, see ibid., p. 234.
84  Cited in Barker, 1950, p. 120.
85  The KKE eventually abandoned and condemned this policy. See Kofos, 1964, p. 221-3.
86  For the million-strong estimate, see Poulton, 1995, p. 171. The US Department of State alleges the existence of only 20,000 to 50,000 Slavophones, and is furthermore silent on their national identity. See US Department of State, 1991, p. 1166-1175. See also MRG Greece et al, 1994, p. 14-5 for other estimates. It should also be stressed that 'an internationally binding definition of the concept of minority still does not exist' (Stavros, 1995, p. 9). Perhaps the most commonly accepted definition is the one by Francesco Capotorti. He defines a minority as 'a group numerically inferior to the rest of the population of the State, in a non-dominant position, whose members—being nationals of the State—possess ethnic, religious or linguistic characteristics differing from those of the rest of the population, and show, if only implicitly, a sense of solidarity, directed towards preserving their culture, traditions, religion or language (ibid.). The major weakness of this definition is its failure to give a more precise indication about the numerical strength required in order for a group to constitute a minority.
87  Karakasidou, 1993a, p. 5. See also Danforth, 1995, p. 116; Karakasidou, 1997a, p. 92 and Karakasidou, 1997b, p. 21-2.
88  For repressive measures during the Metaxas dictatorship, see Carabott, 1997; Close, 1995, p. 51; Gounaris, 1997b, p. 104 and Karakasidou, 1997b, p. 187. For example, Slavophones were sometimes harassed for not speaking Greek, and there was also compulsory night schooling in Greek history and language. For the general repression during the Colonel's dictatorship, see Kofos, 1992, p. 274.
89  See Kofos, 1964, p. 186 and MRG Greece et al 1994, p. 13. Almost certainly implausibly, FYROM sources claim that the exodus involved some 213,000 people. See Human Rights Watch/Helsinki, 1994, p. 8.
90  Close, 1993a, p. 10. Significantly, many of the Slavophones who remained in Greece had cooperated with the right-wing authorities against the KKE and supported the maintaining of a unified Greek state. See Theodoropoulos et al, 1995, p. 45.
91  See Angelopoulos, 1997.
92  See Gounaris, 1997b, p. 107.
93  See MRG Greece et al, 1994, p. 16.
94  See Mihailidis, 1997, p. 141 fn 21 and *Eleftherotypia*, 24 September 1996, p. 25. It is interesting to compare these numbers with the some 20,000 Filipinos and 50,000 Poles residing in Athens alone. See *E Kathimerini*, 25 May 1997, p. 27.
95  Mihailidis, 1997, p. 141 fn 21. This is certainly a far cry from claims of a million-strong group. Thus, it can at least be concluded that 'it is debatable whether this group (although a vocal one) is numerically so strong as to warrant the creation of separate educational institutions; according to international standards, a minority population needs to be sufficiently numerous for such a demand to be justified' (Roudometof, 1996, p. 272). It should be admitted however, that Roudometof is not explicitly referring to the Rainbow Party and its supporters.
96  See *Eleftherotypia*, 22 June 1999, p. 7.

97  For a more complete presentation of accusations against the Greek government, see Danforth, 1995, p. 108-41; Human Rights Watch/Helsinki, 1994; Karakasidou 1993a; MRG Greece et al, 1994; Poulton, 1991/1993, p. 173-92 and Poulton, 1995, p. 162-71. See also Pollis 1992 and Stavros, 1995.

98  This translation of the Greek law is cited in Human Rights Watch/Helsinki, 1994, p. 27. See also Danforth, 1995, p. 122 and *Eleftherotypia*, 17 May 1997, p. 26-7.

99  Apparently, this law has recently been relaxed. During a visit to Skopje, I met a woman who had left her village in Greece in 1949 at the age of ten. She was sent by forces loyal to the KKE to Hungary, while her parents were sent to Poland and Romania. After years of efforts, the family managed to re-unite in the Soviet Union. This woman was first allowed to visit Greece again in April 1997. A somewhat ingenious solution (which I witnessed), was practised at the Greek border. A temporary visa was given to her, in which she wrote her name not in Slavic as it appeared in her passport but in Greek. It also happened that this was the name with which she was born, and was used by her until she left Greece in 1949. At any rate, the result was that the woman was allowed to go and visit a relative in Athens. It is also worthwhile reporting that some prominent Greek politicians suggested to me that the 1982 law might change in the near future. However, the country's government has recently altered the border visa arrangements, and made them somewhat tougher. Visas will now have to be obtained at the Greek mission at Skopje, and not at the border. See *Exousia*, 9 October 1997, p. 6. More than 1,300,000 visas have been granted to FYROM citizens wishing to visit Greece since October 1995! See *Eleftherotypia*, 23 December 1998, p. 4.

100 For the rejection of the centre's creation, see Danforth, 1995, p. 128-9 and Human Rights Watch/Helsinki, 1994, p. 20-1. For the adjudication of this case by the European Court of Human Rights, see *Exousia*, 11 July 1998, p. 6. Concerning accusations for not permitting minority educational arrangements, see Human Rights Watch/Helsinki, 1994, p. 37-44. The issue of whether a Macedonian language exists constitutes an important part of this debate. For a discussion of this issue, see Ioannidou, 1997.

101 See Danforth, 1995, p. 116-25 and Vlasidis and Karakostanoglou, 1995, p. 165. Many of these human rights activists are actually considered by the Greek government to be foreign agents. For example, in an interview on 23 December 1996, Papaconstantinou pointed out that a prominent activist (Mr Sidiropoulos), while virtually penniless, has managed to continually travel around the world expressing his views. The implication was that he was receiving funding from sources (or countries), that do not share Greece's Macedonian policies.

102 See Human Rights Watch/Helsinki, 1994, p. 23-4. The exception that is often mentioned, is that of Father Tsarknias. See ibid., p. 53 and MRG Greece et al, 1994, p. 17. The source of some of his legal troubles was that he was defrocked. However, he was not defrocked because of any human rights activities, but was actually 'convicted in an ecclesiastical court on charges of homosexuality and disobedience to his superiors' (Danforth, 1995, p. 133). Importantly, the critical to the Greek government Human Rights Watch/Helsinki report concludes that the organisation 'does not know of any ethnic Macedonian who is currently serving a prison sentence for the peaceful expression of his or her views' (Human Rights Watch/Helsinki, 1994, p. 25). See also a brief but extremely critical review of Human Rights Watch/Helsinki, in Kozyris J. Phaedon. (1996), *Journal of Modern Greek Studies*, vol. 14, p. 358-61.

103 For an account of several instances of friction between Greece and Yugoslavia over Macedonia, see Mertzos, 1992, p. 403-46.

104 For an impressive analysis of FYROM's school textbooks dealing with this issue, see Kofos, 1994a, p. 14-20. See also Kofos, 1976, p. 14-7. Perhaps the most popular Greek response is Martis, 1983. For a more scholarly and comprehensive effort, see Sakelariou, 1994, p. 30-191.
105 Roudometof, 1996, p. 284. See also Kofos, 1986, p. 168.
106 See Appendix I.
107 For a comprehensive analysis of FYROM's constitution, see Tzonos, 1994. See also Hayden, 1992, p. 659-60 and Kofos, 1994b.
108 Cited in ibid., p. 48.
109 See ibid., p. 48.
110 Ibid., p. 49.
111 The amendments were inserted on 6 January 1992, and can be found in ibid.
112 This point was stressed in all the interviews that were conducted with FYROM officials for the purposes of this thesis.
113 This fact concerning EPC's member states was readily acknowledged in almost all of the interviews that were conducted for this thesis.
114 This passage from Karamanlis' letter can be found in Valinakis and Dales, 1994, p. 109.
115 Interview with Mr Mitsotakis on 10 April 1997.
116 Interview with Mr Papaconstantinou on 23 December 1996.
117 Interview with Mr Tzounis on 14 April 1997.
118 See Appendix IV.
119 Similar arguments concerning Greece's interest in the war not spreading to FYROM were made in interviews with Ms Damanaki on 30 January 1997, Mr Kofos on 5 January 1997, Mr Lengeris on 27 August 1997, Mr Papayannakis on 10 January 1997 and Mr Skilakakis on 15 April 1997.
120 The possibility of a Balkan War was also accepted by FYROM's former (until late November 1998) Assistant Minister of Foreign Affairs Mr Dimovski, during an interview on 29 September 1997. His ultimate argument was that FYROM's existence was in Greece's interest.
121 Cited in Kyrkos, 1994, p. 19. Papandreou's statement was made on 13 January 1994. When asked to comment on this statement, Mitsotakis said that he was in complete agreement, and suggested that he had also summarised the dangers from the war spreading to FYROM in a very similar, if not identical way. The implication was that Papandreou had 'borrowed' this analysis from Mitsotakis (interview with Mr Mitsotakis on 10 April 1997).
122 Glenny, 1996, p. 143.
123 Interview with Mr Papaconstantinou on 23 December 1996.
124 These figures are taken from Doudoumis, 1996, p. 123. See also Perry, 1992a, p. 44; Perry 1992b, p. 12 and Perry, 1997, p. 263. The Interim Agreement can be found and is analysed in Rozakis, 1996.
125 See Economides, 1995, p. 114.
126 Interview with Mr Risteski on 29 September 1997. Essentially the same argument was made in interviews with all FYROM officials. More recently, FYROM officials were quoted characterising Greece as a 'strategic investor' and a 'strategic ally' as regards the realm of economics. See *Eleftherotypia*, 23 December 1998, p. 4.
127 Interviews with Mr Mertzos on 18 December 1996, Mr Mitsotakis on 10 April 1997, Mr Papaconstantinou on 23 December 1996, Mr Papathemelis on 11 January 1997, Mr Samaras on 24 December 1996 and Mr Tzounis on 14 April 1997.
128 Interview with Mr Papaconstantinou on 23 December 1996.

129 See Valden, 1996, p. 198.
130 Saritza, 1996, p. 239. The same argument was made almost verbatim by the Director of FYROM's Ministry of Foreign Affairs Directorate of Economic Affairs Ms Vasileva, during an interview on 29 September 1997. Perhaps more significantly, FYROM's current Prime Minister Ljupco Georgievski concurred with this analysis during an interview in which he invited Greek investment, stating as advantages '[geographic] proximity...low labour costs...[and] access [via FYROM] to the markets of neighbouring states' (*To Vima*, 20 December 1998, p. A36).
131 See Table II.
132 See *E Kathimerini*, 23 December 1998, p. 1.
133 Ibid.
134 See *Eleftherotypia*, 9 October 1996, p. 11; *Exousia*, 9 May 1997, p. 1; *Exousia*, 13 May 1997, p. 31 and *Ependytis*, 25 October 1997, p. 15. For a brief account of investment plans that Greek companies have for FYROM see *Eleftherotypia*, 2 November 1996, p. 4 and *To Vima*, 13 October 1996, p. D15.
135 See *E Kathimerini*, 27 December 1998, p. 5.
136 See ibid.

# 4 The Politics of Greek Cooperation, June 1991-January 1992

This is the hour of Europe.
-Jacques Poos, Luxembourg's Minister of Foreign Affairs, 27 June 1991.

### A. Yugoslavia Disintegrates, EPC Mediates and Greece Cooperates

The end of the Second World War found Marshall Tito and his communist partisans in control of Yugoslavia, which consisted of six republics: Bosnia-Hercegovina, Croatia, Macedonia, Montenegro, Serbia, and Slovenia.[1] In addition to outright suppression and propaganda, Tito attempted to bridge ethnic differences by creating a state with a strong centralised government (until 1974, when more powers passed to the republics), and by allowing a somewhat liberalised economy. His break with Stalin and the subsequent pursuit of a high profile non-aligned foreign policy made him popular at home, and won sympathy (and financial aid) from the West. Yugoslavia became particularly prosperous (by socialist standards), 'with an average annual economic growth [for the years 1965-89] of 6.3 per cent.'[2]

Despite its apparent affluence and stability, the country was actually travelling along a perilous path. Although an analysis of its demise belongs to a different inquiry, it can be mentioned that contributing factors include the death of Tito in 1980 and the rise of the Serbian politician Slobodan Milosevic.[3] Since the mid-1980s', Milosevic had begun 'garnering mass support, both within the party and among the Serbian population at large by openly playing the nationalist card' and especially by stressing both perceived and actual Serb grievances over the fate of Kosovo (a region in Serbia populated by 90 per cent ethnic Albanians).[4] In doing so, Milosevic brought nationalism and its accompanying passions to the forefront of Yugoslav politics.[5] Furthermore, the end of the Cold War and the dissolution of the Soviet empire largely discredited the socialist ideology and created a situation in which Yugoslavia ceased to have the same international and strategic importance. Subsequently, the resurfacing of old nationalistic aspirations, enmities and traumas was accelerated. During the 1990 elections, nationalists came to power in all of the republics and tensions intensified greatly.[6]

Given the prospects for instability, EPC adopted a stance advocating a 'united and democratic Yugoslavia.'[7] However, this chapter will demonstrate that EPC's members eventually sanctioned Yugoslavia's dissolution, and were confronted with the issues of recognising the country's former republics, as well as with a series of other problems. In attempting to deal with them, EPC utilised a variety of its decision-making procedures. As will be shown, particular emphasis was placed upon imposing sanctions and promising aid for the cooperating republics. Furthermore, numerous declarations were issued and conference diplomacy was practised. Innovative decision-making procedures included the creation of an Arbitration Commission (AC), and the sending to Yugoslavia of monitoring missions.

Initially attempting to bolster the chances of a united Yugoslavia, at the beginning of June 1991 the Commission's President Jacques Delors went to Belgrade and informed the Yugoslavs that 'financial support of between $4 and $5 billion would be made available.'[8] On 24 June, the Third Financial Protocol between the Community and Yugoslavia, worth ECU 730 million for the period ending on 30 June 1996 was signed.[9] Despite the utilisation of these economic decision-making procedures, the process of Yugoslavia's disintegration soon became irrevocable.

On 25 June 1991, Croatia and Slovenia declared their independence.[10] The war in Yugoslavia began two days later, when the Serb-controlled Yugoslav National Army (JNA) attacked Slovenia. On the same day, EPC's Foreign Ministers were meeting at Luxembourg and it was immediately decided that the intergovernmental Troika be dispatched to Yugoslavia.[11] It proposed a plan that included the suspension of all declarations of independence for three months, the return of the JNA to its barracks, as well as other measures that aimed at solving the country's constitutional crisis.[12] Although all sides agreed to these measures, none of them was implemented. The Troika was thus forced to go back on 30 June, this time threatening the suspension of aid.[13]

While hostilities continued in Slovenia, the republic's army proved surprisingly successful in its operations against the JNA.[14] In order to increase the pressure and achieve a meaningful settlement, the Extraordinary EPC Ministerial meeting of 5 July 1991 decided that EPC would impose an arms embargo on all Yugoslav republics, and urged the members of the international community to follow suit.[15] Greece endorsed this decision, as well as the warning that unless agreement was reached, the Second and Third Financial Protocols with Yugoslavia would be suspended. These protocols constituted 'the largest aid package which the EC has ever given to an individual state,' worth some $1 billion.[16]

On 5 July, the Committee of Senior Officials (CSO), of the Conference on Security and Cooperation in Europe accepted the EPC plan, which primarily called for the cessation of hostilities.[17] This acceptance also signalled the fact that the CSCE was essentially relinquishing its responsibilities for the resolution of the war in Yugoslavia. Perhaps for the first time in several decades, EPC's members were being assigned the leading and almost exclusive role in dealing with an important international crisis.[18]

EPC efforts to reach a settlement seemed to culminate with the signing of the Brioni Accord on 7 July.[19] The agreement provided for the withdrawal of the JNA forces from Slovenia, and thus marked the end of a limited war that had lasted ten days. There was also agreement to begin negotiations on all aspects of the future of Yugoslavia before 1 August. Finally, it was decided to introduce EPC observers. Unarmed and known as the ice-cream men because of their white uniforms, their

> role, and value...was to improve by their presence the chances of fragile cease-fires holding...[though] the greatest threat that they could make was to withdraw their services, which was regularly done when they met with particularly serious obstacles.[20]

As a result of the Troika missions and the Brioni Accord, a brief period of time was bought, the war having ended in Slovenia and not having yet moved to any other of the Yugoslav republics. Nevertheless, it had become apparent to most observers that, in the words of Jacques Delors: 'the Yugoslav federation in its present form has had its day.'[21] On 13 July the Dutch Presidency sent a telegram to the other EPC members, suggesting that they move towards the 'voluntary redrawing of internal borders as a possible solution.'[22] The Greek government disagreed, but its negative assessment did not cause any problems. The Dutch proposal to tinker with borders prior to recognition failed to win any EPC adherents, and was thus not pursued any further.[23]

During the month of August, war broke out in Croatia, where the JNA proved more efficient than in Slovenia, achieving control of almost a fourth of the republic by early September. Faced with this unwelcome development, Greece agreed that the Ministerial meeting of 27 August express EPC's dismay, and make perfectly clear that the Serb irregular forces in Croatia and the JNA were being considered as responsible for the outbreak of violence in

Croatia.²⁴ The Greek Foreign Minister Antonis Samaras also decided together with his EPC counterparts to establish a Peace Conference and an Arbitration procedure within its framework.²⁵ According to Germany's Foreign Minister Hans-Dietrich Genscher, the idea for this procedure (which represents an innovative decision-making procedure of the regime EPC), emanated from France, though at the EPC meeting it was presented as a joint Franco-German initiative.²⁶ The procedure was supposed to consist of a five member Arbitration Commission, with two members being appointed by the Yugoslav Federal Presidency. The Yugoslav representation failed to materialise, and the AC eventually consisted solely of EPC member state appointees, who were also Presidents of their country's Constitutional Court. It was chaired by the French Robert Badinter, who was joined by colleagues from Belgium, Germany, Italy and Spain.²⁷ The importance of the fact that there was no Greek representative will be discussed and analysed subsequently.

During the 27 August EPC meeting, Samaras expressed his government's concern over what eventually became an extremely contentious issue, by submitting a Greek memorandum on Yugoslav Macedonia.²⁸ Since the beginning of the war in Yugoslavia, this was the first official Greek attempt to raise awareness and present within EPC a position on the name and implications of an independent Yugoslav Republic of Macedonia.

The Memorandum began by suggesting that Kosovo and Yugoslav Macedonia might require different EPC approaches than the ones pursued in Slovenia and Croatia.²⁹ In an academic-like, diplomatic but ultimately alarmist tone, it argued that a declaration of independence by Yugoslav Macedonia would create serious problems. The state would not be economically viable, while its huge Albanian minority would be a source of instability and perhaps even war. Such a new state would most likely be involved in serious disputes and confrontations with Albania, Serbia and Bulgaria. Hence, the warning that 'there seems to be a clear danger of a triangular, if not of a quadrangular conflict in the region.'³⁰

Given this perception of a potentially explosive situation, it becomes evident that the Greek government did not welcome a declaration of independence. However, since such an action was imminent, the Memorandum did not propose attempts to block or postpone it. Rather, it endeavoured to clarify possible actions that would have been considered unfriendly and provocative by Greece. Thus, the issue of the new state's name came to the forefront:

> The Greeks also strongly contest the use of the traditionally Greek name of Macedonia for identifying *a Slavic people*...the Greeks believe that the

Macedonian name is part of their own historical heritage and should not be used to identify, *in an ethnic sense*, another nation.³¹

Although the sensitivity surrounding the name Macedonia was made evident, the Memorandum did not indicate a precise position on the name issue. The objection to the ethnological use of the name Macedonia, together with the fact that the document describes five times the inhabitants of Yugoslav Macedonia as Slav-Macedonians, possibly suggested that Greece might have been flexible to a compromise name that would have included the word Macedonia.³²

## B. The Intensification of Greek Cooperation

On 8 September 1991, the Yugoslav Republic of Macedonia held a referendum on its independence, with a turnout (according to the official results) of 72.16 per cent.³³ Of those voting, 96.44 per cent expressed their support for a 'sovereign and independent state of Macedonia, with the right to enter in a future union of sovereign states of Yugoslavia.'³⁴ On the basis of this referendum, the Assembly of the Yugoslav Republic of Macedonia declared the state's independence on 17 September.³⁵

Greece's Prime Minister Konstantinos Mitsotakis responded to these results in a rather moderate way, by emphasising that 'the position of [his] government, as regards the name that [the inhabitants of the Yugoslav Republic of Macedonia] use is given, self-evident and shared by the entire Greek nation.'³⁶ This statement sent a strong message about the importance of the new republic's name, though it did not entail any specific proposal, thus allowing substantial scope for negotiation and a possible compromise.³⁷ Mitsotakis' statement represents an early example of his flexibility on the name issue, which would eventually lead to a confrontation with Samaras.

Despite the use of diplomatic and calm language by the Prime Minister, it soon became evident that his 'government was deciding to abandon...the low key policy [on the Macedonian Question which was practised] since the time of the Civil War.'³⁸ During a CSCE meeting in Moscow on 27 September 1991, Greek Ambassador Stathatos denied accusations made by Yugoslav representatives, and also distributed a copy of his country's position on the Macedonian Question that was made during the 25 June 1990 Copenhagen CSCE meeting. Together, these two interventions represent an outburst against what was considered to be the falsification of history, the twisting of facts and the ills bestowed upon Greece by Slavomacedonians (significantly, the term is used in the Moscow document).³⁹ Accusations vary from what is considered to be the unjustified appropriation of the ancient Greek Macedonian heritage of Alexander the Great and Aristotle, to the kidnapping of 28,000 children after the conclusion of the Civil War.⁴⁰ Thus, the international community was given evidence of the resentment and determination of Greece to follow closely and possibly contest developments in the Yugoslav Republic of Macedonia.

Nevertheless, Greek cooperation within EPC both continued and intensified, being made manifest in three key issue areas. The first involved the singling out and verbal condemnation of the Serbian side as responsible for the atrocities and the spreading of the war to Croatia. Instances of Greek cooperation on this issue are numerous, and include the 6 October 1991 informal meeting of the Ministers of Foreign Affairs that condemned the JNA, as well as the 27 October EPC declaration on Dubrovnik which consisted of a strongly worded and largely justified attack on Serbian military actions.⁴¹ EPC's frustration, anger and condemnation of the Serbs (endorsed by Greece), are best illustrated by the declaration on the situation in Yugoslavia that was issued on the following day:

> The European Community and its member States are appalled at constant violations of [the] principles [of no unilateral change of borders, and protection of human rights, and rights of ethnic and national groups]. In this context they refer to the Serbian position in the Conference, the coup d'etat by four members of the Federal Presidency and their announcement of a plan aimed at the establishment of a greater Serbia. The statements and actions of JNA, which were condemned in the Declaration on Dubrovnik of 27 October 1991, should also be seen in this light.⁴²

EPC's condemnation of the Serbs was not only limited to EPC's decision-making procedure of declaratory diplomacy, as it soon incorporated the application of additional economic sanctions, while simultaneously giving preferential treatment to the cooperating republics, including FYROM. These developments constitute a second area in which Greece cooperated constantly without creating any problems to its EPC partners.

Thus, on October 6 1991 EPC's Foreign Ministers threatened to terminate the Cooperation and Trade Agreement with Yugoslavia;⁴³ and on 8 November, there was an EPC decision on the imposition of the following measures:
- immediate suspension of the application of the trade and cooperation Agreement with Yugoslavia and a decision to terminate the same Agreement,
- restoration of the quantitative limits for textiles,

- removal of Yugoslavia from the list of beneficiaries of the General System of Preferences,
- formal suspension of benefits under the PHARE programme. Yugoslavia has not been invited to take part in the next Ministerial meeting of G-24 on 11 November 1991.[44]

EPC's intention to request the imposition of an oil embargo by the UN's Security Council was also stated. Again, it was made perfectly clear that these punitive actions would be taken only against the parties that were not cooperating 'in a peaceful way towards a comprehensive political solution on the basis of the EC proposals.'[45]

The cooperating republics were eventually rewarded in the 2 December General Affairs Council meeting, which decided a series of positive measures that reversed most of the 8 November sanctions. They included:

- a Regulation reinstating, as from 15 November 1991, most of the preferential trade arrangements under the pre-existing Co-operation Agreement with Yugoslavia;
- reinstatement of PHARE programme coverage...with the proviso that humanitarian aid is to continue for the benefit of all of the population of Yugoslavia;
- a request to the European Investment Bank that it agree to the use of the ECU 100 million balance under the 2nd EEC-Yugoslavia Financial Protocol, denounced by the Community, to finance projects in the Republics concerned and that it resume payments for ongoing projects, where the situation permits it.[46]

On the same day, a Council Regulation was issued 'concerning the arrangements applicable to the import of products originating in the Republics of Bosnia-Herzegovinia, *Macedonia*, Slovenia and Croatia.'[47] Given Greece's Memorandum on Yugoslav Macedonia and subsequent actions, it is striking to see that the phrase Republic of Macedonia is used in an official Council document. This did not suggest an intention to recognise the state with this name, since Foreign Minister Samaras had made his agreement to these measures conditional upon the incorporation of the following statement: 'the Twelve [are] anxious to point out that the adoption of these measures was entirely without prejudice to the question of recognising the Republics.'[48]

The use of the phrase Republic of Macedonia in this document subsequently proved an embarrassment for Samaras. There seems to have been at least one attempt on his behalf to imply that the person responsible for this Council decision was his country's Permanent Representative to the European Community, Ambassador Vagenas.[49] However, efforts to suggest that he was not present at the meeting can not stand close scrutiny, since the published account of the decisions of the 1539th Council meeting reveals that Greece was represented by 'Mr Antonio [sic] SAMARAS, Minister for Foreign Affairs.'[50] Furthermore, in an interview on 24 December 1996, he did not deny his presence at that meeting.

Regardless of the subsequent political controversy, the decision to accept these positive measures for the 'Republic of Macedonia' does not constitute an incomprehensible blunder. As will be demonstrated in the following chapter, it was a deliberate decision that fitted exceedingly well with Greece's cooperative strategy.

A third area of cooperation involved decisions that encouraged various Yugoslav republics to request Community recognition. On October 6, Greece with its EPC partners

> Agreed that a political solution should be sought in the perspective of *recognition* of the independence of those republics wishing it, at the end of a negotiating process conducted in good faith and involving all parties.[51]

A similar statement was included in the EPC Declaration of 28 October 1991.[52] Undoubtedly, they paved the way for FYROM to request recognition, though Greece did not attempt to utilise this early opportunity in order to express concerns or insert conditions regarding a possible application by FYROM.

On 7 December 1991 the AC published its first opinion, which concluded that 'the Socialist Republic of Yugoslavia is in the process of dissolution.'[53] Consequently, it was becoming increasingly difficult for the EPC member states to avoid facing the issue of recognising at least some of the Yugoslav republics.

## C. The Issue of Recognition

The issue of recognition was confronted by the Greek government during the 4 December 1991 Cabinet meeting.[54] According to the minutes, there was a decision to support the continuation of a united Yugoslavia.[55] Furthermore,

> The government set three conditions to the Skopje Republic [FYROM], which must be accepted, if recognition is wanted: First, [it must] change the name 'Macedonia' *which has a geographic but not an ethnic basis*, second, [it must]

acknowledge that it has no territorial claims against our country, and, third, [it must] acknowledge that no 'Macedonian Minority' exists in Greece.'[56]

It is noteworthy that the condition regarding the republic's name was suggested in the Cabinet meeting by the internationally renowned composer (and Minister Without Portfolio) Mikis Theodorakis.[57] Thus, the issue that would come to dominate the country's politics in the following months, was first formulated by a former active member of the KKE, and not by any leading right-wing politician or by those who subsequently made it the centrepiece of their rhetoric and foreign policy preferences.

That the Cabinet's decision under the heading 'Policy in the Balkans' is mostly devoted to FYROM, suggests that Greek policy towards the dissolution of Yugoslavia was becoming preoccupied with this state; it would soon be obsessed, devoted and in a sense taken hostage by the issue of its name. Some major cooperative decisions were to precede these developments.

As the Maastricht Summit approached, German pressure for the recognition of Croatia and Slovenia intensified. On 27 November 1991, Chancellor Kohl promised to recognise the two republics before Christmas;[58] and on 14 December, Kohl's spokesperson Dieter Vogel confirmed Germany's intention to move towards recognition, regardless of 'whether any, all, or none of the European states join us.'[59]

It was under these developments that an Extraordinary EPC Ministerial Meeting was convened in Brussels on 15 December 1991.[60] It was dramatic, lasted for ten hours, and the agreement that was reached early in the morning signalled the official and irreversible end of the Socialist Federal Republic of Yugoslavia. The meeting also provides an example of the importance of the intergovernmental part of EPC's defining norm, since the most important decisions about the future of Yugoslavia were reserved for discussion and were made by an intergovernmental body. More specifically, EPC's Ministers adopted a common position on the conditions whose satisfaction would have to precede recognition of the various republics.[61] Applications were to be submitted by 23 December, and it was agreed that the AC would provide advice concerning the merits of the various applications.

The stance of the German Foreign Minister was instrumental in determining these decisions. According to Samaras, it amounted to a 'de facto *coup d'état*, complete with a grand theatrical gesture.'[62] He is alluding to Genscher's leaving the room and calling twice Chancellor Kohl, only to eventually explain that Germany remained adamant in its position and thus determined to unilaterally recognise at least some of the Yugoslav republics.[63] Given this development and in order to at least preserve a semblance of the principle of solidarity, EPC's Foreign Ministers accepted Germany's position.

Samaras has never denied that he had serious misgivings about the consequences of the 16 December decisions. Because of the circumstances however, the Greek Foreign Minister believed that vetoing all of the meeting's decisions would have been counter-productive. In order to adequately address his country's legitimate concerns, he forcefully insisted that a paragraph stating additional conditions that would apply to FYROM's probable application for recognition be inserted. According to Genscher, 'Samaras...was afraid that the recognition of Slovenia and Croatia could lead Macedonia to pursue its independence and make demands on Greek territory, including Thessaloniki.'[64]

Italian Foreign Minister de Michelis insisted that FYROM be recognised but was rebuffed by Samaras who thus became the target of an undiplomatic verbal assault. The former Greek Foreign Minister claims that de Michelis angrily yelled at him: 'You are a pirate and a blackmailer! This is piracy!'[65]

Eventually, there was agreement on the following three conditions:

> The Community and its member States also require a Yugoslav Republic to commit itself, prior to recognition, to adopt constitutional and political guarantees ensuring that it has no territorial claims towards a neighbouring Community State and that it will conduct no hostile propaganda activities versus a neighbouring Community State, *including the use of a denomination which implies territorial claims.*[66]

Of these conditions, the first two proved somewhat less contentious. FYROM possibly understood that the blatant conduct of hostile propaganda and the making of territorial claims against Greece, was contrary to the expectations and standards required of states aspiring to EPC recognition. As a result, some important (though not necessarily sufficient), alterations to the state's constitution were subsequently inserted.[67] However, the third condition that required the applicant state not to use a 'denomination which implies territorial claims,' proved controversial.

The former Foreign Minister believes that the phrasing of the third condition clearly implied the word Macedonia. He has often pointed out that prior to Yugoslavia's break-up, the official name used for the republic was the Socialist Yugoslav Republic of Macedonia. Since the words Socialist, Yugoslav, or Republic could not possibly imply territorial claims, Samaras concludes that one is necessarily left with the name Macedonia.[68]

The argument is both logical and persuasive as regards the name Macedonia, although it is significant that the phrasing of the third condition did not include this term. Samaras insists that the actual phrasing 'covered everything' including any subsequent inventive or ingenious FYROM proposal.[69] 'What would happen if they decided to call their republic Thessaloniki?' he asked rhetorically during an interview.[70]

Samaras also insists that during the 16 December meeting, he fulfilled his government's 4 December instructions about FYROM.[71] This claim is accurate as regards the new republic's name: the phrasing of the third condition is consistent with both the 4 December Cabinet meeting decision and the Memorandum on Yugoslav Macedonia. The possibility though that according to these documents, a name in the line of Upper Macedonia or Vardar Macedonia was at the very least debatable, if not acceptable was however underestimated or misunderstood.[72]

News of the 16 December agreement on the three conditions was met with enthusiasm in Greece. The government announced 'a great national success,' while the Panhellenic Socialist Movement (PASOK) which was the main opposition party, declared that the agreement constituted a 'positive event.'[73] Mitsotakis telephoned the subsequent Foreign Minister Michalis Papaconstantinou and urged him to go to the airport in order to welcome Samaras.[74] Former conservative Prime Minister Georgios Rallis, while listening to the Greek Foreign Minister explain his accomplishments in a radio interview on 17 December, 'felt remorseful for having in the past doubted his abilities.'[75]

The official and celebratory Greek statements did not include a *restrictive* interpretation of the third EPC condition, according to which the use of the word Macedonia would have been excluded in every possible way from FYROM's name. Prime Minister Mitsotakis somewhat vaguely stated that the third condition obliges FYROM 'to change its name so that no misunderstandings will be created as regards the historical continuity [of Macedonia].'[76] Samaras stressed that the three conditions constituted a national victory against those who 'unhistorically wanted to falsify the historical meaning of the word Macedonia.'[77]

These statements illustrate that both the Greek Prime Minister and Foreign Minister made no effort to argue in a coherent and clear way that FYROM's name should not include the word Macedonia. This was left to Stelios Papathemelis and Ioannis Charalambopoulos, who as prominent PASOK MPs and former Ministers declared that 'the decision of the Twelve, if it subtracts entirely the name Macedonia from Skopje, [it then] corresponds to the consciousness of Hellenism and indirectly settles the historical truth.'[78]

At that point, they merely represented their personal opinions, though things were about to change.[79]

A significant incident took place on 22 December 1991. Nikos Marakis, one of Greece's most respected and knowledgeable journalists, asked the Foreign Ministry's press spokesperson the following question: 'if our [EPC] colleagues pressure us for a synthetic name [i.e. one including the term Macedonia], will we deny it?'[80] Ambassador Kalamidas replied that 'it is self-evident, there is no issue of us retreating. What does a synthetic name mean?'[81]

This exchange is of particular importance, because it constitutes the first indication of a possible restrictive interpretation of the third EPC condition. However, there was an element of vagueness in Kalamidas' response. Furthermore, such an interpretation could not have possibly been deduced from any document, Cabinet decision or statement that the Prime Minister had made following the 16 December EPC meeting. In other words, this was not the official position of the Greek government. Nevertheless, in the following months it was precisely this restrictive interpretation that gradually became official policy, as well as the cornerstone of Greece's foreign policy towards former Yugoslavia.

Meanwhile, FYROM had applied for Community recognition on 20 December, announcing its intention to satisfy all necessary conditions.[82] The new republic's Parliament inserted two amendments to the constitution on 6 January 1992, the first of which denied that FYROM harboured any territorial ambitions towards neighbouring states, while the second promised that 'the Republic shall not interfere in the sovereign rights of other states and their internal affairs.'[83] In addition to these amendments, a series of answers and documents were provided to the Badinter Commission.[84]

While the AC was deliberating, Greece gave further indication of the importance that was being placed on FYROM's name. In a 3 January 1992 letter to the Community Heads of Government, Greek President Konstantinos Karamanlis wrote that the republic's name was of *'fundamental importance to Greece...This republic has absolutely no right, neither historical nor ethnological, to use the name Macedonia'*.[85] Significantly, this phrasing did not clearly endorse a restrictive interpretation of the third EPC condition.

On the same day, representatives of FYROM's and Greece's Foreign Ministries met in a central Athens Hotel.[86] It was the first instance of the two states talking directly and publicly since the disintegration of Yugoslavia had begun, and was related to the 16 December 1991 EPC meeting where Samaras had agreed that his country would make an effort, at a bilateral level, to resolve the dispute with FYROM.[87] The decision to hold this meeting can be viewed as another example of the politics of cooperation and moderation that were being pursued by Greece.

During the discussions, Ambassador Ailianos stressed that his government would be willing to cultivate bilateral economic relations, as well as help improve the new republic's relations with the EC—a scenario though that largely depended on the name that FYROM would adopt. Ailianos stressed that this was for Greece *'conditio sine qua non'*.[88] Ambassador Kofos gave a lengthy and well-documented presentation, covering the historical aspects of the Macedonian Question.[89] Using 'forceful language,' he accused FYROM for practising 'cultural imperialism' and usurping the name Macedonia.[90] According to Kofos, the adoption of this name suggested territorial ambition, given the fact that FYROM holds 'only 39 per cent [of the geographic region of Macedonia].'[91]

To this barrage of 'name-centred' criticisms, FYROM's representatives countered that they had no authorisation to discuss this issue. For them, the meeting was viewed as merely the first in a series that would aim at discussing various bilateral problems and disputes. The fact that they had specific instructions not to address the third EPC condition, reduced significantly the substantive value of the meeting. Ambassador Kalamidas who was also present (but not a direct participant), called Samaras to inform him of developments, and then proceeded to give a press conference announcing that because of the inability to discuss the new republic's name, talks were being abandoned.[92]

A few days later (11 January), the AC ruled that FYROM fully complied with EPC's guidelines for recognition, and emphasised the republic's undertaking to refrain from the conduct of hostile propaganda.[93] Most importantly, it took the view

> That the Republic of Macedonia has, moreover, renounced all territorial claims of any kind in unambiguous statements binding in international law; [and] that *the use of the name "Macedonia" cannot therefore imply any territorial claim against another State.*[94]

Fortunately for Greece, the Badinter Commission also ruled against the recognition of Croatia and Bosnia-Herzegovina, a development that presented Greek diplomacy with an opportunity.[95] Thus, seeking EPC support, Mitsotakis flew to Rome and Bonn on 14 January, and during his meetings with Prime Minister Andreotti and Chancellor Kohl argued that the recognition of FYROM under the name Macedonia would represent a tremendous defeat to his government, imperilling its slim parliamentary majority of two.[96] This could have led to the return to power of the much more 'troublesome' Leader of the

Opposition, Andreas Papandreou. As a result of such arguments, Mitsotakis gained German and Italian support, to the extent that there would be no recognition of FYROM unless the republic complied with EPC's three conditions. Crucially, he also seems to have pledged his government's support for the recognition of Croatia. Eventually, on 15 January 1992 EPC's member states decided to largely ignore the advice of the AC and recognise Slovenia and Croatia, but not FYROM.[97] Given the events and diplomatic efforts that had preceded these decisions, it appears (and will subsequently be analysed), that EPC's principle of solidarity was probably not operational in this instance.

These recognitions mark the end of a period during which the Greek government practised politics of cooperation and moderation towards former Yugoslavia and FYROM. Between June 1991 and 17 January 1992, it cooperated fully and completely within EPC on almost all the issues that arose from the dissolution of Yugoslavia. The country's veto power was not utilised and essentially never even threatened with use. Greece supported the June 1991 position to maintain a united Yugoslavia, but also signed the 16 December 1991 EPC declaration that formalised the acceptance of Yugoslavia's dissolution. There was also cooperation on the verbal condemnation of Serbia, on the selective application of sanctions that primarily targeted the Serbs, as well as in the establishment of the Peace Conference, the creation of the Arbitration Commission and the recognition of Croatia and Slovenia.

As regards Greece's policy towards FYROM, it was marked by moderation and a willingness to cooperate and reach a compromise. On the most contentious issue that involved the republic's name, the disagreement on the name Macedonia was made evident. Nevertheless, the possibility of a compromise name such as Upper Macedonia or Vardar Macedonia was consistently left open in almost all major Greek decisions, documents and statements. They include the 27 August 1991 Memorandum on Yugoslav Macedonia, Mitsotakis' response to FYROM's referendum on independence, the intervention in the Moscow CSCE meeting, the 4 December 1991 Cabinet meeting decisions and Karamanlis' 3 January 1992 letter to the Community's Heads of Government. Significantly, the possibility of a compromise on FYROM's name was allowed under the conditions agreed in the 16 December 1991 EPC meeting. These conditions further demanded that FYROM refrain from the conduct of hostile propaganda and the making of territorial claims against its larger neighbouring country, though such demands can only be judged as fair and reasonable. Finally, Greece organised a bilateral meeting between Foreign Ministry representatives of the two states on 3 January 1992, and even signed a document that referred to the Republic of Macedonia on 2 December 1991.

The nature, extent and scope of these politics of flexibility, moderation and cooperation began to alter in a substantial manner after mid-January 1992. Eventually, the name-issue came to dominate not only responses towards former Yugoslavia and FYROM, but Greek domestic politics as well. However, before analysing these developments, the politics of Greek cooperation will be explained in a way that is largely consistent with the theory of institutionalism.

## Notes

1. See Map I. 'Serbia [also] contained...the autonomous province of Vojvodina and the autonomous region of Kosovo-Metohija' (Singleton, 1985, p. 209). For a general history of Yugoslavia, see Pavlowitch, 1971 and Singleton, 1985. The origins and first years of the state are best analysed in Ivo Banac's magisterial *The National Question in Yugoslavia* (Banac, 1984). For developments during the years 1962-1991, see Ramet, 1984/1992. For some interesting reflections on the history of Yugoslavia, see Pavlowitch, 1988.
2. *The Economist*, 2 February 1991, p. 45.
3. For a succinct and important discussion of the reasons that led to the demise of Yugoslavia, see especially Holbrooke, 1998, p. 21-9. As regards Milosevic, see Zimmermann, 1995 for a scathing critique of his actions and character. Zimmermann was the last US Ambassador to Yugoslavia. For a perceptive profile of the Serbian leader, see Djilas, 1993. Many episodes of Milosevic negotiating that are particularly revealing of his character, soul and intentions are presented in Holbrooke, 1998. Milosevic's rise to power is analysed in Ramet, 1984/1992: chapter 11. Ramet's chapter also includes an important account of the seminal episode that elevated Milosevic into being the key proponent and representative of Serbian nationalism. See ibid., p. 229-30, as well as Holbrooke, 1998, p. 114.
4. Glenny, 1990, p. 121. For some important, informative and in a sense complementary histories of Kosovo, see Malcolm, 1998, Muertus 1999 and Vickers, 1998. See also Chomsky 1999; Fromkin, 1999; Kofos, 1998, *The New Republic*, 8 June 1998, p. 34-40; Veremis and Kofos, 1998 and Veremis and Triantaphyllou, 1999.
5. On nationalism, see Anderson, 1983/1991; Gelner, 1983; Hobsbawm, 1990; Hutchinson and Smith, 1994; Kedourie, 1970 and 1960/1993; Mayall 1990 and Smith, 1991. For particularly perceptive reflections on Greek nationalism that arose from the country's dispute with FYROM, see Mouzelis, 1994.
6. Montenegro was possibly the only exception. For an analysis of the 1990 elections, see Woodward, 1995, p. 117-25. For the election results in the Yugoslav Republic of Macedonia, see Valinakis and Dales, 1994, p. 32-3.
7. EPC Press Release P. 35/91, 26 March 1991; emphasis added. See also EPC Press Release P. 42/91, 8 May 1991.
8. Gow and Freedman, 1992, p. 99. The position for a united Yugoslavia coincided with that pursued by the United States. In his visit to Belgrade on 21 June 1991, US Secretary of State James Baker declared that his country would not recognise the would-be breakawa[y republics] "under any circumstances"' (*The Economist*, 29 June 1991, p.

41). For Baker's account of his Belgrade visit, see Baker, 1995, p. 478-83. His effort to downplay the fact that the US' official policy was advocating a united Yugoslavia, is particularly noteworthy. For a critical assessment of the consequences of this visit, see Holbrooke, 1998, p. 27.

9   For the terms of the protocol, see Official Journal of the European Communities (hereafter OJ), No C 134/6, 24.5.91.
10  For details, as well as for the reactions of various countries, see *Financial Times*, 26 June 1991, p. 1.
11  See Bull. EC 6-1991, p. 8. The Troika was comprised by Gianni de Michelis, Jacques Poos and Hans van den Broek, Foreign Ministers of Italy, Luxembourg, and Holland respectively.
12  See Gow and Freedman, 1992, p. 102.
13  On the same day, the Presidency of the Community passed to the Netherlands. As a result of this change, de Michelis' place in the Troika was taken by Portugal's Foreign Minister Joao de Deus Pinheiro.
14  For accounts of the 'ten day war' in Slovenia, see Cohen, 1993, p. 224-5; Crnobrnja, 1994, p. 160-3; Glenny, 1992, p. 96-7 and Owen, 1995, p. 34. For an interesting appraisal of the various arguments seeking to explain the JNA's lacklustre performance in Slovenia, see Woodward, 1995, p. 166-8.
15  See EPC Press Release P. 61/91, 5 July 1991.
16  *The Times*, 6 July, 1991, p. 10. See also Weller, 1992, p. 573. It is noteworthy that '40 per cent of Yugoslavia's trade was with the Community' (Gow and Freedman, 1992, p. 99), a fact that further made Yugoslavia vulnerable to EC pressure.
17  For an account of the CSO's powers and mandate, see Weller, 1992, p. 573. For further details of the EPC plan, see Gow and Freedman, 1992, p. 105-6.
18  According to the memoirs of the then US Secretary of State James Baker, 'the Bush administration felt comfortable with the EC's taking responsibility for handling the crisis in the Balkans' (Baker, 1995, p. 636). Baker cites as the main reason for this policy the absence of vital US interests, in contrast to 'European interests [that] were directly threatened' (ibid.), and furthermore argues that the EC was seen as a potentially successful mediator with long experience in dealing with the region.
19  For the text of the Brioni Accord, see European Political Cooperation Documentation Bulletin (hereafter EPCDB), Vol. 7, 1991, p. 334-8. See also *Financial Times*, 8 July 1991, p. 1; Gow and Smith, 1992, p. 10; Silber and Little, 1996, p. 201; cited in Holbrooke, 1998, p. 29; Weller, 1992, p. 573-4 and Woodward, 1995, p. 168-72.
20  Nuttall, 1994b, p. 21. Several observers were actually killed.
21  Delors made this statement on 9 July 1991 during a debate in the European Parliament on the situation in Yugoslavia. See OJ No 3-407/68, 9.7.91.
22  The text of the telegram can be found in Owen, 1995, p. 2-3.
23  For a counter-factual defence of the Dutch proposal, see Owen, 1995, p. 33-4 and Telloglou, 1996, p. 27. Both fail to properly appreciate the telegram's acknowledgement that any voluntary redrawing of the borders 'would entail daunting problems' (cited in Owen, 1995, p. 32).
24  For the declaration on Yugoslavia produced by this meeting, see EPCDB, Vol. 7, 1991, p. 389-90. For the response by FYROM's Assembly to this declaration, see *Balkan Forum*, Vol. 1, (November 1992), p. 169-70. See also Genscher's account of this meeting in Genscher, 1997, p. 786-8.
25  The Peace Conference commenced at the Hague on 7 September 1991, and was chaired by former British Foreign Secretary Lord Carrington. Former US Assistant Secretary of

State for European and Canadian Affairs Richard Holbrooke has characterised Carrington as 'an urbane man of legendary integrity' (Holbrooke, 1998, p. 30).
26  See Genscher, 1997, p. 787.
27  This is why the Arbitration Commission is often referred to as the Badinter Commission.
28  For the text of the Memorandum (in English), see Skilakakis, 1995, p. 258-60. It should be noted that unless otherwise indicated, all references are to documents, articles or books written in Greek and translated into English by me.
29  It is particularly noteworthy the this was the first time that the prospect of instability in Kosovo was stressed. The concerns of the Greek governmnet materialised in March 1999.
30  Ibid., p. 260.
31  Ibid.; emphasis added.
32  See Skilakakis, 1995, p. 42-3. Skilakakis suggests that the name Northern Macedonia might have been acceptable under the arguments made in the Memorandum. This is a correct assessment, to which names such as Upper Macedonia, Vardar Macedonia and perhaps Slavomacedonia could be added.
33  They can be found (in English) in Valinakis and Dales, 1994, p. 38-9. The voting procedure is generally considered to have been fair. For a forcefully argued contrary view, see a speech delivered by the Greek MEP Mr Nianias that can be found in OJ No 3-408/91, 10.9.91. It should also be noted that the leaders of the Albanian and Serbian minorities had urged the referendum's boycott. Furthermore, the referendum was unusual for permitting non-FYROM citizens to participate, though their votes were counted separately and did not contribute towards the official result. This measure aimed at 'conflat[ing] the categories of nationality and citizenship...and contributed powerfully to the construction of a transnational national community of Macedonians who identify with the newly emerged republic of Macedonia' (Danforth, 1995, p. 100). In an interview on 11 April 1997, FYROM's Head of Mission to Greece Mr Arsovsky, explained that this arrangement was made after intense pressure from FYROM's nationalist party, the Internal Macedonia Revolutionary Organisation-Democratic Party of Macedonian National Unity (VMRO-DPNE).
34  Cited in Valinakis and Dales, 1994, p. 38.
35  For the text of FYROM's declaration of independence (in English), see Valinakis and Dales, 1994, p. 40-2.
36  Skilakakis, 1995, p. 46. This statement was made during a press conference in Thessaloniki on 8 September 1991.
37  Mitsotakis made several similar statements until the 4 December 1991 Cabinet meeting. For an account of the more important ones made in mid-November 1991, see Lygeros, 1992, p. 104-5 and Tarkas, 1995, p. 64.
38  Kofos, 1996, p. 3.
39  For the text of the Greek statement in the Moscow CSCE meeting, see Valinakis and Dales, 1994, p. 43-6. For the Copenhagen CSCE statement, see Valinakis, 1992, p. 345-52.
40  For an evaluation of the rather sensational charge that concerns the kidnapping of children, the interested reader should consult Lagani, 1996. In her important study, Lagani objectively analyses this particularly complicated issue, and confirms that in the final stages of the Greek Civil War, thousands of children left Greece. Estimates range from 25,000 to 30,000. This largely forced exodus was primarily carried out by forces loyal to the KKE, though a few of the children left war-ravaged Greece voluntarily and

accompanied by their parents (most of them were subsequently and dramatically separated). About 11,000 children were relocated to Yugoslavia. This number was admitted in a letter written by Tito as well as by a high ranking Greek diplomat (see ibid., p. 64 and 117). Although all children were Greek citizens, some were also Slavophones. Those who were not, originally received education in Greek, although this practice ended abruptly following the Tito-Stalin break. Eventually, fewer than 600 children returned to Greece; and after 1951, the Greek government ended the 'internationalisation' of the issue and stopped pressing for their return. Fear of 'brainwashed' children having adopted anti-Greek positions and pressure from the US and UK accounted for Greece's new position. See also Baerentzen 1987 and Poulton, 1991/1993, p. 180, in conjunction however with Lagani, 1996, p. 107. Some interesting but regrettably brief comments on this topic can be found in Koliopoulos, 1995b, p. 213-9.

41 See the statement made by EPC's Ministers of Foreign Affairs on 6 October 1991, that can be found in EPCDB, Vol. 7, 1991, p. 476-7. For the EPC's declaration on Dubrovnik, see EPC Press Release P. 105/91, 27 October 1991.
42 EPC Press Release P. 106/91, 28 October 1991.
43 See EPCDB, Vol. 7, 1991, p. 476-7. See also Woodward, 1995, p. 468 fn 104.
44 EPC Press Release P. 109/91, 8 November 1991.
45 Ibid.
46 Council of the European Communities General Secretariat (hereafter Council) 9558/91 (Presse 220-G), 2.12.91. For further positive measures that also included Montenegro, see Council 4392/92 (Presse 12-G), 3.2.92.
47 OJ No L 342/1, 12.12.91; emphasis added.
48 Council, 9558/91 (Presse 220-G), 2.12.91.
49 See *Eleftherotypia*, 22 October 1992, p. 12.
50 See Council, 9558/91 (Presse 220-G), 2.12.91.
51 See EPCDB, Vol. 7, 1991, p. 476; emphasis added. See also Genscher, 1997, p. 792-3.
52 See EPC Press Release P. 106/91, 28 October 1991.
53 *International Legal Materials* (hereafter ILM), Vol. 31, No. 6, (December 1992), p. 1494. As the journal suggests, subsequent references to this issue will be cited as 31 *ILM*, followed by the relevant page number, (1992). It should also be noted that the opinion was actually written on 29 November 1991.
54 For important accounts of this meeting, see Skilakakis, 1995, p. 62-3 and Petridis, 1997, p. 391.
55 The minutes can be found in Papaconstantinou, 1994, p. 419.
56 Ibid.; emphasis added.
57 See Petridis, 1997, p. 391.
58 See Genscher, 1997, p. 796. Genscher points out that the date of recognition that was promised by Kohl was actually two weeks later from the one suggested by Hans van den Broek. The Dutch Foreign Minister had mentioned as a possible time limit the date of 10 December 1991. He did so in a statement given to an Austrian newspaper on 18 October 1991. See ibid., p. 793. However, he was talking about a common EPC decision, and not unilateral action.
59 *The New York Times*, 15 December 1991, p. A1.
60 The account of this meeting is partly based on interviews with Mr Kofos on 5 January 1997, Mr Mitsotakis on 10 April 1997, Mr Samaras on 24 December 1996 and 3 February 1997 and Mr Skilakakis on 15 April 1997, as well as on Genscher's account, that can be found in Genscher, 1997, p. 797-9. See also Holbrooke, 1998, p. 31; Skilakakis, 1995, p. 63-4 and Tarkas, 1995, p. 67-9.

61  See EPC Press Release P. 128/91, 16 December 1991. These conditions were also to apply for the recognition of new states in Eastern Europe and the former Soviet Union.
62  Interview with Mr Samaras on 3 February 1997.
63  That two phone calls were made to Chancellor Kohl is accepted by Genscher in his memoirs. See Genscher, 1997, p. 798.
64  Ibid. Genscher states that he considered the possibility of FYROM making territorial claims against Greece to be rather remote. See ibid.
65  Interview with Mr Samaras on 24 December 1996. Significantly, according to Samaras FYROM's Foreign Minister was waiting in the building. After the meeting's conclusion, he immediately had a meeting with de Michelis, who in a sense had assumed at that point the role of championing the republic's claims within EPC. There also seems to have been some sort of antagonism between Greek and Italian diplomacy, dating back to at least 1990, when Greece had managed to essentially exclude Italy from a meeting of Balkan Foreign Ministers. See Glenny, 1997, p. 74.
66  EPC Press Release P. 128/91, 16 December 1991; emphasis added.
67  See Kofos, 1994b, p. 49.
68  For an interview transcript (15 April 1992) where Samaras makes this argument rather passionately, see Ioannou, 1992, p. 110-1. The former Foreign Minister also made the same point during an interview on 24 December 1996.
69  Interview with Mr Samaras on 3 February 1997. Thessaloniki is the largest city in Northern Greece.
70  Interview with Mr Samaras on 3 February 1997.
71  This is how Samaras justifies the fact that he did not contact his Prime Minister during the marathon 16 December 1991 meeting. In an interview on 10 April 1997, Mitsotakis expressed his indignation and frustration for not having been contacted by his Foreign Minister. According to Samaras, the 4 December Cabinet decision requiring FYROM to denounce claims about the existence of a 'Macedonian minority' in Greece, was covered by the clause in the EPC decision that required the applicant state not to conduct hostile propaganda (interview with Mr Samaras on 24 December 1996).
72  For example, the 4 December 1991 Cabinet meeting had decided that the name Macedonia 'has a geographic...basis' (Papaconstantinou, 1994, p. 419). This wording clearly permitted the discussion of names such as Upper Macedonia. Furthermore, in an interview on 5 January 1997, Mr Kofos explained that after being informed about the third condition, no member of the Greek delegation that was in Brussels for the 15 December meeting and was also affiliated with the Ministry of Foreign Affairs, had considered at that point an interpretation that would have had excluded entirely the word Macedonia from FYROM's name.
73  The official government announcement is quoted in Tarkas, 1995, p. 70. PASOK's statement can be found in *Eleftherotypia*, 18 December 1991, p. 4. For other celebratory comments by leading Greek politicians and academics, see ibid., p. 4-5.
74  Interview with Mr Papaconstantinou on 23 December 1997. Papaconstantinou who was then the Minister of Justice, claims to have accepted Mitsotakis' urging with a 'heavy heart,' since he believed that given its ambiguity, the third EPC condition could not have possibly constituted a national success.
75  Rallis, 1995, p. 30. Rallis claims that on reading the following day the actual EPC decision, he concluded that names such as Slavomacedonia or New Macedonia were permissible under the third condition. See ibid., p. 31.
76  *Makedonia*, 18 December 1991, p. 1.
77  Ibid.

78  Ibid., p. 7.
79  Their opinions however, carried particular weight. Charalambopoulos was a former Foreign Minister and Papathemelis was a former Minister of Macedonia-Thrace. As Mr Kofos explained during an interview on 5 January 1997, the latter was also PASOK's 'ideologue' and 'educator' on the Macedonian Issue. His knowledge of the history, various aspects and complexities of this issue is impressive, and became evident during an interview on 11 January 1997. In addition, Papathemelis was Papandreou's chief advisor on this issue. His prominent role within his party at that point as regards foreign policy, is illustrated by the fact that he was chosen by the Leader of the Opposition to represent PASOK in an official briefing given by Samaras about foreign policy developments. See *Makedonia*, 28 December 1991, p. 1.
80  Cited in Tarkas, 1995, p. 77.
81  Ibid.
82  See *Makedonia*, 21 December 1991, p. 20.
83  See 31 *ILM*, p. 1511 (1992).
84  For FYROM's answers (in English), to the most important questionnaire that was sent by the AC, see Valinakis and Dales, 1994, p. 54-62.
85  For Karamanlis' letter, see Ioannou, 1992, p. 101-2; emphasis added.
86  FYROM was represented by Mr Tounte, a diplomatic advisor to President Gligorov, Mr Arsovski, a diplomat and Mr Merchev, a Professor of Constitutional Law. Greece was represented by Ambassador Ailianos, Head of the Greek Foreign Ministry's Division for Balkan Affairs and Ambassador Kofos, the leading Greek expert on Balkan affairs and history. The account of this meeting is based on interviews with Mr Kofos on 5 January 1997 and Mr Arsovski on 3 February 1997. Both of whom were present at the meeting. Interviews with Mr Samaras on 23 December 1996 and Mr Papayannakis on 10 January 1997 were also utilised. Of particular assistance was *To Vima*, 5 January 1992, p. A15, that contains a summary of what took place, including several crucial leaked passages from the various presentations. See also Tarkas, 1995, p. 83-4.
87  Interviews with Mr Kofos on 5 January 1997 and Mr Samaras on 3 February 1997.
88  *To Vima*, 5 January 1992, p. A 15.
89  Arsovski seems to have resented the length and manner in which Kofos gave his presentation. In an interview on 3 February 1997, he argued that 'diplomats do their preparation at home. In negotiations, they discuss.'
90  *To Vima*, 5 January 1992, p. A 15 and interview with Mr Kofos on 5 January 1997.
91  *To Vima*, 5 January 1992, p. A 15.
92  In an interview on 3 February 1997 Arsovski maintained that the members of his delegation were rather resentful of the way in which the meeting broke down. Interestingly enough, in an interview on 5 January 1997, Mr Kofos agreed that it was done in a non-diplomatic and almost suspicious way.
93  For the AC's opinion, see 31 *ILM*, p. 1507-12 (1992). The Greek Ministry of Foreign Affairs criticised the AC's ruling for relying only on documents and arguments provided by FYROM. For the text of the announcement of the Greek Ministry of Foreign Affairs, see *Eleftherotypia*, 15 January 1992, p. 4. The announcement also condemns the AC for ignoring the arguments presented by FYROM's various minorities. In an interview on 3 February 1997, Samaras was particularly upset that a lengthy meeting between Greek Ambassador Lyberopoulos and Mr Badinter produced no positive results for Greece. For a scathing critique of the AC's ruling on FYROM, see Ioannou, 1992, p. 35-8. See also Sarlis, 1993, p. 139-41.
94  31 ILM, p. 1511 (1992); emphasis added.

95  For the AC's opinions on Croatia and Bosnia-Hercegovina, see ibid., p. 1501-7 (1992).
96  See Lygeros, 1992, p. 117 fn 64.
97  See EPC Press Release P. 9/92, 15 January 1992. One of the most critical public reactions to Greece's insistence that EPC should not recognise FYROM under the name Macedonia came from the Danish Foreign Minister Uffe Ellemann-Jensen. See *The Independent*, 21 January 1992, p. 4.

# 5 The Politics of Greek Cooperation: Explanation and Decline

Greece has ceased to be a protagonist in the Macedonian theatre, and has contended herself to playing second fiddle. Still, Greek attitudes toward Macedonian developments are so emotional that Greeks tend either to magnify well out of proportion events or situations connected with Macedonia, or keep a discreet silence.

-Evangelos Kofos, *The Macedonian Question: The Politics of Mutation*, 1986.

### A. The Problematic Nature of the Politics of Greek Cooperation

The Greek government practised politics of cooperation, moderation and flexibility during the June 1991-January 1992 period. However, as will be shown in this chapter, these politics included some decisions that are of a rather problematic nature, since they were contrary to perceived national interests, or were expected to produce negative results for the region.

During the early stages of the Yugoslav disintegration and war, Greek cooperation was helped by the rejection of the Dutch Presidency's proposal to consider the redrawing of the internal borders of the various Yugoslav republics. Had its acceptance been seen as a realistic possibility, Greece would probably have adopted a more interventionist stance, since discussions on the borders of Yugoslav Macedonia would have been on the agenda.[1]

Nevertheless, even in this early phase, certain problematic Greek cooperative decisions can be found, centring on the unwillingness to either block the creation, attempt to impose a national representative, or limit the jurisdiction of the Arbitration Commission. That the AC would consider the case of recognising the Yugoslav Republic of Macedonia was if not absolutely certain, at least extremely likely. Hence, the possibility of a favourable AC ruling for FYROM was risked—an outcome that was probably made more likely by the fact that there was no Greek representative on the commission. Furthermore, the likelihood that such a favourable ruling would influence actors outside EPC could not have easily been ignored. This outcome was admitted by Samaras in a letter sent to his EPC colleagues on 17 January 1992, which noted that

> The announcement [of the AC's ruling on FYROM]...had an immediate negative impact on the region. Bulgaria sought to capitalise on the opportunity offered...[and] rushed to recognise Skopje [on 15 January 1992].[2]

The excuse that he agreed to the AC's creation because its rulings would only constitute recommendations that could have been vetoed subsequently merely states the obvious: Greece could veto any EPC decision.[3] However, it is rather peculiar that there was agreement to the creation of the AC, if the ultimate intention was to simply veto its rulings. Such a course of action does not only incur the political cost of blocking a probable EPC decision, but also incurs the costs associated with opposing the views of people who are supposed to be by profession, disinterested and objective arbiters of Justice; and it allows the party that has received a favourable ruling to appear as a victim.

Turning to the period during which cooperation intensified, it is important to explain the several occasions on which Greek decision-makers consciously participated in actions that they regarded as unfair, catastrophic and contrary to at least certain national interests. Crucially, such examples include the full cooperation within EPC in the condemnation and penalisation of Serbia, the proper appreciation of which requires a brief discussion of what amounted to a special Greco-Serbian relationship.

Serbs and Greeks share the same Christian denomination (Eastern Orthodox), and have not fought against each other in a war for several centuries. This is a rare record for Balkan or even for many Western European peoples. Despite the occasional differences of opinion and points of friction, ties between the two nations have been reinforced in the Twentieth Century by fighting on the same side in both Balkan and World Wars, a fact often stressed by politicians.[4]

At the time of Yugoslavia's disintegration, Greek-Serbian relations were perceived by most decision-makers in Athens as particularly valuable for determining the new balance of power in the region.[5] The two states were supposed to have a similar geopolitical outlook, since both 'view[ed] Turkey's aspirations in the region as a possible threat,' and both were apprehensive about developments in Albania.[6]

Serbia had also signalled its intention not to antagonise Greece's concerns and actions towards FYROM. During a visit to Athens on 16 April 1991, Milosevic diplomatically hinted that he was at the very least agnostic about Greek positions on the Yugoslav Republic of Macedonia.[7] In the subsequent months, Serbia adopted a mush more supporting stance. Characteristically, on 30 April 1992 Milosevic stated that 'Serbia was not going to make any movement on the Skopje issue, that could hurt or damage Greece's interests.'[8]

The degree of affinity between the two countries was demonstrated during an interview with Samaras, who proudly declared that he often informed Milosevic of EPC developments and even had meetings with him in Belgrade before flying to Brussels.[9] Significantly, the former Foreign Minister also claims that Milosevic proposed in early November 1991, that a large number of Serbs 'move' to FYROM, thus essentially taking over the state and ending any possible problems for Greece. Serbia's proposal only vaguely disguised the fact that it would have included a military attack against FYROM, which would have been the necessary consequence of a huge Serbian population transfer to a neighbouring republic that had already declared its independence.[10]

The Serbian leader further suggested to Mitsotakis that their states pursue such an attack jointly and then partition FYROM! The making of this proposal was accepted by Mitsotakis in an interview on 10 April 1997 and is also confirmed by the minutes of an official meeting with his Italian counterpart Andreotti, during which he bluntly stated that 'in the beginning of the crisis, Serbia had proposed that we divide Skopje'.[11]

Prudently and wisely, Greece's Prime Minister refused to pursue such Machiavellian and opportunistic plans. Having done otherwise would have ensured international condemnation, and would have probably brought his country perilously close to becoming a direct participant in the Yugoslav War. Nevertheless, the mere fact that these proposals were discussed suggests a special relationship between the two states.

Given this relationship, the consistent participation in EPC's condemnation and penalisation of Serbia is surprising, since it resulted to the weakening of a state with which history, religion, fears, interests, geopolitical outlook and information were shared. Hence, an explanation of why Greece unfailingly approved and never vetoed EPC's anti-Serb decisions is required and will subsequently be provided.

Explanation is also required for the series of Greek actions that amounted to a rather moderate, flexible and 'gentle' treatment of FYROM. Although there were strenuous objections to FYROM being recognised with the name Macedonia, this position was more than counterbalanced by several cooperative and moderate decisions. Most importantly, the Greek government consistently maintained a stance allowing a compromise name such as Vardar Macedonia or Upper Macedonia, and did not try to block any attempt by FYROM to request Community recognition.

In order to appreciate these actions, it must be kept in mind that FYROM was in a very precarious position. With war raging in other parts of former Yugoslavia, there was no certainty that it would not spread to this republic as well.[12] Also, the fact that FYROM's Albanian and Serbian minorities had boycotted the referendum for independence, suggested the possibility of ethnic tension and strife.[13] Furthermore, FYROM was essentially defenceless, having a negligible army and a virtually non-existent air-force.[14]

Taking into account these realities, it is surprising that a more forceful and confident strategy towards the new state was not pursued by Greece. Given FYROM's uncertain situation, the timing would have probably been opportune. A strategy among these lines might have involved a 'stick' option, such as the threat of an economic embargo.[15] The question of why despite grievances and apprehensions, the Greek government pursued a 'gentle' approach towards FYROM will be answered subsequently.

Another puzzling instance of Greek cooperation involves the recognition of Croatia. First of all, this decision was contrary to the 4 December Cabinet meeting decision that had advocated a unified Yugoslavia. Secondly, the move towards recognising Croatia constituted yet another blow to Serbia. This is because Serbia's enemy would have been entitled to all the benefits enjoyed by a recognised sovereign state, while Serbia would remain unrecognised.

Most importantly, EPC's decision was considered to be premature, with negative effects for the region. Lord Carrington's 2 December 1991 warning that recognition 'would undoubtedly mean the break-up of the [Hague Peace] Conference and might well be the spark that sets Bosnia-Herzegovina alight,' was widely shared by Greek decision-makers.[16] It is noteworthy that the author has found almost no person in Greece who has expressed a favourable opinion of this decision. Comments about the recognition of Croatia typically range from 'criminal' to 'unfortunate'.[17]

On the basis of the above, the problematic nature of a series of Greek cooperative decisions becomes apparent. Explanations are required for the country's failure to seriously pressure a vulnerable FYROM, its participation in EPC's condemnation and penalisation of Serbia, as well as for the decisions to recognise Croatia and allow the creation of the potentially damaging AC.

The desire to provide answers for such a record of decision-making almost invites the application of the theory of institutionalism. As was analysed in Chapter 1, the theory argues that regimes affect state behaviour by creating important incentives for cooperation, despite 'conflict[ing]...perceptions of self-interest held by governments.'[18] It will be shown that regime influence does offer an explanation to most of the Greek cooperative decisions, including the problematic ones. However, a brief examination of the Greek government's most significant foreign policy objectives will be presented first, because it was these regime-related goals that determined to a considerable extent the country's EPC foreign policy towards former Yugoslavia and FYROM.

## B. Greek Foreign Policy Objectives

During the period of June 1991-January 1992, Greece's government had formulated in a coherent and pragmatic way a hierarchy of foreign policy goals. More specifically, the geographic proximity to warring Yugoslavia had a negative impact on the national economy: 'With 40 per cent of...trade passing through Yugoslavia, Athens estimates losses up to $18 million per day.'[19] As a result of this situation, an important objective was to achieve an EPC decision providing monetary compensation.[20]

Thus, after a period of sustained cooperation, the 8 November 1991 annex of the EPC Declaration on Yugoslavia stated that

> If the economy of a member State is seriously affected by Yugoslav countermeasures, then the Community and its member States will show their solidarity by taking effective and concrete corrective measures towards the member State concerned.[21]

This declaration amounted to an EPC commitment to compensate Greece. An example of the granting of such aid can be found in a 25 February 1992 Council regulation.[22] It accepts the arguments made by the Greek government about the negative results on sectors of the national economy that used the Yugoslavia route for the export of products; and it specifically offers ECU 4 million as 'temporary compensation for the consequences of the situation in Yugoslavia on transport of some fresh fruit and vegetables from Greece.'[23]

Another major goal that was to be achieved during the Maastricht Treaty negotiations, was to obtain an increase of structural funding towards Greece.[24] This objective, which is related to the Community's regional policies, was of immense importance for the state's decision-makers and hence a brief explanation is required.

Regional problems are accentuated by a process of economic and monetary integration, partly because it ultimately deprives from countries the ability to use as an economic tool the revaluation of their currencies.[25] Furthermore,

> Economic integration may encourage concentration of new industry and relocation of existing industry in certain areas of the economic union which give superior infrastructure, lower transport costs and availability of skilled labour.[26]

Following years of discussions and planning, the Community eventually managed to initiate a regional policy in 1975, with the creation of the European Regional Development Fund (ERDF). The Community's policy, aiming at reducing regional disparities and problems, reached a new and more important plateau as a result of the Single European Act (SEA).[27] Its admonitions of the SEA were implemented in 1988 with a series of reforms which resulted to the doubling of the Structural Funds for the 1987-93 period.[28] It was estimated that by 1993, structural appropriations would 'increase to ECU 14 billion...or about 25 percent of the total Community budget.'[29] The practical implications of those reforms for a country like Greece were immense. For example, funds were targeted to what were called Objective 1 regions, defined as areas in which the per capita Gross Domestic Product (GDP) was less than 75% of the Community average.[30] Greece as a whole fell under this category, and thus Objective 1 appropriations for the period 1989-1993 were ECU 6,667 million, which represented 69,4 ECUs per inhabitant, as well as 18,4% of all such allocations.[31]

The advent of the Maastricht Summit was seen by Greece, as well as by the other 'poor' EPC members, as an opportunity to achieve an increase in structural allocations. Their desire for such an increase was clearly communicated. Eventually, the TEU reaffirmed the goal of 'strengthening...economic and social cohesion' and furthermore established the Cohesion Fund which was an entirely new fund unrelated to ERDF or to the other Structural Funds.[32] As described in the Protocol on Economic and Social Cohesion that was attached to the Maastricht Treaty, the Cohesion Fund was to provide funding for environmental and infrastructure projects to Community members with GNP per capita of less than 90 per cent of the Community average. In the words of the Commission, the 'Cohesion Fund given the go-ahead at Maastricht will be to...Greece, Ireland, Portugal and Spain...what the structural policies are to the regions.'[33] Its creation was clearly considered by Mitsotakis as an important victory.[34]

Probably the most important foreign policy objective of the Greek government was to achieve the country's accession to the WEU during the

Maastricht Summit.³⁵ As mentioned in Chapter 2, the WEU was born in 1955 from the ashes of the failed attempt to create EDC.³⁶

Greece applied for WEU membership in 1987, primarily because of its Article V, according to which

> If any of the High Contracting Parties should be the object of an armed attack in Europe, the other High Contracting Parties will, in accordance with the Provisions of Article 51 of the Charter of the United Nations, afford the Party so attacked all the military and other aid and assistance in their power.³⁷

It was believed that Article V would provide Greece with important security guarantees against a possible attack by Turkey—guarantees that were impossible under NATO rules where both countries are members.³⁸ Andreas Papandreou who was in 1987 the socialist Prime Minister, summarised this logic during a parliamentary debate, by succinctly stating that 'our interest in applying to join the WEU was in order to be able to face Turkey as a non-ally.'³⁹

By the time of the Maastricht Summit, WEU membership was also viewed as an opportunity to participate in what was becoming a potentially more important actor in international affairs.⁴⁰ Arguments that the WEU should assume a larger role in the Western institutional landscape dealing with security and foreign policy issues, were increasing in both volume and weight.⁴¹ Greek decision-makers undoubtedly wanted their country to be part of an enhanced in significance WEU.⁴²

The importance bestowed upon gaining WEU membership is also illustrated by the fact that Prime Minister Mitsotakis had communicated to his EPC partners that accession to the WEU was essential in order for Greece to sign the Maastricht Treaty.⁴³ This strategy was publicly (if somewhat misleadingly), admitted by Samaras during a Parliamentary debate on 20 December 1991, when he stated that 'we declared that we were not going to sign the entire Maastricht package unless we signed at the same time the WEU agreement in its entirety.'⁴⁴ The Maastricht Treaty did not actually involve any such signing ceremony, though an attached declaration included the invitation leading to guaranteed membership that had eluded Greece since 1987. It plainly stated that 'States which are members of the European Union are invited to accede to the WEU...or become observers if they so wish.'

The insistence to join the WEU also seemed vindicated by the fact that the Maastricht Treaty created the potential for the organisation to assume in the near future an important role as regards defence issues. According to Article J.4.2

> The Union requests the Western Union (WEU), which is an integral part of the development of the Union, to elaborate and implement decisions and actions of the Union which have defence implications.

Greece officially acceded to the WEU on 20 November 1992, although the importance of membership had by then decreased dramatically.[45] The 19 June 1992 Petersberg Declaration had provided the Greek government with a bitter disappointment, since it

> Stressed that the security guarantees and defence commitments in the Treaties which bind the member States within Western European Union and which bind them within the Atlantic Alliance are mutually reinforcing and will not be invoked by those subscribing to Part III of the Petersberg Declaration in disputes between member States of either of the two organisations.[46]

Given the fact that Turkey was a member of NATO (and was also en route to becoming a WEU associate member), this wording amounted to the suspension of Article V in case of hostilities between Greece and Turkey, thus cancelling the main reason that membership had been desired by Greek decision-makers.[47]

## C. Institutionalist Relevance

Institutionalist theory emphasises the role of institutions and essentially ignores domestic politics. As regards this approach, the theory seems to be vindicated in explaining Greece's foreign policy during the period between June 1991 and 17 January 1992. In these months, domestic politics simply did not play a significant role.

More specifically, there were almost no particular domestic developments that determined or influenced to any important degree the politics of Greek cooperation and moderation. The one major exception is related to Greece's failure to present an acceptable nominee to the AC. The country lacks a Constitutional Court, and the closest equivalent is the Council of the State (Semvouleo tis Epikrateias).[48] Its President Mr Vasilis Botopoulos, although perfectly qualified, was considered to be affiliated with PASOK. As a result, he was side-stepped and Prime Minister Mitsotakis nominated a more politically friendly Vice-President of the Council, Mr Konstantinos Degleris.[49]

Not surprisingly, given the stipulation of the EPC decision that only Presidents of Constitutional Courts were to be nominated, Mr Degleris failed even to be considered for appointment, thus depriving Greece of a chance to have a national representative on the AC. However, even if a proper candidate was nominated, there would have been no guarantee of appointment.[50]

In analysing institutionalist relevance, it is crucial to stress that Greek decision-makers including the then Prime Minister and Foreign Minister, believed that it was essential that their state be viewed by its EPC partners as contributing to the solution of the Yugoslav conflict. They also desired to portray Greece as a country with legitimate concerns in the region, the ultimate goal being to create a reputation of trustworthiness and responsibility, as well as a sense of debt, goodwill and understanding.[51]

These reputational concerns and goals were ultimately produced by the 'shadow of the future' cast by the regime EPC. Greek officials were fully aware that the regime would be responsible for many subsequent decisions that would almost certainly be of considerable importance to their country.[52] Such anticipated regime decisions covered developments in Yugoslavia, as well as the foreign policy goals analysed in the previous section.

Greek decision-makers aimed at ensuring that their country not acquire the reputation of contributing, or being a part of the region's problems, and this prudent goal dictated a series of cooperative decisions.[53] Hence, the government never considered vetoing the establishment of the Hague Peace Conference, or of the Arbitration Commission.

The same rationale explains the participation in EPC's condemnation and penalisation of Serbia. Despite the existence of common interests and history, Greece did not want to be seen as a close ally actively aiding Serbia, given the perception that the republic was primarily responsible for the war and its accompanying atrocities. In other words, reputational concerns superseded the Greco-Serbian special relationship. As Mitsotakis explained while referring to this issue:

> [Within EPC] there exists an interesting balance. No country can actually follow exclusively its policies. One must often compromise or even follow policies with which one disagrees, in order to attain other more important goals *in the future*.[54]

Another example of Greek behaviour being influenced by reputational concerns and EPC's 'shadow of the future', was related to the goal of gaining Community aid as compensation for the Yugoslav War's negative effects on the national economy. The government considered its EPC behaviour and reputation as a key test and condition for achieving such aid. It was believed that the securing of aid would be greatly helped if Greece demonstrated its consistent willingness to cooperate even on issues with negative consequences to some of the country's interests. In this way, the existence of the regime EPC with its continuous decision-making function created incentives for co-operation.[55]

The 'gentle' stance towards FYROM was partly influenced by the fear (discussed in Chapter 3), that the possible descent into war and disintegration of the new republic could have probably had detrimental effects, possibly producing a Third Balkan War. However, EPC's 'shadow of the future' also influenced the flexibility on the issue of FYROM's name, to the extent that a compromise name in the line of Upper Macedonia was at the very least not rejected. Furthermore, EPC's 'shadow of the future' helps explain the failure to block FYROM from applying for EPC recognition, or attaching conditions prior to 16 December 1991. In interviews with Samaras, the former Foreign Minister boasted (with justification), and kept repeating essentially the same rationale behind these cooperative decisions.

An example is illustrative. Concerning the 2 December 1991 Council document referring to the 'Republic of Macedonia,' he emphasised that

> I did not want to take what would have been perceived as an extremist position. Such a position could have created the impression that Greece could have territorial ambitions against Skopje...Furthermore, I wanted to create a positive climate [for Greece] with our European partners; and there were also our goals at Maastricht.[56]

Thus, it can be concluded that the institutionalist prediction that regimes 'link the future with the present,' create reputational concerns and thus ultimately increase pressure for cooperation, stands vindicated.[57] Considerations of reputational concerns and the 'shadow of the future' though, do not suffice to explain entirely the politics of Greek cooperation. An analysis of the 2 December 1991 document suggests additional regime-related reasons of crucial importance. More specifically, it has already been mentioned that Samaras referred in an interview to his government's goals at Maastricht. A telegram of the Ministry of Foreign Affairs also explained that *'although Greece did not agree with this [2 December 1991] decision, it would not block a decision, because of the upcoming Maastricht Summit.'*[58] The stated link between cooperation and Maastricht deserves examination.

Institutionalist theory argues that goods provided uniquely by a regime, high issue density and the possibility of side-payments help achieve and foster cooperation. All of these regime-produced incentives were present at the Maastricht Summit. WEU membership and the establishment of the Cohesion Fund were 'goods' that could have been provided uniquely by the regime EPC. In addition to the support of the other 'poor' Community countries, the Greek government also believed that the reputation of a cooperative state would increase the chances of achieving greater monetary allocations from the Structural Funds. Furthermore, it was hoped that a positive reputation and a cooperative stance on Yugoslavia and on other issues, would assist accession to the WEU.[59]

The granting of Greece's Maastricht foreign policy goals can be viewed as an important side-payment which facilitated the signing of the TEU.[60] According to Greek decision-makers, it also represented a reward for their country's cooperation on Yugoslavia.[61] Institutionalism predicts that the existence of high issue density facilitates such side-payments and thus increases the chances for cooperation.[62] This was undoubtedly the case prior and during the Maastricht Treaty negotiations, when issue density reached a peak.

Furthermore, institutionalist theory emphasises the importance of reciprocity. This concept is helpful in explaining Greece's agreement to EPC's 15 January 1992 decision on the recognition of the former Yugoslav republics.[63] Greece did not veto the recognition of Croatia on the condition that this cooperative action be reciprocated by the refusal to recognise FYROM. In this instance, the state of Greek domestic politics was used as an additional argument by Mitsotakis, who warned his German and Italian counterparts that the recognition of FYROM with the name Macedonia would imperil the survival of his government.

Reciprocity can perhaps also be used in explaining Samaras' agreement to sign the 16 December 1991 EPC decisions. For endorsing a document that he believed would produce negative results for the region, Samaras achieved the three EPC conditions on the recognition of FYROM. The former Foreign Minister claims that he was essentially presented with a *fait accompli* because of Germany's intransigence, and argues that vetoing the declaration would have bestowed upon his state the reputation of a non-cooperating member, and would have also incurred the wrath of Germany.[64] Possibly then, reputational concerns played a role in this decision as well.

On the basis of the above, it can be concluded that Greek cooperation is largely explained by the theory of institutionalism. Institutionalist concepts such as the 'shadow of the future,' high issue density, side-payments, reciprocity, goods offered uniquely by regimes and regime-related reputational concerns, are central in understanding Greek foreign policy towards former Yugoslavia and FYROM. The degree of regime influence even superseded concerns that a series of cooperative decisions would have had consequences that were contrary to perceived national interests. Also, the fact that domestic politics played only a marginal role, further contributes to the vindication of institutionalist analysis.

## D. The Decline of the Politics of Greek Cooperation

The decline of the politics of Greek cooperation begins with the 17 January 1992 letter that Samaras sent to his EPC counterparts, the official English translation of which is published here for the first time.[65] Its tone is alarmist and the possibility that the war in Yugoslavia might spread to the other Balkan states is suggested several times. The tone of the letter is also very aggressive: Samaras accuses the AC for considering only FYROM's arguments and criticises Bulgaria for the decision to recognise FYROM.

The most sustained and fierce attack is reserved for the new republic, or 'Skopje' as it is repeatedly called.[66] FYROM is described as an artificial state which Tito created in order to satisfy his imperialist goals against Greece and Bulgaria. The country's government is presented as engaging in hostile propaganda and making territorial claims against Greece. Importantly, the Foreign Minister concluded that FYROM had failed to comply with EPC's 16 December 1991 conditions.

As regards FYROM's name, EPC's Foreign Ministers were reminded the following:

> For 45 years, the Macedonian name became the major vehicle for territorial and cultural expansionism encroaching upon Greek territory. Because of the continued use and abuse by Skopje of the hellenic civilization and traditions in order to promote expansionist aims, any further use of the Macedonian name by an independent state would ipso facto imply territorial claims against Greece.[67]

Given this argument, the letter concluded that

> The term "Macedonia", if used in the denomination of the Skopje Republic, is unacceptable as it contains by itself an expansionist notion...Thus, the adoption of the Macedonian name...carries the clear message that the Republic's jurisdiction extends over the Macedonian provinces of all neighbouring states.[68]

This passage contains a restrictive interpretation of EPC's 16 December 1991 third condition, thus signalling the abandonment of the flexible policy on the name issue.

Despite the attacks on FYROM, the letter also made it clear that Greece was

> Prepared to help create a regional arrangement to meet the security needs of Skopje, as well as those of its neighbours...In addition, Greece could extend to the new Republic special economic privileges, open prospects for an all round economic cooperation, and set in motion the process for a solution to all bilateral issues.[69]

On 21 January 1992, Karamanlis sent a letter to Italy's Prime Minister Andreotti, in which he objected to FYROM being named Macedonia, though there was no clear adoption of the restrictive position on the name issue.[70] Importantly, Karamanlis attempted to explain Greece's 'vital national interest' in this dispute. More specifically, the President accepted that the new republic did not pose a direct military threat, but emphasised that 'a combination of forces' [i.e. neighbouring countries] in addition to FYROM, could constitute a threat for Greece.[71]

Andreotti replied on 27 January, noting the importance bestowed upon 'maintaining the EC's cohesion,' and pointing out that Greece's national interests were taken into consideration to the extent that the AC's recommendation was made subject to a 'necessary political evaluation.'[72] In other words, it was essentially ignored. Andreotti also made an important reference to the issue of recognising the "Macedonian Republic of Skopje,' thus suggesting a possible (and creative) compromise name, aiming at ending the dispute.[73]

The acceptance of a name among the lines suggested by Andreotti would have required the abandonment of the restrictive position on the name issue. However, it was the hard-line stance that actually received a major boost as a result of the huge demonstration that took place on 14 February 1992 in Thessaloniki, Greece's historic second largest city.[74] It was organised by the Macedonian Committee, a non-governmental organisation.[75]

The committee's founding declaration that was issued on 17 January 1992, emphasised the Greek history and culture of Macedonia and Thessaloniki, and also attacked the AC's ruling.[76] Significantly, FYROM was called several times the 'Republic of Skopje'.[77] The arguments and goals of this declaration set the tone and provided part of the rationale for the decision to organise the Thessaloniki demonstration. One of the committee's major goals was to demonstrate that its positions on Macedonian history and politics enjoyed tremendous popular support.

The decision to hold the demonstration was taken unanimously by the Macedonian Committee. Earlier, Nikos Mertzos (a committee founder and demonstration supporter), attempted to inform Mitsotakis that such a decision was imminent. As a friend and advisor to the Greek Prime Minister for Macedonian-Thrace issues, he felt that it was his duty to do so. However, Mitsotakis was on holiday in Italy, and it proved impossible for Mertzos to get in touch with him.[78]

The undertaking of the demonstration was publicly announced on 7 February 1992 by the Mayor of Thessaloniki, Mr Kosmopoulos. It appeared somewhat misleadingly as an initiative of Thessaloniki's local administration, though in a press conference Mr Kosmopoulos did acknowledge that the Macedonian Committee had played an important role.[79] It also became known that during the demonstration, the city's universities, all public and private sector businesses, as well as all schools would remain closed. Finally, a scathing declaration was released, which included the following passage:

> Macedonia is Greek...Righteous wrath is produced...[by FYROM's] insistence to be internationally recognised with our name...The usurpation is evident, and even more evident through this [usurpation] is imperialism. They take away our name and...demand the international legitimisation of their crime![80]

Mitsotakis met with the demonstration organisers in early February at the Thessaloniki airport.[81] During their meeting, he expressed some concerns and objections.[82] According to Mayor Kosmopoulos, the organisers eventually managed to 'secure [the Prime Minister's] silent agreement.'[83] Publicly, Mitsotakis announced that the planned demonstration 'constitutes a national contribution.'[84]

In addition to not having been informed in time of the decision to hold the Thessaloniki demonstration, Mitsotakis was also not informed about its various details. Most importantly, he was never aware of the exact phrasing of the resolution that the organisers intended to pass.[85] Mayor Kosmopoulos though, had called Samaras and read to him over the phone the text of the resolution. The Foreign Minister expressed no objections.[86]

On 14 February, the demonstration took place and its size and passion surprised everyone, even the most optimistic of the organisers.[87] It is estimated that about one million people participated, a fact that at the very least suggests the sensitivity of the Greek people for the Macedonian Issue which is probably not unrelated with the tumultuous and traumatic historical events in the region that were presented in Chapter 3. The overwhelming majority of the participants came from Thessaloniki and the neighbouring provinces. Present were also officials representing the Greek Orthodox Church, all the political parties, professional groups and local administration bodies. The only notable absence was that of the KKE, which refused to be associated with the event.

The KKE ignored any considerations of political cost. Furthermore, it resented the fact of not having been consulted about the demonstration's planning and content, and condemned the organisational role played by the Macedonian Committee.[88] Although the party castigated the propaganda practised by FYROM against Greece, it concluded that the demonstration would probably concentrate on the republic's name, and would ultimately amount to a 'nationalistic, chauvinistic, anti-Communist delirium.'[89]

Despite such predictions, there was almost something mystical about the demonstration.[90] As people flooded Thessaloniki's central square, many were in tears, and most seemed to be declaring their Greek identity which they felt was being threatened, usurped and falsified by FYROM.[91] It should also be stressed that the demonstration was entirely peaceful.[92] The crowd heard speeches from the bishop of Thessaloniki, and the mayor of the historic nearby town of Veroia. The keynote speaker Mr Kosmopoulos provided in his address an eloquent summary of the arguments used to prove that Macedonia has a Greek history spanning more than three thousand years. Furthermore, what he considered to be the conduct of hostile propaganda by FYROM was clearly condemned. A special plea was reserved for Greece's EPC partners, who were urged to act according to the principle of solidarity. Towards the end, Kosmopoulos asked both rhetorically and emphatically: 'If they are named Macedonians, then what are we going to be named?'[93] Nevertheless, no specific policy recommendations were contained in the speech.

The demonstration culminated with the reading and passing of a resolution which condemned what was considered FYROM's attempt to usurp the Greek name of Macedonia.[94] FYROM was also castigated for 'hostility and expansionism against [Greece].'[95] At its very end, the Thessaloniki resolution contained a passage that proved consequential:

> The [Greek] government is called upon to stand by the spirit and message of [this] resolution and demonstration. The people of Macedonia and Thessaloniki request *from the Foreign Minister* that he continues to fight, *and not accept the recognition of the state of Skopje with a name or designation that will include the name Macedonia.*[96]

This phrasing clearly coincided and provided support for the position on FYROM's name that was included in Samaras' 17 January letter to his EPC counterparts.

The Thessaloniki mass demonstration linked the issue of FYROM's name with the passion, patriotism and nationalism that only one million demonstrators could provide. Prior to that date, all diplomatic efforts and positions were reached by diplomats and politicians. The Thessaloniki demonstration however, courted and achieved the participation and backing of almost a tenth of the country's population on a particular position. In effect, the people became important and active actors in Greece's diplomatic efforts. After 14 February, foreign policy, domestic politics and nationalism begin a process of conflation.

Following the demonstration, Samaras flew to Lisbon for a General Council meeting. EPC member states had pledged that the Greek government would be given one opportunity to present its case on the dispute with FYROM at the intergovernmental Council, regardless of any time constraints. Thus, the 17 February 1992 meeting demonstrates once again EPC's strong intergovernmental aspects. Many experts and diplomats in the Greek Ministry of Foreign Affairs had worked on this presentation (published here for the first time) for several weeks.[97]

Samaras' address lasted for more than half an hour and was well researched and argued. He explained that his country was not afraid of a smaller and essentially unarmed republic, but rather was concerned that if FYROM 'was given recognition in its own terms it...will create great instability in the region.'[98] The possible sources of this instability would be the ensuing strife among FYROM's various ethnic groups, or Serbian attempts to dominate the new republic. Also de-stabilising would be a possible Bulgarian bid to 'embrace' FYROM, given the country's past territorial claims for the region and recent position that a Macedonian nation does not exist.[99]

Greece's Foreign Minister attacked FYROM for failing to meet EPC's three conditions and explained in detail that the various constitutional 'amendments, passed with the ease and speed of a simple government decree' did not satisfy the condition that FYROM refrain from making territorial claims.[100] Furthermore, Samaras presented a series of important examples of hostile actions and propaganda being conducted by FYROM against Greece. Perhaps most sensational was the decision of FYROM's Parliament to establish a navy, despite the fact that it is a landlocked country!

As regards the third condition, he argued that the name Republic of Macedonia implied territorial ambitions against his country, as well as an 'assault on our Hellenic cultural heritage.'[101] Samaras then proposed several possible names that if adopted, would have been consistent with his restrictive interpretation of the third EPC condition:

There are many good options. Prior to the Communist era, the administrative name of the region...was Vardar Banovina. Immediately before that, during the last phase of Ottoman rule, it was known as Skopje Sanjak. The Slav insurgents of 1903 proclaimed it, the "Krusevo Republic" and there is much in the name to unite its inhabitants without disturbing its neighbours.[102]

The Foreign Minister stressed that unlike other neighbouring countries, Greece harboured no territorial ambitions against FYROM. He also emphasised that if the dispute was resolved, his government would be willing to assist financially the new republic, as well as guarantee its security.

Towards the end of his presentation, Samaras made references to popular passions and opinions, pointing out that the Thessaloniki demonstration was the 'biggest demonstration ever held in Greece.'[103] At the beginning of the meeting, he had distributed to his counterparts an envelope which included photographs documenting what was considered to be the provocative propaganda practised by FYROM. Most importantly, the package included a copy of a Greek newspaper featuring on its front page a splendid aerial photograph of the huge Thessaloniki demonstration.[104]

According to Mr Evangelos Kofos who was present at the meeting, EPC's impressed Foreign Ministers concentrated on the newspaper to such an extent, that they seemed to simply ignore the first parts of Samaras' presentation.[105] The Greek Foreign Minister's ultimate message, both visual and verbal, had thus been made clear: in addition to having justice on its side, popular passions were of such magnitude that it meant 'that to grant Skopje recognition as Macedonia...[was] politically impossible for any Greek government.'[106]

Following Samaras' presentation, it was decided to postpone any decision on the recognition of FYROM, and also agreed that the Portuguese Presidency would undertake an initiative aiming to resolve the dispute between FYROM and Greece. This is the origin of what eventually became known as the 'Pinheiro Package.' As is customary, the meeting's decisions were made public through an EPC Press Release, which in its original version acknowledged that there was discussion on the recognition of the Republic of Macedonia. When Samaras was informed of this, he returned from his way to the airport, protested and secured a change in the wording, as well as an oral apology from the Portuguese Presidency, which was announced through speakerphones in the place where the meeting was held. The final version simply mentioned that 'The Community and its member States will continue to follow very closely all developments concerning the possible recognition of other Republics.'[107] In a sense, this episode signals Samaras' adoption of a consistent, consequential and often public hard-line strategy on the issue of FYROM's name that will be analysed in the following chapter.[108]

## Notes

1  Samaras argued that this would have indeed been the case during an interview on 24 December 1996.
2  The official English translation of this letter is published for the first time in Appendix II. It should also be noted that Turkey recognised FYROM on 6 February 1992.
3  This excuse or explanation was argued by Mr Samaras during an interview on 24 December 1996.
4  An interesting and important example of potential conflict between Greece and Yugoslavia (though not exactly Serbia, although Serbs probably played the dominant role in Yugoslavia's politics) occurred on 28 October 1940. On that day, 'the Yugoslav Government...debated, and for a moment appeared to favor, entering Greece at the rear of her fighting Army in Albania, in order to take possession of Thessaloniki. Only Greece's ability to drive back the Italians seems to have saved the city at that time' (Kofos, 1964, p. 96).
5  Interviews with Mr Kofos on 5 January 1997, Mr Mitsotakis on 10 April 1997 and Mr Samaras on 3 February 1997.
6  Krause, 1995, p. 55. Serbia had to contemplate the possibility of a nationalist uprising in its predominantly Albanian region of Kosovo. The events that occurred in 1999 demonstrated, that these fears were not unfounded. As regards Greece, it has been claimed that 'hav[ing] a history of strained relations with Albania...[it] would certainly side with Serbia [in case Albania was drawn in the Yugoslav War' (Crnobrnja, 1994, p. 242). See also Austin, 1993. The most important reason behind Greece's strained relations with Albania is related to the existence of a Greek minority in that country. For an analysis of the history, politics and treatment of this minority, see Veremis et al, 1995.
7  This was Milosevic's first official foreign visit as President of the Yugoslav Republic of Serbia. The fact that he chose Greece was probably not coincidental, and aimed to underscore the special relationship and ties between the two states. This was not missed by Mitsotakis who was pleased by this choice, and used it as an opportunity to recount some of the historical Greco-Serbian ties. For Milosevic's and the Greek Prime Minister's comments, see *Makedonia*, 17 April 1991, p. 13.
8  Quoted in Doudoumis, 1996, p. 20. Serbia eventually recognised FYROM as the Republic of Macedonia on 8 April 1996 This decision was considered in Greece as nothing less than a betrayal. For the almost furious responses of the government, political parties and the press, see *Makedonia*, 9 April 1996, p. 1 and 5. However, Greek indignation did not take into account the numerous instances in which their country had participated in EPC's condemnation of Serbia during the previous years. For an analysis of the decision for mutual recognition between Serbia and FYROM, see especially Krause and Markotitch, 1996. See also Tarkas, 1997, p. 204-11 and 472-3 and Woodward, 1997, p. 121.
9  Interview with Mr Samaras on 3 February 1997.

10  Both Mitsotakis and Samaras accepted in interviews on 10 April 1997 and 3 February 1997 respectively, that a Serbian population transfer would have almost certainly also entailed a military attack against FYROM.
11  Tarkas, 1995, p. 91. See also Perry, 1997, p. 232. In an interview on 3 February 1997, Samaras confirmed that the population transfer and partition proposals were essentially the same. See however Tarkas, 1995, p. 36.
12  The intense fear of the war spreading to the republic during that period, was confirmed in an interview with Mr Risteski on 29 September 1997. Similar points were made in interviews with Mr Arsovski on 3 February 1997 and Mr Dimovski on 29 September 1997.
13  For subsequent accounts of strife among FYROM's ethnic groups, see *The Economist*, 26 July 1997, p. 28 and *Eleftherotypia*, 26 February 1997, p. 14.
14  See Perry, 1992, p. 16 and Perry, 1997, p. 267.
15  Embargoes were eventually imposed by Greece on FYROM, though under different circumstances. For example, when Greece imposed its most severe embargo in February 1994, the threat of the war spreading to the new republic had receded substantially.
16  Woodward, 1995, p. 184.
17  The characterisation 'criminal' was made during an interview with Mr Mertzos on 18 December 1996. In an interview on 10 January 1997, Mr Papayannakis described the decision as 'unfortunate.'
18  Keohane and Nye, 1977/1989, p. 259. See also Haggard and Simmons, 1987, p. 508.
19  *The New York Times*, 9 November 1991, p. A1. It should also be noted that in a 17 January 1992 letter to his EPC colleagues, Samaras claimed that 'almost 60% of the total Greek exports are exported from northern Greece via Yugoslavia, to Central and Western Europe.' See Appendix II.
20  Interviews with Mr Mitsotakis on 10 April 1997, Mr Samaras on 24 December 1996, Mr Skilakakis on 15 April 1997 and Mr Tzounis on 14 April 1997.
21  EPC Press Release P. 109/91, 8 November 1991. On 4 November 1991, 'The Council had asked the Commission to submit at the earliest opportunity proposals in favour of Greece, which is the Member State most affected by the proposed measures and generally by the economic consequences of the Yugoslav crisis, based on the notion of "disproportionate damage," as the Twelve have assured Greece of complete solidarity' (Council 8943/91 Presse 187-G 4.11.91).
22  See OJ No L 58/1, 3.3.92.
23  Ibid. For the subsequent Community implementation of this policy, see OJ No L 187/28, 7.7.92; OJ No L 350/1, 1.12.92; OJ No L 96/22, 22.4.93 and OJ No L 154/4, 21.6.94.
24  Interviews with Mr Mitsotakis on 10 April 1997, Mr Papaconstantinou on 23 December 1996, Mr Samaras on 24 December 1996, Mr Skilakakis on 15 April 1997 and Mr Tzounis on 14 April 1997.
25  See Hannequart, 1992a, p. 1; Hitiris, 1988/1991, p. 233 and O'Donnell, 1992, p. 29. Regional problems refer to 'disparities in levels of income, in rates of growth of output and employment, and in general in levels of economic inequality between the geographic regions of a country' (Hitiris, 1988/1991, p. 232).
26  Hitiris 1988/1991, p. 234.
27  See Article 130.a. These policies were to be implemented through the Structural Funds, which included the ERDF, the European Social Fund (ESF) and the European Agricultural Guidance and Guarantee Fund (EAGGF). The European Investment Bank (EIB) was also to be involved. See SEA, Article 130b.
28  For an account of the reforms, see Commission, 1989.

29 Marks, 1992, p. 192.
30 Other objectives were also included, though Objective 1 was the most important to Greece in terms of monetary allocations. For a brief discussion of the other Objectives, see ibid., p. 206-10.
31 These figures are taken from Urzainqui and de Andres, 1992, p. 93.
32 Title XIV. Article 130a.
33 COM(92) 2000 final, p. 23.
34 During an interview on 10 April 1997, Mr Mitsotakis could hardly contain his pride while referring to the establishment of the Cohesion Fund.
35 Based on interviews with Mr Kofos on 5 January 1997, Mr Mitsotakis on 10 April 1997, Mr Papaconstantinou on 23 December 1996, Mr Samaras on 24 December 1996, Mr Skilakakis on 15 April 1997 and Mr Tzounis on 14 April 1997.
36 The aim was to 'make the WEU an active consultative body for the Europeans in security policy matters, a kind of...EPC in the field of security' (Wegener, 1991, p. 272). The WEU remained dormant between 1973 and 1984. The declarations signalling and confirming the reactivation of the WEU were made in Rome on 27 October 1984 and in Bonn on 23 April 1985. They can be found in Bloed and Wessels, 1994, p. 53-60 and 61-4 respectively. The fact that Denmark, Greece and Ireland were not WEU members was considered an advantage, as these countries often posed particular challenges to EPC decision-making. For additional reasons that led to the WEU's reactivation, see Cahen, 1989, p. 6-7 and Wegener, 1991, p. 272-3.
37 For the text of the entire Treaty that includes Article V, see Bloed and Wessel, 1994, p. 1-6. Article 51 of the UN Charter states that 'Nothing in the present Charter shall impair the inherent right of individual or collective self-defence if an armed attack occurs against a Member of the United Nations, until the Security Council has taken measures necessary to maintain international peace and security. Measures taken by Member in the exercise of this right shall be immediately reported to the Security Council and shall not in any way affect the authority and responsibility of the Security Council under the present Charter to take at any time such actions as it deems necessary in order to maintain or restore international peace and security' ([UN] Department of Public Information, 1989, p. 27-8).
38 In interviews with Mr Papaconstantinou on 10 January 1997 and Mr Tzounis on 14 April 1997, it was stressed that the language used in the WEU's Article V in support of a member that is being attacked is stronger than that which is provided by NATO. However, its importance is lessened by the fact that the WEU lacks NATO's integrated command, organisational structure and experience. See Cahen, 1989, p. 27 and Wegener, 1991, p. 273-4.
39 The debate took place on 20 December 1991. Papandreou's speech can be found (translated into English), in Couloumbis and Veremis, 1992, p. 283-5. This speech is stressed and commented in Tsakaloyannis, 1996, p. 205 fn 27, who also presents an excellent discussion of additional reasons and developments that prompted the Greek socialists to apply for WEU membership in 1987. See ibid., p. 191-2.
40 See for example van Eekelen, 1991 for an account of the WEU's reaction to developments in the Gulf in 1987 and especially in 1990, though prior to the outbreak of war. Van Eekelen was the then Secretary-General of the WEU.
41 See for example the passages of a 1987 speech by Jacques Delors, cited in Cahen, 1989, p. 15.
42 Interviews with Mr Samaras on 3 February 1997 and Mr Tzounis on 14 April 1997.

43  Interview with Mr Mitsotakis on 10 April 1997. In the same interview, Mitsotakis explained that he never actually used the word veto; nor was he ever forced to threaten its use.
44  Samaras was responding to a question asked by Maria Damanaki, the then leader of the party Synaspismos. Their exchange can be found (translated into English), in Couloumbis and Veremis, 1992, p. 289.
45  For the Council of Ministers Communique that announces the accession of Greece to the WEU, see Bloed and Wessel, 1994, p. 159-62.
46  Ibid., p. 143-4.
47  Furthermore, insult was added to injury when Article X was suspended in the case of Turkish associate membership. According to Article X, disputes between WEU members should be referred to the International Court of Justice (ICJ) at the Hague. Most Greek decision-makers consider that an ICJ adjudication over Greek-Turkish disputes in the Aegean would almost certainly lead to a ruling favourable for their country. Subsequently, the WEU concession to Turkey concerning Article X was viewed as a further blow to Greek interests. For the WEU's Article X, see Cahen, 1989, p. 72-3. For the decision suspending Article X, see the first paragraph of the minutes of the 20 November 1992 WEU Council of Ministers meetings, that can be found in Bloed and Wessel, 1994, p. 165.
48  See Legg and Roberts, 1997, p. 124.
49  This account is partly based on interviews with Mr Lengeris on 27 August 1997, Mr Papaconstantinou on 23 December 1996, Mr Papathemelis on 11 January 1997, Mr Tarkas on 9 April 1997 and Mr Vrahatis on 30 August 1997.
50  This fact is often omitted from discussions of this episode. See for example Tarkas, 1995, p. 91.
51  Based on interviews with Mr Kofos on 5 January 1997, Mr Mertzos on 18 December 1996, Mr Mitsotakis on 10 April 1997, Mr Papaconstantinou on 10 January 1997, Mr Samaras on 24 December 1996 and 3 February 1997, Mr Skilakakis on 15 April 1997 and Mr Tzounis on 14 April 1997. The degree of agreement among them is remarkable.
52  Based on interviews with Mr Kofos on 5 January 1997, Mr Mertzos on 18 December 1996, Mr Mitsotakis on 10 April 1997, Mr Papaconstantinou on 10 January 1997, Mr Samaras on 24 December 1996 and 3 February 1997, Mr Skilakakis on 15 April 1997 and Mr Tzounis on 14 April 1997.
53  Interviews with Mr Kofos on 5 January 1997, Mr Mertzos on 18 December 1996, Mr Mitsotakis on 10 April 1997, Mr Papaconstantinou on 10 January 1997, Mr Samaras on 24 December 1996 and 3 February 1997, Mr Skilakakis on 15 April 1997 and Mr Tzounis on 14 April 1997.
54  Interview with Mr Mitsotakis on 10 April 1997; emphasis added.
55  Based on interviews with Mr Kofos on 5 January 1997, Mr Mertzos on 18 December 1996, Mr Mitsotakis on 10 April 1997, Mr Papaconstantinou on 10 January 1997, Mr Samaras on 24 December 1996 and 3 February 1997, Mr Skilakakis on 15 April 1997 and Mr Tzounis on 14 April 1997.
56  Interview with Mr Samaras on 3 February 1997.
57  Axelrod and Keohane, 1993, p. 94.
58  Skilakakis, 1995, p. 57; emphasis added. This telegram was sent by the Greek Ministry of Foreign Affairs to the Greek Embassy in Belgrade on 3 December 1991. In an interview on 1 April 1997, Mr Skilakakis revealed that although not in quotation marks in his book, this is the exact wording of the telegram.

59  Based on interviews with Mr Mitsotakis on 10 April 1997 and Mr Samaras on 3 February 1997.
60  The signing of the TEU by Greece could not have been considered as a foregone conclusion. This is because there was little doubt that some of the Treaty's articles, and especially those referring to Economic and Monetary Union (EMU), would produce strains and hardship to the Greek economy and society.
61  Interviews with Mr Mitsotakis on 10 April 1997, Mr Papaconstantinou on 10 January 1997 and Mr Samaras on 3 February 1997.
62  For example, see Keohane, 1983, p. 155 and Keohane, 1984, p. 91.
63  See EPC Press Release P. 9/92, 15 January 1992.
64  Interview with Mr Samaras on 3 February 1997.
65  See Appendix II. Mitsotakis claims that he was not informed about this letter at the time that it was sent, although there was no subsequent public denunciation. More certain is the fact that the Greek Cabinet was not informed of the letter immediately after it was sent (interviews with Mr Mitsotakis on 10 April 1997 and Mr Skilakakis on 15 April 1997).
66  See Appendix II.
67  Ibid.
68  Ibid.
69  Ibid.
70  The letter is published in Valinakis and Dales, 1994, p. 83-4.
71  Ibid., p. 83.
72  Svolopoulos, 1997, p. 616, Vol. 12.
73  Ibid. In a memorandum that was written on 14 April 1993, Mr Kofos analysed the advantages and disadvantages for Greece of the various names with which FYROM could have been recognised. He considered the name Macedonian Republic of Skopje to have the advantage of allowing FYROM's citizens to be called Skopjans. Kofos' memorandum which is of exceptional quality is published in Tarkas, 1997, p. 171-4.
74  The account of events related to the Thessaloniki demonstration is based on interviews with Ms Damanaki on 30 January 1997, Mr Kofos on 5 January 1997, Mr Kosmopoulos on 5 February 1997, Mr Lengeris on 30 August 1997, Mr Mertzos on 18 December 1997, Mr Mitsotakis on 10 April 1997, Mr Papaconstantinou on 23 December 1996, Mr Papayannakis on 10 January 1997, Mr Samaras on 23 December 1996, Mr Skilakakis on 15 April 1997, Mr Tsohatzopoulos on 3 August 1997, Mr Tzounis on 14 April 1997 and Mr Vrahatis on 30 August 1997. Of particular assistance was also the videotape *Eimaste Edo* [We Are Here], produced in 1992 by Thessaloniki's local administration TV station, TV 100. This tape, full of interviews and covering the entire event, is essential to an analysis of the Thessaloniki demonstration.
75  Its membership was comprised of some of the most prominent and respected citizens of Thessaloniki. Among them were Thessaloniki's Mayor Mr Kosmopoulos, the Aristotle University's Chancellor Mr Trakatellis, former Ministers Zartinides, Papathemelis and Tzitzikostas, as well as many successful and important businessmen, such as Mr Bakatselos. They were affiliated with all the major Greek political parties, with the exception of the KKE though the overwhelming majority had close ties with the then governing party of New Democracy.
76  The privately published and hard to obtain declaration is reproduced in Appendix III. It was written by Mr Mertzos and includes a list of the committee's members.
77  See Appendix III.

78  According to Mertzos, this was both unfortunate and unacceptable: 'Greece does not go on holiday' he poignantly stressed in an interview on 18 December 1996.
79  *Makedonia*, 8 February 1992, p. 1. The role of the Macedonian Committee in organising the Thessaloniki demonstration was much more crucial and central than what Mr Kosmopoulos implied in his press conference, a fact that he accepted during an interview on 5 February 1997.
80  *Makedonia*, 8 February 1992, p. 7.
81  Mitsotakis was en route to Athens, returning from Davos in Switzerland.
82  Based on interviews with Mr Kosmopoulos on 5 February 1997, Mr Mertzos on 18 December 1996, Mr Papathemelis on 11 January 1997 and Mr Tsohatzopoulos on 3 August 1997.
83  Interview with Mr Kosmopoulos on 5 February 1997.
84  *Makedonia*, 11 February 1992, p. 1.
85  Interview with Mr Skilakakis on 15 April 1997.
86  Based on interviews with Mr Samaras on 24 December 1996 and Mr Kosmopoulos on 5 February 1997.
87  Samaras' reaction and interest in the Thessaloniki demonstration was described by Mr Kofos in an interview on 5 January 1997. More specifically, Kofos says that he was in a meeting in Samaras' office preparing for the 17 February Lisbon General Council meeting. A secretary informed them that the demonstration was taking place in Thessaloniki. The various experts, Kofos included, did not pay particular attention. The politician Samaras however, reacted differently: he abandoned the meeting and stayed glued in front of a television set, appearing very pleased.
88  The analysis of the position taken by the KKE is based on *Rizospastis*, 9 February 1992, p. 3 and on an interview with Mr Lengeris that was conducted on 27 August 1997. Mr Lengeris is a member of the KKE's Central Committee, and is partly responsible for the party's international relations section. During the interview, it was explicitly and repeatedly clarified that all the views that he expressed, also represented in an exact and accurate way, the views of the KKE's General Secretary Ms Aleka Papariga. As I was told while trying to arrange KKE-related interviews: 'there is only one view in the party[!]'.
89  *Rizospastis*, 9 February 1992, p. 3.
90  In an interview on 24 December 1996, Mr Samaras called the demonstration 'a Dionysian expression of the Greek people.'
91  Having talked to many friends and relatives, I am amazed to report that most admit having cried at least at some point during the demonstration.
92  Characteristically, a huge banner read: 'Peace, Security, Cooperation in the Balkans.'
93  Based on the viewing of TV 100's *Eimaste Edo*, 1992.
94  The resolution had been collectively written and approved by the Macedonian Committee (interview with Mr Kosmopoulos, 5 February 1997).
95  *Makedonia*, 15 February 1992, p. 5.
96  Ibid.; emphasis added. The specific mentioning of Greece's Foreign Minister and not of Greece's Prime Minister or government is noteworthy. It is perhaps explained by the fact that Samaras had been informed of the resolution's precise phrasing, and had explicitly expressed his support and approval. It is doubtful whether Mitsotakis would have passed a similar judgement.
97  See Appendix IV.
98  Ibid.
99  Ibid.

100 Ibid.
101 Ibid.
102 Ibid.
103 Ibid.
104 Samaras distributed the 15 February 1992 copy of the newspaper *Makedonia*.
105 Interview with Mr Kofos on 5 January 1997. Kofos believes that more that 50 per cent of the impression produced by Samaras on 17 February 1992 was not caused by the elaborate and lengthy research and work undertaken by the Ministry of Foreign Affairs experts. Rather, it was produced by the copy of the newspaper that was distributed, since it made explicit the degree of popular passion on the dispute with FYROM.
106 See Appendix IV.
107 EPC Press Release P. 8/92, 17 February 1992.
108 The Greek press was informed of Samaras' intervention in altering the text of the EPC declaration. As expected, his actions received favourable coverage. See *Makedonia*, 18 February 1992, p. 12.

# 6 The Challenge of Samaras, February-April 1992

A foolish consistency is the hobgoblin of little minds, adored by little statesmen and philosophers and divines.

-Ralph Waldo Emerson.

### A. The Political Parties Respond to Popular Discontent

After returning from Lisbon, Samaras participated on 18 February 1992 in an unusual meeting of the leaders of the Greek political parties that were represented in Parliament.[1] This meeting was the first in a series of events that followed the momentous 14 February Thessaloniki demonstration that belong firmly to the realm of Greek domestic and partisan politics, and ultimately determined the country's EPC foreign policy towards former Yugoslavia and FYROM.

The 18 February First Council of the Political Leaders was chaired by the President of the Hellenic Republic, Konstantinos Karamanlis. Participants included Prime Minister Mitsotakis, the Leader of the Opposition Andreas Papandreou, Maria Damanaki, leader of the small leftist party Synaspismos, and Aleka Papariga, General Secretary of the KKE. This meeting, as well as the subsequent Parliamentary debate on 24 February 1992, represented the initial responses of the political parties to the rise of popular emotions and to the Thessaloniki demonstration. In a sense, the Greek people had succeeded in preceding and upstaging their elected representatives.

At the beginning of the meeting, Samaras gave an account of what had taken place at the Lisbon General Council.[2] In the following four hours, all major foreign policy issues were discussed in a civilised and calm manner. As regards the dispute with FYROM, the Prime Minister suggested that a compromise on the name might become necessary.[3] Importantly, Karamanlis, Papandreou and

Papandreou and Mitsotakis pronounced the third EPC condition vague, thus indirectly criticising Samaras.

In the official announcement of the Presidency, it was noted that 'convergence of views was ascertained on vital national issues [however there] remain differences on others.'[4] On the dispute with FYROM though, there was unanimous agreement that Greece ought to pursue a settlement on the basis of the 16 December 1991 EPC conditions. That there was agreement on this point, was made perfectly clear in the press conferences given by the leaders after the meeting's conclusion. Mitsotakis declared that 'as regards the Balkans and [our] policy towards Skopje, there was agreement.'[5] Papandreou noted that there was agreement on the '"Macedonian" [issue] and on Balkan policy.'[6] Similar statements were made by Maria Damanaki and Aleka Papariga.[7] It was also decided that given 'extraordinary situations,' a similar meeting could be held in the future.[8]

The leader's views on foreign policy issues were discussed publicly during a Parliamentary debate on 24 February 1992, the tone and conduct of which was uncharacteristically serious, moderate, calm and non-demagogic.[9] The agreement on Greece's policy towards its dispute with FYROM was reiterated by all the speakers. Mitsotakis emphasised this fact and could not resist the temptation to tease the KKE's representative for his participation in this agreement (the KKE is usually a lonely and contrarian voice in Parliament).

Despite any personal misgivings or privately expressed doubts, Mitsotakis also declared that 'the Foreign Minister did [on 16 December 1991] in Brussels a wonderful job.'[10] Furthermore, the Prime Minister completely overlooked the Thessaloniki resolution's argument that FYROM's name should not include the word Macedonia, judging the demonstration significant only to the extent that it informed the world community about Greece's arguments and disagreements with FYROM. This 'public relations' interpretation of the Thessaloniki demonstration ignored what appeared to be genuine popular concern about FYROM's name.

Papandreou's reference to the same event was rather vague. He stated that 'Greece can not recognise the name Macedonia to Skopje. The enormous Thessaloniki demonstration proved this. It was a reawakening of the nation.'[11] Although Papandreou paid lip service to what had happened in Thessaloniki, he was not clear as to whether he actually accepted the contents of the Thessaloniki resolution. It can only be ascertained with certainty that he would have been opposed to FYROM simply being named Macedonia.

In his speech, Papandreou criticised the Greek government's agreement in the 16 December 1991 EPC meeting. His criticism though, only passingly implied that the three conditions were inadequate. Rather, he primarily argued that Samaras should have utilised his veto power and thus blocked a decision that essentially sanctioned Yugoslavia's break-up. Finally, the Leader of the Opposition condemned the government's decision to allow the creation of the Arbitration Commission, as well as its failure to ensure that the country was represented on it.

This Parliamentary debate revealed broad agreement on Greece's strategy and goals in the dispute with FYROM. The various dissensions that were expressed concerned primarily tactics. Mitsotakis never defended or even presented the Greek position on FYROM's name that was included in Samaras' 17 January 1992 letter to his EPC counterparts; and the opposition's representatives were either vague or silent about supporting a maximalist position on the name issue. Nevertheless, and despite not being advertised, the official Greek stance on FYROM's name remained maximalist. It remained so though more as a diplomatic manoeuvre than a position 'cast in stone.'[12] Mitsotakis commented on the potential flexibility of this position during an interview, by stressing that 'a country does not enter a dispute arguing for the minimum of its demands.'[13]

Greece's governing and opposition parties had thus responded to popular concerns without resorting to populism, nationalistic rhetoric, or even a clear adoption of the restrictive position on what FYROM ought to be named. In doing so, they underestimated the radicalism and passion of at least a certain segment of the population; and at any rate, their positions and discourse soon changed in a dramatic, undisputed and consequential way.

Perhaps more in accordance with the people's feelings was the official sanctioning of some limited trade difficulties against FYROM, that provide the first indication of what eventually became the politics of Greek confrontation. More specifically, the Greek border authorities created a number of bureaucratic obstructions in an attempt to prevent or delay goods from being brought into FYROM via Greece. Their actions 'delayed or halted cargoes of food, oil, medicine and other imports bound for Skopje.'[14] The consequences were potentially harmful for the new republic, since the totality of its oil requirements, as well as many other vital products, were imported from Greece. However, as would have probably been expected of any such enterprise undertaken in the Balkans, even these limited measures were implemented in a less than full-proof and exemplary way.[15]

On 26 February, Karamanlis responded privately to developments by sending a note to Samaras that referred to the situation in the Balkans and to Greece's dispute with FYROM.[16] The key paragraph and argument (which is subsequently elaborated in the note), stated that

Reason thus demands that all the measures that will avert major disturbances in the Balkans, be taken; and at any rate nothing should happen which could deteriorate the situation; and what would certainly undermine stability and perhaps even peace in the Balkans would be the recognition of Skopje with the name Macedonia. Such an action would not only constitute the falsification of history...Above all it would undermine security and peace in the region.[17]

Samaras says that he often utilised the arguments presented in this note, which he regarded as supportive of his position on FYROM's name. A closer examination though, reveals that Karamanlis' wording does not coincide with an endorsement of the Thessaloniki resolution and Samaras' preferred stance. The President only states his opposition to FYROM being named Macedonia, while he maintained an ambiguity on names such as for example Vardar Macedonia. By doing so, Karamanlis seems to have been signalling his support, or at least was not rejecting the possibility of a compromise name that would had resolved Greece's dispute with FYROM. During an interview, Samaras conceded that this is the correct interpretation based on the actual phrasing of the note. However, he stressed that the period when it was written must also be taken into account, and hence 'one must necessarily conclude that the note must be interpreted as something that denies a synthetic name for FYROM.'[18]

On the day that Karamanlis was communicating his note to Samaras, George Trangas, an important journalist, judged that Denmark, Italy and Holland were rather unresponsive and unfriendly to Greece's positions and concerns over FYROM's name. He thus urged the listeners of his morning radio show to boycott imported products from these countries. His recommendation was taken seriously, and a spontaneous nation-wide boycott began to take place. One of Greece's largest supermarket chains facilitated the boycott by placing signs that indicated products originating from the targeted countries. At the same time, one of the best private hospitals proudly and very publicly declared that it would seize having any sort of transactions with Holland.[19] It was estimated that in less than two days, demand for Italian and Dutch products had decreased by 25 per cent.[20]

The boycott represents the clearest possible indication that the dispute with FYROM elicited passionate popular reactions. For the second time in the month of February, the people had preceded and upstaged their political leaders, albeit now in a less than responsible and productive way. The government's spokesperson condemned the boycott by saying that 'these spontaneous initiatives express some of the people's feelings...[However] the government does not agree and recommends self-restraint.'[21] This stand was endorsed by the EP in a resolution that noted

> That it is totally unacceptable for political disagreements between Member States to be pursued by economic means; [the EP] welcomes the condemnation of popular initiatives of this sort by the authorities of the Member State concerned.[22]

The fact that the non-intergovernmental EP had expressed its opinion on this issue, illustrates that it does play a certain role, thus ensuring that the defining norm of the regime EPC is not that of strict intergovernmentalism.

A contrary opinion was held by Samaras, who was supportive of the boycott. In a letter to the Greek Prime Minister written on 17 March 1992, he described it as 'spontaneous, pure and patriotic.'[23] Samaras considers himself fortunate to have been given an opportunity to express publicly his support.[24] He claims that he came across by chance a *Reuters* wire report mentioning that according to sources in the Dutch Foreign Ministry, he had condemned the boycott of Dutch products. This being untrue, he instructed that the Foreign Ministry issue the following statement:

> The Minister of Foreign Affairs Ant. Samaras expressed to his Dutch counterpart that [the boycott involves] spontaneous popular reactions which are happening for the first time in Greece. [These] reactions however are due to the diffuse perception [concerning] Holland's total stance on our national issues, and especially on the Skopje [one].[25]

This statement does not only fail to condemn the boycott, but actually passes the blame to the Dutch government because of its position on Greece's dispute with FYROM. In other words, it accepts Trangas' rationale for the boycott! Furthermore, the difference with the government's official position is enormous. Thus, an additional indication was provided of the growing rift between Samaras and Mitsotakis.

Given these developments, rumours of a Samaras resignation began to circulate, though the Foreign Ministry's spokesperson denied them on 27 February 1992.[26] Samaras' high-stakes campaign to ensure that Greece adopt permanently his restrictive stance on FYROM's name was nevertheless being pursued, his strongest weapon being the threat of resignation. At this point, it must be explained that such a development was expected to have serious political ramifications. Coming from a patrician family, charismatic, well educated, eloquent, wealthy, and having attained some of the highest political offices at a remarkably young age, Samaras was the 'coming man' of the Greek Centre-Right.[27] An indication that he was at the height of his power and popularity is offered by the fact that a Samaras speech at the Athens Hilton Hotel was attended by some seventy government MPs.[28] Since New Democracy's 152 MPs constituted a majority of only two, fears that his resignation would bring down Mitsotakis' government can be properly appreciated.[29]

## B. Samaras Attacks His Government

In the beginning of March 1992, the Greek government was facing a potentially explosive situation. Its responses to developments stemming from the dissolution of Yugoslavia were rapidly being reduced and dominated by the issue of what would be an acceptable name with which FYROM should be recognised, while all other considerations were becoming of secondary (if any), importance.[30] At the same time, the citizens seemed to be supporting a hard-line and passionate stance, demanding that the word Macedonia be excluded entirely from FYROM's name.[31] The government's own Foreign Minister considered this to be the only appropriate and defensible policy, and began campaigning for its permanent and uncompromising adoption, not being covered by the 17 January 1992 letter that represented his country's maximum but negotiable position on FYROM's name.[32] On the other hand, Mitsotakis favoured a compromise on this issue. For Greece's Prime Minister, probably the only encouraging developments were that the President and opposition parties had not yet accepted or campaigned publicly for a non-negotiable hard-line position.

On 5 March 1992, US Secretary of State James Baker sent a letter to Samaras which is published here in its entirety for the first time.[33] Baker suggested a meeting with his EPC counterparts in order to discuss the issue of recognising Serbia and Bosnia-Herzegovina. He also supported the recognition of Macedonia (he did not use the term FYROM):

> I must tell you that it is our judgement that failure to recognize what is now known as Macedonia in a reasonably timely fashion will contribute to instability and encourage other Yugoslav elements to adventurism which could rapidly escalate to open conflict. This surely would not be in the interest of Yugoslavia's neighbors, the European Community, or the United States.[34]

This letter alarmed the Greek government, and a meeting chaired by Mitsotakis was called on the following day, aiming to discuss how to respond to the new development.³⁵ It must be stressed, that this meeting did not and could not reach any definitive conclusions concerning Greece's official policy towards FYROM and its name, since such decisions could only be taken by the Cabinet or by the Council of the Political Leaders. The meeting's value lies in the fact that it reveals the policy and tactical preferences of its most important participants.

Mitsotakis suggested that the possibility of a compromise on FYROM's name be discussed, because his Foreign Minister might be confronted with such a proposal during his forthcoming meetings with Baker and Genscher, as well as at the US-EC Foreign Minister's meeting. Samaras adamantly opposed any discussion on the basis of a compromise, requested that he receive written instructions on how to handle any discussions, and argued that an even better solution would involve written instructions emanating from a new meeting of the Council of the Political Leaders.

His insistence on written instructions was calculated to avert the translation of moderate views into official policy. Samaras correctly sensed that given popular feelings and passions, advocates of a more moderate approach towards FYROM's name would be unwilling to commit their position in an official document providing instructions to the Foreign Minister. At the end of the meeting, it was decided that Mr Moliviatis seek out in writing the positions of Karamanlis and Papandreou on a possible compromise. Not surprisingly, a series of meetings and discussions in the following few days failed to produce any written instructions for Samaras.³⁶

The Greek Foreign Minister flew to Brussels feeling confident that a combination of his country's veto power and the undergoing Pinheiro initiative would neutralise any US pressure for the recognition of FYROM. He was vindicated in his analysis. In the words of James Baker: 'since it was clear that the Greeks would continue to veto any EC move on Macedonia, I backed off and devoted my energies to Bosnia.'³⁷ Thus, the 10 March 1992 US/EC declaration merely stated

> That positive consideration should be given to the requests for recognition of [Bosnia-Herzegovina and FYROM], contingent on the resolution of the remaining European Community questions relating to those two republics.³⁸

Returning from this meeting, Samaras continued his campaign to commit the Greek leadership to a non-negotiable hard-line course. His next 'target' was the President. Karamanlis was the founder of the New Democracy party and one of the greatest statesmen in modern Greek history.[39] Samaras' attempt to influence such an 'Olympian' figure involved a somewhat audacious action. During a meeting with Karamanlis on 13 March 1992, he 'forgot' an envelope containing an important and critical letter.[40]

In this letter, Samaras referred to the March 6 meeting and emphasised that all the other participants were favourably disposed towards a compromise solution on FYROM's name. Most importantly, he criticised the President for failing to take a position on such a course of action.[41] He wrote: 'Mr Moliviatis failed to receive any specific view on the burning issue of the name by the President of the Republic or by the Leader of PASOK,' and thus implied that Karamanlis possibly favoured a compromise.[42]

Samaras demanded the immediate meeting of the Council of the Political Leaders chaired by the President, in order to 'develop a *final* position' on FYROM's name.[43] The use of the word final provides further evidence that the maximalist position included in Samaras' 17 January 1992 letter to his EPC counterparts was negotiable. This demand also represents an inadvertent and indirect admission that the third EPC condition was rather vague, since otherwise no new meeting would have been required to specify Greece's position on FYROM's name.

The letter ended with a thinly veiled threat of resignation. The Foreign Minister warned that unless 'a stance of no compromise is adopted...I can not be the one who represents the country in the imminent crucial meetings.'[44] Samaras was suggesting that by failing to take a clear (and hostile) stance towards a compromise with FYROM, the President would also be held responsible for his resignation. The conveying of this message was probably the essence of his letter.

The content and consequences of Samaras' preferred policy of 'no compromise' were soon elaborated in his lengthy 17 March 1992 letter to Mitsotakis.[45] Samaras emphasised that FYROM's name is 'the key that unlocks and locks the three [EPC] conditions.'[46] After presenting a historical analysis of FYROM's provocations and dangers for Greece, he urged

> The unanimous decision of the Council of the [Political] Leaders to seal and make official to every direction the weighty message that we do not accept a compromise on the name issue. Hence, it must become most clear that Greece does not discuss any variation, alternation, use, connection, or any synthetic finding which will refer to the name Macedonia.[47]

The meaning and wording of this policy recommendation is similar to the Thessaloniki resolution. The Foreign Minister recommended that the Council of the Political Leaders decision be communicated to the EC states, the US, CSCE members, as well as to all UN member states. These states would also be warned that Greece would block FYROM's entry to international organisations, by relying on its veto power where possible.

Samaras' intended hard-line stance was not limited to such measures. He suggested that if the Pinheiro initiative failed, a series of punitive measures be adopted, that were to include the closing of the border with FYROM. A blockade though would not be sufficient, and it was hence further recommended that the Greek government close down its General Consulate in Skopje, and also expel all FYROM citizens residing in Greece.

Samaras judged that these measures were both feasible and desirable. They would cause the isolation and destruction of FYROM's economy, and thus force the republic's capitulation to Greek demands. Hence, the Foreign Minister's strategy is revealed: while threatening to resign, he believed that a non-negotiable restrictive position on the name issue, supported by tough measures falling just short of a military intervention, would bring victory to Greece in the dispute with FYROM.

## C. The 'Pinheiro Package' and the Break with Samaras

On 1 April 1992, Samaras had a meeting with the Portuguese Foreign Minister Joao de Deus Pinheiro and Ambassador Jose Cutileiro.[48] He was presented with a plan to end the dispute with FYROM, which has subsequently been referred to as the 'Pinheiro Package.'[49] Pinheiro's initiative and proposals provide another example of a decision-making procedure of the regime EPC, and also offers evidence of the important role played by the intergovernmental Presidency.

Following the 16 December 1991 meeting, this was the second major EPC attempt to address the dispute. According to the minutes, Pinheiro clarified that his plan was being submitted on a 'take it or leave it basis.'[50] It was a package deal that FYROM and Greece would have to accept or reject as a whole.

In order to satisfy the first EPC condition, the plan envisioned the signing of a Treaty between the two states. The main points on which agreement was to be reached were as follows:

*Article 1*
The two States Parties to this Treaty hereby confirm their common existing frontier as an enduring and inviolable international frontier.

*Article 2*
The two States Parties undertake to respect the sovereignty, the territorial integrity and the political independence of each other.
*Article 3*
The two States Parties shall refrain from threats or the use of force aimed at the violation of the common existing frontier...
*Article 4*
The two States Parties will work together and cooperate to maintain and ensure an open frontier for the lawful and free passage of goods and persons.[51]

Samaras was in agreement with this part of the plan, and also viewed positively Pinheiro's proposal that FYROM make additional changes to its constitution in accordance with Greek demands. Agreement was then reached on the suggestion that the republic receive Community assistance. It was clarified that it would be conditional upon friendly relations with Greece, and would furthermore be directed via the neighbouring EPC member. In Pinheiro's words: '[we will try] to find ways to help you, so that you can help them.'[52]

During the meeting there was disagreement on two areas. The first involved Pinheiro's suggestion on exactly how FYROM's government should satisfy EPC's first and second conditions. He proposed that it send a legally binding letter, its key part stating the new republic's willingness to

> Take promptly effective measures in order to discourage any acts of hostile activity or propaganda against Greece that are likely to incite violence, hatred and hostility against the Greek people and may offend their cultural and historical values or may place in jeopardy the Greek identity and undermine the loyalty of Greek citizens towards the Greek State.[53]

Samaras requested that a more negative phrasing be included, which would deny in a clear and forceful way the existence of a 'Macedonian' minority in Greece. Portugal's Foreign Minister agreed to accommodate this request.

The second area of disagreement focused on Pinheiro's attempt to find a solution that would satisfy the third EPC condition, by suggesting that FYROM be named New Macedonia. Not surprisingly, Samaras strongly objected to such a name, arguing that it 'was not in accordance with the interpretation that Greece gives to the third condition.'[54] Ambassador Cutileiro in a rather remarkable exchange with Samaras, implied that the Greek Prime Minister was in favour of a compromise:

*Mr Cutileiro*: I hope that the decision of Greece's political leadership on the issue of the name will eventually be different than yours.
*Mr Samaras*: You understand why I do not want to comment on what you are saying.

*Mr Cutileiro*: I said it as a joke![55]

Pinheiro also insisted that FYROM's and Bosnia-Herzegovina's recognition be discussed together in the upcoming 6 April EPC meeting. Samaras wanted to avoid such a development, because it would increase considerably the pressure on the Greek side. A persuasive excuse was found, since Mitsotakis was going to be away on an official visit to Hungary, and the Greek Foreign Minister thus argued that not enough time existed to discuss the proposed package deal and reach a decision. Pinheiro agreed, but pointed out that he would stress in the meeting that a final decision must be reached by 1 May 1992.

Two days after the meeting, Samaras sent new letters to Karamanlis and Mitsotakis. In his letter to the President, he argued that his negotiating credibility was weakened because of the lack of a national position on the issue of FYROM's name.[56] He urged Karamanlis to undertake an initiative to call a second meeting of the Council of the Political Leaders on 11 April 1992, suggesting somewhat vaguely that such a gathering on that date would allow some twenty days for an 'extraordinary special programme aimed at averting unpleasant developments on our national issue.'[57]

In the letter to Mitsotakis, he pointed out that his position regarding FYROM's name had been consistent, clear and vocal—unlike the Prime Minister's silence.[58] According to Samaras, Mitsotakis' evasive stance had prevented the 'crucial clarification' of the third EPC condition.[59] It is noteworthy that the vagueness of the third condition is once again inadvertently implied and accepted. The Foreign Minister then wondered why Mitsotakis did not 'proceed to my immediate replacement' if he held an opposing view.[60]

The letter ended with a repetition of the proposal made to Karamanlis for a new meeting of the Council of the Political Leaders on 11 April 1992. The rationale remained the same, though in this letter it was linked to an ultimatum:

> If this does not happen, Mr President [of the government], you will have to agree with me, that my staying at the Ministry of Foreign Affairs beyond this date, would be aimless, not to say decorative.[61]

Given the government's slim Parliamentary majority and grim electoral prospects, this was a serious threat.[62]

The Prime Minister responded on 5 April, explaining that he was 'astonished' by Samaras' letter.[63] Despite previous public praise, he accused him for failing to achieve a clear and satisfactory condition on FYROM's name.[64] The Foreign Minister was also condemned for not studying the consequences of a possible Greek rejection of EPC's package proposal, in which case a series of undesired unilateral recognitions would be likely. Most importantly, Mitsotakis rejected Samaras' ultimatum, stressing that the Council of the Political Leaders was not a constitutionally recognised decision-making body, though the possibility of a meeting at a later date was left open. Mitsotakis added that he would interpret any 'premature resignation' as a cowardly attempt to 'avoid battle'—a stance that he would have to condemn publicly.[65] The description of a possible resignation by Samaras as 'premature' essentially accepted that such a development was becoming increasingly likely.

Samaras' request was also rejected by the President in the letter of 7 April 1992, in which he pointed out that an initiative to convene the Council of the Political Leaders required their unanimous consent;[66] and the consent of at least Mitsotakis was clearly lacking. Karamanlis also poignantly suggested that such requests ought to be submitted by the Prime Minister himself, and not by mere Ministers. Furthermore, the President judged the third EPC condition vague, and implied that given his differences with government policy, Samaras should consider resigning.

While his confrontation with Mitsotakis and Karamanlis was rapidly reaching a crisis point, Samaras travelled to Brussels for an EPC Ministerial meeting on 6 April 1992. According to the minutes, Lord Carrington supported the recognition of Macedonia (the term is used throughout the minutes).[67] Samaras stated that 'on Macedonia he would only be able to a go a limited way in terms of a declaration.'[68] The representatives of the UK, Luxembourg, Belgium, the Netherlands and Denmark signalled their desire for an early recognition of FYROM. However, they certainly were aware that Samaras was equipped with veto power, and that EPC-sponsored negotiations were being conducted. Pinheiro suggested that the negotiations would be concluded in two weeks; and the Greek Foreign Minister assured his counterparts that 'a package deal was possible on or about 1 May.'[69] It should be pointed out though, that this statement did not provide a clear guarantee that the negotiations would be completed successfully by that date. The meeting's declaration stated that

The Community and its member States also heard a report from the Presidency about its efforts to reach a solution on the issue of the recognition of another republic [FYROM]. They expect these efforts to produce results soon.[70]

The issue of Bosnia-Herzegovina's recognition was also discussed in the same meeting. In the previous months, war had subsided in Croatia, where the deployment of a UN peace-keeping force had begun.[71] However, the situation in Bosnia was correctly assessed to be explosive. The most ethnically mixed of all the Yugoslav republics, Bosnia had held a referendum on 1 March 1992, which had ominously been boycotted by the republic's Serb Population.[72] On a turnout of 64.4 per cent, 99.7 per cent had voted for independence.[73]

Despite the prospects for instability and the beginning of hostilities among Bosnia's ethnic groups, EPC's Foreign Ministers decided to recognise the republic as an independent state.[74] Samaras cooperated in this decision notwithstanding the fact that he judged such an action 'premature' and believed that it would produce negative consequences for the region.[75]

Returning to Athens, Samaras sent new letters to Karamanlis and Mitsotakis. To the former, he denied that the third EPC condition was vague and argued that given FYROM's previous name (Socialist Republic of Macedonia), only the word Macedonia could imply territorial threats.[76] As was previously explained, this logic does not necessarily apply to names such as Upper Macedonia or Northern Macedonia. Samaras also castigated the President for failing to publicly declare his position on whether the word Macedonia should be part of FYROM's name.

In the letter to Mitsotakis, the Foreign Minister reiterated his demand for a meeting of the Council of the Political Leaders on 11 April.[77] Most importantly, he used language that was unapologetic, rough and offensive, thus almost seeking a final break in their relation.[78] The Prime Minister was accused for 'political hypocrisy' for claiming to having supported Samaras.[79] His interpretation of the third EPC condition constituted 'a gift to the opposing [i.e. FYROM's] propaganda' and is almost 'laughable,' as was the charge that Samaras was attempting to avoid battle.[80] Furthermore, for raising doubts on the feasibility of closing the Greek borders, Mitsotakis was charged with putting on the same level 'country and counting-office.'[81]

This letter is also significant because it contains one of the most clear and succinct explanations of Samaras' hard-line stance on FYROM's name:

Among the three [EPC] conditions, the commanding guarantee is the eradication of the name 'Macedonia', which when eradicated, essentially kills the danger of territorial claims, as well as that of propaganda.[82]

In his 9 April written reply, Mitsotakis announced his intention to end the practice of exchanging letters with Samaras, given their 'unacceptable tone.'[83] The Prime Minister stressed that the government had not reached a decision on how to respond to developments, urged Samaras to participate and contribute to the decision-making process, and resign only if he disagreed with its outcome. He reminded his Foreign Minister that Turkey and not FYROM constituted the most important security threat to Greece, and maintained his judgement that the third EPC condition was vague by stating that otherwise there would have been 'no need to exchange letters today.'[84] Finally, Mitsotakis granted Samaras' demand for a new meeting of the Council of the Political Leaders (eventually scheduled to take place on 13 April 1992).

### D. The Point of No Return: 13 April 1992

The consequences and aftermath of the Second Council of the Political Leaders constitute the kind of paradox that makes the study of politics fascinating. On 13 April 1992, Samaras' hard-line view on FYROM's name finally became Greece's official, non-compromising and near unanimous policy. However, on the very same day of his policy triumph, he was dismissed from office.

The Foreign Minister entered the meeting together with Mitsotakis, gave a brief analysis of recent developments, and then presented the participants with a document containing seven proposals.[85] The first suggested that the Council issue an announcement making it absolutely clear that 'the name Macedonia is non-negotiable under any form.'[86] The second proposal recommended that in the case that Greece's demands were not met, border passages with FYROM be closed. At the same time, Samaras urged that Greece utilise its veto power to block FYROM's Community recognition, though this policy recommendation ignored the possibility of EPC member states recognising FYROM unilaterally.

The remaining proposals aimed at informing important states and actors of Greece's position. Mitsotakis was to call an extraordinary meeting of the European Council, while an extraordinary session of the Greek Parliament would pass a resolution and distribute it to the national Parliaments of the EC states, as well as to the European Parliament. The Greek political leaders were urged to meet with their EC counterparts and Jacques Delors, Cyrus Vance and Lord Carrington would be invited to Athens in order to receive a comprehensive briefing. Finally, the President of the Hellenic Republic would inform the EC Ambassadors, and Samaras would brief his EC counterparts.

Having concluded his presentation, Samaras became the target of a verbal outburst by Karamanlis. Most likely, the elder statesman considered inappropriate the fact that a mere Minister who was four decades his junior, was giving policy recommendations to both him and to the other political leaders. Samaras' proper role in the meeting should have been to simply provide information concerning developments. Although Samaras claims that he had received permission from Mitsotakis, the Prime Minister was not responsible for making such a decision for a meeting that was chaired by the President.[87]

After Samaras was excused, the meeting began in earnest. Mitsotakis submitted a 'top secret' memorandum written by the 72-year old diplomat Ioannis Tzounis which examined the consequences of three possible scenarios following a Community recognition of FYROM with the name Macedonia.[88] According to the memorandum, a Greek refusal to recognise FYROM both *de jure* and *de facto* would produce a series of negative consequences, and would certainly fail to alter the position of the other EPC member states. Furthermore, qualified majority voting would allow the new republic to develop economic relations with the Community, and even decisions subject to a Greek veto could eventually be implemented on the basis of a series of bilateral agreements. Tzounis also argued that Greek enterprises located in FYROM would suffer considerably, while the closing of the borders would affect negatively tourism and Greek trade with the Community.

A decision to deny the *de facto* and *de jure* recognition of FYROM would force the closing of the Greek Consulate at Skopje, an important source of information; and it would push FYROM towards friendship with countries considered hostile to Greece like Turkey. Tzounis argued that ultimately, such a policy position would degenerate into having 'the fate of the Hallstein doctrine.'[89]

A *de facto* recognition of FYROM would keep the Consulate open, and ameliorate the negative consequences described in the previous scenario. However, it would not pressure FYROM to change its name. But even this approach would eventually have results similar to the long-standing non-*de jure* recognition of Israel. The final scenario of Greece doing absolutely nothing is dealt with in a brief sentence emphasising its ridiculous and absurd nature.

Tzounis ended his memorandum by arguing that given the existence of 'nationalistic frenzy' in Greece, FYROM's recognition by the US and the EC states would unleash anti-American and Anti-European feelings with unfortunate results.[90] Given the prospect of a serious diplomatic defeat, he concluded that the 'persistence in our present policy offers no exit and leads to an impasse [and to] total self-entrapment.'[91]

In the discussion that took place afterwards, there was no decision in accordance with the policy implications of the Tzounis memorandum. There was also disagreement on what punitive measures should possibly be applied against an uncooperative FYROM. Papandreou adopted a hard-line stance, arguing for the validity of Samaras' second proposal, but was met with the objections of Mitsotakis, Damanaki and Papariga. It was decided to discuss this issue in a subsequent meeting of the Council of the Political Leaders.[92]

During the meeting, Mitsotakis argued that in case the Greek stance on FYROM's name led to diplomatic failure, a proposal that FYROM be named 'Northern Macedonia' or 'Vardar Macedonia' be submitted and accepted, but there was no agreement on this point.[93] Furthermore, the meeting's substantive decision seriously undermined any such future approach. This was because Greece's

> Political leadership, with the exception of the KKE, decided that Greece will recognise an independent Skopje state only if the three conditions that the EC set on 16 December '91 are kept, with the *self-evident clarification that in the name of this state the word Macedonia will not exist*.[94]

The consequences of this decision were immense. Its phrasing marks the official and non-negotiable hardening of the Greek stance towards FYROM's name. We can perhaps even talk of its 'ossification,' since this position did not change in the subsequent years; and this despite EPC's pressure and incentives, the Prime Minister's desire to change it, and Greece's international reputation constantly reaching new lows.

A second consequence was the automatic rejection of the 'Pinheiro Package' that had advocated the name New Macedonia. Finally, the Second Council of the Political Leaders signalled the clear and public adoption of a hard-line stance by Andreas Papandreou. Afterwards, he even stressed to reporters that Samaras' 'positions correspondent...to ours, such a correspondence exists.'[95] By doing so, the Leader of the Opposition was essentially declaring that his relative silence and unusual self-restraint over the government's handling of the 'Skopje Issue' were coming to an end. He was now competing with Samaras on hard-line views, and cleverly positioning himself to reap popular dissatisfaction in case of a compromise or ignominious diplomatic defeat. The adoption of this position by Papandreou radically limited Mitsotakis' ability for diplomatic manoeuvres, since he was being forced to confront hostility and criticism by PASOK, as well as from within his party by Samaras and his allies.

After the meeting's conclusion, Mitsotakis announced that he was personally replacing Samaras, while Ioannis Tzounis was named second Deputy Minister for Foreign Affairs.[96] The Prime Minister implied that Samaras was being removed for posing unacceptable ultimatums to the government, and also admitted for the first time publicly the existence of more than one policy preferences within his administration.[97] In a sense, this 'double talk' ended by the adoption of Samaras' policy on the issue of FYROM's name. By accepting this view (which was in accordance with popular will but contrary to his own), Mitsotakis denied the young politician any pretext to overthrow the government.[98] Given the new popular policy, any such attempt would have been perceived as grounded on base personal motives.

Amazingly given his previous correspondence with the Prime Minister, Samaras was surprised by his dismissal.[99] Clearly disappointed, he was reduced to endorsing the decision of the Council, and vaguely warning that eventually 'a compromise will be baptised a victory.'[100] Mitsotakis' strategy had worked—for the time being. His government was secure, and he won a Parliamentary vote of no-confidence in the following days. The price however was the politics of limited Greek cooperation and eventually confrontation.

## E. The Beginning of Institutionalist Breakdown

The January-April 1992 period is characterised by the gradual decline of the politics of Greek cooperation, the rise of popular passions and the dominance in importance of the issue of FYROM's name. All other issues arising from the dissolution of Yugoslavia became of lesser and subordinate significance, or simply irrelevant. During this period, the value of institutionalism in explaining Greek foreign policy is reduced substantially. The reason is related to the immense rise in importance of domestic and partisan political developments and considerations.

Institutionalism can perhaps make a claim in at least explaining part of the policy contained in the 17 January 1992 letter that Samaras sent to his EPC counterparts. By adopting a restrictive position on FYROM's name, this letter signalled the beginning of the decline of the politics of Greek cooperation. At that point though, it did not represent a non-negotiable position.[101] According to Greece's Ministry of Foreign Affairs resident-expert on the Macedonian Question:

No one, but no one, had ever thought that it was possible for the name of this state [FYROM] not to include the word Macedonia or a derivative [of this name]. No one. I had not even heard such a thing from Samaras.[102]

In addition to the tough but negotiable position on FYROM's name, the letter also contained an offer to meet the republic's security needs and provide financial assistance. This seems to have been influenced by EPC's 'shadow of the future:' the Greek government desired to create a favourable reputation and impression within EPC since the regime would certainly be dealing again with disputes or issues related to Greece and FYROM.[103] It was judged that the offer of assistance would contribute towards the attainment of a reputation of a reasonable country willing to reach a compromise and end the dispute.

Institutionalist theory can also make a justified claim in explaining the Greek vote for the recognition of Bosnia at the 6 April 1992 EPC meeting, a decision that is almost universally condemned in Greece.[104] Characteristically, Mitsotakis argues that it had much worse consequences for the war in Yugoslavia than the decision to recognise Croatia.[105] In an interview, Samaras explained that his government's decision was not based on the principle of solidarity. Rather, the aim was to 'procrastinate in reaching [an EPC] decision on the name with which Skopje was to be recognised.'[106] This rationale is consistent with the institutionalist concept of reciprocity: the Greek government agreed on a decision that it considered as being seriously mistaken and premature, in order to achieve a postponement in discussing the name with which FYROM was to be recognised. This also provides a good illustration of how, as far as the country's foreign policy was concerned, the issue of FYROM's name had subordinated all other issues arising from the disintegration of Yugoslavia.

Despite Bosnia's recognition and some of the policy provisions contained in the 17 January 1992 letter, institutionalist theory proves entirely inadequate in explaining all other events and developments, since they are firmly rooted in domestic politics. The Thessaloniki demonstration and the boycott of Dutch, Danish and Italian products constitute important examples. Both are events whose undertaking and execution was completely unrelated to any EPC influence. They are crucial however, for understanding why the 17 January 1992 hard-line but negotiable position on FYROM's name became Greece's official and uncompromising position on 13 April 1992.

Domestic developments showed that there was tremendous and almost exclusive popular interest and sensitivity on the issue of FYROM's name. Furthermore, the demonstration of popular opinions and passions unequivocally and overwhelmingly supported the restrictive view on FYROM's name. Inevitably, the Greek government and political parties were forced to bestow particular importance on the position that the populace favoured overwhelmingly.

The defining significance of domestic and partisan considerations is also evident in the 13 April 1992 Council of the Political Leaders, which adopted the non-negotiable hard-line position on FYROM's name, and thus caused the automatic rejection of the 'Pinheiro Package.'

Mitsotakis who signed the 13 April decision even though he was in disagreement, offers three reasons that purport to explain and justify his action.[107] First of all, a restrictive interpretation of the third EPC condition was consistent with the will of the people. In democratic regimes, politicians ought to respect and take under serious consideration popular opinions. Secondly, failure to adopt this position would have caused his government's downfall. By sacking Samaras and agreeing with most of his positions, he got rid of what he considered a politically dangerous and over-ambitious Minister, while preserving New Democracy's hold on power.

The former Greek Prime Minister admits that leadership and convictions often require making politically unpopular decisions with negative consequences for someone's political career. However, he argues that there were not enough votes in Parliament to pass the 'Pinheiro Package' and thus honourably end the dispute with FYROM. Such an attempt would have also cost him the next general election. In an interview, he stressed:

> If [my government] fell then, there would be elections, and the elections would take place with the issue of Skopje open. And the Greek people would express themselves. How...? They would express themselves in favour of the extreme national position that the word Macedonia must not be in the name of this young republic. Result: not only would I not help the country, but I would...capture it in a policy, which would not then be able to change for many years.[108]

In other words, Mitsotakis argues that the third reason for agreeing on 13 April was that otherwise a general election would have been fought in an atmosphere of nationalism, and would have produced a PASOK government with views at least as hard-line as those of Samaras.

History will eventually evaluate the merit of Mitsotakis' apparently sincere yet tortured arguments. For the purposes of this study, it will suffice to stress that all of the reasons behind Mitsotakis' rationale to endorse the 13 April decision lie solely in the realm of domestic and partisan politics. There is not even a hint of regime influence or importance. Furthermore, there seems to be an almost universal acceptance among politicians and decision-makers of the fact that the 'Pinheiro Package' was rejected because of domestic political reasons.[109] Interestingly, when asked in an interview why his initiative failed, Pinheiro considered as responsible 'reactions inside Greece, which were represented with determination by Antonis Samaras.'[110]

Domestic and partisan considerations also influenced the decisions by Papandreou and Damanaki to sign the 13 April decision. PASOK's leader probably did not want to be superseded in nationalistic rhetoric by the young and popular Samaras. In addition, the restrictive position was extremely popular (at least at that point), within his party's ranks. As one of his closest and most trusted political associates remarked during an interview: 'within PASOK, there was virtually no disagreement.'[111] Finally, according to perhaps Papandreou's most important advisor on this issue, it was his 'instinct' that showed him the proper (and politically advantageous it should be added), way.[112]

Damanaki today is self-critical about her role in the 13 April Council, readily accepting that she miscalculated about the possibility that the Council's decision would have changed soon. Furthermore, she stresses that 'I also had to confront my intra-party problem.'[113] In the words of a leading Synaspismos member: 'Maria's [Damanaki] hands were tied. She could not resist.'[114] Both are referring to the fact that many party heavyweights favoured the restrictive position on FYROM's name, thus denying Ms Damanaki any room for flexibility.[115] Also, given the fact that many Synaspismos members (including Ms Damanaki), were previously affiliated with the KKE, it was important that their new party be differentiated from its communist rival, since a position coinciding with the one taken by Ms Papariga might have created confusion, and opened a debate about the role and exact ideology of Synaspismos.[116]

On the basis of the above analysis, it can be concluded that the institutionalist explanatory relevance largely breaks down during the January-April period. Institutionalism possibly manages to explain the decision to recognise Bosnia, and probably also explains some of the 17 January 1992 positions of the Greek government. On the other hand, institutionalist theory can not account for momentous and consequential events such as the Thessaloniki demonstration, or the spontaneous and popular boycott. Furthermore, it can not explain the 13 April non-negotiable adoption of the restrictive position on FYROM's name and thus the rejection of the 'Pinheiro Package.' Had Pinheiro's attempts proved successful, substantial evidence would have been produced of institutionalist importance and influence. However, it was rejected because of considerations based on domestic and partisan politics.

The neglect of such politics is the main reason for institutionalism's reduced explanatory power. This 'Achilles Heel' of institutionalism will prove central in the analysis of the politics of limited Greek cooperation and confrontation that will be presented in the next chapter.

## Notes

1   This was not the first time in modern Greek history that a Council of Political Leaders had been held. For example, a similar Council had taken place in 1951, with the aim to achieve agreement on a national strategy that was to be followed on Cyprus. In that instance, the Greek leaders exhibited a high and unusual degree of prudence, moderation and agreement. See Lagakos, 1996, p. 44-6.
2   The account of this meeting is based on interviews with Ms Damanaki on 30 January 1997, Mr Lengeris on 27 August 1997, Mr Mitsotakis on 10 April 1997, Mr Samaras on 24 December 1996 and 3 February 1997 and Mr Skilakakis on 15 April 1997. Of particular assistance were Papandreou's hand-written notes of the meeting, published in Papandreou, 1997, p. 516-30 and also the account given in Skilakakis, 1995, p. 93-6. It is allegedly based on an 'analytical presentation' (ibid., p. 93) that Mitsotakis made to Skilakakis and has largely been corroborated in interviews. On the importance of Skilakakis' account of the meetings of the Council of the Political Leaders, see footnote 85.
3   Further evidence on this point is provided by Papandreou's hand-written notes of the meeting. See Papandreou, 1997, p. 518.
4   Ioannou, 1992, p. 79. The 'others' referred to Greek-Turkish relations.
5   *Makedonia*, 19 February 1992, p. 1.
6   Ibid., p. 12.
7   See ibid.
8   Ibid., p. 1.
9   The speeches of Mitsotakis and Papandreou are reproduced in their entirety in *Makedonia*, 25 February 1992, p. 1, 8, 9 and 14. The newspaper's coverage also includes important sections from the speeches of Maria Damanaki and Mitsos Kostopoulos, the KKE's representative.
10  Ibid., p. 8.
11  Ibid., p. 9.
12  Based on interviews with Mr Kofos on 5 January 1997, Mr Mitsotakis on 10 April 1997, Mr Samaras on 23 December 1996, Mr Skilakakis on 15 April 1997 and Mr Tzounis on 14 April 1997.
13  Interview with Mr Mitsotakis on 10 April 1997.
14  *The New York Times*, 1 April 1992, p. A18. See also *The Economist*, 8 February 1992, p. 56.
15  For revealing documents that strongly suggest that this was the case, see Tarkas, 1995, p. 140-5.
16  See ibid., p. 120-3.
17  Ibid., p. 121.
18  Interview with Mr Samaras on 24 December 1996. Samaras also gave a football analogy to support his interpretation of Karamanlis' note. Although obscure to anyone not familiar with Greek football, I have decided to report it. More specifically, in emphasising

the importance of the period that the note was written, Samaras told me: 'It is like saying that Panathinaikos [a popular Athens football club] is not playing well. This does not suffice. One has to clarify whether this comment is being made when Zaets or Rotsa is [the club's] manager.'
19  See *Makedonia*, 27 February 1992, p. 12.
20  See *Makedonia*, 28 February 1992, p. 11. The boycott began to decline in effectiveness and intensity in early March 1992.
21  Cited in Ioannou, 1992, p. 79.
22  OJ No C 94/295, 13.4.92.
23  Skilakakis, 1995, p. 269.
24  Interview with Mr Samaras on 24 December 1996.
25  Ioannou, 1992, p. 80.
26  The relevant statements can be found in Tarkas, 1995, p. 126.
27  See Seitanidis, 1997, p. 255-63.
28  This was despite the fact that the government urged MPs to attend the Parliamentary session and thus ignore Samaras' speech. The speech took place in early April 1992. See Lygeros, 1992, p. 121 fn 69. Another indication of Samaras' popularity is that in June 1992, 62.7 per cent of all voters and 86.8 per cent of New Democracy voters held a favourable opinion towards him. In November 1992, the numbers were 68.4 per cent and 80.5 per cent respectively. See Loulis, 1995, p. 397.
29  Papandreou's PASOK had governed Greece during the 1981-89 period. Sensing a defeat in the polls, the ailing and scandal-ridden socialist leader changed the electoral law, making it considerably more difficult for a single party to achieve an absolute majority in Parliament. This was the case in the June 1989 election, which resulted in an unprecedented conservative-communist coalition government. New elections were called in November 1989, only to lead to the formation of a short-lived all-party government, under the octogenarian Xenophon Zolotas. Eventually, in the April 1990 elections Mitsotakis' New Democracy captured 150 seats. A defection from a small right wing party and an Elections Court decision raised the number of conservative MPs to 152.
30  The existence of this situation was explained in many interviews, including the ones with Mr Mitsotakis on 10 April 1997, Mr Papaconstantinou on 10 April 1997, Mr Samaras on 3 February 1997 and Mr Tzounis on 14 April 1997.
31  Popular passions had many outward manifestations. For example, it was reported that 'the Macedonian star, the emblem of the ancient empire, appears in stickers on shop windows and street-lamps. Men wear the star in their lapels, and women have them on brooches and earrings' (*The New York Times*, 17 April 1992, p. A9).
32  This was confirmed in an interview with Mr Samaras on 3 February 1997.
33  See Appendix V.
34  Ibid. Although Baker favoured FYROM's recognition, he was also aware of Greece's opposition to such a decision. See Baker, 1995, p. 640-2.
35  Also present during the meeting were Samaras, Mr Moliviatis who represented President Karamanlis, Mr Tzounis who was a diplomatic advisor to Mitsotakis, Mr Ailianos, Head of the Greek Foreign Ministry's Balkan Affairs Division, Mr Karagiannis, Greek Ambassador to Belgrade and Mr Tsilas, head of the Prime Minister's diplomatic office. The account of this meeting is based on interviews with Mr Mitsotakis on 10 April 1997, Mr Moliviatis on 9 January 1997, Mr Samaras on 3 February 1996, Mr Tzounis on 14 April 1997, as well as on the account given in Tarkas, 1995, p. 157-61.

36  These meetings and discussions are described in Tarkas, 1995, p. 162-71. Incredibly, transcripts of telephone conversations between Samaras and Moliviatis are included in these pages! However, they do not contain any information of great importance.
37  Baker, 1995, p. 642.
38  EPC Press Release P. 32/92, 10 March 1992.
39  Konstantinos Karamanlis served as Prime Minister of Greece longer than any other politician. He was Prime Minister during 1955-63 and 1974-80 and also President during 1980-85 and 1990-95. Perhaps the greatest achievement of his long and controversial career was ensuring his country's accession to the EC. He also managed the bloodless and exemplary transition to democracy in 1974, establishing for the first time a truly democratic and republican Greece. Many books have been written about Karamanlis. For what amounts to an account of his soul by an intimate friend and also President of the Hellenic Republic, see Tsatsos 1984. Karamanlis' political philosophy is analysed in Tzermias, 1990. Useful selections of the statesman's letters, speeches and documents can be found in Kartakis, n.d. and Lambrias 1995. For a collection of important (and favourable), essays analysing Karamanlis' statesmanship and personality, see Ahrweiller et al, 1995. See also the brief but extremely perceptive and balanced comments in Diamantopoulos, 1996, p. 52-6. Finally, Karamanlis' recently published magisterial twelve-volume 'Archives' (Svolopoulos, 1997—they are in a sense his memoirs), provide essential material on the statesman's thoughts and actions.
40  The text of the letter can be found in Tarkas, 1995, p. 177-81.
41  This provides indirect confirmation that Karamanlis' 26 February 1992 note was not supportive of a restrictive interpretation of the third EPC condition.
42  Ibid., p. 180. Samaras is correct only to the extent that he did not receive any written instructions approved by the President. It is misleading though, to imply that Karamanlis was completely silent on the issue of FYROM's name. The previously presented interpretation of his 26 February 1992 note to Samaras suggests that he had communicated his views.
43  Ibid., p. 181; emphasis added.
44  Ibid.
45  The letter can be found in Skilakakis, 1995, p. 264-85.
46  Ibid., p. 265.
47  Ibid., p. 275.
48  Ambassador Jose Cutileiro had been appointed by his country's Presidency as the Community Coordinator for the International Conference on Yugoslavia.
49  The main parts of the 'Pinheiro Package' can be found (in English), in Valinakis and Dales, 1994, p. 87-90.
50  Skilakakis, 1995, p. 282.
51  Valinakis and Dales, 1994, p. 88-9.
52  Skilakakis, 1995, p. 284.
53  Valinakis and Dales, 1994, p. 89.
54  Skilakakis, 1995, p. 284.
55  Ibid.
56  The letter is published in Tarkas, 1995, p. 240-2.
57  Ibid., p. 242.
58  The letter can be found in Tarkas, 1995, p. 242-6.
59  Ibid., p. 244
60  Ibid.
61  Ibid., p. 246.

62  On 30 March 1992, Mikis Theodorakis decided to abandon the ranks of New Democracy and sit in Parliament as an independent deputy, thus reducing the government's majority to one. The government's unpopularity had become manifest in a by-election that took place on 5 April 1992, in Greece's largest and bell-weather constituency of B Athens. New Democracy had decided not to contest the election, but on a heavy turnout of 68 per cent, PASOK received 66 per cent of the vote—almost a third more than it had received in the previous election. For further analysis, see Loulis, 1995, p. 350-4 and Lygeros, 1996, p. 213-5. For the most comprehensive and sophisticated analysis of the decline of the popularity of Mitsotakis' government, which begins in November 1991 and ends with the October 1993 electoral defeat, see Loulis, 1995, p. 318-73 and 393-475.
63  Mitsotakis' letter can be found in Tarkas, 1995, p. 249-52.
64  Ibid., p. 249.
65  Ibid., p. 251.
66  Karamanlis' letter can be found in Tarkas, 1995, p. 253-4.
67  They are published in Skilakakis, 1995, p. 288-90.
68  Ibid., p. 289.
69  Ibid., p. 290.
70  EPC Press Release P. 40/92, 6 April 1992.
71  This force was established by the 21 February 1992 UN Security Council Resolution 743 (see 31 *ILM*, p. 1447-9, 1992). Its full deployment began on 16 March. For an analysis, see Gow and Smith, 1992, p. 40-6.
72  For an illuminating map of Bosnia's ethnic distribution by district, see Woodward, 1995, p. 226-7. For Bosnia's history, see Malcolm, 1994. Two important books on the war in Bosnia are Rieff, 1995 and Vulliamy 1994.
73  The data is taken from Cohen, 1993, p. 237.
74  See *The New York Times*, 7 April 1992, p. A3.
75  Interview with Mr Samaras on 3 February 1997. The characterisation of the decision to recognise Bosnia by Samaras as 'premature' has been recorded in the minutes of the 6 April 1992 meeting. See Skilakakis, 1995, p. 289.
76  The text of Samaras 8 April 1992 letter to the President can be found in Tarkas, 1995, p. 258-60.
77  For the text of the letter, see ibid., p. 260-7.
78  Curiously, in an interview Samaras denied that this was the case. Although he admitted that the language was tough, he stressed that it was a private letter. 'I did not give [the letter] to anyone else at that time' he revealingly added in an interview on 3 February 1997.
79  Tarkas, 1995, p. 262.
80  See ibid., p. 262-6.
81  Ibid., p. 265.
82  Ibid., p. 264.
83  Tarkas, 1995, p. 268.
84  Ibid., p. 270.
85  The account of this meeting is based on interviews with Ms Damanaki on 30 January 1997, Mr Lengeris on 27 August 1997, Mr Mitsotakis on 10 April 1997, Mr Moliviatis on 9 January 1997, Mr Papathemelis on 11 January 1997, Mr Samaras on 24 December 1996 and 3 February 1997 and Mr Skilakakis on 15 April 1997. Also of great assistance was the account given in Skilakakis, 1995, p. 133-43, that was completely corroborated in interviews and is supposedly based on the notes that Mitsotakis took during the

meeting. The fact that Ms Damanaki and Ms Papariga (as Mr Lengeris explained) do not dispute a single word of these 'notes' is significant. As was hinted in the interviews with Mr Mitsotakis and Mr Skilakakis, and was made more explicit in the interview with Mr Lengeris, these notes are actually part of the meeting's official minutes. Because the participants agreed to keep the minutes unpublished, it was impossible for Skilakakis to claim that he was simply quoting from them. The rather ingenious solution was to claim that his account was based on notes that the then Prime Minister supposedly kept. It is noteworthy that in the recently published Karamanlis Archives the account of the 13 April 1992 meeting is almost exclusively comprised from an extensive quotation of Mitsotakis' 'notes' as they appear in Skilakakis' book. See Svolopoulos, 1997, p. 632-4, Vol. 12. Skilakakis also utilised Mitsotakis' notes for his account of the 14 June 1992 third meeting of the Council of the Political Leaders. Again, not a word has been disputed, and I strongly suspect that the 'notes' are again part of the official minutes. Even if this is not the case, on the basis of the interviews that were conducted for this thesis, it must be concluded that Mitsotakis is a gifted and exceptionally accurate keeper of notes. On the 13 April 1992 Second Council of the Political Leaders, see also Tarkas, 1995, p. 282-91. Crucially, extensive excerpts from Papandreou's handwritten notes from all three meetings of the Council of the Political Leaders have been published in his last wife's memoirs. See Papandreou, 1997, p. 516-39. These are normal, brief notes, and they must be contrasted with Mitsotakis', who in comparison comes across as a person with the skills of a stenographer. Furthermore, what can be deduced from the excerpts of Papandreou's hand-written notes, does not contradict in any way the account given in Skilakakis. As regards the document containing Samaras' proposals, it can be found in Valinakis and Dales, 1994, p. 91-2.

86   Ibid., p. 91.
87   Samaras made the claim that he had received permission from Mitsotakis during an interview on 3 February 1997.
88   Although the memorandum discusses a Community [i.e. an EPC] recognition of FYROM, this would have been impossible given Greece's veto power. Tzounis was actually referring to the possibility of all EPC states recognising FYROM as Macedonia unilaterally. Despite its top secret status, it was leaked to the press the following day. The journalists had a field-day asking questions to a hapless government spokesperson, who described the memorandum as a 'working document' containing 'scientific and not political appraisals' (see *Eleftherotypia*, 15 April 1992, p. 6). However, memoranda of such a nature are not labelled 'top secret' and distributed to leaders of political parties at an extremely crucial meeting. The memorandum can be found in *Eleftherotypia*, 14 April 1992, p. 16.
89   Ibid. According to the Hallstein Doctrine, West Germany refused to recognise diplomatically any state that had recognised East Germany, with the sole exception of the Soviet Union. See Hanrieder, 1989, p. 160.
90   *Eleftherotypia*, 14 April 1992, p. 16.
91   Ibid.
92   The commitment to hold such a meeting was made clear in their joint communique. See Valinakis and Dales, 1994, p. 93.
93   'Northern Macedonia' was Mitsotakis' proposal according to Skilakakis, 1995, p. 140. On the basis of Papandreou's hand-written notes, it was 'Vardar Macedonia.' See Papandreou, 1997, p. 539.
94   Valinakis and Dales, 1994, p. 93; emphasis added. After the meeting's conclusion, Papariga managed a rambling anti-US and anti-EU tirade. She rhetorically asked 'who

has enunciated the EC to the UN of the Balkans?' (*Makedonia*, 14 April 1992, p. 11); and insisted that 'true patriotism is to raise your voice against the EC's hegemonic forces, [and] against the United States' (ibid.). The KKE's stance in this meeting is explained by a number of reasons. The party's past actions and positions on the Macedonian Question, as well as the desire to satisfy party activists in Western Greek Macedonia and be perceived as a progressive party, were certainly important in determining its stance. See Karakasidou, 1993b. The KKE has consistently argued that focusing on FYROM's name was a mistake. Apparently, it seems that the party concluded that after 16 December 1991, a restrictive position on the name issue would ultimately be unattainable. According to Papandreou's hand-written notes of the 13 April meeting, Papariga had claimed that 'the issue was closed' (Papandreou, 1997, p. 538). Subsequently, as far as the KKE was concerned, Greece should have concentrated on issues of propaganda practised by FYROM. This analysis of the KKE's stance (partly explained during an interview with Mr Lengeris on 27 August 1997) is mostly devoid of ideological constraints and is primarily based on a *Realpolitik* evaluation of developments. Surprisingly, it is very close to the positions taken by the US and other EPC member states. It is also noteworthy that the KKE's consistent adherence to its original analysis and positions was praised in interviews with (among others), Mr Mitsotakis on 10 April 1997, Mr Papaconstantinou on 23 December 1996, Mr Samaras on 24 December 1996, Mr Tzounis on 14 Aril 1997 and Mr Vrahatis on 30 August 1997. Although most said that the KKE had the correct position for the wrong reasons, a feeling of envy was palpable. This is because the KKE was able to stick to its position, ignore considerations of political cost, and not face any significant internal dissension. As a result, the KKE is the only Greek party (albeit a rather small one), that can claim a consistent and uniform position on Greece's dispute with FYROM.

95   *Makedonia*, 14 April 1992, p. 10. Papandreou did remain critical of Samaras' handling of a series of decisions, such as the 16 December 1991 EPC conditions and the failure to achieve Greek representation on the AC.
96   During their meeting, Mitsotakis had informed the other leaders of the political parties of his intention to dismiss Samaras. He did not reveal that he was going to replace him personally. Tzounis remained on his post until 7 August 1992. The other Deputy Foreign Minister was Mr Papastamkos, who was responsible for issues concerning the Hellenic Diaspora.
97   For Mitsotakis' comments, see *Makedonia*, 14 April 1992, p. 1, 10.
98   Mitsotakis acknowledged the fact that the Greek people supported the decision of the Second Council of the Political Leaders on FYROM's name, during a Parliamentary debate on 27 March 1993. See Kyrkos, 1994, p. 11-2 fn 1.
99   When asked in an interview on 24 December 1996 if he expected his dismissal, Samaras simply and revealingly replied to me: 'Of course not.'
100  Cited in Tarkas, 1995, p. 289.
101  Confirmed in interviews with (among others), Mr Kofos on 5 January 1997, Mr Mitsotakis on 10 April 1997 and Mr Samaras on 24 December 1996.
102  Interview with Mr Kofos on 5 January 1997. He is referring to the period prior to 17 January 1992.
103  Interview with Mr Samaras on 3 February 1997.
104  No person whom I have interviewed has expressed a positive opinion of this decision.
105  Interview with Mr Mitsotakis on 10 April 1997.
106  Interview with Mr Samaras on 3 February 1997. Samaras actually used the word procrastinate in English.

107 Interview with Mr Mitsotakis on 10 April 1997.
108 *Oikonomikos Tachydromos*, 5 October 1995, p. 5. Mitsotakis made the same argument in a letter that he sent to the same magazine on 22 February 1994, and can be found in Valinakis and Dales, 1994, p. 201-2. The former Greek Prime Minister reiterated the same argument during an interview on 10 April 1997.
109 Interviews with Ms Damanaki on 30 January 1997, Mr Mertzos on 18 December 1996, Mr Mitsotakis on 10 April 1997, Mr Papaconstantinou on 23 December 1996, Mr Papayannakis on 10 January 1997, Mr Papathemelis 11 January 1997 and Mr Skilakakis on 15 April 1997.
110 *Eleftherotypia*, 5 July 1993, p. 7.
111 Interview with Mr Tsohatzopoulos on 3 August 1997. The same point was made during an interview with Mr Papathemelis on 11 January 1997.
112 Interview with Mr Papathemelis on 11 January 1997.
113 Interview with Ms Damanaki on 30 January 1997. Ms Damanaki much later managed to change her party's position, by publicly declaring that achieving two and a half out of the three EPC conditions would suffice (see Kyrkos, 1994, p. 60 fn 11). What she had in mind, was a name for FYROM that also included the word Macedonia. As Damanaki explained to me in an interview, she passionately believes that this position cost Synaspismos its parliamentary representation in the October 1993 elections. Damanaki subsequently resigned her position as Party President.
114 Interview with Mr Papayannakis on 10 January 1997.
115 Such a position was certainly favoured by Mr Lentakis (who later joined Mr Samaras' party), and Mr Androulakis. Ms Damanaki in an interview on 30 January 1997 and Mr Papayannakis in an interview on 10 January 1997, suggested that the restrictive position on FYROM's name was also supported by Synaspismos' subsequent President, Mr Konstantopoulos. In support of this argument, see *Ta Nea*, 25 November 1997, p. 7. In an interview on 30 August 1997, Konstantopoulos' Chief of Staff Mr Vrahatis, argued that no *public* speech (his emphasis), statement or article exists, in which Mr Konstantopoulos made a hard-line argument. Although it is impossible to determine with absolute certainty what was said in closed Synaspismos meetings during the period covered in this thesis, it is most likely that Mr Konstantopoulos had originally adopted, or at least not rejected the restrictive position. His later opposition strategy towards Ms Damanaki also included the issue of what party body was responsible for taking decisions on foreign policy issues. More specifically, Konstantopoulos argued that the party's Parliamentary group should not be responsible for taking decisions on foreign policy issues. At any rate, the result was that Ms Damanaki undoubtedly faced constraints in formulating the party's positions because of inter-party opposition.
116 This argument was suggested in interviews with Mr Papayannakis on 10 January 1997 and Mr Vrahatis on 30 August 1997.

# 7 The Politics of Limited Greek Cooperation and Confrontation, April-December 1992

Statesmen are not called upon only to settle easy questions. These often settle themselves. It is where the balance quivers, and the proportions are veiled in mist that the opportunity for world-saving decisions presents itself.

-Sir Winston S. Churchill, *The Gathering Storm*, 1948.

### A. Limited Greek Cooperation: The Road to Lisbon

The months following the sacking of Samaras were consequential for Greece's EPC foreign policy towards former Yugoslavia. As will be analysed in this chapter, a series of major EPC decisions in Guimaraes, Lisbon and Edinburgh as well as the O'Neil initiative, influenced developments and also proved the crucial significance of EPC's intergovernmentalism. At the same time, the Greek government pursued politics of limited cooperation within EPC and confrontation against FYROM, that were ultimately the result of domestic and partisan politics.

In late April, wishing to exploit his enhanced status as the only EPC Foreign Minister who was also a Prime Minister, Mitsotakis had meetings with the Foreign Ministers of Germany, Italy, Portugal and the UK. They produced results that were rather favourable for Greece. In deference to Greek concerns, de Michelis noted that 'there is no reason to be in a hurry.'[1] Genscher (who was Mitsotakis' personal friend), stressed that 'when countries have vital interests...they can count...every time on our support.'[2] Portugal's Prime Minister and Foreign Minister exhibited an important degree of understanding for Greek concerns.[3] After their meeting, Mitsotakis insisted that Greece was primarily interested in finding a solution to the dispute with FYROM, and also confirmed the paramount importance bestowed upon FYROM's name: 'the issue of the name we separate, in an absolute way' he declared.[4] Finally, Douglas Hurd insisted that 'it was certain that we do not wish to create difficulties for Greece on this issue.'[5] According to the former Greek Prime Minister, this outpouring of support by EPC's Foreign Ministers represents an illustration of EPC's principle of solidarity.[6]

With these meetings, Mitsotakis prepared the ground for the informal gathering of EPC's Foreign Ministers in Guimaraes on 1 and 2 May 1992.[7] It produced the first EPC declaration devoted solely to Greece's dispute with FYROM, and also provides another example of important EPC decisions being made in intergovernmental bodies.[8] During the meeting, it was originally suggested by Genscher that FYROM be recognised under the name Republic of Skopje. As the meeting proceeded, Mitsotakis felt anxious, hoping that there would be no alteration of this suggestion. Unfortunately, the French and Italian Ministers revisited the issue, raising certain important objections that did not centre on the specifically proposed name. They argued that it was inappropriate and unacceptable for EPC's Ministers to choose a name and 'baptise' FYROM, without having first consulted with the republic.

Eventually, the EPC member states decided that they

Are willing to recognise that State [FYROM] as a sovereign and independent State, within its existing borders, and *under a name that can be accepted by all parties concerned.*[9]

This constituted a new EPC position, since for the first time it was clearly stipulated that any solution to the name dispute would be conditional upon FYROM's acceptance.

An additional indication of EPC's growing frustration and disappointment with Greece was related to the declaration's praising of the 'Pinheiro Package.' Greece and FYROM were urged to 'do their utmost to resolve the pending questions on [its] basis.'[10] Given his favourable opinion of the package, Mitsotakis could endorse such language, though he was unable and unwilling to alter the decision of the second Council of the Political Leaders and thus 'rescue' Pinheiro's initiative.

After the conclusion of the Guimaraes meeting, it became absolutely clear to Mitsotakis that Greece's reputation and credibility with its European partners had reached a very low point.[11] He thus decided to pursue actions that would allow Greece to be portrayed as a cooperative partner, believing that this would help his country achieve the best possible result in the dispute with FYROM.[12] In other words, he aimed at reproducing the politics of cooperation and moderation that were successfully practised during the period between June 1991 and January 1992. Such politics now had to take into account the limits imposed by the combination of a slim Parliamentary majority, a hostile Samaras and Papandreou, and the 13 April 1992 decision. As a result, the scope for cooperation was severely restricted.

On 9 May 1992, Mitsotakis sent a letter to Gligorov.[13] Using language that was similar to the 17 January 1992 letter, it offered security guarantees and financial assistance.[14] A previously unpublished document reveals the scope and extent of projects and actions that Greece wanted to pursue in a joint and mutually beneficial way with FYROM.[15] They included the pursuit of schemes in the Vardar-Axios valley, 'substantial financial assistance,' and even support for the signing at a later date of an association agreement between FYROM and the Community.[16] Mitsotakis' offer though, demanded that FYROM accept a name that would be consistent with the restrictive Council of the Political Leaders interpretation of the third EPC condition. Not surprisingly, it was turned down by Gligorov.

Greece's dispute with FYROM was discussed at the 11 May General Council meeting in Brussels.[17] Despite the Guimaraes decision, the Danish and Dutch Foreign Ministers suggested that FYROM ought to be recognised in accordance with the recommendations of the AC. As was undoubtedly expected, the Greek Prime Minister objected and the issue remained unresolved.

On 15 May, Mitsotakis sent a telegram to the Greek Embassies in all EC member states, as well as to various other countries. This previously unpublished telegram provided arguments and guidelines that were to be utilised in discussions concerning FYROM.[18] It is important for two reasons. First, it provides further evidence that the Greek position on FYROM's name was non-negotiable: 'It is not a simple negotiable position of the Greek government, but a demand of all the Greek people.'[19]

Secondly, the telegram includes an interesting comment by Mitsotakis on the Guimaraes decision, in which he states that

> The postponement of reaching a decision does not constitute a solution. The only solution is the recognition [of FYROM] that Greece desires as much as [our EPC] counterparts. The necessary prerequisite for this to take place is, as was decided in GUIMARAES, that Greece agrees on the name of this new republic.[20]

This appears to be a somewhat incredible statement, which seems to fail to grasp the significance of what had taken place in Guimaraes. Greece was always in a position to veto any EPC decision, especially one linked to an issue that was considered of extreme importance to the country's population and decision-makers. It was FYROM, a non-recognised and non-EPC member state that lacked this capability; and it was precisely this capability that was given to FYROM (as regards its name), in Guimaraes.

Despite the awkward and misleading phrasing of the telegram, the Greek Prime Minister had actually achieved a victory of sorts. The Guimaraes decision obliged FYROM to seek a name within the EPC framework, where Greece had veto power. Hence, the young republic could not simply reject an EPC proposed name and then seek UN recognition under the name Republic of Macedonia.[21]

After Guimaraes and the subsequent developments, Mitsotakis decided that Greece should participate in the intensification of EPC sanctions against Serbia and Montenegro. During the preceding months, the Bosnian Serbs had embarked on an offensive aimed at conquering 65 per cent of Bosnia.[22] This campaign involved some of the worse atrocities perpetrated in Europe since the Holocaust.[23] Most notable was the practice of 'ethnic cleansing': an orchestrated and murderous effort to drive the Muslim and Croat population out of certain areas. Confronted with these events, Mitsotakis agreed with his EPC partners that

> By far the greatest share of the blame falls on the JNA and the authorities in Belgrade which are in control of the army, both directly and indirectly by supporting Serbian irregulars.[24]

Serbia was also seen as the main culprit by the UN Security Council, which on 30 May 1992 passed Resolution 757, aiming at imposing a severe trade embargo on Serbia and Montenegro.[25] The most important of the measures that were decided included the prohibition of the importing and exporting of all products with these republics. An 'air' embargo was also imposed, prohibiting aircraft from flying to, or originating flights from these territories. Exceptions to this strict embargo were made only for humanitarian flights, as well as for foodstuffs and products related to medical purposes.

On the next day, EPC's member states announced their willingness to enforce these measures.[26] The UN Security Council was additionally requested to adopt 'an embargo on oil and petroleum products...and to freeze assets, financial transactions and payments' with Serbia and Montenegro.[27] Mitsotakis agreed to all these measures, despite the Greco-Serbian special relationship that was analysed previously.

Another Greek cooperative decision of this period benefited Turkey. For over two years, the Greek government had vetoed

The adoption of the so-called 'redirected' or renovated Mediterranean policy...because it wanted to ensure that Turkey would not benefit from the latter's 'horizontal aspect' envisaging financial assistance to all the Mediterranean countries linked by association or cooperation agreements with the EC.[28]

This veto was lifted in late June 1992, and Turkey was made eligible for receiving some 300 million ECUs over five years, that were to be used primarily for environmental projects. Nevertheless, even this limited cooperative gesture was criticised harshly by PASOK. A party spokesperson declared that Greece appeared as a 'totally unreliable [country]...susceptible to all kinds of pressures on all our unresolved [national] issues.'[29]

Prior to the Lisbon European Council meeting, Mitsotakis made one more important proposal that he considered as being somewhat cooperative and capable of providing a reasonable solution to the dispute. It involved a dual name for FYROM: the republic would receive an official UN name that would not include the word Macedonia, while for internal purposes Greece would allow and tolerate FYROM to use any name of its choice. The expectation was that the name chosen would be the Republic of Macedonia. However, the most significant part of the dual name proposal (FYROM's official UN name) was consistent with the hard-line decision of 13 April 1992. This undermined considerably the proposal's alleged cooperative intention and character.

On 14 June, Mitsotakis informed the participants of the third Council of the Political Leaders about his intention to pursue a solution on the basis of the dual name formula.[30] The meeting lacked the drama and consequences of the previous one, no decision to alter the restrictive stance on FYROM's name was taken, and the dual name formula was not adopted.[31] Only Ms Damanaki spoke in support of it.[32] The new element in the leader's communique was the declaration of their 'steady decision...[that] Greece avoid any military entanglement in the Balkans.'[33]

Mitsotakis first informed EPC's Foreign Ministers of his intention to propose a dual name formula during the 15 June General Council meeting, by suggesting that FYROM's UN name should be Vardar Republic.[34] The republic would then be allowed to select for domestic purposes any name that it desired. The French Foreign Minister subsequently mentioned this proposal publicly, and thus the Greek press took notice and attempted to get an answer from the Foreign Ministry's spokesperson Mr Avramopoulos, who indirectly confirmed the proposal's existence.[35] Andreas Papandreou reacted with a public and harsh condemnation, emphasising that 'the ridiculous is now added to the handlings of the government...we will lose any trace of authority in the international community with proposals of this kind.'³⁶

Mitsotakis reiterated the dual name proposal in a letter that he sent to his EPC counterparts on 23 June 1992, whose tone was utterly alarmist.³⁷ The Greek Prime Minister stressed several times the danger of the war spreading to the North of Yugoslavia unless the dispute with FYROM was solved 'before it is too late.'³⁸ He even noted that Gligorov had recently admitted the existence of extreme nationalist groups in his country that were beyond his government's control. Mitsotakis warned that if these groups undertake 'action...I simply tell you that no one will be in a position to control the reaction of the Greek people.'³⁹ He had in mind reports that FYROM's nationalist party (VMRO-DPNE) had held meetings to discuss terrorist bombing attacks in Thessaloniki.⁴⁰

Mitsotakis also indicated some willingness to compromise, by admitting that a decision at the upcoming Lisbon European Council meeting did not have to 'satisfy [the Parties involved] totally.'⁴¹ Most importantly, he suggested that

1. The Community can simply state that it is ready to recognise Skopje under any name that this Republic chooses, with the condition that it will not include [the name] Macedonia. [or]
2. We can tell to Skopje that we will recognise them with any name that they choose, which will not include [the name] Macedonia, but they will have the freedom to call themselves any name that they desire.⁴²

The latter option amounted to an official proposal of the dual name formula. The Prime Minister stated that given a speedy decision, he would be able to persuade the Greek people of the virtues of such a compromise. By doing so, he essentially implied that there was not sufficient public support for a solution among these lines.

On the eve of the Lisbon European Council, Papandreou raised the tone of his criticisms to the level of demagoguery. He flew to Thessaloniki and announced that the government was 'selling off parts of our country...The people do not stand any more this sell-out and submissive policy.'⁴³ He also demanded the immediate holding of national elections. A serious defeat in Lisbon would have undoubtedly strengthened the impact of such demands and rhetoric.

Somewhat more encouraging to Mitsotakis was an EP resolution on the issue of FYROM's name. The resolution, which provides evidence of the actions of the non-intergovernmental bodies that 'dilute' the intergovernmentalism of the regime EPC, declared:

> As for the name by which [FYROM] may be recognized internationally, [the EP] believes that the conditions set by Greece are aimed at safeguarding peace, cooperation and stability throughout the region, and are therefore of crucial importance for the European Community.[44]

However, this resolution did not refer to the dual name formula.[45] The intergovernmental European Council that took place in Lisbon on 26 and 27 June 1992, produced an important declaration on Greece's dispute with FYROM:

> The European Council reiterates the position taken by the Community and its Member States in Guimaraes on the request of the former Yugoslav Republic of Macedonia to be recognized as an independent State. It expresses its readiness to recognise the republic within its existing borders according to their Declaration on 16 December 1991 *under a name which does not include the term Macedonia*. It furthermore considers the borders of this republic as inviolable and guaranteed in accordance with the principles of the UN Charter and the Charter of Paris.[46]

This declaration was interpreted by Mitsotakis as a great national triumph, who explained that it was the 'final and definitive' EPC decision on the dispute. Having achieved the 'main reason for which I became Foreign Minister,' he announced his intention to resign the post.[47] Despite the fact that the Lisbon Declaration made no reference to the dual name formula, Mitsotakis seized the opportunity to reiterate publicly this proposal. He depicted the decision as the fulfilment of the first (and most important to Greece), part of the dual name solution. The Prime Minister then explained that the people of FYROM can 'domestically use...any name that they want,' and pledged that 'we will help them financially so that they will survive.'[48]

Samaras said that he was 'full of joy' for this decision. Such sentiments were not shared in FYROM, where the republic's Foreign Minister Dr Denko Maleski resigned.[49] The same fate awaited the Prime Minister Nicola Kljusev and his Cabinet, who resigned on 7 July 1992. The only person who seemed sceptical of the Lisbon decision was Andreas Papandreou.[50] Responding to the jubilant statements made by Mitsotakis, he suggested caution, and reminded journalists of the celebrations following the 16 December 1991 EPC conditions and Greece's WEU accession that had proved painfully unjustified.

Papandreou's scepticism was vindicated. Celebrations in Athens and despair in Skopje proved premature.

The Lisbon Declaration was perceived as a victory in Athens because it seemed to be endorsing the Greek restrictive and non-cooperative stance on FYROM's name. However, one of its key parts stating that the European Council...reiterates the position taken...in Guimaraes' was not properly analysed.[51] This reference amounted to an EPC signal that the Lisbon and Guimaraes declarations were to be read in conjunction. As previously argued, according to the Guimaraes declaration any resolution of the conflict would have required the agreement of both FYROM and Greece. In other words, although the decision in Lisbon was that the word Macedonia should not be part of FYROM's name, this provision also had to be accepted by FYROM.

On 3 July 1992, FYROM's Assembly rejected the part of the Lisbon Declaration that referred to the republic's name.[52] Nevertheless, based on interviews, the claim has been forcefully made that at that point, Gligorov was sending to Athens strong signals that he was ready to compromise on a name such as New Macedonia or perhaps even Slavomacedonia.[53] This has also been fully confirmed by the then Prime Minister Mitsotakis.[54] At any rate, the Greek government rejected these overtures since they were not consistent with the 13 April decision. The politics of Greek confrontation were to follow.

## B. Greek Confrontation

On 30 July 1992, President Gligorov sent a letter to the UN's General Secretary, requesting that the organisation recognise his country;[55] and on 11 August, FYROM's Parliament passed a law endorsing a new national flag. Its design depicted the 'Star of Vergina,' which was found in Philip the Second's tomb and is considered to have been the emblem of the Macedonian dynasty.[56] Crucially, no Slavs lived in the region during the reign of Alexander the Great's father. In Gligorov's words: 'We do not have any relation to Alexander the Great. We are a Slavic people who arrived here [in Macedonia] in the sixth century.'[57] Given this fact, FYROM's adoption of a new flag was perceived by the incensed Greeks as a serious provocation.[58]

The response of the Greek government was harsh. It condemned the action as a 'shameless, provocative, and unacceptable usurpation of a Greek historical symbol;'[59] and most importantly on 21 August Mitsotakis announced that 'Greece temporarily suspends the passage of oil products towards the North.'[60] This decision was supposed to end international criticism that Greece had been violating the UN embargo and permitting oil shipments into Serbia.

In reality, it amounted to the imposition of an oil embargo against the new republic. Mitsotakis has explained that international criticism simply provided an adequate pretext for Greece to implement punitive economic measures against FYROM.[61]

The effects of the embargo were mitigated by oil shipments entering FYROM via Bulgaria.[62] Nevertheless, the Greek government's attitude had become confrontational, a fact that is well illustrated by the 'story of the labels.'[63] It originated in a series of proposals made by the Commission, in order to increase the effectiveness of the Community embargo against Serbia.[64] Based on these proposals, the Council of Ministers decided that

> The export to the Republic[s] of Bosnia...Croatia as well as the *territory* of the former Yugoslav Republic of Macedonia of all commodities and products originating in or coming from the Community shall be subject to the presentation of a prior authorization for export...to be issued by the competent authorities of the Member States.[65]

It is noteworthy that after intense Greek pressure, FYROM is merely described as a territory. Furthermore, the Greek government later ensured the explicit Community clarification that the name that was supposed to be used in all such authorisations was that of FYROM.[66]

The practical consequences of this policy would have been extreme for FYROM, since the republic's authorities label products with the words Republic of Macedonia. As a result, strict adherence to the Community policy would have caused the end of all Community trade with the republic! Mitsotakis realised that insisting on this policy would have been both problematic and counterproductive. Thus, he did not object to the other Member States *de facto* ignoring these provisions.[67] Nevertheless, the political capital that Greece spent on a technical issue in order to succeed to characterise the republic as a territory, and cause the maximum possible problems in its trade, is indicative of Greek policy and feelings during this period.

Meanwhile, as war was raging in Bosnia, the UK (which had assumed the Community Presidency on 1 July), and the UN, organised the London Conference on 26 and 27 August 1992. More than thirty countries were represented, in what was another example of the conference diplomacy decision-making procedure of the regime EPC.[68] The dispute between FYROM and Greece was not central to the proceedings, and was not mentioned in any of the speeches by the representatives of the US or of the EPC member states.[69] The same applied to the Russian Foreign Minister, despite his country's recent recognition of the republic.[70]

Greece was represented at the London Conference by the new Foreign Minister Michalis Papaconstantinou.[71] He was fluent in several languages, author of numerous books (several of which on Macedonian history and politics), and unusually well educated for a Greek politician. In his intervention, Papaconstantinou reaffirmed his country's cooperation and support for the UN sponsored arms and trade embargoes.[72] In tune with mainstream Western opinion, he condemned the use of violence and emphasised the importance of protecting minorities, delivering humanitarian aid, and ensuring that the conflict be at least contained. He also stressed that if FYROM complied with the Lisbon Declaration, 'Greece will be ready to extend its full cooperation and friendship to the new Republic.'[73] The tone of the intervention was pragmatic and devoid of any references to the glorious but ancient Greek history in the region. It was thus characteristic of Papaconstantinou's approach to the dispute, though it was not inconsistent with the Greek hard-line policy on FYROM's name.

Kiro Gligorov who also participated in the Conference, made a passionate plea for recognition.[74] He noted that FYROM was a democratic society respecting human and ethnic rights, and also emphasised that

> We have acquired our independence and sovereignty and we control our own frontiers, we have preserved peace and internal stability within the Republic. This situation has prevented the escalation of war...For the peace and democracy for which the Republic of Macedonia had received high marks by the whole international community, it has also gained silently an unseen punishment, p. it remained the last to await recognition.[75]

Gligorov used this opportunity to reject once again the Lisbon Declaration, arguing that any change of name was 'insulting' and would amount to his country 'defacing itself.'[76]

The London Conference was significant to the extent that it signalled the UN's taking over the leading role from EPC as regards developments in Bosnia. However, EPC would remain primarily responsible for dealing with the dispute between FYROM and Greece until December 1992. The Greek government supported the Conference's conclusions which made no reference to FYROM.[77] Thus, Greece once again participated in a harsh verbal condemnation of Serbia: 'If...Serbia and Montenegro...do not comply [with the Conference's decisions] the Security Council will be invited to apply sanctions leading to their total international isolation.'[78]

On 12 September, EPC's Foreign Ministers met at Brocket Hall in England. After a suggestion by the British Presidency, it was decided to enlist the services of the retired British diplomat Robin O'Neil, who was to undertake an initiative aiming to solve the dispute between Greece and FYROM.[79] This initiative also represents the capability of the intergovernmental Presidency to provide new decision-making procedures and to a degree set the agenda. At any rate, it must be stressed that according to O'Neil, his mission was 'unusual, difficult and impertinent.'[80]

At the same time, pressure to end the Greek oil embargo against FYROM was mounting.[81] A thinly veiled criticism was even included in the 16 October 1992 declaration of the European Council meeting in Birmingham:

> In the light of the deteriorating economic situation in the former Yugoslav republic of Macedonia, the European Council stressed the need for appropriate measures to prevent this republic from bearing the unintended consequences of UN sanctions.[82]

While O'Neil was making a series of trips to both Greece and FYROM, there was renewed talk in Athens about ending the dispute on the basis of the dual name formula.[83] Samaras objected strenuously to such a compromise and declared it a 'dual theft.'[84] Faced with this opposition, Mitsotakis called on 21 October 1992 a meeting of New Democracy's MPs aiming to receive their backing for his preferred foreign policy positions.

The meeting was dramatic, lasted for seven hours and is of particular importance because it influenced subsequent foreign policy developments.[85] It also marked the beginning of the process that eventually led to the creation of a political party by Samaras (Politiki Anixi), as well as to the downfall of the Mitsotakis government.[86]

In his speech, the Prime Minister somewhat mildly criticised Samaras for his handling of the 16 December 1991 EPC conditions, and supported the dual name formula by arguing that the republic's official UN name was what really mattered.[87] An exasperated Mitsotakis stressed that to deny FYROM's citizens the right to call themselves for domestic purposes what they wish would confirm 'what they write about us [unjustly,] that we are a paranoid country.'[88]

Mitsotakis threatened MPs that a rejection of his proposal would force him to call an early national poll. Given the government's unpopularity, this was a serious threat.[89] He concluded by suggesting that MPs opposing the dual name formula for reasons of conscience should resign their seats, in order not to jeopardise New Democracy's Parliamentary majority.

In his previously unpublished speech, Papaconstantinou stressed that the issue of FYROM's recognition had to be resolved as soon as possible.[90] He revealed that Greece had faced considerable hostility from the Danish Foreign Minister in Birmingham, and clarified that there were no indications concerning the prospects of O'Neil's initiative.

Papaconstantinou argued that the pressure that Greece exhorted on FYROM was of particular importance. Political and financial circles within the young republic had begun to request the normalisation of relations between the two states. Furthermore, FYROM had failed to secure membership in any international organisation and had committed an almost universally condemned error by adopting the Star of Vergina on its flag. At the end of his speech, the Greek Foreign Minister warned that he was 'afraid that unless we achieve a solution of this issue [at the upcoming European Council meeting] at Edinburgh, we will then have to confront our own isolation.'[91]

Samaras' speech (extensive excerpts of which are published here for the first time), was less structured but far more dramatic and consequential.[92] He proposed that the dual name formula be rejected because its acceptance would imply that FYROM's arguments concerning the use of the name Macedonia were at least partly justified.[93]

There was also a clarification of his intentions in case the proposal failed:

> I consider that its rejection will have, for me at least, direct political consequences. In matters of conscience, there is no room for majority. If the Parliamentary group has not been persuaded by what I have said, if I am [in the] minority, I hold my basic obligation, human, ethical, political...to resign from the office of Member of Parliament...[94]

Samaras' proposal received only four votes, the overwhelming majority of MPs expressing their support for 'the decision of Lisbon according to which the recognition of [FYROM] is only accepted with one name not carrying...the name Macedonia *for all its foreign relations* [sic].'[95]

Despite the fact that the Lisbon Declaration made no such distinction, this was a victory for Mitsotakis, especially since Samaras resigned later that afternoon his seat as an MP. However, it was only a pyrrhic victory for the Greek Prime Minister, given that the three MPs who had joined Samaras in rejecting the dual name formula sufficed to bring down the government.[96] This was a crucial fact that had to be taken into consideration by Mitsotakis, before any compromise was reached on the basis of the dual name formula.

On 3 November 1992, Papaconstantinou sent a letter to his EPC counterparts (published here for the first time), clarifying Greece's positions.[97] Referring to Ambassador's O'Neil initiative, Papaconstantinou noted that 'to this day, no apparent progress has been registered.'[98] This amounted to almost an understatement, after the disastrous meeting that had taken place between Papaconstantinou and O'Neil on 12 October 1992.[99] O'Neil claims that he warned the Greek government that the oil embargo was actually hurting their aims, and that by insisting on a hard-line policy on FYROM's name, they risked the state being eventually recognised as Macedonia.[100]

On the other hand, the Greeks had concluded that O'Neil lacked objectivity and discussed arbitrarily only a one name solution, abandoning entirely the dual name formula.[101] The retired British Ambassador also seemed to ignore the various aspects of the 'Pinheiro Package.'[102]

An alarmed Papaconstantinou attempted to rectify these negative developments with the 3 November letter, in which FYROM is accused for adopting the Star of Vergina flag, as well as for 'attributing to [Greece] aggressive intentions and territorial claims.'[103] The Greek Foreign Minister suggested that FYROM might have been under the impression that the Lisbon Declaration could be reversed in Edinburgh, and recommended that 'we should take care that no mixed signal reach Skopje.'[104] He then made the following recommendation:

> The Portuguese Presidency prepared a "package deal" which, in addition to the name problem, could resolve all the outstanding issues connected with recognition. This package should be part of the discussions currently being carried out by Ambassador O'Neil.[105]

Papaconstantinou was not suggesting a compromise on the basis of the name New Macedonia, which would have been contrary to the 13 April Council of the Political Leaders decision. The pragmatic politician was actually making an important and commendable (if futile), effort to depart from the absolute focus on the name issue, to which even O'Neil seemed to have succumbed. He was thus attempting to ensure that the issues of FYROM conducting hostile propaganda and making territorial claims against Greece return on the agenda.

Greece's Foreign Minister made certain cooperative gestures towards FYROM, by implying in somewhat unclear terms his government's support for a dual name formula, and by reiterating Greece's willingness to guarantee FYROM's security. He clarified that given the satisfaction of certain technical conditions, oil shipments towards the new republic would resume. Humanitarian shipments of oil would also be available upon FYROM's request.[106] Ominously though, Papaconstantinou warned that 'we have reached the "end of the rope."'[107]

Meanwhile, Ambassador O'Neil was still in search of a compromise. In late November, he stated that 'I believe we are as close to a solution as you can be. It is for the government of Skopje to take the decision.'[108] This was an entirely misleading statement, perhaps though fitting for what was becoming an exercise in futility. As regards the Greek government, the most crucial meeting between O'Neil and Papaconstantinou had taken place on 22 November. The British retired diplomat announced that FYROM was willing to accept the name Macedonia-Skopje. Papaconstantinou claims to have explained that the Greek government would not be in a position to accept such a name.[109]

O'Neil delivered his report on 3 December 1992.[110] The fact that the Greek government had been almost entirely informed in advance about its contents, constitutes evidence of the principle of information of the regime EPC.[111] The O'Neil Report provides a somewhat lengthy account of the major EPC-related developments in the dispute between Greece and FYROM. The 16 December 1991 conditions, the opinion of the AC, the efforts of the Portuguese Presidency and the decisions at Guimaraes and Lisbon are all revisited.

Having presented this background information, O'Neil enters the more substantive part of his report, by arguing that FYROM is in an especially precarious situation: the republic's economy is suffering from the oil embargo, as well as from observing the UN embargo against Serbia, and ethnic tensions with the Albanian minority seem to be rising.[112]

Given this rather grave situation, the British diplomat informs that FYROM is willing to accept a compromise name, with the full expectation of Community recognition at the upcoming Edinburgh European Summit: 'The Government of FYROM...[is]...ready to accept the name for the state of Republic of Macedonia (Skopje) *for all international purposes*.'[113]

This sentence contains the essence of his initiative. It is noteworthy that unlike the proposal presented to the Greek government on 22 November (Republic of Macedonia-Skopje), FYROM's proposed name in the Report is distinguished by a parenthesis.[114] Furthermore, the clarification that this name would be utilised for international purposes constitutes an acceptance of the dual name formula. However, neither this formula, nor a name containing the term Macedonia was part of the Lisbon Declaration. O'Neil accepts this awkward fact, and states that 'this offer does not correspond to the positive offer expressed in the European Council declaration at Lisbon;'[115] and he has also admitted that his 'task was to persuade Macedonia to change its name to something new which did not include the word Macedonia, not to suggest that the EC should change its mind.'[116]

By ignoring the terms of his mandate, O'Neil essentially judged that the arguments made by FYROM's officials had particular merit, and especially that changing their name in a more radical way could not have achieved the required Parliamentary support. More importantly, by virtue of his proposal, the Ambassador had accepted that

> The term Macedonia describes accurately the national identity of the majority of the population, that it describes accurately the geographical situation of the Republic, and that the name Macedonia has been chosen and approved by all the minorities, who are not themselves of Macedonian stock.[117]

Not surprisingly, the Greek Ministry of Foreign Affairs was instructed on 4 December to issue a brief statement noting that the O'Neil Report was not considered objective.[118] This suggests the bitter disappointment felt towards the British diplomat. In an interview, Papaconstantinou kept repeating that 'the man [O'Neil] was biased.'[119] Mitsotakis also made similar comments and stressed that the Greek arguments were entirely ignored.[120] Furthermore, according to Papaconstantinou, positive initiatives taken by the Greek government were only given brief mention in the O'Neil Report. He primarily had in mind the Greek-organised 12 November 1992 declaration of all neighbouring to FYROM countries, that they would respect the young republic's territorial integrity and borders.[121]

The dispute between Greece and FYROM was discussed extensively at the 7 December meeting of EPC's Foreign Ministers, which began with a brief intervention by Ambassador O'Neil.[122] Papaconstantinou then gave a lengthy, passionate and at times furious speech attacking the O'Neil Report as being 'in bad faith and unreliable.'[123] He then presented several criticisms, focusing primarily on the fact that the retired British diplomat had ignored his mandate.[124] The Greek Foreign Minister communicated in categorical terms his country's intention to reject the O'Neil Report at the forthcoming Edinburgh European Council.

Papaconstantinou concluded his speech by suggesting that FYROM be named Vardar Republic, and also repeated the by then standard Greek offers of financial aid and security guarantees, given a favourable to Greece resolution of the dispute. Faced with Greece's intransigence, Douglas Hurd suggested that the issue be discussed at the subsequent Edinburgh meeting.

Prior to the Edinburgh Council, Karamanlis and Mitsotakis sent letters to their EPC counterparts. The purpose of Karamanlis' 24 November 1992 letter was to avert any EPC abandonment of the Lisbon Declaration.[125] The Greek statesman dismissed the argument that the non-recognition of FYROM may lead to the war spreading to that republic, and poignantly stressed that the recognition of Croatia and Bosnia produced no improvements but rather 'complicated [things] dangerously.'[126]

The President emphasised that his country had no interest in FYROM's dissolution, and suggested that financial help and security guarantees to FYROM would follow a satisfactory resolution of the dispute He then proceeded to stipulate a grave threat. If the Lisbon Declaration was abandoned

> In order to protect its security and national dignity [Greece would be forced to] close its borders [with FYROM] with painful results for Skopje and unpleasant [ones] for Greece and the Community.[127]

The fact that this warning was made by the immensely respected and 'moderate' on this dispute Karamanlis, illustrates the potential extent and quality of the politics of Greek confrontation.

In his 10 December 1992 letter, Mitsotakis reiterated Karamanlis' conditional offer to FYROM, but made no explicit reference to the possibility of closing the borders.[128] He also emphasised the importance that Greece attached to EPC maintaining the Lisbon Declaration. In doing so, he essentially rejected the substance of the letter that Kiro Gligorov had sent to him on 2 December.

In this previously unpublished letter, Gligorov urged that his republic be recognised, since it had fulfilled all EPC conditions.[129] Furthermore, FYROM's President rejected the Lisbon Declaration and castigated Greece:

> The Lisbon Declaration requires from us to erase the term Macedonia from the name of our country. This is a precedent in the history of nations and beyond the international standards. This request by the Republic of Greece was being followed by economic pressures and blockades on the Republic of Macedonia.[130]

Despite this rejection and prior to the Edinburgh meeting, Gligorov ignored considerations of political cost and proceeded in undertaking a major cooperative action.[131] On 9 December 1992 he went to his republic's Parliament, declaring that his government intended to accept the name Republic of Macedonia (Skopje).[132] This name was to have been adopted 'for all international purposes...not just for relations with the EC. The legal [i.e. for domestic purposes] name of the Republic of Macedonia would not however be changed.'[133] Gligorov warned that if this name was rejected in Edinburgh, he would then request UN membership under the name Republic of Macedonia.[134] According to the then government's Vice President Mr Risteski, this decision was also reached as a result of 'certain internal circumstances. Our country had not yet stabilised politically or economically, nor was it recognised yet,' he stressed in an interview.[135]

On the following day, a huge demonstration took place in Athens. Organised by local administration authorities, it successfully followed the blueprint of the 14 February 1992 Thessaloniki demonstration.[136] Some 1,300,000 people assembled in what was probably the largest gathering of people to ever take place in Greece's capital. The main (and somewhat misleading) slogan was 'Macedonia is Greek.'[137] Little doubt was thus left about the passions, sensitivities and interests of the Greek people. The success and emphasis of the Athens demonstration probably minimised any room for diplomatic manoeuvre and cooperation in Edinburgh.

The political parties (except the KKE) were represented, as were most professional and labour unions and the Greek Church. The keynote speaker was the Mayor of Athens, Leonidas Kouris, who stressed the importance and Greekness of the name Macedonia, and also warned of the danger of Turkey increasing its influence in the region as a result of the crisis.[138] The resolution that was subsequently passed condemned what were perceived to be provocations by FYROM, but made no reference to a solution on the basis of the dual name formula. Following the October meeting of New Democracy's MPs, that had become a dangerous (for the government) option.

The most crucial passage of the Athens resolution, the wording of which is consistent with the essence of the resolution in Thessaloniki, stated the 'demand that the three conditions of the Lisbon decision be confirmed and imposed.'[139] However, the Thessaloniki resolution created considerable pressure for the non-negotiable adoption of the restrictive position on FYROM's name, whereas the Athens resolution merely confirmed stated Greek policy, though it did ensure that any bold cooperative action in Edinburgh would meet with popular disapproval, and almost certainly guarantee the government's downfall.

At the 11 December 1992 Edinburgh European Council, and as regards the dispute with FYROM, Greece was essentially alone.[140] At the parallel meeting of the Foreign Ministers, an intransigent Papaconstantinou was the target of a sustained attempt by all EPC members to persuade him that a compromise on the name issue was necessary. On the following day, there was a renewed attempt among the same lines. Feeling isolated and frustrated, Papaconstantinou threatened to veto the declaration on the former Yugoslavia that the meeting was expected to produce, and implied that Greek non-cooperation on issues relating to Yugoslavia would be extended, perhaps indefinitely.[141] His threat illustrates the importance of the fundamental rule of consensus of the regime EPC, and if actualised would have destroyed any semblance of EPC solidarity on Yugoslavia.

Faced with this development, Hurd asked for a brief break and attempted to persuade Papaconstantinou in private. The Greek Foreign Minister was especially revealing in explaining to his British counterpart why a compromise on the name issue was not possible:

> *Our government will fall* and that which will come [into office] after the elections will not be able to follow another policy. With the people's verdict being recent it will be even tougher on its stance.[142]

Given Greece's intransigence, the Edinburgh declaration on former Yugoslavia did not include a rejection of the Lisbon Declaration, though it made evident EPC's concern over FYROM's fate and precarious condition.[143] A Security Council resolution establishing a UN force in the republic was welcomed.[144] Furthermore, the European Council 'stressed the need for appropriate measures to prevent [FYROM] from bearing the unintended consequences of UN sanctions.'[145] This constituted a thinly veiled criticism of Greece's oil embargo, as well as to the Greek attempts to prevent FYROM from benefiting from international organisations. Evidently, the Greek government's decision to 'release 40,000 tons of the embargoed oil prior to Edinburgh' had failed to assuage its EPC partners.[146] Finally, it was decided that FYROM would receive from the Community financial assistance worth some ECU 50 million.

Referring to these decisions, Mitsotakis declared that 'we managed finally to win the battle.'[147] This was true only to the extent that there was no abandonment of the Lisbon Declaration. However, after Edinburgh, there were no other important EPC initiatives to solve the dispute between Greece and FYROM. The 'war' moved away from Europe to New York, and the UN became the battlefield were FYROM attempted to achieve recognition. A study of these events would reveal new protagonists and concerns, as well as a Greek diplomacy acting skilfully and often brilliantly.[148] Such an analysis though, belongs to a different inquiry.

## C. The Continuation of Institutionalist Breakdown

The period between April-December 1992 is characterised primarily by the politics of Greek confrontation. The Greek government insisted unfailingly on a restrictive position on FYROM's name, was involved in the 'story of the labels,' imposed an oil embargo and threatened to close its borders with the new republic, rejected the O'Neil Report and Gligorov's gestures after Lisbon, and even threatened to veto the decisions on former Yugoslavia in an EPC meeting. It will subsequently be demonstrated that these acts were ultimately the result of domestic and partisan considerations.

During the same period, a record of limited cooperative Greek decisions also exists. For example, Greece continued to participate in EPC's condemnation of Serbia, which involved agreement to various harshly worded declarations, the adoption of strict sanctions on 31 May 1992, as well as agreement to the conclusions of the August London Conference. Mitsotakis explains that these cooperative actions were undertaken in order to persuade EPC members that Greece could be a reasonable and cooperative partner.[149] The aim was to attempt to change the country's horrible reputation as nothing less than EPC's 'black sheep.'[150]

Importantly, Papaconstantinou had adopted a different analysis of Serbia's strategic importance to Greece. In an interview, he stressed:

> With Serbia we have nothing in common. I do not think [that we have any common interests]. The Serbs would not be very much interested in Turkey, and I do not think that it would be possible to agree [with them] on Albania...and after all [FYROM's citizens] and Bulgarians are also Christian Orthodox.[151]

This observation is significant to the extent that it lessens the value of Greece's cooperation in EPC's condemnation of Serbia. If the perception was that no or few common interests were involved, then such cooperation could not have possibly damaged national interests, and was thus much easier to be pursued.

Another cooperative gesture involved the Greek government's decision to lift its veto and allow Turkey to receive some ECU 300 million from the Community's renovated Mediterranean policies. Mitsotakis makes it absolutely clear that this concession to his country's main regional rival was a gesture aimed at pleasing the other EPC states and altering his country's reputation as an obstinate troublemaker.[152] Crucially, Mitsotakis' government was fully aware that the Maastricht Treaty would have allowed these monetary contributions to be made on the basis of qualified majority voting, thus ensuring the by-pass of the Greek veto.[153] Furthermore, Greece did not lift its veto on the far more important Fourth Financial Protocol between the Community and Turkey, which involved some ECU 800 million.[154]

Some cooperative aspects can also be found in the letter that Mitsotakis sent to Gligorov on 9 May 1992, as well as in Papaconstantinou's previously unpublished 3 November letter to his EPC counterparts. Both demanded a resolution of the dispute on the basis of the 13 April decision on FYROM's name. This lessened significantly their cooperative nature, despite the fact that they offered financial assistance and security guarantees to FYROM.

The first letter was part of the Greek attempt to achieve the Lisbon Declaration, while the second aimed at maintaining it. These letters were influenced by EPC's 'shadow of the future;' and both tried to achieve their goal by incorporating cooperative measures that would help present Greece as a reasonable country. This would have reduced reputational costs and helped ensure that future EPC decisions were favourable to Greece.[155] The same goal was behind Greece's 12 November 1992 initiative to persuade FYROM's neighbours to announce their respect for the new republic's borders.[156]

It can perhaps also be argued that Greece's proposal for a dual name formula may be viewed as being somewhat cooperative. According to several key Greek decision-makers, it constituted a sincere effort aiming to resolve the dispute and demonstrate that Greece was not part of the problem in Yugoslavia.[157] The ultimate goal was to reduce reputational costs and alter a situation of relative isolation within EPC.[158] The cooperative importance of the dual name formula was however lessened substantially, since it insisted that FYROM's official UN name should not include the word Macedonia.

On the basis of the above, it can be concluded that institutionalism can claim to explain a few Greek cooperative decisions during the April-December 1992 period. The institutionalist emphasis on reputational concerns and on the 'shadow of the future' proved to be of some relevance. Nevertheless, it must be stressed that these cooperative actions were always of limited and reduced significance. They included offers of financial assistance to FYROM and Turkey, and the dual name formula that provided for all international purposes a vindication and implementation of the 13 April Council of the Political Leaders hard-line decision. Furthermore, although the participation in EPC's condemnation of Serbia continued, the country's alliance and strategic importance to Greece was judged by the new Foreign Minister as of limited value; and at any rate, these regime-influenced cooperative actions were dwarfed in degree and consequence by the Greek government's politics of non-cooperation and confrontation, that were determined by domestic politics.

The decision to impose an oil embargo against FYROM, as well as the 'story of the labels,' illustrate the threatening quality of Greek confrontation. Both measures aimed at wrecking the economy of a new and virtually unarmed republic, which was facing the possibility of war spreading inside its borders. According to both Mitsotakis and Papaconstantinou, there was continuous pressure from Greece's EPC partners to end these confrontational tactics, as well as various hints that the Lisbon Declaration might be overturned.[159] The Greek government simply ignored pressures and reputational concerns and refused to cooperate; and on 24 November 1992 in a letter to his EPC counterparts, Karamanlis even threatened the closing of his country's borders with FYROM. These confrontational actions were part of a strategy of pursuing a resolution of the dispute, while continuing to adhere to the decision of 13 April. As was analysed in the previous chapter, this fundamentally important to all developments decision was the result of domestic and partisan politics.

The significance of domestic politics was also manifested in the December Athens demonstration, which showed that popular passions and concerns about the dispute with FYROM remained important. At the level of domestic and partisan politics, PASOK's role should be emphasised. The largest opposition party was always extremely critical of even minor cooperative acts. Harsh condemnations were reserved for the decisions to allow minor Community monetary allocations to Turkey, or pursue a solution on the basis of the dual name formula.

Domestic and partisan considerations condemned the prospects of a solution based on the dual-name formula. Although Mitsotakis won the backing of New Democracy's Parliamentary Group on 21 October 1992, the three MPs that had voted with Samaras against the formula sufficed to eliminate the government's parliamentary majority. In an interview, Samaras proudly revealed that he subsequently sent several messages to Mitsotakis, explaining the implications for the government's future if there was any agreement based on this formula.[160] Eventually, he even sent to Mitsotakis a letter on 15 March 1993, which is published here in its entirety for the first time, ominously stating that 'any idea of a compromise on the Skopje issue must be abandoned.'[161]

Hence, the Greek government's room for a diplomatic compromise, or pursuit of significant cooperative actions, became extremely limited. This was the result of the combination of the continual adherence to the 13 April Council of the Political Leaders decision, popular passions, harsh criticisms by PASOK, and a slim Parliamentary majority constantly threatened by Samaras and his loyalists. This situation (produced exclusively by domestic and partisan considerations), meant that the acceptance of Gligorov's post-Lisbon compromise gestures or of the O'Neil Report and hence the name Macedonia (Skopje), would have guaranteed the government's downfall.[162] As Papaconstantinou stressed, he was essentially 'chain bound,' and thus even obliged to threaten to veto the decisions of the Edinburgh EPC meeting on 12 October 1992.[163]

In conclusion, it becomes apparent that institutionalism fails to elucidate to a satisfactory degree Greek foreign policy during the April-December 1992 period. It only provides an explanation for a series of rather minor, peripheral and limited cooperative decisions. As was the case for the period between 17 January and April 1992, domestic and partisan politics prove more important than institutions, in explaining the politics of Greek confrontation, non-cooperation and adherence to a hard-line stance on the name issue. Given this serious failure, amendments to the theory's conditional nature will be discussed and proposed next. They will be followed by some conclusions and lessons on the often problematic nature of Greek foreign policy-making.

## Notes

1. *Makedonia*, 16 April 1992, p. 1.
2. *Makedonia*, 17 April 1992, p. 17. This statement was made after Genscher had a meeting with Karamanlis. The extremely interesting minutes of their meeting are published in Svolopoulos, 1997, p. 639-40, Vol. 12.
3. See *Makedonia*, 21 April 1992, p. 1.
4. Ibid.
5. *Makedonia*, 24 April 1992, p. 9.
6. Interview with Mr Mitsotakis on 10 April 1997.
7. The account of the meeting at Guimaraes is primarily based on an interview with Mr Mitsotakis on 10 April 1997, the important report in *Makedonia*, 5 May 1992, p. 1 and on Skilakakis, 1995, p. 158.
8. See EPC Press Release P. 53/92, 4 May 1992.
9. EPC Press Release P. 53/92, 4 May 1992; emphasis added.
10. Ibid.
11. Mitsotakis makes an important reference to this negative climate in a crucial speech that he delivered on 21 October 1992. See *Makedonia*, 22 October 1992, p. 12. He made the same point during an interview on 10 April 1997.
12. Interview with Mr Mitsotakis on 10 April 1997.
13. See Tarkas, 1995, p. 307 and Valinakis and Dales, 1994, p. 229.
14. For the 17 January 1992 letter see Appendix II.
15. See Appendix VI.
16. Ibid.
17. The account of this meeting is based on *Makedonia*, 12 May 1992, p. 15; Tarkas, 1995, p. 308 and *To Vima*, 17 May 1992, p. A16. The last provides the most authoritative account, which at times is both amusing and troubling.
18. For the text of the telegram, see Appendix VII.
19. See ibid.
20. Ibid.
21. This explanation of the Guimaraes decision is based on interviews with Mr Mitsotakis on 10 April 1997 and Mr Skilakakis on 15 April 1997. In an interview on 29 September 1997, Mr Risteski argued that it was FYROM's mistake not having abandoned earlier the pursuit of an EPC solution, and suggested that his country ought to have requested immediately UN recognition.
22. See Glenny, p. 1992, p. 167.

23  For a judicious documentation of crimes committed in Bosnia during this period, see Helsinki Watch Report, 1992.
24  EPC Press Release P. 56/92, 11 May 1992.
25  It can be found in 31 *ILM*, p. 1453-8 (1992).
26  EPC Press Release P. 63/92, 1 June 1992. For the Council regulations implementing this decision, see OJ No L 151/4, 3.6.92; OJ No L 151/7, 3.6.92; OJ No L 151/20, 3.6.92 and OJ No L 166/35, 20.6.92.
27  Council 6774/92 (Presse 99-G), 4 June 1992.
28  Ioakimidis, 1996, p. 77.
29  *Makedonia*, 27 June 1992, p. 15.
30  The participants of the third Council of the Political Leaders were the same who were present at the 13 April meeting, with the exception of Samaras. It should also be added that Mitsotakis had mentioned briefly and essentially rejected the dual name formula during the first meeting of the Council of the Political Leaders that had taken place on 18 February 1992. According to Papandreou's hand-written notes, such a formula was then judged to have only 'small chances' of success. See Papandreou, 1997, p. 518.
31  The account of this meeting is based on interviews with Ms Damanaki on 30 January 1997, Mr Lengeris on 30 August 1997, Mr Mitsotakis on 10 April 1997 and Mr Skilakakis on 15 April 1997. Of particular importance was Skilakakis, 1995, p. 167-70. His account of the meeting was based on 'notes' that Mitsotakis kept. For an analysis of the exact nature of Mitsotakis' 'notes,' see chapter 6, footnote 85.
32  Interview with Ms Damanaki on 30 January 1997. This point was confirmed by Mr Mitsotakis in an interview on 10 April 1997.
33  Valinakis and Dales, 1984, p. 96.
34  Interview with Mr Mitsotakis on 10 April 1997.
35  See *Makedonia*, 19 June 1992, p. 15.
36  Cited in Skilakakis, 1995, p. 170.
37  The letter can be found in Valinakis and Dales, 1994, p. 97-9.
38  Ibid., p. 99.
39  Ibid., p. 97.
40  Interviews with Mr Papaconstantinou on 23 December 1997 and Mr Skilakakis on 15 April 1997. Significantly, VMRO-DPNE's discussions of possible terrorist attacks were not denied during interviews with Mr Arsovski on 3 February 1997 and Mr Dimovski on 29 September 1997. However, it must be stressed that FYROM's government never encouraged, endorsed or participated in such discussions.
41  Valinakis and Dales, 1994, p. 97.
42  Ibid., p. 98.
43  *Makedonia*, 27 June 1992, p. 1.
44  OJ No C 176/201, 13.7.92. The resolution was made on 11 June 1992.
45  The dual name formula also won the backing of the US. Mitsotakis was informed of this support during the Lisbon European Council. See Tarkas, 1995, p. 320.
46  Bull. EC 6-1992, p. 22; emphasis added.
47  Cited in *Makedonia*, 28 June 1992, p. 40. For the entire transcript of Mitsotakis' speech and press conference after the conclusion of the Lisbon European Council, see ibid.
48  Ibid.
49  Cited in Skilakakis, 1995, p. 175.

50  For Papandreou's comments, see *Makedonia*, 28 June 1992, p. 40. See also his subsequent statements in *Makedonia*, 30 June 1992, p. 13, in which the attack on the dual name formula should be noted.
51  Bull. EC 6-1992, p. 22.
52  For the text of the Assembly's declaration (in English), see Valinakis and Dales, 1994, p. 103-5.
53  Interviews with Mr Mertzos on 18 December 1996, Mr Papaconstantinou on 23 December 1996, Mr Samaras on 3 February 1997 and Mr Tzounis on 14 April 1997. Mr Kofos, in an interview on 5 January 1997 further stressed that President Gligorov was on record saying that the 'game of the name' was at times almost lost. Kofos argues that such a possibility was faced by FYROM after Lisbon, (as well as after 16 December 1991).
54  Interview with Mr Mitsotakis on 10 April 1997. The former Greek Prime Minister acknowledged Gligorov's overtures, but did not mention the exact compromise names that had been suggested. In an interview on 29 September 1997, Mr Risteski characterised the Lisbon Declaration as 'useful but *not fully* accepted' (emphasis added). The use of the phrase 'not fully accepted' in this carefully worded comment, suggests that a compromise name that included the term Macedonia was at the very least contemplated by FYROM's government. This is probably why Mr Risteski did not state that the Lisbon Declaration was rejected at that time in its entirety. If this is indeed the case, his comment provides further (though indirect), evidence in support of the claims made by Greek decision-makers concerning FYROM's post-Lisbon cooperative gestures.
55  The letter can be found (in English), in Papaconstantinou, 1994, p. 429-30.
56  For a depiction of FYROM's flag, as well as for a pictorial representation of the ancient Star of Vergina, see Appendix VIII. See also Danforth, 1995, p. 163-74 for a discussion of the flag issue. A magisterial biography of Philip II is Hammond 1994. For an exciting account of the tomb's discovery by the renowned archaeologist Manolis Andronikos, see his private notes published in *Ta Nea*, 16 October 1997, p. 24-5.
57  Cited in Danforth, 1995, p. 46. Not all FYROM citizens accept Gligorov's argument. For a devastating critique of the more ridiculous and outrageous claims concerning the Slav 'descendants' of the ancient Macedonians, see Kofos 1986. In an interview on 29 September 1997, Mr Risteski admitted that claims directly linking his people with the ancient Macedonians were examples of 'revolutionary romanticism' and 'mythology'. He then proceeded to partly accept these false claims, on the basis that they nevertheless constitute a real part of his people's tradition, and hence a necessary and important component of their identity. This 'true lies' argument not only stretches credulity, but is also revealing of the degree of historical distortion, falsification and logical implausibility that is required in order to mount arguments whose basis is admittedly spurious. Mr Risteski somewhat qualified his position by stating that the ancient Macedonians are 'part of our history but also belong to the Greeks.' Mr Arsovski on 3 February 1997 and Mr Dimovski on 29 September 1997 made exactly the same point, which requires some elaboration. The thesis that is advanced is that through intermarriage with the descendants of the non-Greek barbarian ancient Macedonians, all late-comers to the region can make a claim to the ancient Macedonian cultural and historical heritage. Perhaps to someone not familiar with the region's history, this all-inclusive argument might seem appealing. The problem is that it is based on spurious and unacceptable assumptions. Although a thorough refutation would require a separate thesis, it is sufficient to note that given the argument's 'logic', anyone residing in geographic Macedonia can make equally compelling claims to simultaneously being a descendant

and sharing equally in the history and culture of Albanians, Armenians, Bulgarians, Greeks, Jews, Pomaks, Roma, Serbs and Turks (to name just a few). In other words, and taken to its extreme logical conclusion, this 'multicultural' argument collapses from its own audacity, improbability and basis on historical falsification.

58  In an interview on 3 February 1997, FYROM's Head of Mission in Greece Mr Arsovsky also accepted that the adoption of the flag could have been viewed as provocative by the Greeks. Interestingly, in an interview on 29 September 1997, FYROM's former Assistant Minister of Foreign Affairs Mr Dimovski stressed that FYROM's flag only contained an imitation of the Star of Vergina. An examination of Appendix VIII allows for an evaluation of this claim. Also, during an interview on 29 September 1997 with the then Vice President of FYROM's government Mr Risteski, a fascinating account of former (and in some cases much older) flags utilised by nationalist groups was presented. They contained a star or a sun, and one even had a unicorn that apparently represented Alexander the Great's horse Buchephalas. However, no previous flag contained the actual Vergina symbol.

59  Cited in Lygeros, 1992, p. 210 fn 129. This statement was issued after the adoption of the new FYROM flag and before the imposition of the Greek oil embargo. As a result, the claims of Ljupco Georgievski, leader of VMRO-DPNE in *Le Monde Diplomatique*, that 'the Greeks revolted only 8-10 months [after the adoption of the flag, otherwise]...we would have chosen the lion' (cited in Tsirkinidis, 1994, p. 332), are lies.

60  Cited in Tarkas, 1995, p. 327. This decision was consistent with the decision in Council 6774/92 (Presse 99-G), 4 June 1992.

61  Mitsotakis admitted this logic behind the embargo in an interview on 10 April 1997, as well as during a crucial speech to his party's MPs. See *Makedonia*, 27 October 1992, p. 12.

62  Part of a document that provides evidence for this fact was published in Tarkas, 1995, p. 331. See Appendix IX. This practice was also confirmed in an interview with Mr Arsovsky on 3 February 1997.

63  Papaconstantinou, 1994, p. 171. See also the previously unpublished letter that Papaconstantinou sent to his EPC counterparts on 12 October 1992, that can be found in Appendix IX.

64  See COM(92) 424 final, 11 August 1992.

65  OJ No L 266/27, 12.9.92; emphasis added.

66  See OJ No L 276/18. 19.9.92.

67  See Lygeros, 1992, p. 217.

68  Among them were representatives from the US, Russia, and Japan, as well as the leader of the Bosnian Serbs, Radovan Karadzic. All of the speeches, statements and interventions can be found in the academic edition of David Owen's 1995 *Balkan Odyssey CD-ROM* (hereafter Owen-CD). Passages will be cited according to the CD-ROM reference.

69  The issue of FYROM's recognition was raised however by Serbia's Prime Minister Milan Panic, and the Foreign Ministers of Bulgaria and Slovenia. See Owen-CD, 1995: T: LC 26/8/92 Ganev statement and T: LC 26/8/92 Rupel statement. Papaconstantinou claims in his memoirs that they were asked by Gligorov to address this issue. See Papaconstantinou, 1994, p. 81-2.

70  Russia recognised FYROM as the Republic of Macedonia on 5 August 1992. It appears that the decision was made somewhat suddenly and whimsically by Russian President Boris Yeltsin. See Crow, 1992.

71  Papaconstantinou who was 73 years old, was sworn as Greece's Foreign Minister on 8 August 1992.

72  See Owen-CD, 1995: T: LC 26/8/92 Papaconstantinou intervention.
73  Ibid.
74  Owen-CD, 1995: T: LC 26/8/92 Gligorov statement.
75  Ibid.
76  Ibid.
77  See 31 *ILM*, p. 1537-43 (1992). The Conference also decided that Lord Owen, a former UK Foreign Secretary, would replace Lord Carrington.
78  Cited in Silber and Little, 1995/1996, p. 262.
79  See Papaconstantinou, 1994, p. 115. For O'Neil's account of his initiative, see O'Neil, 1997.
80  Ibid., p. 7.
81  Interview with Mr Papaconstantinou on 23 December 1996.
82  Bull. EC 10-1992, p. 10. In Birmingham, there was also an informal meeting of EPC's Foreign Ministers, that discussed Greece's dispute with FYROM. Most notably, the Danish Foreign Minister asked for the republic's recognition. As expected, Papaconstantinou reacted negatively to this suggestion, and thus no decision was made. See *Makedonia*, 17 October 1992, p. 13 and Papaconstantinou, 1994, p. 178-82. Also based on an interview with Mr Papaconstantinou on 23 December 1997.
83  According to O'Neil, one of his most immediate problems was how to travel to Skopje. Finding train travel slow and uncomfortable, he eventually opted for a Greek car driving him to the border, at which point he was picked up by an official FYROM car. O'Neil also provides evidence of the consequences of the oil embargo, noting that in one of his 100 mile long trips from the Greek border to Skopje, he only saw three cars. See O'Neil, 1997, p. 2 and 4.
84  Cited in Lygeros, 1992, p. 220 fn 139.
85  Particularly good coverage of the meeting can be found in *Eleftherotypia*, 22 October 1992, p. 1-14.
86  On 7 and 9 September 1993, two New Democracy MPs defected to Samaras' Politiki Anixi, forcing Mitsotakis to call a general election. On 10 October 1993, a triumphant PASOK received 46.88 per cent of the vote and 171 seats (out of 300). New Democracy received only 39.30 per cent, Politiki Anixi 4.87 per cent and the KKE 4.54 per cent. Synaspismos failed to win Parliamentary representation. See Lygeros, 1996, p. 242-3 and 251.
87  See *Makedonia*, 22 October 1992, p. 1, 12 and 15.
88  Ibid., p. 15.
89  Proof of the government's unpopularity was a nation-wide poll that was released in November 1992. Only 25.1 per cent of respondents declared their willingness to vote for New Democracy, whereas 33.5 per cent opted for PASOK. See Loulis, 1995, p. 423.
90  See Appendix X.
91  Ibid.
92  See Appendix XI. Samaras also submitted three supporting documents. The first was the previously analysed 23 June 1992 letter that Mitsotakis sent to his EPC counterparts. The others are published here for the first time. For Samaras' speech, and his various exchanges with New Democracy MPs, see also Skilakakis, 1995, p. 191-2 and 194-6.
93  Interview with Mr Samaras on 24 December 1997.
94  Appendix XI.
95  *Makedonia*, 22 October 1992, p. 1; emphasis added.

96  In an interview on 24 December 1996, Samaras explained that he had specifically advised his closest allies not to vote with him against the dual name formula, but three of them ignored his explicit request. Samaras argues that in addition to them, many more were in support of his position. Given subsequent defections to his party, this is almost certainly an accurate assertion.
97  See Appendix XII.
98  Ibid.
99  Interview with Mr Papaconstantinou on 23 December 1996.
100  See O'Neil, 1997, p. 6.
101  O'Neil essentially confirms the legitimacy of this complaint. He argues that following his visits to Skopje, he concluded that only the names Macedonia (Skopje) or FYROM (the latter though as a 'possible fall-back position'), could provide plausible solutions to the dispute. See ibid., p. 6. Both are single names that are incompatible with the Lisbon Declaration.
102  Based on an interview with Mr Papaconstantinou on 23 December 1996.
103  Appendix XII.
104  Ibid.
105  Ibid.
106  In an interview on 10 April 1997, Mr Papaconstantinou clarified that FYROM never made such a request.
107  Interview with Mr Papaconstantinou on 10 April 1997.
108  *Financial Times*, 24 November 1992, p. 4. O'Neil made this statement knowing that Gligorov was willing to accept the name Macedonia (Skopje). See O'Neil, 1997, p. 8. However, he ought to have been in a position to guess the negative Greek reaction to such a proposal.
109  Interview with Mr Papaconstantinou on 23 December 1996. This point is confirmed by O'Neil. See O'Neil, 1997, p. 8.
110  His report can be found (in English) in Papaconstantinou, 1994, p. 431-9.
111  Interview with Mr Papaconstantinou on 23 December 1996.
112  It was estimated that 'Skopje's enforcement of UN sanctions against Serbia cost...$1.9 billion per year' (Perry, 1995, p. 44).
113  Papaconstantinou, 1994, p. 437; emphasis added. FYROM's government also accepted to change Article 49 of the constitution. It was to contain the following language, p. 'The Republic cares for the status and rights of Macedonians living abroad, assists their cultural development and promotes link with them' (ibid., p. 438).
114  In an interview on 23 December 1996, Mr Papaconstantinou argued that this change made O'Neil's proposal even less appealing to the Greek government. However, based on O'Neil, 1997, there is no indication that the originally proposed name was Macedonia-Skopje. Perhaps though, reference to this change might have been considered as an unnecessary and technical detail for his audience.
115  Papaconstantinou, 1994, p. 439.
116  O'Neil, 1997, p. 4.
117  Ibid., p. 437.
118  Interview with Mr Papaconstantinou on 23 December 1996.
119  Interview with Mr Papaconstantinou on 23 December 1996. Papaconstantinou personally issued those instructions. It is also noteworthy that in his lavishly illustrated memoirs, the only photograph showing him grim-faced was taken during a meeting with O'Neil. In the same interview, when confronted with this observation, he admitted that it was done intentionally.

120 Interview with Mr Mitsotakis on 10 April 1997.
121 See *Makedonia*, 11 November 1992, p. 1 and *Makedonia*, 12 November 1992, p. 1. Although somewhat ignored by O'Neil, this initiative of the Greek government was praised in more certain terms by the EP. See OJ No C 337/197, 21.12.92, paragraph 17.
122 The account of this meeting is based on Papaconstantinou, 1994, p. 220-44, on an interview with Mr Papaconstantinou on 23 December 1996 and on the lengthy and important report in *Makedonia*, 8 December 1992, p. 1 and 12. It must be noted though, that EPC's official press release though, merely states that 'The Ministers...held a discussion on the subject [of O'Neil's Report].' See Council, 10523/92 (Presse 235-G), 7 December 1992.
123 *Makedonia*, 8 December 1992, p. 1.
124 See Papaconstantinou, 1994, p. 221-2. Also based on an interview with Mr Papaconstantinou on 23 December 1996. For O'Neil's response to these criticisms, see O'Neil, 1997, p. 8. O'Neil 'took comfort from the fact that the Greek government had, incidentally, criticised and dismissed in almost identical terms [the AC's opinion]' (ibid.).
125 It can be found in Valinakis and Dales, 1994, p. 108-10.
126 Ibid., p. 109.
127 Ibid.
128 See *Makedonia*, 12 December 1992, p. 1. Mitsotakis also warned that an abandonment of the Lisbon Declaration would 'cause the tragic destabilisation of our region' (ibid.). Read carefully and in conjunction with the 24 November 1992 Karamanlis letter, it may be argued that this phrase hints to the closing of the borders with FYROM. Admittedly though, it is less than absolutely clear.
129 See Appendix XIII. During my research, I have not found any proof of this letter having been published in any Greek or English publication. However, it has been impossible to find out whether it has been published in any unofficial FYROM publication.
130 Ibid.
131 That such a decision entailed political cost should not be doubted. Characteristically, FYROM's current Assistant Minister of Foreign Affairs stressed that any 'politician who agrees to a change of FYROM's constitutional name could say good-bye to his political career' (interview with Mr Dimovski on 29 September 1997).
132 See *Makedonia*, 10 December 1992, p. 18.
133 O'Neil, 1997, p. 8.
134 In an interview on 29 September 1997, Mr Risteski explained that not having gone directly to the UN requesting recognition was probably a mistake on behalf of FYROM's government.
135 Interview with Mr Risteski on 29 September 1997 It should be noted that '1992 was [financially] anything but a successful year for [FYROM]. The gross social product decreased by 15 per cent and investment by 24 per cent, while the real depreciation of salaries was 34 per cent...As a result of Resolution 577 of the United Nations alone, [FYROM's] economy...suffered damage to the extent of 1,3 billion [US] dollars. The damage caused by the Greek embargo amount[ed] to an additional 1 billion [US] dollars' (Reuter, 1999, p. 39). Of importance is also the fact that Mr Dimovski provided precisely the same explanation with Mr Risteski during an interview on 29 September 1997. The fact that Gligorov clearly and publicly accepted a compromise name other than Macedonia, has proved an embarrassment for FYROM's hard-line politicians who argue that the name Macedonia 'is our identity, our existence' (interview with Mr Risteski on 29 September 1997), thus implying that no compromise is possible. The

problem of course is that having accepted once precisely such a compromise, evidence exists that the name Macedonia has not always been 'sacred' or non-negotiable.
136 Primarily responsible for the organisation of the demonstration was the Central Committee of Municipalities and Communities in Greece (KEDKE).
137 For an astute analysis of the slogan's logic, problems and implications, see Kofos 1999, p. 235.
138 For his speech, see *Makedonia*, 11 December 1992, p. 15. This point was also reiterated by the various other speakers. See ibid.
139 Ibid.
140 However, some two hundred Greek mayors had flown to Edinburgh in order to demonstrate their support for Greece's restrictive position (interview with Mr Kosmopoulos on 5 February 1997).
141 Interview with Mr Papaconstantinou on 23 December 1996.
142 Papaconstantinou, 1994, p. 231; emphasis added.
143 See Bull. EC 12-1992, p. 10.
144 This was UN Security Council Resolution 795, that can be found (in English) in Valinakis and Dales, 1994, p. 125-6.
145 Bull. EC 12-1992, p. 10.
146 Petkovski et al, 1993, p. 34.
147 *Makedonia*, 13 December 1992, p. 1.
148 When I first contacted Papaconstantinou in order to arrange some interviews, I explained to him over the phone that my thesis would deal with events up to the Edinburgh European Council. Although he was in complete agreement with this cut-off point, he commented on the fact that the UN battle would not be included by saying: 'This is unfortunate...this is unfortunate.'
149 Interview with Mr Mitsotakis on 10 April 1997. The same argument was made (among others) by Mr Tzounis in an interview on 14 April 1997.
150 See Skilakakis, 1995, p. 147-53.
151 Interview with Mr Papaconstantinou on 23 December 1996. The former Foreign Minister did stress however that Greece should have good relations with Serbia, 'as with all countries' (ibid.). Papaconstantinou's argument is partly based on the fact that the Eastern Orthodox Churches have tended to be closely associated with the state to which they belong. See Karakasidou, 1997b, p. 82-3. They have subsequently failed to act as a force limiting antagonism and hostilities among the various Orthodox countries. Greece and Bulgaria provide a significant historical record and illustration of warring Orthodox nations. Such examples are underestimated by Samuel Huntington, who in his theory of the 'Clash of Civilisations' talks about a Slavic-Orthodox civilisation, to which Greece seems to belong. See Huntington 1993 and Huntington 1996, p. 126-7 and 162-3.
152 Interview with Mr Mitsotakis on 10 April 1997.
153 Admittedly though, at that time the ratification of the Maastricht Treaty was not necessarily a foregone conclusion. This is because in the 2 June 1992 referendum, the Danish people had rejected the TEU. They subsequently reversed their decision in the 18 May 1993 referendum. See Duff et al, 1994, p. 54-5 and 63.
154 See *Makedonia*, 27 June 1992, p. 15.
155 Based on interviews with Mr Mitsotakis on 10 April 1997 and Mr Papaconstantinou on 23 December 1996.
156 Based on interviews with Mr Mitsotakis on 10 April 1997, Mr Papaconstantinou on 23 December 1996, Mr Skilakakis on 15 April 1997 and Mr Tzounis on 14 April 1997.

157 Based on interviews with Mr Mitsotakis on 10 April 1997, Mr Papaconstantinou on 10 April 1997, Mr Skilakakis on 15 April 1997 and Mr Tzounis on 14 April 1997.
158 Based on interviews with Mr Mitsotakis on 10 April 1997, Mr Papaconstantinou on 10 April 1997, Mr Skilakakis on 15 April 1997 and Mr Tzounis on 14 April 1997.
189 Interviews with Mr Mitsotakis on 10 April 1997 and Mr Papaconstantinou on 10 April 1997. These pressures were also reflected in various EPC decisions. See for example Bull. EC 10-1992, p. 10.
160 Interview with Mr Samaras on 24 December 1996.
161 See Appendix XIV. In an interview on 24 December 1997, Samaras explained that he had in mind any name or formula not strictly adhering to the decision of the 13 April Council of the Political Leaders.
162 Interviews with Mr Mertzos on 18 December 1996, Mr Mitsotakis on 10 April 1997, Mr Papaconstantinou on 10 April 1997, Mr Samaras on 24 December 1996, Mr Skilakakis on 15 April 1997 and Mr Tzounis on 14 April 1997. It must also be stressed though, that O'Neil did not assist his initiative by managing to be perceived by Greek decision-makers as a biased diplomat.
163 Interviews with Mr Mitsotakis on 10 April 1997 and Mr Papaconstantinou on 23 December 1996 and 10 April 1997.

# 8 Conclusions

It was an extraordinary period of testing, but statesmen do not have the right to ask to serve only in simple times.

-Henry Kissinger, *Years of Upheaval*, 1982.

### A. The Theory of Institutionalism Reconsidered

The application of institutionalist theory required that EPC be viewed as an international regime. Thus, in the book's concluding section, this argument and its ramifications will be evaluated, and a more comprehensive account of the regime EPC presented. However, this discussion will be preceded by an examination of the theoretical consequences for institutionalism, emanating from the empirical research that was undertaken.

More specifically, in the previously analysed case-study, the desire that the war raging in parts of former Yugoslavia not spread to FYROM constituted the most fundamental common interest that also satisfied institutionalism's conditional nature. Given the presence and actions of EPC, and the existence of various other common interests during the entire period of June 1991 to December 1992 (as presented in Chapter 3), the practice of cooperation could have been expected on the basis of institutionalism. However, it was precisely when shared interests became more significant, that the politics of limited cooperation and confrontation were practised.[1]

Subsequently, certain serious problems arise for the theory, though it can not be discarded entirely since it largely explains Greece's foreign policy towards former Yugoslavia and FYROM between June 1991 and 17 January 1992.

As was shown in Chapter 4, during these months the Greek government practised politics of cooperation, moderation and flexibility, signing all EPC decisions on Yugoslavia and never threatening to use its veto power. Furthermore, EPC's condemnation and penalisation of Serbia was endorsed, regardless of the special Greco-Serbian relationship. Greece also agreed to the establishment of the Hague Peace Conference and the creation of the Arbitration Commission, while the formalisation of Yugoslavia's dissolution was accepted despite grave misgivings.

Concerning FYROM, Mitsotakis' government pursued a rather 'gentle' and moderate policy, arranging a meeting between representatives of Greece's and the new republic's Foreign Ministries aimed at resolving the dispute, and perhaps most importantly, maintaining a moderate and flexible position on the name issue. Although a name consisting solely of the word Macedonia was clearly rejected, the option of a compromise name related to FYROM's geographical location (i.e. Upper Macedonia or Northern Macedonia), was consistently maintained.

In Chapter 5, it was shown that this cooperative record is explained by institutionalism. During this period, domestic politics (which are ignored by the theory), played only a limited role, while concepts used in institutionalism such as reciprocity and the 'shadow of the future' proved consequential. More precisely, Greek decision-makers were conscious of the fact that EPC would be responsible for reaching most subsequent decisions on Yugoslavia and on their country's dispute with FYROM—a realisation that made reputational concerns particularly acute, and hence dictated the concerted efforts aimed at creating goodwill and achieving for Greece a reputation of a trustworthy and responsible partner. This is how the flexible policy pursued towards FYROM, the acceptance of the AC and the Hague Peace Conference, and the participation in Serbia's condemnation are primarily explained.

Reputational concerns deriving from EPC's 'shadow of the future' were also connected to the pursuit of some specific and significant Greek foreign policy goals that included accession to the WEU, monetary compensation for damages to the national economy due to the Yugoslav War, and the creation of the Cohesion Fund. These were 'goods' that could only be provided by EPC; and the attainment of most of them was actually possible during the Maastricht Treaty negotiations which were characterised by high issue density and by the increased possibility of side-payments.[2] Together with acute reputational concerns, they created considerable (and successful), incentives and pressure for the Greek government to pursue politics of moderation and cooperation.

Finally, the concept of reciprocity proved important in explaining the decision to recognise Croatia, given the implicit agreement that there would be no EPC recognition of FYROM as the Republic of Macedonia, despite the AC's opinion. Furthermore, reciprocity explains Samaras' agreement on 16 December 1991 to Germany's positions on former Yugoslavia, since during the same meeting he achieved the three conditions on the new republic's recognition. Certain reputational concerns connected with the possible wrath of Germany against a non-cooperating Greece, probably also influenced the stance of the young Foreign Minister.

The decline of the politics of Greek cooperation begins with the letter that Samaras sent to his EPC counterparts on 17 January 1992, arguing that the word Macedonia had to be excluded entirely from FYROM's name. At that point, this was the maximalist but negotiable position of his government. As analysed in Chapter 6, it became non-negotiable after the conclusion of the 13 April 1992 Second Council of the Political Leaders, in which all of them (with the exception of the KKE's General Secretary), espoused the restrictive interpretation of the third EPC condition.

The immediate result of this agreement was the rejection of the 'Pinheiro Package,' according to which the new republic would have been named New Macedonia. A subsequent EPC effort carried out by the retired British Ambassador Robin O'Neil under the auspices of his country's Presidency, met with the same fate. His report suggested that the name Macedonia (Skopje) be adopted for FYROM, and was thus also contrary to the 13 April decision. During the EPC meeting in Edinburgh on 12 December 1992, Foreign Minister Michalis Papaconstantinou not only rejected the O'Neil Report, but actually threatened to veto the meeting's conclusions on Yugoslavia (and possibly subsequent ones as well).

The politics of non-cooperation were not limited to the issue of FYROM's name. As Chapter 7 showed, a more direct confrontation was pursued with the imposition of an oil embargo against the new republic in August 1992. Furthermore, the 'story of the labels' and threats of sealing the borders, illustrate the degree and quality of Greek confrontation which aimed at seriously damaging FYROM's already fragile economy.

During the period between mid-January and December 1992, there were also cooperative decisions, though their scope and significance were rather limited. Perhaps most importantly, Mitsotakis' government agreed to EPC's recognition of Bosnia, despite near certainty that the results would be catastrophic. As was shown in Chapter 6, this decision is explained by the concept of reciprocity: the aim was to procrastinate and thus postpone an EPC decision on the name with which FYROM was to be recognised. This episode reveals the fact that Greek foreign policy towards former Yugoslavia was being almost completely dominated by the name dispute with FYROM.

A second action of this period that can be viewed as being cooperative involved the proposal of the dual name formula. Its cooperative nature was lessened however, since FYROM's international name had to be consistent with the 13 April restrictive interpretation of the third EPC condition. The making of this specific proposal seems to have been connected to reputational concerns deriving from EPC's 'shadow of the future.' The same concerns also influenced the frequent offers to guarantee FYROM's security and provide financial assistance, given of course a resolution of the dispute that was favourable to Greece; and they also affected the continuous participation in EPC's condemnation and penalisation of Serbia.

Despite such partial 'successes,' institutionalist theory fails to provide an adequate explanation for the major developments of this period. By ignoring domestic politics, it is unable to incorporate into its analysis events such as the Thessaloniki demonstration of 14 February 1992, or the subsequent spontaneous and popular boycott of Dutch, Italian and Danish products. These events, clearly belonging to the realm of domestic politics, demonstrated the nature and intensity of popular passions. Furthermore, at the same time Samaras began his high-stakes campaign to force his government to accept a non-negotiable restrictive position, while the Leader of the Opposition gradually began to raise the tone of his rhetoric and to publicly converge with the Foreign Minister's views.

The result of these domestic and partisan developments was the consequential decision of 13 April and the elimination of Mitsotakis' ability to achieve a diplomatic compromise. The Prime Minister had to confront the opposition tactics of both Samaras and Papandreou, feared the overthrow of his government that was based on a slim Parliamentary majority, and faced near-certain electoral defeat in such an eventuality. Subsequently, Mitsotakis was pressured into endorsing the politics of confrontation and limited cooperation. Thus, it can be concluded that after mid-January 1992, as regards the causation of Greek foreign policy, almost all significant decisions are explained and produced at the domestic level. EPC's influence on the country's foreign policy towards former Yugoslavia (which at that point had been reduced to the name dispute with FYROM), can at best be judged of limited consequence.

In addition to explaining cooperation on the basis of regime influence, it was demonstrated in Chapter 1 that institutionalism is connected with liberal theories and is severely criticised for its approach towards the issue of relative gains. As regards the 'emasculated liberalism' that characterises the theory, it can be argued that it proved of limited consequence to events.[3] The potential for mutual economic gains (analysed in Chapter 3), within an environment of relative economic openness that could have been safeguarded by EPC, did not influence in any important degree the quality and fervour of the dispute. Nor did the series of offers of financial aid provide a solution, although all these factors were taken into consideration by most decision-makers.[4] Nevertheless, these conclusions are not necessarily at odds with institutionalist expectations and assumptions.

Institutionalism stands vindicated in its analysis of the conditional nature of relative gains considerations. No evidence was found that concerns about relative gains were part of Greece's decision-making process and strategic planning.[5] An explanation might lie in the fact that the difference in capabilities and resources between FYROM and Greece were so immense, that it made almost no sense to think of the dispute in terms of relative gains. Hence, institutionalist theorists seem to argue correctly that relative gains considerations are conditional upon circumstances and the desire to exploit them.[6]

Thus, on the basis of the case-study presented in this book, it can be concluded that institutionalism explains events between June 1991 and January 1992, but mostly fails to do so for the 17 January-December 1992 period. As a result of this conclusion the theory can not be abandoned, though some amendments become necessary. More specifically, institutionalism would retain its predictive and explanatory relevance if its conditional nature was expanded. In other words, it is being proposed that given the combination of certain conditions in a specific issue-area, and despite the existence of common interests, the application of the theory be suspended.

The expansion of its conditional nature would require situations satisfying specific characteristics. They would certainly have to involve highly politicised issues with particular emotional relevance for the people. Such issues are firmly entangled with popular perceptions concerning matters of national interest and identity. They tend to be the result of traumatic historical events that may involve long-standing and possibly even ancient disputes. The Macedonian Question with its complexities, controversies and conflicts that were analysed in Chapter 3, provides a paradigmatic illustration. It is thus not coincidental that in interviews conducted for this book in both Greece and FYROM, phrases like 'the name is our soul' or 'the name is our identity' where often uttered in a forceful manner, and were clearly expressed in events such as the Thessaloniki demonstration. In instances when the people and many of their elected representatives judge that cooperation might address and adversely affect important interests and deeply held beliefs, the desire and scope for the pursuit of cooperative actions will inevitably diminish.

The chances for cooperation as predicted and explained by institutionalism are further reduced, if there also exists an unstable domestic political situation in which it is difficult for the government to reach important decisions. Reliance on petty personal and partisan calculations, coupled with the overwhelming fear of upsetting vital supporters or losing power, can only produce politics of timidity, delay and undue caution. This was clearly the case with Mitsotakis' government that was unable to back the Prime Minister's preferred foreign policy positions, being hostage to Samaras and Papandreou and facing a hostile electorate in the event of any significant compromise.

Finally, the achievement of cooperation is certainly not assisted when the regime involved is rather weak and lacks the power and tools to greatly affect outcomes. As will be discussed in the following section, EPC provides an example of such a regime, especially given its rule of consensus and its inability to contest developments through military means.

Hence, it can be concluded that highly politicised and emotional issues, important considerations of perceived national interest and identity, a rather weak regime and an unstable domestic political situation, are conditions whose combination ought to 'trigger' the suspension of institutionalist analysis. These conditions were present in Greece and hence influenced the country's non-cooperative and confrontational foreign policy record during the period between mid-January and December 1992. Similar conditions might perhaps be present in other places like Palestine, Bosnia or Kosovo. Solutions to those disputes must first and foremost be political acts confronting domestic and partisan realities.[7] Relying exclusively or primarily on regimes, or even on important common interests, will probably prove counter-productive and ineffective.

## B. EPC as an International Regime: An Evaluation

The 'breakdown' of EPC into its principles, norms, rules, decision-making procedures, scope and organisational form that was attempted in Chapter 2, provided certain important advantages, not least because it permitted the application of institutionalist theory. Thus in this section, there will be an evaluation and elaboration of the regime EPC, on the basis of the book's case-study.

More specifically, as regards EPC's principles, that of solidarity requires particular attention, especially since the agreement on its significance among the major protagonists of this book's case-study is striking. FYROM's President Kiro Gligorov explained in an interview:

> Among the principles that underpin the working of the European Union is the principle of solidarity. For this reason you [the Greeks] had behind you the European Union, [you] had its backing. In the recent dispute with us, if it [can be called] a dispute, you had an ace in you hands.[8]

In a similar manner, former Foreign Minister Papaconstantinou stressed that

[EPC's member states] were supportive and truly saw Greece as a friend, even though they mostly believed that we were wrong [on the dispute with FYROM]; and no one can claim that it was their [national] interest that dictated such a stance. No! It was precisely solidarity.[9]

Agreeing with Papaconstantinou, Samaras expressed with certainty his belief that solidarity was in operation in EPC affairs, and insisted that had it not been for this principle, it would have been impossible for Greece to hold out on the issue of FYROM's name.[10] Mitsotakis also made essentially identical comments.[11]

Despite these assurances about the significance of solidarity, a case can be argued against it, since various EPC decisions were apparently reached regardless of any considerations of this principle. Thus, the 16 December 1991 EPC decisions were primarily the result of the uncompromising German position and pressure. Regarding the conditions for FYROM's recognition, reciprocity and possibly certain reputational concerns seem to have been of crucial importance. The fact that an unanimous decision was eventually reached was more of an attempt to preserve a facade of solidarity, than its sincere expression.

As previously explained, reciprocity was involved in the 15 January 1992 EPC decision to recognise Croatia and not FYROM, despite the contrary opinions of the Arbitration Commission. Also, as shown in Chapter 6, the EPC decision of 6 April 1992 to recognise Bosnia was signed by the Greek government not because of a desire to exercise solidarity, but rather as a way of postponing an EPC decision on FYROM's recognition. Furthermore, solidarity was clearly not practised by Papaconstantinou when he threatened to veto the EPC declaration on Yugoslavia during the 12 December 1992 meeting in Edinburgh.

This decision-making record and its explanation is actually accepted by the advocates of the importance of solidarity.[12] In defence of their position though, certain EPC-related developments and decisions must also be analysed. For example, after assuming the office of Foreign Minister, Mitsotakis had several meetings with a number of EPC leaders and Foreign Ministers. Despite the frustration with what was considered to have been the mishandling (at best) of the dispute by the Greek government, a tremendous amount of goodwill and support was expressed towards him. It is most likely that this support was at least partly the result of the principle of solidarity; and at any rate, Mitsotakis is convinced that this was the case.[13]

According to Greek decision-makers, solidarity was operational and consequential in the declaration of the 26-27 June 1992 Lisbon European Council.[14] Although not exactly the triumph that it was then portrayed to have been, it certainly strengthened Greece's position. Mitsotakis, Papaconstantinou and Samaras also make an additional and crucial argument in favour of the importance of solidarity.[15] They explain that although their arguments and positions on the dispute with FYROM were often (and unfairly) little understood or appreciated by the other EPC member states there nevertheless was a constant and mostly genuine effort by their partners to reach a solution that would have been acceptable to Greece.[16] Without the principle of solidarity, Greek concerns might have received a summary, and perhaps not even a polite, dismissal. An argument could perhaps be advanced to the extent that the country's positions were tolerated because it possessed veto power over all aspects of EPC's decision-making. However, this argument ignores the fact that EPC states could have unilaterally recognised FYROM as the Republic of Macedonia. That they did not proceed to such unilateral and veto-bypassing actions, is probably testimony to the potential importance of the principle of solidarity.[17]

Thus, it can be concluded that the principle of solidarity constitutes a noteworthy parameter in understanding EPC; and viewing EPC as an international regime allows this principle to become part of the analysis of EPC actions. Despite its potential importance though, it is not being argued that solidarity supersedes entirely considerations of national interest. Nor is there an implicit recommendation that EPC member states should rely exclusively or even primarily on this principle.

As regards EPC's principles of information and confidentiality, they were generally honoured. There were few leaks, and at least Greek decision-makers were mostly satisfied with the degree of information that they received.[18] Characteristically, they were largely aware of the contents of the O'Neil Report, prior to its official presentation and publication.

Attention must also be given to Papaconstantinou's comments on the importance of the principle of parallel membership between the Community and EPC. According to the former Foreign Minister, this principle allowed his country to have 'other wings' in its dispute with FYROM.[19] This is why Papaconstantinou considers Karamanlis (who was almost solely responsible for Greece's accession to the Community), together with Eleftherios Venizelos, as the greatest Greek statesmen of the Twentieth Century.

Turning to the examination of EPC's norm of 'diluted' intergovernmentalism, it must be stressed that intergovernmental bodies were responsible for almost all important discussions and decisions. For example, it was the Council of Foreign Ministers that decided on 16 December 1991 the consequential guidelines for the recognition of the former Yugoslav republics, while the European Council concluded the negotiations and reached all final decisions that led to the signing of the Maastricht Treaty, and also issued the crucial Lisbon Declaration. Furthermore, the role exercised by the Presidency must be noted, since the 'Pinheiro Package' and O'Neil's initiative were undertaken by the Portuguese and British Presidencies respectively.

As regards the non-governmental bodies, the European Parliament had a distinct but not particularly consequential role. For instance, it condemned the popular boycott of Danish, Dutch and Italian products, and supported prior to the Lisbon European Council (admittedly somewhat vaguely), the importance that Greece bestowed upon FYROM's name. Although the EP received information and often gave advice, it was never judged as significant in interviews by major decision-makers.[20] Finally, the role of the Commission was limited to implementing decisions regarding the granting of financial aid and the imposition of sanctions.[21] Hence, it can be concluded that on the basis of this case-study, the analysis of EPC's norm of 'diluted' intergovernmentalism that was presented in Chapter 2 holds true.

This book also verifies the crucial importance of EPC's rule of consensus. All decisions were taken unanimously, and although the threat of veto was rarely exercised, such an action was always possible and thus had to be taken into account.[22] This was certainly the case in Edinburgh on 12 December 1992, when Papaconstantinou announced his intention to veto EPC's declaration on Yugoslavia and also threatened to act similarly in future occasions.

Concerning the implications of the rule of consensus, this book does not validate the argument that it leads to decisions representing EPC's lowest common denominator. EPC decisions actually tend to represent, or at least approach, something of a median line among the views of its member states. The 16 December 1991 EPC meeting provides an example. Adherence to the lowest common denominator would not have produced any decision; and although the final outcome was close to representing the German point of view and perceived interests, Greece also managed to gain some important 'concessions,' by securing the three conditions that applied to FYROM's recognition.

Another illustration involves the Maastricht Treaty negotiations. Reliance on the lowest common denominator would have either produced paralysis, or a Treaty much less ambitious and comprehensive than the one that was actually signed. The case of Greece is again illustrative. The country's government realised the difficulties for the national economy and society that EMU would have produced. However, the gaining of WEU membership and agreement on the establishment of the Cohesion Fund (goals that were not necessarily shared by all other member states), allowed the endorsement of the TEU's final draft.

It could perhaps be argued that given the fact that Greece maintained its hard-line stance on FYROM's name, EPC's decision-making on the unresolved dispute was actually based on the lowest common denominator. Such a conclusion though, would ignore the series of important Greek cooperative actions during the period of June 1991 and mid-January 1992. But even afterwards, examples of cooperation also exist, and include Greece's constant agreement with EPC's condemnation and penalisation of Serbia, the recognition of Bosnia and to a more limited extent the dual name formula proposal. The existence and evaluation of this entire cooperative record firmly tilts the balance towards the median line approach.

Concerning EPC's decision-making procedures, this book confirms previous practices but also reveals certain innovations. EPC issued (as usual), numerous declarations on every aspect of the war in Yugoslavia. Conference diplomacy was also practised: examples are provided by the August 1992 London Conference on the war in Yugoslavia and the Hague Peace Conference chaired by Lord Carrington.

EPC though was not limited to the practice of declaratory and conference diplomacy, since on several occasions various other tools were utilised. Thus, in attempting to reach a solution, EPC member states sent observers to monitor cease-fires, imposed an arms and oil embargo on Yugoslavia, as well as additional sanctions to the non-cooperating (with EPC), Yugoslav republics.

An innovative decision-making procedure included the establishment of the Arbitration Commission, which was comprised by a panel of judges and was responsible for addressing legal issues arising from the dissolution of Yugoslavia. The Presidency-backed initiatives that produced the O'Neil Report and the 'Pinheiro Package' also represent important decision-making procedures. Their goal was to find a solution to the dispute between Greece and FYROM through a series of diplomatic negotiations and meetings in the two countries. Hence, it can be concluded that EPC's decision-making procedures are plentiful and at times even innovative. However, their potential effectiveness is restricted by EPC's scope.

The scope of EPC proved broad enough to cover all foreign policy issues, as well as the economic and political aspects of security. Such issues included the recognition of new republics, and the imposition of sanctions during the war in Yugoslavia. EPC's scope clearly did not include the military aspects of security, and subsequently the possibility of an effective military intervention in Yugoslavia was never entertained or threatened. The inability to pursue such actions significantly reduced EPC's strength and effectiveness; and together with the rule of consensus, they potentially preclude the pursuit of a coherent and influential EPC foreign policy.

Thus, on the basis of this book it can be concluded that the regimes approach is sufficiently comprehensive to incorporate into its analysis all the EPC actions that were described in the previous chapters. Perhaps most importantly, viewing EPC as a regime and 'dissecting' it into its principles, norms, rules, decision-making procedures, organisational form and scope, can allow the application of institutionalism to a series of events (given of course the satisfaction of the theory's conditional nature).[23] As this study demonstrated, EPC did operate as a regime and hence the institutionalist analysis proved of particular relevance, especially for the period of June 1991-January 1992. However, despite the advantages of this approach, additional empirical research is required in order to reach more comprehensive and sophisticated theoretical conclusions.

## C. Lessons on the Conduct of Greek Foreign Policy

The analysis of Greece's actions towards former Yugoslavia that was contained in this book contributes to the understanding of this turbulent period, and furthermore leads to some important lessons concerning the conduct of Greek foreign policy. More specifically, this study examined in great detail the series of Greek cooperative decisions (often contrary to perceived national interests), that included full cooperation within EPC and a flexible, moderate stance towards FYROM during the period of June 1991 to mid-January 1992. These actions are either completely ignored or not sufficiently emphasised (and certainly not analysed) in the existing literature.[24]

In explaining this cooperative record, an original analysis of the circumstances and ways under which EPC influenced Greek foreign policy was presented. It was shown how EPC created strong incentives eliciting cooperation through high issue density, issue linkages, side payments, and also by institutionalising reciprocity and ultimately making reputational concerns more acute. This institutionalist explanation demonstrating EPC's potential cooperative effects is completely lacking from all the standard works on Greek foreign policy-making, and even from more specialised studies of the interplay between EPC and Greece.[25]

It must also be stressed that during the period when politics of cooperation were practised, a clear hierarchy of foreign policy goals existed and was effectively pursued. WEU membership was of the utmost importance because it was linked to Greece's most significant security threat, emanating from Turkey.[26] The hope was to receive additional security guarantees and possibly assistance in the instance of a conflict with the neighbouring state. The economic aspects of foreign policy were also not neglected, since compensation for damages to the national economy due to the war in Yugoslavia were sought. At the same time, there was a determined effort aiming at the creation of the Cohesion Fund which would lead to substantial monetary allocations for Greece.

Certain conclusions must also be deduced from the period when politics of non-cooperation and confrontation were pursued. Perhaps of the greatest significance was that a price was ultimately paid by Greek diplomacy. Thus, as was previously explained, the importance of the cherished goal of WEU membership was substantially diminished as a result of the 19 June 1992 Petersberg Declaration which effectively suspended the WEU's Article V in case of a conflict between Greece and Turkey.

Furthermore, there can be no doubt that Greece's reputation within EPC lay in tatters, a development that probably contributed to the fact that there was no final and favourable for Greece resolution of its dispute with FYROM within EPC. The failure to reach a satisfying EPC agreement may constitute the ultimate price that Greece paid for its confrontational stance.

On the basis of the account of the Greek politics of confrontation, evidence is also found in support of the view according to which:

> Greek foreign policy can be properly be accounted for...by seriously taking into consideration three factors: public opinion, the role of personality and the interplay between personalities and society/public opinion.[27]

Thus, this study demonstrated that popular opinion and actions often proved of crucial significance. Consequential events such as the Thessaloniki and Athens demonstrations, the boycott of Italian, Danish and Italian products, as well as the consistent popular approval of a hard-line non-negotiable position on the name issue, can firmly be ascribed to this category.

The mass demonstrations and popular feelings and the ways in which they influence Greek foreign policy, deserve some additional attention. First of all, it must be stressed that such occurrences have not been rare or unusual in modern Greek history. For example, in a major new study Yannis Yanoulopoulos has shown that passions and mass demonstrations affected negatively Greek foreign policy between the years 1897 and 1922.[28] This period was especially traumatic and tumultuous since it included the First World War, the two Balkan Wars, the Asia Minor Campaign and the subsequent '1922 Catastrophe.'[29] In the coming decades, the various developments and vicissitudes of the Cyprus Issue were invariably linked to demonstrations, always expressing feelings of nationalism, and usually limiting the necessary flexibility that is required for the effective pursuit of diplomacy.[30]

Despite the existence of this historical record, any lessons from the interplay between popular passions and the usually not positive results for Greek foreign policy, seem to had been forgotten by the time that the latest phase of the Macedonian Question erupted. There are several reasons for this development. First, since 1967 almost no major demonstrations linked exclusively to foreign policy issues had taken place in Greece. It thus perhaps appeared plausible that such practices belonged firmly to the past. Furthermore, the Cold War had in effect 'frozen' history (and borders) in the Balkan Peninsula. The Macedonian Question in particular seemed to many of mere historical relevance, unable to mobilise passions or elicit strong opinions.[31] Finally, any attempt to confront or criticise the expression of popular passions linked to national issues or issues of identity was always bound to be a delicate undertaking, promising various political and personal costs. Perhaps this also explains the almost extraordinary Greek scholarly neglect to study adequately such episodes.

This book however offers some lessons concerning the role of popular passions and actions in the making of Greek foreign policy. Perhaps most importantly, and given the history of the modern Greek state, a major conclusion is that an outburst of popular feelings is always possible, even if they have remained dormant for decades.

Secondly, what makes popular passions especially potent and hence influential for Greek foreign policy, is that they are related to historical traumas, important national issues and matters of identity. Furthermore, popular opinions are expressed or encouraged by the Church, at least some major politician and political parties, the mass media and several intellectuals.[32] They thus receive respectability, legitimacy and ultimately become more important.

As regards the Thessaloniki demonstration that has been analysed for the first time to such an extent in this book, it must be pointed out that it was a moving event, as well as a huge organisational success that proved to the world that the Greek people were concerned about FYROM's name and policies.[33] However, in terms of foreign policy-making, Mitsotakis should have followed the decision to hold the demonstration and its implementation more closely. Once the decision was taken, there were three possible outcomes, all potentially consequential. The demonstration's failure would have undermined the government's negotiating power, since it would have shown the lack of interest of the people on this issue. On the other hand, a successful demonstration without, or at least with a vaguely worded resolution, would have had in a sense defeated and ridiculed its purpose, rendering all organisational efforts essentially aimless. The final possibility, a successful demonstration with a resolution advocating a specific policy stance is what actually took place; and it produced substantial pressure that eventually helped the adoption of a non-negotiable restrictive position on FYROM's name.

Hence a further lesson can be deduced. Unless there is absolute certainty about specific goals and strategy, the holding of mass demonstrations must be viewed with caution. Encouraging or orchestrating the expression of popular passions can cause events to get out of control. Self-entrapment, the simplification of foreign policy dilemmas and the demonisation of opponents may then become real dangers. Hence efforts by a country's political leadership must be made in order to avoid what Yanoulopoulos has called 'our noble [self] blindness.'[34]

Turning to the interplay between political personalities and public opinion, as was explained previously in detail it was also highly consequential. For example, it ultimately determined the decision of the 13 April 1992 Second Council of the Political Leaders, as well as the Greek government's subsequent inability and unwillingness to alter the official position on the name issue.

At this point, it should be stressed that a foreign policy that is even partly based on popular passions, strong personalities and their interplay will almost certainly be emotional, erratic and prone to crises.[35]

An additional danger looms since (as Henry Kissinger has cautioned):

> The public does not in the long run respect leaders who mirror its own insecurities or see only the symptoms of crises rather than the long-term trends. The role of the leader is to assume the burden of acting on the basis of a confidence in his own assessment of the direction of events and how they can be influenced. Failing that, crises will multiply, which is another way of saying that a leader has lost control over events.[36]

As regards the cast of characters of this study, it can be argued that it featured some impressive personalities, whose actions often proved fateful. Sophocles has written that 'the exercise of power reveals a man's soul' and equipped with this penetrating observation, certain comments will be made about the major protagonists

For the President of the Hellenic Republic, it can be concluded that he was impeccable in carrying out his duties.[37] Hailing from Macedonia and having lived through most of this century's momentous events in the region,

Karamanlis had an 'acute personal problem' when it came to Greece's dispute with FYROM.[38] The President attempted to utilise his international reputation and prestige by sending a series of letters to the leaders of various states, though it was rather unfortunate for Greece that health problems prevented him from pursuing personal diplomacy by visiting other countries. As his close aide Mr Moliviatis commented, there is a difference between 'letters and personal contacts.'[39]

Despite his political affiliation, Karamanlis never pursued partisan goals. For example, he allowed and chaired meetings of the Council of the Political Leaders only after having secured their unanimous agreement, and not because of pressure emanating from various other sources. Greece's President took his constitutional role and powers seriously, and by successfully managing to stay above the partisan fray, ensured that his reputation, prestige and historical legacy remain unscathed from his country's entanglement with FYROM. However, the President's powers are severely restricted by the constitution, and hence although Karamanlis' influence on events was overall positive, its impact was relatively limited.

Unlike Karamanlis, Papandreou was in charge of a major party, and had to pursue a more partisan role. He believed that Mitsotakis' policies towards former Yugoslavia and FYROM were at best amateurish, and accused the government for lacking a clear, coherent and long-term vision of Greece's post-Cold War foreign policy goals in the region.[40] At the same time, the popular concerns and passions over FYROM's name were undoubtedly appreciated by the socialist leader. Having always placed importance on FYROM's propaganda and irredentist claims, Papandreou also realised the domestic political importance and possible long-term regional implications of FYROM's name.[41]

Given Papandreou's analysis, an endorsement of Mitsotakis' actions would have been tantamount to accepting a dangerous incompetence, while to ignore popular passions would have probably invited political annihilation, and would have certainly gone against his populist tendencies.[42] Hence, after February 1992 PASOK's leader completely abandoned his stance of relative restraint, flexibility and moderation, adopted a hard-line position on the name issue, and always criticised harshly even minor Greek cooperative actions, occasionally utilising demagogic language and rhetoric. Although it seems that he believed in the positions that he was advocating, the style and manner of his opposition were not always constructive and helpful to his country's foreign policy-making.[43]

Contrary to Papandreou, Papaconstantinou aimed at shifting the nature and tone of his Greece's foreign policy. A pragmatist, and one of the few

Greek politicians with a deep knowledge of the Macedonian Question, he immediately abandoned the emphasis on ancient history. Lacking any further political ambition, his goal was to reach a solution within EPC.[44] Domestic and partisan politics precluded any such development, and Papaconstantinou was even reduced to threatening to veto an EPC decision on Yugoslavia. His political gifts and experience were better demonstrated during FYROM's subsequent attempt for UN recognition. It was an epic battle, and contrary to expectations Greece managed to avoid defeat.[45]

Mitsotakis who is one of the most experienced and controversial Greek politicians, was ultimately responsible for the foreign policy pursued by his country towards former Yugoslavia and FYROM.[46] Being friends with many of the world's most important statesmen, he became acutely aware of what he considered to be the ruining of Greece's international reputation; and he also agonised about the relative neglect of vital national interests.

The Prime Minister's actions exhibit pragmatism, as well as a sharp grasp of the problems at the international level. Above all, Mitsotakis desired an honourable and lasting solution to the dispute with FYROM, and most of his efforts aimed at achieving this goal. Characteristically, he used the outcome of his finest hour at Lisbon on 26-27 June 1992, in order to secure a compromise on the basis of the dual name formula.

Mitsotakis found himself in a truly unenviable position. Having a slim Parliamentary majority that was constantly threatened by Samaras and his allies, it was almost impossible for him to reach a compromise and avoid the devastating political consequences associated with such a decision. Furthermore, it was possible that any compromise would have been overturned by the subsequent government.

Whereas Mitsotakis pursued a solution, Samaras pursued victory. The young Foreign Minister probably felt betrayed and politically exposed, when he realised that the position on FYROM's name that was included in the 17 January 1992 letter to his EPC counterparts on FYROM's name was negotiable. For Samaras, adherence to this position was not merely a matter of political expediency—in his mind, it probably became a matter of conscience. The realisation of this development is essential in order to comprehend his subsequent actions. Thus, in the pursuit of a non-negotiable restrictive position on FYROM's name, Samaras was willing to encourage or accept manifestations of popular emotions, pressure and attack his government, ignore Greece's reputational costs, propose tough measures against FYROM, and even damage his political career. His approach to politics can only be characterised as passionate.

There is an indication after conducting the interviews for this book that all the major decision-makers had good intentions. However, these do not suffice for the exercise of successful statesmanship. To quote a German proverb: 'The road to Hell is paved with good intentions.'[47] At the very least, a hierarchy of threats, dangers and priorities must be established. Such an evaluation must be made on the basis of pragmatism, information and rational thinking, not emotions. Issues that rank low must not necessarily be completely ignored or abandoned. Nevertheless, an attempt must be made to allocate limited resources on the basis of a country's true needs. Prestige, reputation and funds are too scarce and precious to be squandered away.

In the dispute with FYROM, and especially after January 1992, Greek decision-makers should have kept under consideration that at least in the short-term, the new republic could not have posed a military threat. The fact that Turkey constituted the greatest security threat to their country, should have dictated a policy bestowing importance at least equal to FYROM, to the neighbouring large and powerful republic. Statesmen must ultimately pursue and safeguard their nation's most important and long-term interests.

These observations do not intend to suggest that Greece did not have valid grievances against FYROM; nor is there an implicit attempt to devalue the importance of the issue of the republic's name. Nevertheless, the combination of the desire to maintain FYROM's territorial integrity, the young republic's (at least short-term) military impotence, and the more serious threat emanating from Turkey, suggest that Greece could have perhaps pursued a more confident strategy towards FYROM. Compromise on the name issue should not have been a prerequisite under any circumstances. The strengthening of bilateral economic relations though, would have probably constituted an integral part of such a strategy, especially given Greece's comparative advantages and larger economy.

A more successful strategy towards FYROM would have also avoided the dangers of largely conflating foreign policy with domestic and partisan politics. Such a conflation has often produced negative and occasionally catastrophic outcomes in modern Greek history.[48] In a democratic society, foreign policy must be conducted in a way that addresses the concerns, interests and perhaps even passions of a country's citizens. But foreign policy must not be conducted directly by the citizens. This is why they elect governments, fund Ministries of Foreign Affairs and train diplomats. Domestic, partisan and personal political ambitions and considerations must not constrain, limit or hijack the flexibility that is essential to the pursuit of a successful foreign policy. Admittedly, this is a tough and almost impossible balancing act; and it requires statesmanship of the highest order.

For a variety of reasons, the Greek government and political parties failed to pursue statesmanship of the highest order during the period covered in this book. The result was defeat—at least for the time being. In the Balkans there is 'no burial of dead ideas.'[49] The Macedonian Question will probably resurface in the future, perhaps with new complications and parameters, possibly with a different intensity, certainly with new protagonists. Bismarck once remarked that 'fools learn from experience; wise men learn from the experience of others.' Hence, future statesmen must study the experience and mistakes of their predecessors, in order to avoid repeating them. The complexity and limits of decision-making at the European level, as well as the perils of domestic and partisan politics must be fully comprehended and contemplated. It is the author's hope that this study will also contribute towards such a painful but necessary exercise.

## Notes

1. For example, as was explained in previous chapters, these politics took place when the war in Bosnia endangered FYROM's territorial integrity and Greece's reputation was reaching an all-time low.
2. These conclusions contradict Smith 1996, who has argued that EPC is 'not used as a forum for making side payments, threatening sanctions against each other, or linking issues into package deals that occurred in other EC policy sectors or during [Inter Governmental Conferences]' (ibid., p. 9).
3. Long, 1995, p. 496.
4. Based on almost all of the interviews that were conducted for this book. Examples of Greek offers of financial aid for FYROM include Samaras' 17 January 1992 letter, the 16 October 1992 European Council meeting, certain aspects of the 'Pinheiro Package,' Mitsotakis' 9 May 1992 letter to Gligorov, Papaconstantinou's 3 November 1992 letter to EPC's Foreign Ministers and Karamanlis' 24 November 1992 letter to his EPC counterparts.
5. This conclusion is based on all EPC documents examined, as well as on most of the interviews that were conducted for this book.
6. See Keohane, 1993b, p. 283.
7. This lesson seems to have been understood well by the US officials who helped broker the Interim Agreement between Greece and FYROM. They paid particular attention to the then Greek Leader of the Opposition and president of New Democracy, Miltiades Evert. During a visit to the US, unusual arrangements were made for him to meet most of Washington's foreign policy establishment. For the impressive list of contacts and account of these meetings, see Tarkas, 1997, p. 492-5. Mr Evert was highly praised for his moderate style of opposition on the dispute with FYROM. It remained unaltered after his US visit.
8. *To Vima*, 29 June 1997, p. G4. In this passage, Gligorov is referring to events prior to the February 1994 imposition of the Greek embargo against FYROM.
9. Interview with Mr Papaconstantinou on 23 December 1996.

CONCLUSIONS    185

10  Interview with Mr Samaras on 24 December 1996.
11  Interview with Mr Mitsotakis on 10 April 1997. The importance of solidarity was also stressed in interviews with Mr Mertzos on 18 December 1996 and Mr Tzounis on 14 April 1997. During a conversation on 9 October 1996, the current Greek Foreign Minister Mr George Papandreou, emphasised to me his firm belief that the principle of solidarity was fully operational in EPC proceedings. Papandreou also provided several examples that were however unrelated to Greece's dispute with FYROM.
12  Interviews with Mr Papaconstantinou on 23 December 1996, Mr Samaras on 24 December 1996, Mr Mitsotakis on 10 April 1997 and Mr Tzounis on 14 April 1997.
13  Interview with Mr Mitsotakis on 10 April 1997.
14  Interviews with (among others), Mr Mertzos on 18 December 1996, Mr Mitsotakis on 10 April 1997, Mr Papaconstantinou on 23 December 1996, Mr Papathemelis on 11 January 1997, Mr Samaras on 24 December 1996 and Mr Tzounis on 14 April 1997.
15  Based on interviews with Mr Mitsotakis on 10 April 1997, Mr Papaconstantinou on 23 December 1997 and Mr Samaras on 24 December 1997.
16  This point was also made during interviews with (among others), Mr Mertzos on 18 December 1996, Mr Papathemelis on 11 January 1997 and Mr Tzounis on 14 April 1997.
17  Interviews with Mr Mitsotakis on 10 April 1997, Mr Papaconstantinou on 23 December 1997 and Mr Samaras on 24 December 1997.
18  Interviews with Mr Papaconstantinou on 23 December 1996, Mr Samaras on 24 December 1996, Mr Mitsotakis on 10 April 1997 and Mr Tzounis on 14 April 1997.
19  Interview with Mr Papaconstantinou on 23 December 1996.
20  Based on most of the interviews that were conducted for this book.
21  The Commission played briefly a more active role during the Spring of 1994, when it brought a case to the ECJ accusing Greece for imposing an embargo against FYROM. The Advocate General's opinion was eventually in favour of Greece. It must be stressed though, that during these developments EPC was of marginal importance to the dispute between Greece and FYROM, whereas the UN constituted the main battlefield. See Tarkas, 1997, p. 434-9 and 483-4.
22  On this point, see Genscher, 1997, p. 803.
23  As regards EPC's organisational form, it can be concluded that the Secretariat essentially played an unimportant role. It was never mentioned as having even minor significance in any of the interviews that were conducted for this book. Specific comments on its insignificance were made during interviews with Mr Papaconstantinou on 10 January 1997 and Mr Tzounis on 14 April 1997.
24  See for example Gow 1997; Kofos 1999; Lygeros, 1992; Papaconstantinou, 1994; Skilakakis, 1995; Tarkas, 1995 and Veremis, 1995.
25  For example see Couloumbis, 1994; Ioakimidis, 1999; Theodoropoulos, 1993; Theodoropoulos et al, 1994; Theodoropoulos, 1995; Tsakaloyannis, 1993; Tsakaloyannis, 1996; Valinakis, 1997; and Veremis and Couloumbis 1997. However, EPC's socialisation effect on Greek foreign policy has been discussed and analysed. See Valinakis, 1993, p. 268.
26  For an analysis of the serious disputes between Greece and Turkey, see Giokaris et al, 1994. The best Greek studies of Greco-Turkish relations are probably Alexandris et al, 1991 and Theodoropoulos, 1988. See also Kouris, 1997.
27  Ioakimidis, 1999, p. 142. However, given the institutionalist explanation of the politics of Greek cooperation, this thesis does not argue that these are the exclusive causes of Greek foreign policy.

28 Yanoulopoulos, 1999.
29 The best study of Greece's entanglement in Asia Minor is probably Llewellyn-Smith, 1998.
30 See Stefanidis, 1999.
31 During an interview on 5 January 1997, Mr Kofos explained that his colleagues in the Greek Ministry of Foreign Affairs joked (and in a sense taunted him) by often reminding him that by dealing with the Macedonian Issue, his professional duties were ultimately of a purely historical nature.
32 On this point, see especially *Eleftherotypia*, 10 September 1999, p. 15.
33 Compare for example the analyses of the Thessaloniki demonstration in Kofos, 1999 and Veremis, 1995.
34 This is the apt title of Yanoulopoulos' study.
35 See ibid., p. 154-9.
36 Kissinger, 1994, p. 136.
37 For another positive interpretation of Karamanlis' statesmanship during this period, see the analysis written by Mr Moliviatis and published in Svolopoulos, 1997, p. 636-8, Vol. 12.
38 Ibid., p. 638. It should be noted that Karamanlis was born in 1907, a subject of the Ottoman Empire.
39 Ibid.
40 These conclusions are partly based on interviews with Mr Papathemelis on 11 January 1997 and Mr Tsohatzopoulos on 3 August 1997.
41 Interview with Mr Tsohatzopoulos on 3 August 1997.
42 Papandreou's populism was clearly demonstrated during the 1980's, a decade during which he held office and dominated politically.
43 Casting some doubt on Papandreou's sincere advocacy of a hard-line position, is his meeting with US official Jim Williams on 23 March 1993. If William's official account is accurate (which is not at all certain since it was based on memory and includes at least one inconsistency), then Papandreou had explained to him that 'a quick solution to the problem—even if it will not be a positive one for Greece—would be better from leaving matters to continue as they currently are' (Tarkas, 1997, p. 118). Despite this comment, PASOK's leader remained publicly committed to an uncompromising restrictive position on FYROM's name. See for example his comments in the Greek Parliament on 27 March 1993 that can be found in ibid., p. 143-7.
44 The fact that Papaconstantinou did not entertain any further political goals is also accepted by those who generally disagree with his views. See Tarkas, 1997, p. 57. Samaras made a similar argument about Papaconstantinou during an interview on 24 December 1996.
45 See Papaconstantinou, 1994, p. 243-416.
46 On Mitsotakis' long and controversial career, see Diamantopoulos, n.d and Dimitrakos, n.d. See also Loule-Theodoraki, 1996. This is a favourable biography, that is primarily based on extensive interviews with Mitsotakis, and is often revealing of his thoughts and soul in a way that was probably unintentional.
47 This is taken from Telloglou, 1996. His study of German foreign policy towards the disintegration of Yugoslavia is tellingly subtitled 'Years of Good Intentions.' It is an excellent study, and it deserves an English translation so that it can reach a wider audience.
48 See Lagakos, 1996.
49 Brailsford, 1906, p. 1.

# TABLES

## TABLE I The Prisoner's Dilemma

|  |  | Column Player | |
|---|---|---|---|
|  |  | Cooperate | Defect |
| Row | Cooperate | R=3, R=3<br><br>Reward for mutual cooperation | S=0, T=5<br><br>Sucker's payoff, and temptation to defect |
| Player | Defect | T=5, S=0<br><br>Temptation to defect and sucker's payoff | P=1, P=1<br><br>Punishment for mutual defection |

Note: The payoffs to the row chooser are listed first.
R stands for reward for mutual cooperation, and is worth 3 points.
T stands for the temptation to defect, and is worth 5 points.
S stands for sucker's payoff, and is worth 0 points.
P stands for punishment for mutual defection, and is worth 1 point.

*Source:* Axelrod, 1984: 8.

## TABLE II FYROM's imports and exports with Greece

in mil.$

| Greece | 1985 | 1986 | 1987 | 1988 | 1989 | 1990 | 1991 | 1992 | 1993 | 1994 | 1995 | 1996 |
|---|---|---|---|---|---|---|---|---|---|---|---|---|
| import in Greece | 27.0 | 18.3 | 41.1 | 37.5 | 35.9 | 49.7 | 62.1 | | 49.6 | 12.7 | 14.1 | 102.4 |
| % of total import | 4.9 | 3.7 | 6.8 | 5.7 | 5.5 | 4.5 | 5.4 | | 4.7 | 1.2 | 1.2 | 8.9 |
| export from Gr. | 37.2 | 21.1 | 17.7 | 27.6 | 36.6 | 97.6 | 85.4 | | 52.2 | 23.5 | 29.2 | 77.4 |
| % of total export | 4.3 | 2.8 | 2.3 | 3.2 | 3.9 | 6.4 | 6.2 | | 4.4 | 1.6 | 1.7 | 4.8 |
| total trade | 64.2 | 39.4 | 58.8 | 65.1 | 72.5 | 143.3 | 147.5 | | 101.8 | 36.2 | 43.3 | 179.8 |
| % in total trade | 4.6 | 3.2 | 4.3 | 4.3 | 4.6 | 5.6 | 5.8 | | 4.5 | 1.4 | 1.5 | 6.5 |
| trade balance | -10.2 | -2.8 | 23.4 | 9.9 | -0.7 | -49.9 | -23.3 | | -2.6 | -10.8 | -15.1 | 25.0 |

*Source:* FYROM's Ministry of Foreign Affairs, Directorate for Economic Relations, 29 September 1997.

# MAPS

MAPS 193

**MAP I    Post-War Yugoslavia (1945-1991)**

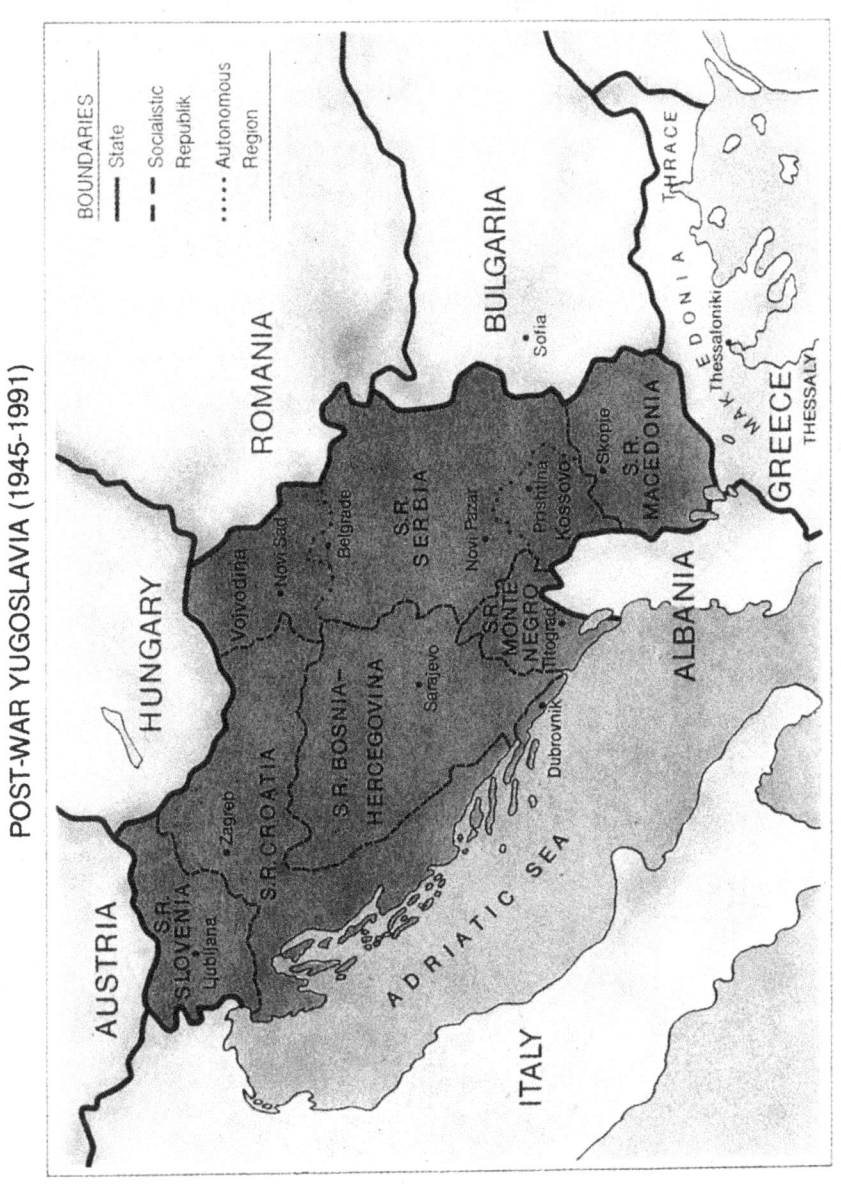

*Source:* Citizen's Movement, 1993: 2.

194  GREECE, EUROPEAN POLITICAL COOPERATION AND THE MACEDONIAN QUESTION

**MAP II  Territorial settlements at the Treaties of San Stephano (1878) and Berlin (1878)**

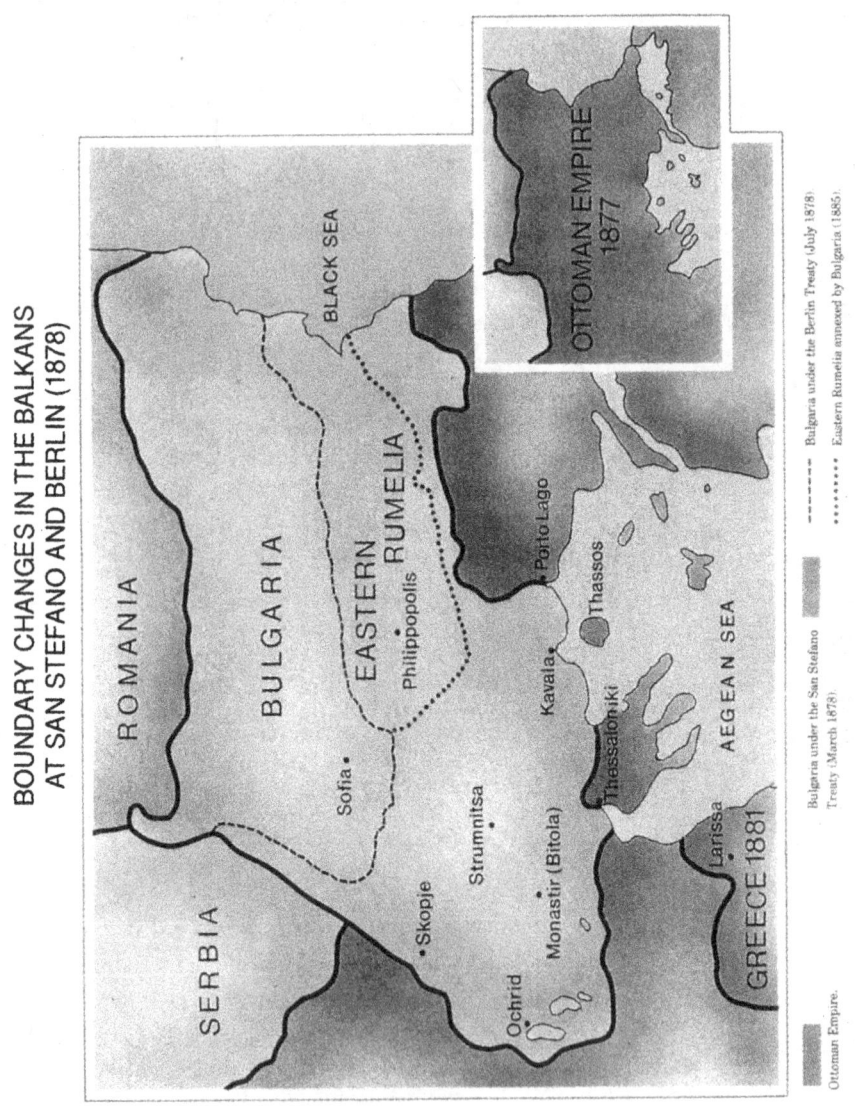

*Source:* Citizen's Movement, 1993: 9.

## MAP III Territorial agreements of the March 1912 alliance between Bulgaria and Serbia

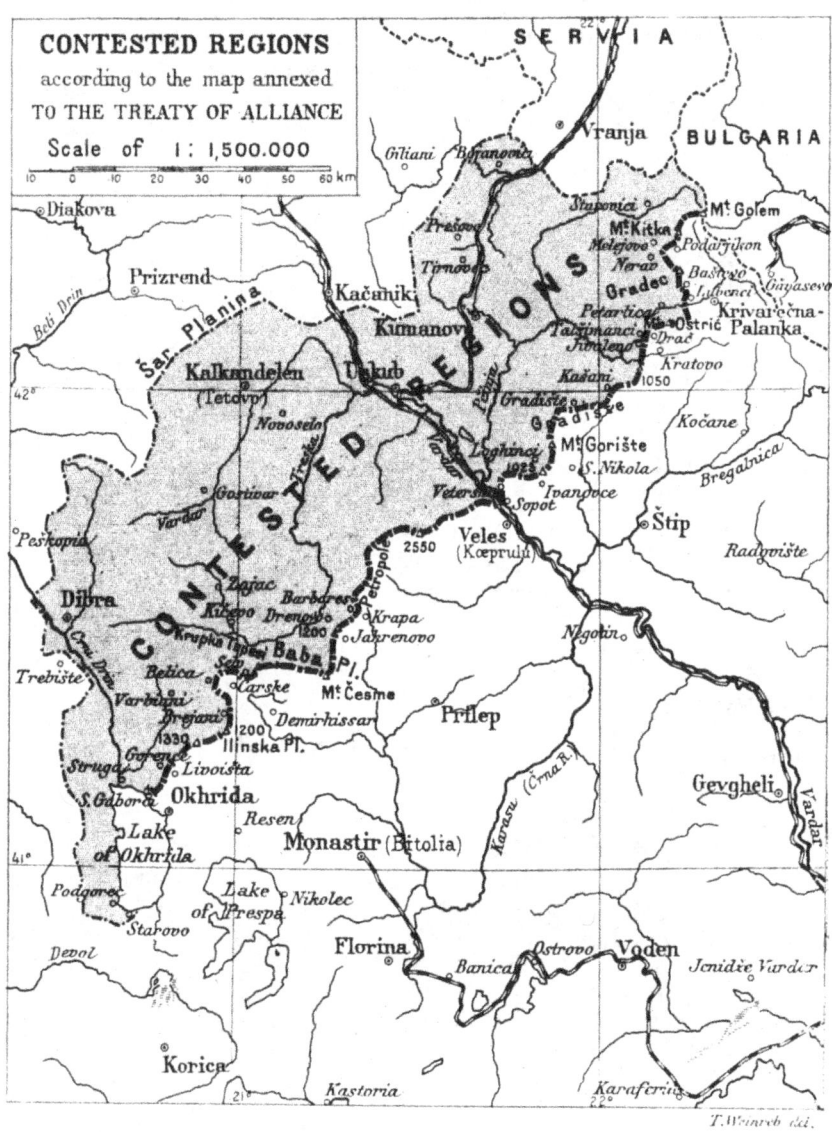

*Source:* Carnegie Foundation, 1914/1993: 45.

**MAP IV  Territorial settlements of the May 1913 London Conference and the August 1913 Treaty of Bucharest**

TERRITORIAL MODIFICATIONS
IN THE BALKANS
1. CONFERENCE OF LONDON   2. TREATY OF BUKAREST

*Source:* Carnegie Foundation, 1914/1993: 70.

MAP V  Bulgaria's conquests during the First World War

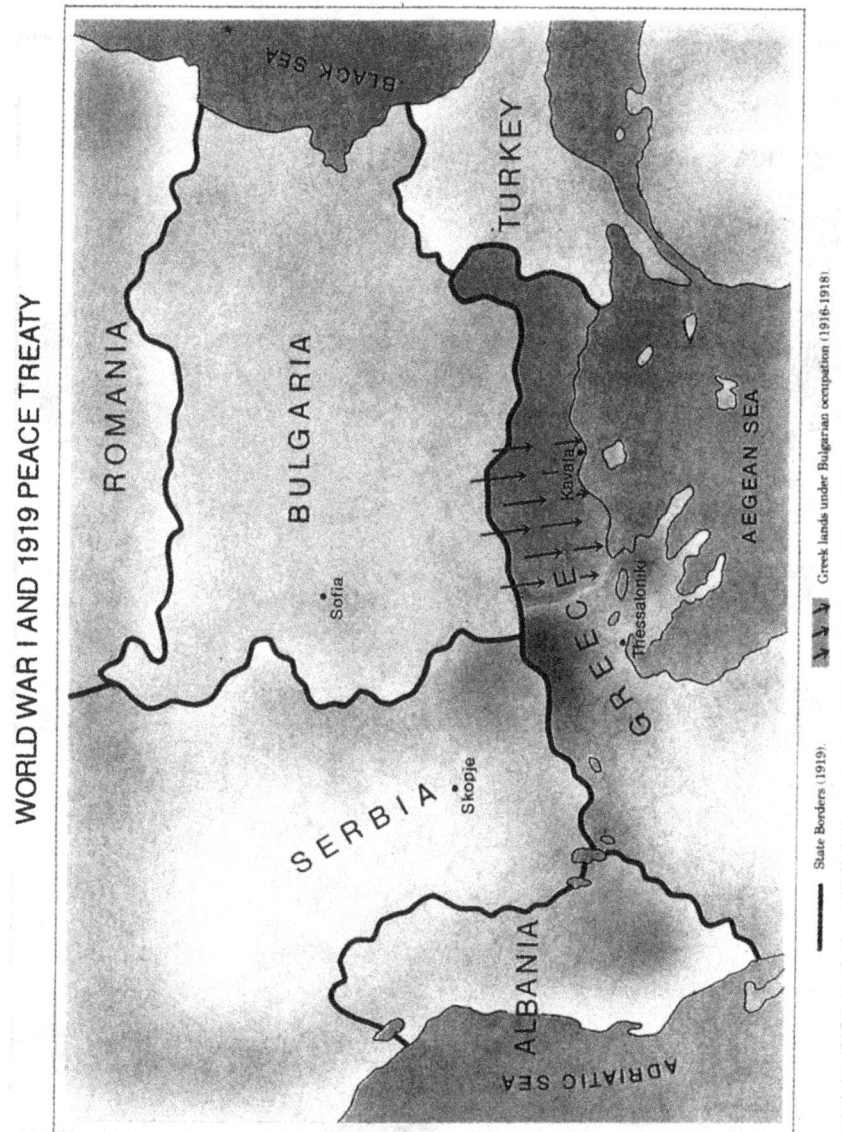

Source: Citizen's Movement, 1993: 10.

**MAP VI** The Balkan States after the First World War and the Treaty of Neuilly

Source: Jelavich, 1983: 123.

## MAP VII Bulgarian conquests during the Second World War

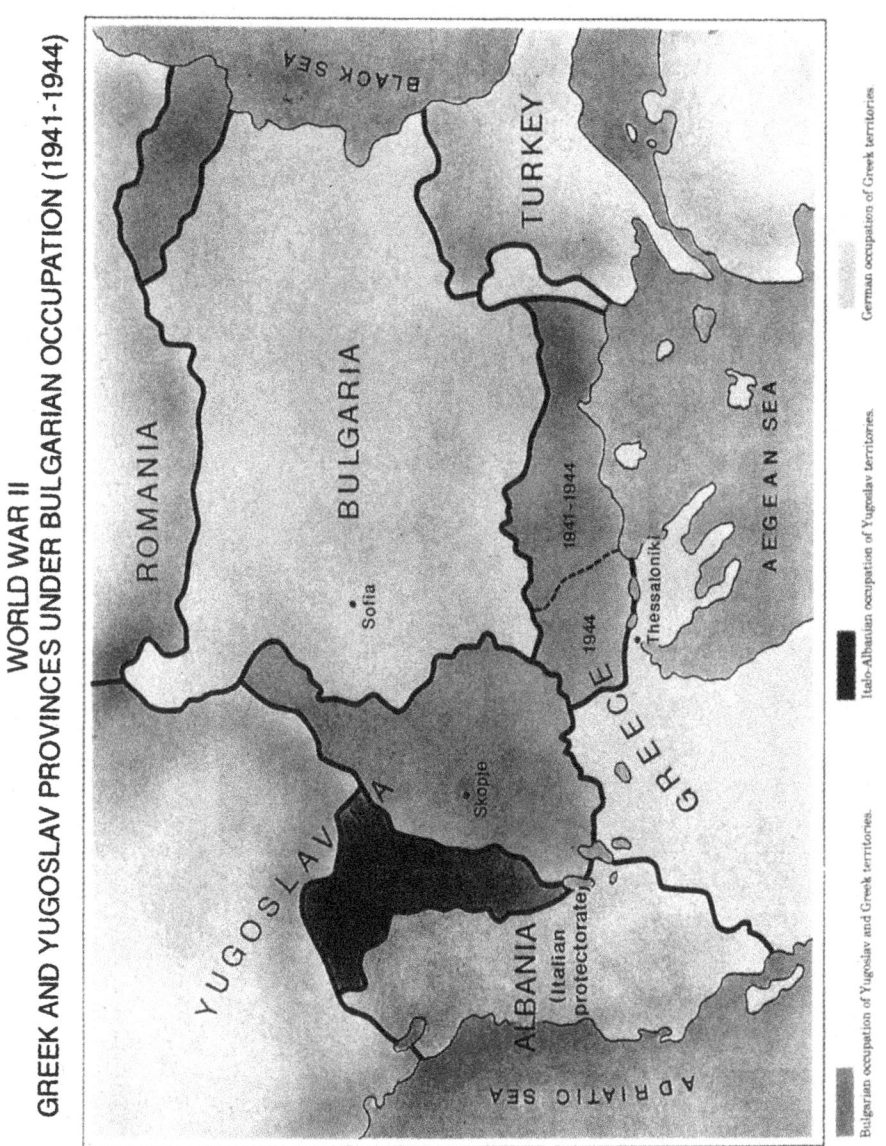

Source: Citizen's Movement, 1992: 11.

MAP VII Brigades' conquests during the Second World War

# APPENDICES

# APPENDIX I

Examples of propaganda practised by FYROM against Greece

**Ia.** Irredentist Map Showing 'Greater Macedonia.'

*Source:* Hellenic Foundation For Defense and Foreign Policy, 1993: 15.

**Ib.** Examples of propaganda Implying territorial threats against Greece

VMRO electoral poster (November 1990) portrays all Macedonian regions as a unified state. The poster is adorned with the Ancient Macedonian dynasty emblem (Vergina Sun). Text on map reads: "Its fate is in your hands" (i.e. the fate of a United Macedonia is in the hands of the voters of the Former Yugoslav Republic of Macedonia).

*Attachment 5*

Car sticker on sale in Skopje kiosks, depicting all three Macedonian regions as a unified Macedonian state.

*Source:* Hellenic Foundation For Defense and Foreign Policy, 1993: 13.

APPENDICES  205

**Ic.** Propaganda map published in a FYROM schoolbook

*Fig. 13*

**"Foreign propaganda in Macedonia"**

The picture speaks for itself. The students of this class are taught that Greece, Bulgaria and Serbia had predatory intentions towards Macedonia. It is nowhere mentioned that these states were struggling to free their subjugated brothers in Macedonia and the other Christian provinces of the Ottoman Empire.
(*Grade 9 History, general stream,* Skopje 1992, page 109).

*Source:* Kofos, 1994a: 28.

**Id.** Calendar depicting the statue of Alexander the Great in Thessaloniki. The words: 'Alexander, Macedonian, Thessaloniki' (in the Cyrillic alphabet) are falsely written on its base

*Source:* Papaconstantinou, 1992: 118.

# APPENDIX II

Letter that Greece's Foreign Minister Antonis Samaras sent to his EPC counterparts on 17 January 1992. The official English translation of this letter is published here for the first time.

THE MINISTER FOR FOREIGN AFFAIRS

Athens, 17 January 1992

Dear Colleague,

You will recall that on Friday, 10 January, we decided that I will present to you in our next meeting the position of my Government concerning the petition for recognition of the Republic of Skopje. And, indeed, I am committed to do so. However, I strongly feel I should provide you at this moment with a written preliminary analysis, prior to that meeting. This has become imperative, especially in the light of the advice of the Arbitration Commission and Bulgaria's premature and unwarranted recognition of the Republic of Skopje.

Let me immediately indicate that I find it impossible to comprehend the fact that, as the Arbitration Commission's report itself indicates, all of its conclusions on "Macedonia" were drawn from data or evidence provided solely by Skopje. (Declaration of the Skopje Assembly, letter of Skopje's Minister of Foreign Affairs, Skopje's response to the Commission's questionnaire, results of the Skopje referendum, the Skopje Constitution, etc). Documentation and objections against the recognition raised by ethnic Albanians, Serbs and Montenegrins, constituting 30-35 per cent of the total population of that Republic, were ignored. Similarly, Greek reservations based on the 16 December 1991, E.C. Ministerial decision, were not taken into consideration. Futhermore, the Arbitration Commission went on to pass judgement on a major political issue -the denomination of the Republic- without substantiating its view, either on legal or on political grounds.

The announcement of this advice, although in no way binding to us Twelve, had an immediate negative impact on the region. Bulgaria sought to capitalize on the opportunity offered. Despite assurances given directly to me by the Bulgarian Foreign Minister just a day prior to the publication of the Badinter report, Sofia rushed to recognize Skopje. It even rushed to recognize Bosnia-Herzegovina, something that was rejected even by the Arbitration Commission because of inherent dangers in premature action.

THE MINISTER FOR FOREIGN AFFAIRS

I must make clear to all colleagues that an immediate threat for the spreading of the conflict to the southern Balkan region has already emerged. Old territorial issues and sensitivities seem to revive. A challenge to the external frontiers of the entire region is already present. There exist, unfortunately, political forces in the neighbourhood of the Skopje Republic which dream today for new territories for their respective motherlands. In this context, if Bulgaria, by its initiative to extend recognition, hopes to lure Skopje into a special bilateral arrangement, the Yugoslav crisis could develop into an all Balkan confrontation. Obviously, the same holds true for other countries geographically close to the region.

The statement of the Presidency, on 15 January 1992, according to which the Community and its member-states have decided to recognize only Slovenia and Croatia, since "there are still important matters to be addressed" for the cases of Bosnia-Herzegovina and Skopje, is certainly a balancing force on which we must build the solution of the existing problems.

In anticipation of our February meeting and in order to facilitate a better understanding of the complex political Macedonian issue, I would like to first invite your attention to the following observations :

1. <u>The Macedonian issue today can only be understood if the history of its development is kept clearly in mind</u>.

The Macedonian issue was reactivated when Marshal Tito set up in 1945 the "People's Republic of Macedonia". It was a political move fitting the Yugoslav leader's hegemonistic plans at the time. The Skopje federative republic was seen as the nucleus -or Piedmont- for the annexation of the adjoining Macedonian provinces of Greece and Bulgaria. I am sure you are well aware that Tito, with Stalin's help, succeeded in forcing the Bulgarian Government of G.Dimitrov to agree to cede Bulgarian Macedonia to Yugoslavia (1947). At the same time, Tito extended his support to the Communist forces in Greece during the Greek civil war, in anticipation of acquiring control of Greek Macedonian provinces. Both plans failed. When Stalin evicted Yugoslavia from the Cominform (1948), Bulgaria stepped back from the Tito-Dimitrov agreement and assumed for a number of years an agressive role on the Macedonian issue, spear-heading Soviet expansionism. As for Greece, with the termination of the Greek civil war (1949), the immediate annexation of Greek Macedonia to Yugoslavia was avoided.

Subsequently, and despite the normalization of Greek-Yugoslav relations (1951), Skopje continued for 40 years to undermine Greek sovereignty over Greek Macedonia. The Macedonian provinces of Greece and Bulgaria were viewed "as not yet liberated", while the "People's Republic of Macedonia", projected itself as the only "free part" of Macedonia, and the "Piedmont" for the unification of all Macedonian regions.

THE MINISTER FOR FOREIGN AFFAIRS

During the same 40-year period and in order to best serve its expansionist plans, Skopje attempted to appropriate and monopolize the Macedonian name. To achieve this goal, Skopje found it necessary to usurp Greek historical and cultural heritage in Macedonia from antiquity to the present. Thus, Alexander the Great and Aristotle have been added to the Skopjan pantheon! So have the Greek apostles to the Slavs, Cyril and Methodius, simply because they were born in Thessaloniki! Even the victories of the Greek army during the 1940-41 war were attributed to the so-called "Macedonians" of Skopje, only because a Greek army division was named Macedonia after the name of the Greek province! Thessaloniki, whose culture, language and traditions have been Greek for 2300 years, is projected as the capital of the future "united Macedonian state".

Evidently, by manipulating a geographical term (Macedonia), Skopje expansionists sought to convert this term into an ethnic name for a Slav nation. In the process, they obviously attempted to deny the Greek people their legitimate right to a major part of their cultural identity.

Thus, for 45 years, the Macedonian name became the major vehicle for territorial and cultural expansionism encroaching upon Greek territory. Because of the continued use and abuse by Skopje of the hellenic civilization and traditions in order to promote expansionist aims, any further use of the Macedonian name by an independent state would ipso facto imply territorial claims against Greece.

2. In view of the historic implication and the nationalist forces behind this issue, the recognition of a Yugoslav Republic as an independent "Republic of Macedonia" would be a constant threat to peace and security in South Eastern Europe now and for many years to come.

As I have explained, Bulgaria claims historical and kin ties with the Skopje region and its slavonic part of the population and has already proceeded to recognize the independence of the Republic. Moreover, very recently, recriminations between Bulgaria and Serbia were exchanged and mutual accusations for important troop movements were also hurled at each other. We all, of course, know that the area of the Republic of Skopje has historically always been the target of conflicting interests, due to its mosaic of different nationalities (Albanians, Bulgarians, Serbs, Turks, Greeks, Roma etc). Unfortunately, 19th century images of "Greater Bulgaria", "Greater Serbia" and "Greater Albania" are still haunting today the region of Skopje, awaiting the signal of its "independence" to stake their claims...

More onimous for the future is the prospect of a Bulgarian national revival among Skopje's Slav population. For 45 years Bulgarian ethnicity has been outlawed and its supporters persecuted. A clash between "Macedonists" and pro-Bulgarians will become inevitable, particularly if Sofia emerges in the

THE MINISTER FOR FORGIGN AFFAIRS

role of a "big brother" for the young Republic. Allow me, for instance, to refer to the two VMRO parties that operate under the same name in both Skopje and Sofia. In fact, the VMRO is presently the majority party in the Skopje parliament, while their active Bulgarian counterpart presently operates as a nationalist Bulgaro-"Macedonian" movement. Both VMROs are committed to extremist nationalist goals; goals aiming at territorial expansionism. May I also remind you that in a very recent NATO document the VMRO Skopje party was qualified as a "terrorist" organization.

A more serious and immediate complication could develop as a result of inter-ethnic conflicts. Already, the ethnic Albanians, comprising almost a third of the total population of the Republic, have registered their opposition to the Skopje Government by demanding self-rule. Their recent plebiscite, although conducted against Government objections and arbitrary police interventions, was a clear sign of troubles to come.

It is obvious that in the long run Skopje, an economically non-viable and ethnically antagonistic entity, surrounded by competing "suitors" and "protectors", could be open to manipulations by stronger powers. The possibility of opening a Pandora's box of Balkan intrigues, guerilla warfare and armed conflict involving neighbouring states, in addition to inter-ethnic strifes in Skopje itself, could simply ignite the whole Balkan area and become a major destabilization factor for the whole of Europe.

Greece will be directly affected by such developments. On the one hand, the economic and social reverberations of a possible armed conflict will be immediately felt, particularly in northern Greece (tourism, trade, movement of people, political and economic refugees). On the other hand, attempts at changing the external borders of the Skopje Republic will upset balances. The "domino effect" we are experiencing in the case of the Yugoslav Republics, will contaminate neighbouring states, including Greece. Let me remind you that almost 60% of the total Greek exports are exported from northern Greece via Yugoslavia to Central and Western Europe. The consequences would thus be devastating for the Greek economy.

It goes without saying that the problems briefly enumerated above are not new. However, they now acquire a particularly acute character after Skopje's request to become an independent state. If in the past, Skopje's rush actions and propaganda activities have been underaken within the framework of Yugoslavia, one can imagine the kind of dangerous adventures it will embark upon were it to become an independent state.

3. In the interest of avoiding past destabilizing experiences and promoting permanent peace and securuty for the future, <u>the prerequisites for the recognition of the independence of Skopje, as endorsed by the Twelve in the "Declaration on Yugoslavia", must be fully respected.</u> Unfortunately, to this date, the authorities of Skopje have failed to implement these conditions. Indeed:

THE MINISTER FOR FOREIGN AFFAIRS

-They have not offered sufficient guarantees, constitutional or other, to ensure that they will have no terrritorial claims.

-They continue carrying hostile propaganda, even at this critical moment, prior to their recognition.

-They have made no attempt to find a suitable denomination for their future independent Republic.

-Greece has spared so far no effort to find fair and equitable solutions. But, despite Greek observations and suggestions concerning various provisions in the constitution raised directly with the Skopje delegation which visited Athens for talks on the implementation of the E.C. decision on 3 January, there has so far been no constructive response.

As you know, the preamble of Skopje's constitution states that the new Republic rests upon "the statehood-legal traditions of the Krushevo Republic" (1903) and the "historical decisions of the Antifascist Assembly of the People's Liberation of Macedonia" (ASNOM), passed in 1944. Let me explain:

The events of 1903 and 1944 highlighted the attempt by the Slavs of Macedonia to establish respectively an autonomous or an independent Macedonian state. A state which would absorb the whole of Macedonia, including the Macedonian provinces of Greece, Bulgaria, and Albania. Indeed, the Krushevo Manifesto, of 2 August 1903, was an appeal to the people to "come beneath the flag of autonomous Macedonia", while the ASNOM Communist-Titoist Manifesto of 1944, issued also on the 2nd of August for symbolic purposes, proclaimed the "just and unique demand for uniting all the Macedonian people with the right to self-determination". It further stated:" let the struggle of the Macedonian Piedmont inspire you... it alone leads to freedom and union of all Macedonian people... Let the artificial boundaries which separate brother from brother... be swept away".

These references in the preamble make it obvious that territorial irredentism and future expansionism are very much part and parcel of the new Constitution. Such a political model is obviously incompatible with the CSCE spirit and fundamental principles.

This is why we consider that the amendments to articles 3 and 49 of the Constitution are simply meaningless and in any way, not of nature to alter its main philosophy and its basic thrust.

-The Gligorov Government, has been engaged in a worldwide "good-will campaign" to impress on world leaders and public opinion the image of a new Republic dedicated to peace and friendly neighbourly relations. The letters sent by Skopje officials to the Arbitration Commission served a similar purpose. Yet, in practice, hostile propaganda against Greece continues unabated.

For example, Skopje leaders during recent months have publicly spoken about territorial claims against Greece. Allow me to cite just two of them:

THE MINISTER FOR FOREIGN AFFAIRS

- - Vasil Tupurkovski, the Skopje representative to the Yugoslav Presidency, has repeatedly spoken about the unification of all the Macedonian lands. Thus, on 20 January 1991, while on the "Macedonian Heritage" TV program in Toronto, he was asked "if Macedonians should struggle for cultural and spiritual unity rather than territorial unity". Tupurkovski replied: " I think that our national ideal cannot be limited; the territorial unity is also part of it". Also, in December 1990, in a radio interview at Perth (Australia), he said that the "new Macedonian state will have as its primary target, the liberation of the enslaved Macedonians and the unification of the wider Macedonian region".

- - President Kiro Gligorov in an interview to NIN magazine, (Belgrade 1 Feb. 1991) spoke of "segments of the Macedonian people in Serbia, Greece and Bulgaria which were divided and subjugated after the Balkan wars" and revealed that the leading "Macedonian" nationalist parties aim at a "Great Macedonia" and do not hide their intention that " the Macedonian power will redraw the borders of Greece and Serbia"!

Skopje has not ceased referring to Greek Macedonia as "Egejska (Aegean) Makedonija", a term used to imply that the whole of northern Greece is part of a wider Slav territory. Only a few days ago, a conference was organized in Skopje dealing with linguistic questions of "Egejska Makedonija". In fact, "hate literature" continues to appear in publications both in the Republic and abroad. A recent typical example is provided on a 1992 calendar with maps on which Greek along with Bulgarian and Albanian Macedonia are shown as part of "Great Macedonia". Those calendars were mailed in thousands of copies throughout Greece; a clear sign of what one should expect after the recognition of independence.

- As for the denomination, Greece has had the opportunity to analyze in detail to the Skopje delegation why the term "Macedonia", if used in the denomination of the Skopje Republic, is unacceptable as it contains by itself an expansionist notion. Indeed, as I have earlier explained, in order to best serve its expansionist plans, Skopje usurped the Macedonian name and purportedly converted it into an ethnic name for its Slav nation. This becomes all the more brazen, when one takes into acount that the geographical region of Macedonia extends across four borders: in Greece (51%), Bulgaria (9.5%), Albania (0.5%) and Yugoslavia (39%). Thus, the adoption of the Macedonian name for the future Republic carries the clear message that the Republic's jurisdiction extends over the Macedonian provinces of all neighbouring states.

It should not be forgotten, dear Colleague, that the Macedonian name was granted by Tito at a time when Moscow was seeking an exit to the Aegean. It will be an irony if, years after the termination of the Cold War, the community would offer, a posteriori, a historical legitimacy to such claims.

4. Despite all the dangers I believe there is still time to find an equitable solution; one that may open the prospects for regional security and cooperation. Greece is the only neighbouring country which harbours no claims against Skopje. If an understanding is reached on the basis of the E.C. terms

MINISTER FOR FOREIGN AFFAIRS

for recognition, Greece is prepared to help create a regional arrangement to meet the security needs of Skopje, as well as those of its neighbours. Thus, mutual suspicions between Skopje and individual neighbours, as well as between neighbouring countries competing for influence or dominance on Skopje would steadily evaporate.

In addition, Greece could extend to the new Republic special economic privileges, open prospects for an all round economic cooperation, and set in motion the process for a solution to all bilateral issues.

In choosing a name for the new Republic, former administrative denominations of the region could probably provide a logical and acceptable solution. It should be noted that prior to Tito's decision to assign to Skopje the Macedonian name, no such denomination had ever been used in the past, either as a state or as an administrative denomination for that region. It is a denomination that was artificially introduced to advance territorial claims and has no historical or cultural validity.

It is more than obvious that the establishment of good relations between Skopje and Greece, is of paramount importance for both the new Republic and the whole Balkan region. First, it will allow the Skopjan Republic to survive. Secondly, it will deflate the aspirations of other powers at its own expense and will thus create the necessary conditions for peace in this highly sensitive area.

In this light, it is a matter of urgency that partners impress upon the authorities of Skopje the need to implement fully, by deeds rather than meaningless declarations, the E.C. ministerial decision of 16 December and to desist from any initiatives that may inflame the region.

If and when Skopje decides to abide by the E.C. terms for the recognition of its independence, I suggest that, at that time, an agreement be concluded between the E.C. and Skopje providing guarantees for the proper implementation of the terms specified by the Community.

Dear Colleague,

This is certainly not the time to create new problems. It is the time to try and find lasting solutions. I am confident that our proposals will meet with your approval and that the Community amd its member-states will continue to act with the same spirit of solidarity as manifested in Maastricht. After all, it is our common goal to establish peace and security in South-Eastern Europe by eliminating any source of friction or conflict.

Sincerely yours

Andonis C. Samaras

## APPENDIX III

Founding declaration of the Macedonian Committee that was issued on 17 January 1992.

### ΕΜΕΙΣ ΟΙ ΜΑΚΕΔΟΝΕΣ ΔΙΑΚΗΡΥΣΣΟΥΜΕ

Εκπροσωπώντας τις πνευματικές, παραγωγικές, πολιτικές και κοινωνικές δυνάμεις της Θεσσαλονίκης, με αρραγή εθνική ενότητα εν δυνάμει και με μια ψυχή συνήλθαμε σήμερα Παρασκευή 17 Ιανουαρίου 1992 σε Συνέλευση μετά από πρόσκληση της Μακεδονικής Επιτροπής, και αφού εξετάσαμε τα γεγονότα που αναφέρονται στα Βαλκάνια και ιδιαίτερα στη γενέτειρά μας Μακεδονία, διακηρύσσουμε προς κάθε κατεύθυνση τα εξής:

1. Είμαστε, ήμασταν και θα είμαστε Μακεδόνες, δηλαδή Έλληνες, πολύ υπερήφανοι διαιολογημένα για την ανεκτίμητη συνεισφορά των προγόνων μας στον ανθρώπινο πολιτισμό και στον Χριστιανισμό. Η Θεσσαλονίκη μας φέρει επί 2.300 χρόνια το όνομα της αδελφής του Μεγάλου Αλεξάνδρου, ο οποίος επικεφαλής των Πανελλήνων δημιούργησε την πρώτη στον Κόσμο πολιτισμική και πολιτική Κοινότητα των Εθνών, θεμελιωμένη στην ισότητα, στην πνευματική ωριμότητα, στην ελευθερία και στην αδελφωσύνη όλων των Εθνών, χωρίς καμμιά διάκριση - ιδεώδη επίκαιρα παρά ποτέ σήμερα και σταθερούς κατευθυντήριους άξονες της Ευρωπαϊκής Κοινότητας προς την ευρωπαϊκή ενοποίηση. Προς εμάς τους Θεσσαλονικείς, στην ελληνική γλώσσα, απευθύνει τις δύο ομώνυμες επιστολές του ο Απόστολος των Εθνών Παύλος, ο οποίος όχι τυχαία επέλεξε τη Μακεδονία για να θεμελιώσει εδώ την πρώτη στην Ευρώπη Εκκλησία του Σωτήρος Χριστού. Συμπατριώτες μας εξ άλλου Θεσσαλονικείς Έλληνες ήσαν οι δύο Ισαπόστολοι, "Ουράνιοι Προστάτες της Ευρώπης", Άγιοι αδελφοί Κύριλλος και Μεθόδιος, οι οποίοι, ανταποκρινόμενοι σε αγωνιώδες αίτημα, έδωσαν στους Σλαβικούς Λαούς της Ευρώπης το Αλφάβητο, τον Χριστιανισμό και τον Πολιτισμό.

2. Κληρονόμοι μιας τέτοιας εθνικής ελληνικής κληρονομιάς, που αποτελεί κοινό κτήμα της Ευρώπης και ασφαλές θεμέλιο της υπό οικοδομούμενη ευρωπαϊκή ενοποίηση, εμείς οι Μακεδόνες είμαστε αποφασισμένοι και υποχρεωμένοι, όπως έπραξαν με αφειδώλευτες θυσίες και οι πατέρες μας επί γενεές γενεών, να υπερασπισθούμε την εθνική, ιστορική, πολιτισμική και ευρωπαϊκή ταυτότητά μας και αυτό τούτο το πανάρχαιο όνομά μας, που μια μικρή ομάδα σλαβικής καταγωγής στην πολυεθνική γιουγκοσλαβική δημοκρατία των Σκοπίων έχει σφετερισθεί μετά το 1944, το χρησιμοποίησε για την κατάπτηση και προσάρτηση της ελληνικής Μακεδονίας και τώρα επιχειρεί να το επιβάλει διεθνώς.

3. Εμείς οι Μακεδόνες, συνεπώς, αισθανόμαστε τουλάχιστον πικρία όταν διαπιστώνουμε ότι τρίτες χώρες χρησιμοποιούν για δικούς τους λόγους τη Δημοκρατία των Σκοπίων και ότι η νομική γνωμάτευση της Επιτροπής Διαιτησίας υπό την προεδρία Μπαντιντέρ, στηριζόμενη σε κενό γράμμα και σε νεκρό τύπο, συνιστά στην ΕΟΚ να αναγνωρίσει διεθνώς υπό το ψευδώνυμο "Μακεδονία" ένα πολυεθνικό κρατίδιο κατά μήκος των βορείων συνόρων της ελληνικής Μακεδονίας μας. Βεβαίως η απαράγραπτη Ιστορία δεν ξαναγράφεται καθ' υπαγόρευση τρίτων, αλλά αντιθέτως τιμωρεί αμείλικτα. Γι' αυτό όσοι επιχείρησαν να την βιάσουν, όπως π.χ. ο ηγεμονιστής Τίτο, ο φασίστας Μουσσολίνι κι άλλοι όμοιοί τους, δεινά μόνο επεσώρευσαν στους Λαούς τους. Ορατό όσο και τραγικό παράδειγμα η σημερινή κατάσταση στη γειτονική Γιουγκοσλαβία.

Επειδή όμως τα φρικτά δεινά δεν περιορίζονται αποκλειστικά σε όσους τα προκαλούν, ούτε στους δυστυχείς Λαούς τους, αλλά επεκτείνονται ραγδαίως, όπως δίδαξαν δύο Παγκόσμιοι Πόλεμοι με Αρμαγεδώνα την Ευρώπη και όπως σήμερα διδάσκει η κατάρρευση του υπαρκτού σοσιαλισμού και του διεθνούς συστήματός του, γι' αυτό οι ίδιοι κατ' αρχήν Λαοί και πρωτίστως η Ευρωπαϊκή Κοινότητα οφείλουν να προλάβουν σήμερα για να μη θεραπεύουν πολλά δεινοπαθήματα αύριο. Αυτό πράττουμε εμείς ως Έλληνες και έχουμε την ήρεμη βεβαιότητα, ως πολίτες της Ευρώπης ότι αυτό θα πράξει η Κοινότητα για όλους τους ευρωπαϊκούς Λαούς και κατά πρώτα θεμιελιώ επιταγήν της για τους Λαούς της ΕΟΚ. Τούτο συνιστά στοιχειώδη πρόνοια προλήψεως και ενισχύσεως για το ευρωπαϊκό σύστημα ασφαλείας γενικά, αλλά αποτελεί και συμβατική υποχρέωση αλληλεγγύης για την Κοινότητα προς τα μέλη της. Πολύ περισσότερο μάλιστα όταν η Κοινότητα, σε επίπεδο αναπτύξεως των περιφερειών της, έχει συμβληθεί ευθέως και θα εξακολουθεί να συμβάλλεται πολλαπλώς με την ελληνική κοινοτική Περιφέρεια της Μακεδονίας - Ανατολικής, Κεντρικής και Δυτικής.

4. Η Θεσσαλονίκη μας είναι επί δύο τουλάχιστον χιλιάδες συνεχή χρόνια μέχρι και σήμερα η πρωτεύουσα της Μακεδονίας. Υπό τρεις αλληλοδιάδοχες πολυεθνικές Αυτοκρατορίες, Ρωμαϊκή, Βυζαντινή και Οθωμανική, μέχρι την απελευθέρωσή της το 1912, υπήρξε ειρηνική γέφυρα των βαλκανικών Λαών, Κεντρική Πύλη της Ευρώπης στην Ανατολή, γόνιμος στίβος πνευματικών ρευμάτων και πολιτικών ιδεών, πνευματικός φάρος της Βαλκανικής, αλλά ποτέ δεν έχασε τον ελληνικό πολιτιστικό και ιστορικό χαρακτήρα της, ούτε άλλωστε αμφισβητήθηκε αποτελεσματικά η ταυτότητά της. Σήμερα, αναδεικνυόμενη και πάλι σε στρατηγικό οικονομικό σταυροδρόμι των Βαλκανίων, οργανική ήδη πόλη και λιμάνι της Ευρωπαϊκής Κοινότητας και εξ αποστολής ανοικτή σε όλες τις ειρηνικές δραστηριότητες όλων των Λαών, όπως άλλωστε μαρτυρεί και η Διεθνής Έκθεσή της καθ' όλο το έτος και κάθε έτος, αποτελεί, χάρις στα μνημεία της, ένα από τα μεγαλύτερα Ζωντανά Μουσεία της Χριστιανωσύνης,

της χιλιετούς βυζαντινής τέχνης και του ελληνικού πολιτισμού σε άμεση σύνδεση και λειτουργικότητα με το Άγιον Όρος μοναδική στον Κόσμο Μοναστική Πολιτεία της Οικουμενικής Ορθοδοξίας, με την Πέλλα Κοσμοκράτειρα άλλοτε πρωτεύουσα του Μεγάλου Αλεξάνδρου, με την Βεργίνα πρώτη πρωτεύουσα και νεκρόπολη των Μακεδόνων Βασιλέων και με το Δίον Ιερά Πόλη των Μακεδόνων στις υπώρειες του Ολύμπου, μυθική καθέδρα των Δώδεκα Θεών του ελληνικού πανθέου. Είναι, λοιπόν, αδιανόητη για κάθε πολιτισμένο άνθρωπο, ιδιαίτερα Ευρωπαίο, και είναι φύσει αδύνατη ιστορικά η πολιτική απόπειρα να της αφαιρεθεί με μίαν απόφαση - και από ποιούς; - η ζώσα επί χιλιετίες ελληνική ταυτότητά της. Εγκυμονεί όμως σοβαρούς, ορατούς και άμεσους κινδύνους για την σταθερότητα των Βαλκανίων και της Ευρώπης κάθε τέτοια απόπειρα, την οποία εντέλει είμαστε αποφασισμένοι και ικανοί να αντιμετωπίσουμε.

5. Με τέτοιο χαρακτήρα, τέτοιο υπόβαθρο και τέτοιαν αποστολή ειρήνης, συναδελφωσύνης των Λαών και πολιτισμού, η σύγχρονη Θεσσαλονίκη, σημάζουσα τώρα εν ελευθερία στην γεωπολιτική αυτή θέση, εργάσθηκε αποδοτικά και ασφαλώς θα συνεχίσει να εργάζεται για τη συνεργασία, την οικονομική ανάπτυξη, το διεθνές εμπόριο και τελικά τον πολιτισμό όλων των Λαών, κυριώτερα των γειτονικών. Αυτή είναι εξ άλλου η ζωή και η ευτυχία της, που μπορούν ελεύθερα και πρέπει να συμμερισθούν όλοι οι γείτονες. Και αυτό έκαμαν παλαιότερα, αλλά και κατά τα τελευταία χρόνια. Με δεδομένον αυτόν τον εμπράκτως αποδεδειγμένο προορισμό η Θεσσαλονίκη και, από αυτήν την Συμπαρευούσά της, όλη η Ελλάδα πιστεύει ακράδαντα ότι οι επιλογές της ηγεσίας των Σκοπίων και της σημερινής βουλγαρικής κυβερνήσεως, που απηχούν κατά τον επιεικέστερο χαρακτηρισμό έμμονες, αλλά πολύ επικίνδυνες εθνιαστικές προλήψεις και εκρηκτικά κατάλοιπα ενός καταδικασμένου από την ευρωπαϊκή Ιστορία και αποτυχημένου στην πράξη ηγεμονισμού, βλάπτουν εξαιρετικά αυτούς τούτους τους Λαούς τους προς τους οποίους εμείς οι Μακεδόνες απευθυνόμεθα ακόμη μια φορά με δεδηλωμένη εμπράκτως αλληλεγγύη και ειλικρινή φιλία, για να τους υπενθυμίσουμε ό,τι άριστα γνωρίζουν εξ ιδίων: η συνεργασία τους με την Ελλάδα αποτελεί γι' αυτούς μονόδρομο ειρήνης, ασφαλείας, ελευθερίας και προόδου. Το ποτάμι δεν γυρίζει πίσω. Και το μέλλον είναι μπροστά. Απελευθερωθείτε από τους φανατισμούς του μεγαλοϊδεατισμού. Δεν νεκροαναστείνεται ούτε έχει τις υλικές προϋποθέσεις να νεκροαναστηθεί, αλλά μπορεί να σκοτώσει όσα πολλά, ζωτικά και μόνιμα μας ενώνουν στον κοινό δρόμο προς την Ενωμένη Ευρώπη. Και προειδοποιούμε: σκληρόν προς κέντρα λακτίζειν.

Αυτό το γραπτό μήνυμα ειρήνης, ευθύνης και αλληλεγγύης μεταφέρουμε από σήμερα, με όλες τις ενεργές δυνάμεις των φορέων της Θεσσαλονίκης και των χιλιάδων επί μέρους συλλογικών οργάνων πρωτοβαθμίων οργανώσεων, επιχειρήσεων, συνδικάτων, ιδρυμάτων και προσώπων μελών αυτής της σημερινής Συνελεύσεως, απ' ευθείας προς τον βουλγαρικό Λαό, προς τον πολυεθνικό πληθυσμό της Δημοκρατίας των Σκοπίων και προς την Ευρωπαϊκή Κοινότητα και τα μέλη της ευρωπαϊκής οικογενείας. Έκαστος εφ' ω ετάχθη. Και αύριον ο Κόσμος θα είναι ασφαλώς καλύτερος.

6. Τέλος εμείς οι Μακεδόνες απευθυνόμεθα προς την Κυβέρνησή μας και τις ηγεσίες όλων των πολιτικών κομμάτων για να εκφράσουμε την βαθειά ικανοποίησή μας, που είναι και ικανοποίηση ολοκλήρου του ελληνισμού, για την ενότητα και την ανυποχώρητη αποφασιστικότητα με την οποία υπερασπίζονται τα υπέρτατα συμφέροντα του ελληνικού Έθνους, των βαλκανικών Λαών και της Ευρώπης. Το μηνυμά μας προς το Έθνος από τον προκεχωρημένο προμαχώνα της Μακεδονίας μας είναι: ενότητα, νηφαλιότητα και δράση.

Θεσσαλονίκη 17 Ιανουαρίου 1992

Ο Δήμαρχος Θεσσαλονίκης
Κων. Κοσμόπουλος

Αριστοτέλειο Πανεπιστήμιο Θεσσαλονίκης
Ο Πρύτανης
Αντώνης Τρακατέλης

Πανεπιστήμιο Μακεδονίας
Ο Πρύτανης
Γιάννης Τσεκούρας

Εταιρεία Μακεδονικών Σπουδών
Ο Πρόεδρος
Καθηγητής Κων. Βαβούσκος

Ίδρυμα Μελετών Χερσονήσου του Αίμου
Ο Πρόεδρος
Καθηγητής Αντώνιος - Αιμίλιος Ταχιάος

Σωματείο "Οι φίλοι του Μουσείου
του Μακεδονικού Αγώνα"
Ο Πρόεδρος
Δημήτρης Ζάννας

Εμπορικό και Βιομηχανικό Επιμελητήριο
Θεσσαλονίκης
Ο Πρόεδρος
Παντελής Κωνσταντινίδης

Εργατοϋπαλληλικό Κέντρο Θεσσαλονίκης
Ο Πρόεδρος
Ηλίας Κοντόπουλος

Σύνδεσμος Βιομηχανιών Βορείου Ελλάδος
Ο Πρόεδρος
Βασίλης Πανούτσος

HELEXPO Α.Ε. Διεθνής Έκθεση
Θεσσαλονίκης
Ο Πρόεδρος
Αλέξανδρος Μπακατσέλος

Δικηγορικός Σύλλογος Θεσσαλονίκης
Ο Πρόεδρος
Χαράλαμπος Νάσλας

Ιατρικός Σύλλογος Θεσσαλονίκης
Ο Πρόεδρος
Νικόλαος Αγγελίδης

Ένωση Συντακτών Ημερησίων Εφημερίδων
Μακεδονίας - Θράκης
Ο Πρόεδρος
Αντώνης Κούρτης

Τεχνικό Επιμελητήριο της Ελλάδος
Τμήμα Κεντρικής Μακεδονίας
Ο Πρόεδρος
Αδρέας Κουράκης

Επαγγελματικό Επιμελητήριο Θεσσαλονίκης
Ο Πρόεδρος
Γιώργιος Τσέντος

Βιοτεχνικό Επιμελητήριο Θεσσαλονίκης
Ο Πρόεδρος
Δημήτριος Πανέρας

Οδοντιατρικός Σύλλογος Θεσσαλονίκης
Ο Αντιπρόεδρος
Στέλιος Μπακατσέλος

Φαρμακευτικός Σύλλογος Θεσσαλονίκης
Ο Πρόεδρος
Αναστάσιος Καραγκούνης

Εμπορικός Σύλλογος Θεσσαλονίκης
Ο Πρόεδρος
Κων. Γραβάνης

Επιτροπή Εθνικών Θεμάτων του Δήμου
Ο Πρόεδρος Σωτήρης Καπετανόπουλος
Πρόεδρος του Δημοτικού Συμβουλίου

Δημήτρης Φατούρος
Καθηγητής Πανεπιστημίου, δημοτικός
σύμβουλος, μέλος της Επιτροπής

Σύνδεσμος Τουριστικών Πρακτόρων
Μακεδονίας - Θράκης
Ο Πρόεδρος
Αργύρης Δούκας

Ένωση Ξενοδόχων Θεσσαλονίκης
Ο Πρόεδρος
Βασ. Μπρόβας

Σύνδεσμος Εμπορικών Αντιπροσώπων
Βορείου Ελλάδος
Ο Πρόεδρος
Ρέμης Χατζησάββας

Ελληνική Εταιρεία Διοικήσεως Επιχειρήσεων
Ο Πρόεδρος
Πάρης Τσουκαλάς

Παμμακεδονική Ένωση Ελλάδος
Ο Αντιπρόσωπος
Ελευθέριος Χαλβατζής

Κέντρο Αποδήμων Μακεδόνων
Ο Διευθυντής
Κων. Πύρζας

Σύλλογος Μακεδονομάχων και Απογόνων
"Ο Παύλος Μελάς"
Ο Αντιπρόσωπος
Χρ. Παπαζαφειρίου

Ένωση Αποστράτων Αξιωματικών
Θεσσαλονίκης
Ο Πρόεδρος
Γεώργιος Δάτσιος

Σύλλογος Αποστράτων Αξιωματικών Στρατού
Βορείου Ελλάδος
Ο Πρόεδρος
Νικ. Κοτλίδας

Λέσχη Ελλήνων Καταδρομέων
Ο Πρόεδρος
Κων. Λυκιστραφίτης

Νικόλαος Ζαρτινίδης
τέως υπουργός

Στέλιος Παπαθεμελής
βουλευτής Θεσσαλονίκης
τέως υπουργός Μακεδονίας - Θράκης

Γιώργος Τζιτζικώστας
βουλευτής Θεσσαλονίκης
τέως υπουργός Μακεδονίας - Θράκης

Αγαμέμνων Γκράτζιος
Επίτιμος Αρχηγός ΓΕΕΘΑ

Δημήτριος Παντερμαλής
Καθηγητής Πανεπιστημίου

Νικόλαος Μουτσόπουλος
Καθηγητής Πανεπιστημίου

Στέλιος Νέστωρ
δικηγόρος

Ν. Ι. Μέρτζος
δημοσιογράφος

Αριστοτέλης Βρίτσιος
Καθηγητής Πανεπιστημίου

Θεμιστοκλής Κουϊμτζής
Καθηγητής Πανεπιστημίου

Ιωάννης Τσαλουχίδης
επιχειρηματίας

Σωτήρης Κιόσης
Γεν. Διευθυντής
Οργανισμού Λιμένος Θεσσαλονίκης

Φίλιππος Παπαδόπουλος
Διευθυντής της Περιφερειακής Διοικήσεως
Βορείου Ελλάδος
της Εθνικής Τραπέζης της Ελλάδος

Φαίδων Γιαγκιόζης
δημοσιογράφος

Άρης Αλεξίου
επιχειρηματίας

Γ. Φιλίππου - Βαλλής
βιομήχανος

Γιάννης Σρενδόνης
αρχιτέκτων

## APPENDIX IV

Previously unpublished Address that was delivered by Greece's Foreign Minister Antonis Samaras to his EPC counterparts in Lisbon on 17 January 1992.

ADDRESS
OF FOREIGN MINISTER ANDONIS SAMARAS

(Lisbon 17 Feb. 1992)

I have come here to discuss an issue that may at a casual glance seem to be a natural outgrowth of the breakup of the Communist world--the desire of a Yugoslav Republic to establish its own identity in the world. But up close where we are, we can see that it is an issue that can cause great friction, wrenching division and open conflict in our region.

Whether that happens or not depends to a large degree on what decisions we make on how to respond to this difficult issue. Since we have lived with every aspect of it, I want to take a little time to indicate where the dangers lie, how to avoid them, and what measures might be adopted to promote cooperation and peace in the Balkans rather than division and conflict.

The issue, of course, is the desire for recognition of a part of Yugoslavia that was known as the administrative region of Vardar Banovina until it was renamed "The People's Republic of Macedonia" in 1945.

The person who gave the region its new name was Marshall Tito and the reason he did so was to use it as a nucleus for the annexation of those parts of Bulgaria and Greece that were once the Macedonia of Alexander the Great. You may remember that Tito, with Stalin's help, forced the Bulgarian government in 1947 to agree to cede Bulgarian Macedonia to Yugoslavia. You may recall, too, that Tito also tried to grab Greek Macedonian provinces by persuading Greek Communist forces in the late 1940's to promise him those areas in exchange for his support of their insurrection.

Fortunately, both plans failed. When Tito broke with Stalin in 1948, Bulgaria broke the agreement to cede its Macedonian provinces and indeed assumed an aggressive posture toward Macedonian areas in Yugoslavia. As for Greece, the defeat of the Communist insurrection in 1949 ended the immediate threat of annexation of Greek Macedonia.

I have gone into a brief historical review to remind you that the re-invention of Skopje as the "Republic of Macedonia" is very recent, was accomplished specifically to advance territorial ambitions, and, in the case of Greece, to do so by promoting armed conflict.

The name "Republic of Macedonia", therefore, is not a phantom fear for us. It is associated with immense pain and suffering by the Greek people and linked with a deliberate plan to take over parts of our territory that have had a Greek identity for more than 2,500 years.

I can anticipate you saying, "Yes, yes, all of what happened was unfortunate, but you should put it behind you and move on. These are different times and circumstances."

We could put it all behind us, and we would, if the territorial ambitions Tito set in motion in 1945 ended with our civil war a few years later or even with the cold war more recently. BUT THEY HAVEN´T.

For all of the 47 years since Tito created "The People´s Republic of Macedonia", its leaders have never stopped trying to undermine our sovereignty over Greek Macedonia, which they call Aegean Macedonia and portray as "occupied" territory that one day will be "liberated".

During the same period, they have published and circulated throughout the region and abroad countless books, articles and pamphlets identifying large areas of Greece as part of "Great Macedonia", and listing Thessaloniki, the second largest city in Greece, as its future capital.

Only a year ago the President of the Republic, Kiro Gligorov, gave an interview to a Yugoslav magazine in which he spoke of "subjugated" Macedonians in Greece, Serbia and Bulgaria and acknowledged that the leading nationalist parties in Skopje vow that "Macedonian power will redraw the borders of Greece and Serbia." At about the same time, the republic´s representative to the Yugoslav presidency, Vasil Tupurkovski, told a radio audience in Perth, Australia that "the new Macedonian state will have as its primary target, the liberation of the enslaved Macedonians and the unification of the wider Macedonian region."

Now, as they pursue recognition, the leaders of the Republic ridicule the concern such efforts have aroused in us by asking how a country of 10 million people like Greece that is a member of both NATO and the EEC could fear a small, weak state of 2.1 million.

Let me tell you right now, that I haven't come here to urge you to move slowly and carefully in considering recognition for Skopje, because the Greek people fear it. We don't. But we know, that if it is given recognition on its own terms it will be encouraged to pursue its misguided ambitions at every opportunity and will create great instability in the region.

We know, too, that if Greece does not recognize and support its independence--and that we cannot do until it follows the example of other communist states like Russia and completely abandons its past--it will become a tempting target for other countries in the region. That will bring the kind of conflict to the Balkans that we haven't seen in decades.

I want to state clearly that Greece is not against the recognition of an independent state to replace the former Yugoslav "Socialist Republic of Macedonia." Since Yugoslavia has unraveled, we accept the emergence of a new independent Republic on our northern borders. It is in our interest to have a small, but truly independent state as a neighbor than a big and powerful one. Such a state would serve our concern, and the concern of the Community, for stability in the region.

Greece, however, will not endorse a rush to recognition that has the potential to trigger open clashes among the various ethnic groups in this small, mosaic of a state, and to revive old territorial ambitions that are certain to send the Balkans to the violent conflicts of the past.

Independence under those circumstances, will put Skopje at risk of falling either into the embrace of Bulgaria, which has always coveted the region and considers most of its people Bulgarians, or under the dominance of its powerful northern neighbor, Serbia, as many in the republic fear. If either happens, Greece cannot remain indifferent, and stability in the Balkans will become a memory.

The only way to clear a safe path to recognition for Skopje is through the procedures we adopted by unanimous decision on 16 December 1991. I quote: "The Community and its member States... require a Yugoslav republic to commit itself, prior to recognition, to adopt constitutional and political guarantees ensuring that it has no territorial claims towards a neighbouring Community State and that it will conduct no hostile propaganda activities versus a neighbouring Community State, including the use of a denomination, which implies territorial claims."

Let us look then at how the Republic and its leaders have responded to the three major requirements in the decision we took last December.

For the past two months, Skopje has launched a well-financed, carefully-orchestrated campaign in Europe and the United States to portray itself as a peaceful, democratic, unarmed state with neither the power nor the desire to threaten any of its neighbors. Their president has travelled to most of the major capitals to give his personal assurances of the republic's good intentions, and its parliament has passed two ammendments to the Constitution that it says give legal binding to the assurance.

But both the statements and the ammendments are only window dressing to conceal the real goods inside.

The ammendments, passed with the ease and speed of a simple government decree, do not alter the substance of the original articles or of the preamble. Let me explain. In article three, they have added an ammendment, which declares that Skopje nurtures no territorial claims against its neighbors. This is obviously accepted CSCE language. But in the same article, they maintain the provision that while their territory remains unviolable, their borders may, nevertheless, be changed in accordance with their constitution! The inherent contradiction is evident. Also, while new language has been added saying that the republic "will not interfere in the internal affairs of other states", it is meaningless, because the constitution leaves intact Article 49, which says that the state will "take care of the status of the rights of the Macedonian people in neighboring countries."

Now all countries feel obliged to look after the rights of their citizens, when travelling abroad, but no nation we know about gives itself constitutional authority to be a special arbiter of the status of citizens of neighboring countries. Article 49 empowers, indeed compels, present and future governments of the republic to do exactly that.

What use do you think that an ultra-nationalist party like V.M.R.O., which was identified as a terrorist organization in a recent NATO document, will make of that authority, if it comes to power in the republic? While you are considering that, let me tell you that V.M.R.O. currently has the largest number of seats in Skopje's parliament and that its 1990 electoral platform, issued jointly with another extremist party, the Democratic Party for Macedonian National Unity, declared that "elements of the Macedonian nation, which live under occupational rule of Greece, Bulgaria and Albania are not an ethnic minority but just occupied and enslaved parts of the Macedonian nation...". The platform also states that "the V.M.R.O. party declares its readiness to conduct talks with neighbouring countries for the unification of Macedonia".

Even more telling is the fact that the preamble to the Republic's constitution has been left intact, and it is in preambles of constitutions that the philosophy of states is reflected.

The preamble to Skopje's constitution states that among the principles on which the new republic will be built are the "legal traditions of the Krusevo Republic and the historical decisions of the Antifascist Assembly of the People's Liberation of Macedonia." Both the Krusevo Republic of 1903 and the Antifascist Assembly held by Tito in 1944 proclaimed expansionist goals best reflected in the Assembly's declaration calling for "unification" of the Greek and Bulgarian provinces with the "People's Republic of Macedonia."

In view of the intentions embodied both in the preamble and in the articles of the republic's constitution, you can see why we don't feel reassured by the ammendments recently enacted by Skopje's government to enhance its chances for recognition, and why they do not constitute "guarantees against territorial claims", as required by the unanimous decision of the Community of last December 16.

The second requirement on Skopje of that decision--to desist from "hostile propaganda" against Greece--has merely prompted a letter by the Republic's Foreign Minister to the Arbitration Commission pledging that it will not carry out such acts against us.

In practice, organizations with strong ties to the Republic's political leadership have been mobilized both at home and abroad to intensify hostile propaganda against Greece.

I can cite numerous examples of what they have done in just the two months, since the Community asked Skopje to end its hostile propaganda, but will limit myself to three representative examples to save time.

--Two weeks ago, immigrants from Skopje demonstrated outside our Copenhagen Embassy and pinned a map and a proclamation outside the door. The map shows Greek Macedonia under occupation and the proclamation is filled with slogans calling for its liberation. What is most important about the protest is that the group that organized it is an affiliate of the extremist V.M.R.O. political party I mentioned earlier, that has the most seats in Skopje's parliament.

--Early in February, another demonstration was organized right at our border with Yugoslavia. Protestors shouted obscenities against Greeks on the other side, passed out hate literature, and carried placards calling for independence and "unification" of all of Macedonia under Skopje's rule.

--On January 15, 1992, a publishing firm in Skopje issued a set of "souvenir" banknotes with the most famous landmark of Thessaloniki, the White Tower, pictured on the note. Indeed Thessaloniki is shown with a Slavic name as Solun. Another banknote appropriates Bulgarian history, depicting the medieval Tsar Samuel as a "Macedonian". Appropriating the history of neighboring countries seems to be a popular occupation in Skopje these days.

Lest anyone think that such efforts are private initiatives, or the work of extremist emigre groups, let me point out that the government of Skopje has hired America's biggest public relations company, "Hill and Knowlton", to conduct its lobbying in the United States. I have included a copy of its contract with "Hill and Knowlton", in the material in your folio, so that you can see that part of its perscribed duties is to promote the interests of "Macedonians" in neighboring countries.

By the way, one of the first initiatives of the lobbyists was to publish data sheets on "The Republic of Macedonia." One of them describes the climate of the "coastal areas" of the republic as "mild Meditteranean". A look at any map of the region makes clear that Skopje is landlocked and the closest coastal areas are around Thessaloniki and the Chalkidiki Peninsula on Greece's northern Aegean coast. It will further amuse you and give you an insight into the true aims of Skopje, to know that we have just received a cable saying that the landlocked Republic unanimously adopted a law a few days ago calling for the creation of an army, an air force, and a ... navy!

It is obvious then that hostile propaganda, both mild and severe, continues unabated against Greece and it is organized and directed by Skopje. The aim of this propaganda is to spread false information about the ethnological composition of Greek Macedonia, to undermine the exemplary human rights record of Greece and create feelings of hostility against our country abroad, to dispute the Greek cultural heritage of Macedonia and to usurp the Macedonian name in order to justify claims on Greek Macedonia.

In view of the continuing attacks on us, it is obvious that Skopje has no intention to meet the community's second requirement for recognition and end hostile propaganda against Greece, but is only trying to make us believe it will. As much as we may want to, the evidence makes clear that we can't.

We now come to the third and final requirement the Community adopted last December for granting recognition--the stipulation that the Republic should not adopt a name that implies territorial claims.

I submit to you now, as I did in the letter I sent earlier, that the denomination "Republic of Macedonia" not only implies territorial claims because it was given to Skopje 47 years ago for the express purpose of taking over parts of Greece and Bulgaria, but also perpetuates them because if a country exists with that name the impression is given that areas in other countries that bear the same name must belong to it.

Dear Colleagues,

The name is the game itself. Were it not for the use of the denomination "Macedonia", which Skopje attempts to monopolize, they would have no basis to put forward any claim whatsoever on other states' territories.

Equally important, the name implies not only territorial claims against Greece but represents an assault on our Hellenic cultural heritage. The culture and history of Macedonia is part of the Greek heritage and has no connection to the Slav people, who now want to call themselves "The Republic of Macedonia."

As Constantine Karamanlis, the President of Greece, who is himself a Macedonian, wrote in a letter to a European political leader, Skopje has "absolutely no right, either historic or ethnic, to use the name Macedonia.

No historical right because the Slavs, who make up the majority of the Republic's present population, first appeared in the history of the region in the sixth century A.D., that is some 1,000 years after the period, when Alexander the Great established Macedonia as a significant part of the Greek world. And no ethnic right, because the present population of this Republic is made up of Slavs, Albanians, Gypsies and other ethnic groups, all of them respected, of course, but none with any connection to Macedonians."

Despite the lack of any real ethnic or cultural tie between the present republic and ancient Macedonia, their leaders, by using its name over the past 47 years, have been able to foster the impression that they are the natural inheritors of Philip and Alexander and the land they once ruled.

We are not so nationally naive, as to be annoyed only because of a fixation on our ancient history. The strong reaction of the Greek people is not due to a sterile ancestor worship. It is due to the fact that for almost half a century the name Macedonia has been used as a weapon for the promotion of expansionist aims. The use of the name is not independent of the desire to seize and control Greek territory. It is an instrument of aggressive policy.

And, of course, if a lie is big enough and is repeated enough times, it will stick. After 47 years the lie about the so-called "Republic of Macedonia" has taken root. There is no better proof of that than the fact that this group of Western European nations is considering recognizing a state with a name it was given at the height of the cold war as a part of a communist strategy to take over large areas of one of its members.

While the republic's claim to links with ancient Macedonia is unsupportable at any level and its ambitions to expand its territory is unjustifiable for any reason, there is ample evidence, including the statements I have cited, that these delusions are deeply imbedded in the long term policies of Skopje. These policies will not be abandoned, if Skopje is given unconditional recognition, even though some of its leaders are now disclaiming a connection to ancient Macedonia in hopes of increasing the chances of winning it.

There is no other conclusion to reach, if the republic's leaders insist on calling their state Macedonia, since it is a name to which they have no connection and was imposed as a vehicle to promote expansion into the territory of neighboring countries. Russia stopped calling itself the "Soviet Union", when it abandoned its Communist and expansionist past. Why does Skopje insist on keeping a name associated with expansionist ambitions in the Balkans unless it still harbors those aims?

I know there is a feeling among some of you that the name of the Republic should not be a cardinal issue, that Greece's insistence on a different name is emotional, and that there are no rational reasons to require a change.

But within the world community, it is unprecedented for a state to use the geographical name of an area, whose greatest part lies outside its borders. As you may be aware, the territory of the Republic extends over 39 per cent of the geographic region of Macedonia, while Greek Macedonia covers 51 per cent and Bulgarian Macedonia 9 per cent.

If the name of a geographic region is allowed to be monopolized by a political entity, which controls only 39 per cent of the territory, the door is left open for claims in perpetuity for the remaining 61 per cent. This is not scare talk. The whole existence of the so-called "Macedonian" nation, since its creation by Tito is based on that assumption. Once recognition is assured, nationalist forces in the republic will use the name as a strong weapon for cultural and territorial aggression. While they will be waving a powerful slogan--"Free Macedonia!"-- against us, we will be left with the impossible task of trying to explain subtle nuances about the history of the region over the past 2500 years.

Some of you may still feel that it would be presumptuous for the Community to ask a state to change its name. But we have before us a petition for recognition by the government of a state under creation, an entity that has never been recognized as a Republic under international law. Its name was assigned to it by a Communist regime for its own expansionist aims, a regime that no longer exists. So in examining the credentials of a candidate state, we have every right to require that it should not be identified with a name and a history, which is associated with territorial claims against a member state of our Community.

Let us remember that the Macedonian name already exists and is in use as a name for a large historical, geographic and administrative region of Greece. In Thessaloniki there is the "Ministry or Macedonia-Thrace", the "Macedonian University", the "Society for Macedonian Studies", the "Macedonian Press Agency", the "Macedonian Conservatory", the "Macedonian Airport of Thessaloniki" and close to 2.5 million people of Northern Greece, who call themselves Makedones! If Skopje is given the right not only to usurp but, as an independent state, to monopolize that name, it will unleash old quarrels and new conflicts in the whole region on a wide scale.

The case is clear. If we do not remove the root of the problem, that is the name, we would merely invite trouble. And we will all come to regret it.

I don't think we are being alarmists or reacting any differently than you would in similar circumstances.

In fact, we have a recent example showing that Central Europeans are just as sensitive about such issues. Last October, the Republic of Slovenia published a new banknote, bearing a watermark of the historical symbol of the old principality of Carinthia. Although it was a temporary banknote, its printing raised a stormy reaction among Carinthian Austrians, who accused Slovenia of fueling nationalistic claims for Carinthia. After a heated debate in the local parliament, the federal government in Vienna was asked to intervene with Slovenian authorities, who finally gave assurances that they have no claims on the province and agreed to substitute the banknote.

I don't need to draw parallels. But if Austrians reacted as they did about a watermark, you can imagine Greek sensitivity after having been subjected to 47 years of provocations.

The fact is that the end of the cold war has unleashed nationalistic forces that are capable of creating hostility and conflict anywhere in the world.
To create a new state called Macedonia in the Balkans is the surest way to revive all these conflicting claims and to plant hostility in the region that is certain to reap a whirlwind of troubles in the future.

For the stability of the region, for the good of Skopje itself, and for the peace of mind of all of us here, the best course for the Republic is to adopt a suitable name. There are many good options. Prior to the Communist era, the administrative name of the region, as I have mentioned, was Vardar Banovina. Immediately before that, during the last phase of Ottoman rule, it was known as Skopje Sanjak. The Slav insurgents of 1903 proclaimed it, the "Krusevo Republic" and there is much in the name to unite its inhabitants without disturbing its neighbors.

I am aware that the Arbitration Commission recommends recognition as Macedonia on the basis of assurances provided by Skopje. But the Commission, which based its recommendation on juridical reasons, failed to observe a basic legal principle: "audiatur et altera pars" (Hear the other side).
Not only did it discount our evidence, it did not listen to the objections raised by ethnic Albanians, Serbs and Montenegrins inside Skopje to recognition. I know you are aware that leaders of the Albanian minority in the republic have sent a letter to the "Twelve" protesting the Commission's recommendation.

It is evident that we cannot follow the Commission's advice on Skopje either because it fails to take into account the political ramifications of recognition and the conflict it will unleash in the Balkans.

Let us look briefly at those implications both in Skopje and on its neighbors.

Skopje, itself, is a mosaic of contentious ethnic and religious groups. In Skopje the principal ethnic groups--Albanians, Bulgarians and Serbs--feel strong allegiance to countries just across the border and they yearn to unite with them. On top of that, religious hostilities that have been brewing for years are reaching a boiling point in the Republic. Albanian Moslems--a third of the population--resent Orthodox Christians, who make up almost half, for trying to dominate them over the past several decades. The Christians in turn see the Moslems as symbols of centuries of Ottoman subjugation. It is only a matter of time before the Republic's Moslems rise to demand their own independence and eventual union with Albania which is predominantly Moslem.

For its part, Albania has not tried to hide its intentions. The Albanian Foreign Minister has made it clear that Tirana sets two conditions for the recognition of Skopje. First, that the Skopje Republic should recognize an independent "Republic of Kossovo" and, second, that Skopje expresses its willingness to aknowledge an autonomous state for its predominantly Albanian western districts. Once autonomy is achieved, the pressure will start for unification.

On Skopje's eastern border stands Bulgaria. Although it became the first country to recognize the republic's independence, there was no jubilation in Skopje because its people suspect Bulgaria's intentions. The day after Bulgaria rushed to recognize the republic, Skopje's leading newspaper, "Nova Macedonia", which is linked to President Gligorov, published an article saying that Sofia's quick recognition may mask plans to play the role of "protector" or "liberator" of the new state and ultimately absorb it.
The Gligorov newspaper has reason to worry because in recognizing Skopje, Bulgaria made it clear that it recognizes a state but not the existence of a Macedonian nation. In other words, it recognizes the name of the land but not the identity of its people!"

Sofia considers the majority of people in the eastern half of Skopje ethnic Bulgarians with a fixed destiny—union with Bulgaria. That was made clear by a statement made just twelve days ago by the former Prime Minister of Bulgaria, Dimitar Popov, at a meeting of the "Independent Public Committee for Ethnic Questions" in Sofia. "The dissolution of Yugoslavia", he said will undermine existing treaties and allow Bulgaria "to seek international support to undo the historical injustice done to her as regards the Bulgarian western provinces." By western provinces, of course, he means parts of the Republics of both Skopje and Serbia.

As for Skopje's northern neighbor, Serbia, its government has indicated that Belgrade will not oppose the Republic's independence, but Serbia's leaders have also made it plain that they will not tolerate Bulgarian domination of the Republic and will act to prevent it.

Of all its neighbors, Greece is the only country that has no designs on its territory. There are tens of thousands of Greeks in the Republic of Skopje. We can make territorial claims of our own on their behalf. We have not, and we are the only country in the region that hasn't. Instead, being the only stable democracy in the area and the only member of the Community, we are in a position to help Skopje most to safeguard its sovereignty and strengthen its economy.

If Skopje is granted recognition on the basis of the December 16 Community decision, which includes a change in name, Greece will do everything possible to help the Republic. We have already worked out proposals and projects to provide fundamental assistance to Skopje, because we believe that the Community has a key role to play in the region. They include two recommendations, one on arrangements for regional security that embrace Skopje, and the other on economic development of the Vardar-Axios Valley.

On the other hand, if Skopje is granted recognition on its own terms, inluding the name" Macedonia", Greece will not be able to help the republic in any meaningful way and will have to take measures to protect its interests. To explain why, let me describe to you the feelings of the Greek people about this issue. As your own missions in Greece may have already reported to you, no issue in decades has inflamed Greeks as much as the possible recognition of Skopje as Macedonia. Passions are particularly strong in Northern Greece, in Greek Macedonia. Our Makedones number 2.5 million, roughly one quarter of our population, that is more people than there are in all of Skopje.

All Greeks feel the same anger over this issue. Petitions signed by officials of local governments, trade unions, professional and business organizations, agricultural cooperatives and student associations, irrespective of political affiliations, are flooding my office. Local and regional radio and television stations are carrying daily reports and debates on the issue, and groups throughout Greece are meeting to discuss ways to show their opposition to the creation of a state called Macedonia.

Only three days ago, on February 14, that resolve was dramatized by the biggest demonstration ever held in Greece. You can see the picture in your folio and judge for yourselves. An estimated one million people rallied in Thessaloniki to demonstrate that Greeks will not tolerate any further encroachment upon their cultural heritage or any claims, stated or implied, against their territory.

What all this means is that to grant Skopje recognition as Macedonia is to make it politically impossible for any Greek government, now or in the future, to help the Republic secure an accepted place in the region. Without Greek support, it will fall victim to encroachment from one or more of its other neighbors sooner or later.

To grant Skopje recognition on its own terms then, will not be doing it a favor but assuring its eventual dismemberment. Morever, such recognition is certain to become an apple of discord in the whole region and trigger hostilities and conflicts in the Balkans for years and decades to come.

Let us for a moment project our minds into the future. As politicians, we must be able to look ahead. Is there anyone in this room, who can guarantee that Democracy will remain alive in this volatile Balkan region in the years to come? Can anyone exclude the possibility of a temporary or even a permanent reversal of the democratic process in any one of the countries in the greater area?

That is why, my friends, it is absolutely imperative that the Community takes its time to consider every aspect of this issue very carefully and to come up with a process for recognition that is firmly anchored in its decision of 16 December 1991.

Now is the time, less than 10 days since the official signing of the Maastricht documents, for the Community to close ranks on this issue, to show its solidarity with one of its members directly involved, and to safeguard peace and security in Southeastern Europe for the benefit of all the peoples in the region. We have agreed on the three special conditions. If they are not met in substance, then the international community will get the message that the European Union does not really mean what it says, and that the vital interest of its smaller members are not given the same consideration as those of its most prominent.

To make our standards and our determination absolutely clear, I would like to make the following proposals concerning the Community's policy:

--We must present a united front that is absolutely solid. We have set a common policy that constitutes a very important test case for the Community.

The first step toward European Union and common international objectives cannot be characterized by uncertainty and lack of solidarity. Therefore, we must first reaffirm our Declaration of December 16.

We must then take the measures to exercise pressure upon the leaders of Skopje and convince them that it is to their interest to comply with our three prerequisites for recognition because they offer the best way to secure both their survival and peace in the Balkans.

If we all agree, I would suggest that the Presidency conveys to the leadership of Skopje a clear message: we are ready not only to recognize their independence but to give them all necessary guarantees for their security and economic development provided they meet the conditions.

It will be up to Skopje's leaders to grasp the opportunities Greece and the Community are prepared to offer, if they will accomodate the concerns of their neighbors. But whatever they do, the Community must stand firm for stability and order in our disquieting world. Any hasty move now will help turn the Balkans as we reach the end of the century into the kind of violent and turbulent region it was at the beginning of it.

I am an optimist and I dream that with patience and resolve, we can turn the Balkans, which a prominent magazine recently called "History's cauldron", into an example of how old rivalries can be forged into new opportunities for cooperation, prosperity and peace.

Thank you for your attention and for your interest in the concerns of my country.

## APPENDIX V

Letter that US Secretary of State James Baker sent to Greek Foreign Minister Antonis Samaras on 5 March 1992. It is published here in its entirety for the first time.

Dear Andonis:

In the aftermath of the Bosnian and Montenegrin referenda and the Security Council decision to begin the process of deploying a UN Peacekeeping Force in Croatia, we clearly face a new situation in Yugoslavia, a situation replete with both opportunities and dangers. President Bush has asked me to propose that I meet, while in Brussels for the NACC Ministerial, with you and the other EC foreign ministers to seek at that time to develop a common approach to dealing with this new phase of the Yugoslav crisis.

From the outset, the United States has strongly supported the efforts of the Community to resolve the crisis, and we highly appreciate the role the Community has played in this effort. If we are able to reach an agreement on March 10 regarding further steps, I believe this will be the best assurance available that the crisis in Yugoslavia can be successfully managed.

In our view, the changing circumstances in Yugoslavia put a particular premium on moving ahead quickly on two fronts. To begin with, we believe we must do all we can to expedite the deployment of the UN Peacekeeping Force, and we hope that the advance party currently on its way to Yugoslavia will be able quickly to obtain the information necessary to refine the cost estimates and enable the Council to take the necessary decision. Secondly, the February 29-March 1 referenda in Bosnia-Hercegovina and Montenegro have completed the process in which most of the Yugoslav people have expressed a preference as to the future. More urgently, the Bosnia-Hercegovina referendum has created a situation in which we believe rapid action is needed to prevent a serious threat of unrest and destabilization in that republic. Already, we see efforts by Serbia, using Serbian organizations in

Bosnia-Hercegovina, to destabilize the situation, and we have sent a strong warning to President Milosevic to cease these activities or run the risk of adverse consequences to Serbia's future relationship with the United States. Likewise, the threat of a breakdown in the ceasefire in Croatia is always present. Finally, we are increasingly concerned about the economic crisis in all the Republics of Yugoslavia. Continued deterioration in the economic situation will mean not only greater instability and privation for the Yugoslav people but also a greater burden for our countries in supporting the inevitable recovery programs.

With these thoughts in mind, I would propose that we meet in Brussels following the NACC Ministerial on Tuesday, March 10 to determine whether we can agree now to move ahead together in dealing with the Yugoslav crisis. As before, we would see the Community taking the leading role, with the United States firmly supporting and assisting that role. In this connection, we would like to seek agreement on March 10 to complete the process of recognizing the independence of those Yugoslav Republics that have requested it. This would mean for the United States recognition of the independence of Croatia, Slovenia, Bosnia-Hercegovina and Macedonia. For the Community, this would involve recognition of the independence of Bosnia-Hercegovina and Macedonia. As I am sure is true for you, we have wrestled with the question of whether recognition of Bosnia-Hercegovina's independence would contribute to stability in that delicately-balanced republic or encourage efforts by the large Serbian minority to destabilize the situation. We have concluded that while there obviously is no external influence that can guarantee the stability and territorial integrity of Bosnia-Hercegovina, we can best contribute to that objective by a collective recognition of that Republic's independence and warning against efforts from within or without to undermine its integrity.

In addition to the question of recognition, we would also need to agree on how to deal with Serbia and Montenegro. Our preliminary thinking would be to agree to recognize those two republics as a common Yugoslav state, provided that satisfactory arrangements can be worked out with the Yugoslav successor states on the many legal and financial issues that would ensue inevitably from the disintegration of the Yugoslav Federation. One key condition we should insist upon with all the Yugoslav Republics is mutual respect for the territorial integrity of all the new states. We should also consider carefully how we can best maintain pressure on the Serbian leadership to extend to national minorities in Serbia, particularly in Kosovo, the same protections that Belgrade seeks for Serbs in Croatia.

We are, as friends and allies, very sensitive to your concerns about Macedonia, as you described them to me at our meeting here in Washington on January 22. Obviously, we have made clear publicly and privately, including to the President of Macedonia, that any effort by that country to call into question the frontier between Greece and Macedonia would be totally unacceptable to the United States and other members of the world community. We have also sought to encourage the Macedonians to take steps that would eliminate any legitimate concern on your part regarding their intentions. In this connection, President Gligorov's public statements here on January 29 following his meeting with Deputy Secretary Eagleburger were encouraging. He stated that Macedonia has no territorial claims against any neighboring state, considers the border of those states inviolate, and is fully committed to the values and principles underlying the CSCE and the EC-sponsored peace conference chaired by Lord Carrington. As Ambassador Sotirhos has told Prime Minister Mitsotakis, we will be prepared to continue our efforts, together with your partners in the Community in order to find a mutually-acceptable solution.

At the same time, I must tell you that it is our judgment that failure to recognize what is now known as Macedonia in a reasonably timely fashion will contribute to instability and encourage other Yugoslav elements to adventurism which could rapidly escalate to open conflict. This, surely, would not be in the interest of Yugoslavia's neighbors, the European Community, or the United States.

Obviously, a key point in any solution must be a successful conclusion of the peace conference organized by the Community under the presidency of Lord Carrington. As before, we are prepared to give all our support to Lord Carrington and use whatever influence we have with the parties to assist him.

Given the urgency of the situation I hope it will be possible for us to meet in Brussels next Tuesday and to reach a common position on how we should deal with the crisis in Yugoslavia. As I said, I think we face a significant opportunity, working together, to resolve the crisis, but I also fear that time is not on the side of those who wish for a peaceful and constructive end to the Yugoslav tragedy.

# APPENDIX VI

Previously unpublished list by Greece's Ministry of Foreign Affairs containing projects aimed at developing economic relations between Greece and FYROM.

### Projects of development of relations with Skopje

The Greek government is examining positively number of spheres of cooperation with the Republic of Skopje after the latter complies with the terms set by the European Community for its recognition:

a) Greece is ready to negotiate with Skopje <u>security</u> and <u>confidence build ing measures</u> in the spirit of CSCE and the documents of Vienna, 1992.

b) Granting substantial financial assistance in the form of grants.

c) Facilities to be granted to Skopje in the port of Thessaloniki.

d) Joint exploitation of Vardar-Axios valley. There is already an important UNDP feasibility study which should be brought up to date.
This project includes the construction of electrical power stations, irrigation plants, ecological protection of the waters, transportation etc. Finance could be provided also by international institutions.

e) Joint projects for the protection of the environmment, especially in border areas. Such projects could be financed by international institutions.

f) Skopje could be included in the Balkan cooperation projects or other regional cooperation schemes and benefit from the cooperation to be developed.

g) Skopje could benefit of additional assistance in know-how etc within the framework of the "Phare" and G-24 projects.

h) Greece will support a possible request of Skopje to sign a cooperation. and later on an association, agreement with the Community.

## APPENDIX VII

Previously unpublished telegram that Greece's Prime Minister Konstantinos Mitsotakis sent to various Greek Embassies on 15 May 1992.

Ύστερα από την κατάσταση που διαμορφώθηκε στο Συμβούλιο Γενικών Υποθέσεων της 11ης Μαΐου (τηλ/μά μας ▓▓▓▓▓▓▓▓) επιβάλλεται να συνεχισθεί η προσπάθεια να καμφθούν οι αντιστάσεις και να δημιουργηθούν οι προϋποθέσεις εκείνες που θα επιτρέψουν την προώθηση του δικαίου ελληνικού αιτήματος ν'αναγνωρισθούν τα Σκόπια με ονομασία που δεν θα περιέχει αναφορά στην Μακεδονία.

Στις επαφές σας με όσο το δυνατό ανωτέρους αρμόδιους αξιωματούχους που θα φροντίσετε να προκαλέσετε παρακαλούμε να υπογραμμίζετε τα εξής:

1) Η αναβολή λήψεως αποφάσεως δεν αποτελεί λύση. Μόνη λύση είναι η αναγνώριση την οποία η Ελλάδα επιθυμεί εξίσου με τους εταίρους. Απαραίτητη προϋπόθεση για να γίνει αυτό είναι, όπως αποφασίσθηκε στο GUIMARAES, να συμφωνήσει και η Ελλάς στο όνομα της νέας Δημοκρατίας.

Η απόφαση του GUIMARAES - την οποία ελπίζουμε ότι όλοι οι εταίροι θα σεβασθούν διότι αλλοιώς καταργείται η βάση της εξωτερικής πολιτικής των Δώδεκα - αυτή καθεαυτή υποδηλοί αλλαγή του σημερινού ονόματος με το οποίο προβάλλονται οι Σκοπιανοί.

2) Η ελληνική θέση γύρω από το όνομα είναι ανυποχώρητη. Δεν είναι απλή διαπραγματευτική θέση της Ελληνικής Κυβερνήσεως, αλλά αίτημα ολοκλήρου του ελληνικού λαού.

Είτε αρέσει στους εταίρους μας η θέση αυτή είτε όχι αποτελεί μία πραγματικότητα, ένα πολιτικό γεγονός που τους καλεί να βγάλουν τα συμπεράσματά τους.

Η πίεση προς την Ελλάδα για αλλαγή στάσεως όχι μόνο δεν έχει την παραμικρή ελπίδα να επιτύχει αλλ'ενέχει σοβαρούς κινδύνους και για την Ελλάδα και για την Κοινότητα. Διότι μιά συμβιβαστική λύσις θα εξησφάλιζε εις το διηνεκές την εναντίωσιν του ελληνικού λαού προς το μόρφωμα των Σκοπίων, το οποίον περιστοιχισμένον, όπως είναι, από κράτη εποφθαλμιούντα μακροχρονίως την ακεραιότητά του, δεν ημπορεί να επιβιώσει άνευ της υποστηρίξεως της Ελλάδος.

Αφ'ετέρου η δημιουργία ισχυρών αντικοινοτικών και υπερεθνικιστικών ρευμάτων που μπορεί να οδηγήσει σε αποσταθεροποίηση όχι μόνο της Ελλάδος αλλά και ολόκληρης της περιοχής, είναι και αυτή από τους εμφανέστερους κινδύνους που ελλοχεύουν.

3) Από τη στιγμή που θα συνειδητοποιήσουν οι εταίροι μας ότι η πίεση προς την Ελλάδα όχι μόνο αναποτελεσματική είναι αλλά και επικίνδυνη για το σύνολο της Κοινότητας δεν απομένει άλλος δρόμος απο την πίεση προς την πλευρά των Σκοπίων ώστε να εγκαταλείψουν το τιτοϊκό παρελθόν τους και να κοιτάξουν προς το μέλλον.

Διότι είναι αναμφισβήτητο ότι μέχρι το Β'Παγκόσμιο Πόλεμο ουδείς ιστορικός αναφέρει την ύπαρξη μακεδονικού έθνους.

Η Δημοκρατία αυτή αποτελεί δημιούργημα του τιτοϊσμού της σταλινικής εποχής και είναι το τελευταίο κατάλοιπο του σταλινικού συστήματος στην Ευρώπη.

Εχουμε επαναλάβει κατά κόρον ότι το κρατίδιο αυτό κατασκευάσθηκε με συγκεκριμένες σκοπιμότητες από τον Τίτο και τον Στάλιν. Οι σκοπιμότητες αυτές είχαν σαν έναυσμα την επιθετική φιλοσοφία του κομμουνισμού εις βάρος του τότε ελευθέρου κόσμου και την υλοποίηση των επεκτατικών προθέσεών του. Η Ελλάς, απο το Β'Παγκόσμιο Πόλεμο συνόρευε με τα κατ'εξοχήν σκληροπυρηνικά κομμουνιστικά καθεστώτα και απετέλεσε προπύργιο του ΝΑΤΟ στην αντίκρουση του κομμουνισμού. Θα ήταν τραγικό, τη στιγμή που ο κομμουνισμός εξουδετερώθηκε, οι σύμμαχοι και εταίροι μας να επιτρέψουν την επιβίωση του τελευταίου αυτού υπολείμματος της σταλινικής ιδεολογίας έναντι των κυρίων εθνικών συμφερόντων της Ελλάδος. Αυτή είναι μία διάσταση την οποία καμμία Ελληνική Κυβέρνηση δεν θα μπορούσε να εξηγήσει στον ελληνικό λαό.

4) Υπό το φως των ανωτέρω αναμένουμε από τους εταίρους μας ότι θα σταθμίσουν την σοβαρότητα της καταστάσεως και θα θελήσουν να ασκήσουν την επιρροή τους προς τα Σκόπια ώστε να δεχθούν το σύνολο των όρων που έχει θέσει η Κοινότητα απο τις 16 Δεκεμβρίου και επανέλαβε στις 2 Μαΐου στο GUIMARAES.

Δεν αρκεί να γίνονται διακηρύξεις με όρους, πρέπει να ασκηθεί και εν τοις πράγμασι πίεση για την αποδοχή των όρων, πράγμα που δεν έχει γίνει μέχρι τώρα.

5) Η Συμφωνία του MAASTRICHT θεσπίζει την κοινή εξωτερική πολιτική. Είναι γνωστό ότι η Ελλάδα διαφωνούσε με τις απόψεις άλλων εταίρων της συναφώς με την κρίση στη Γιουγκοσλαβία, κρίση που είχε και έχει σημαντικές επιπτώσεις για τη χώρα μας. Ωστόσο, στο πλαίσιο της νέας φιλοσοφίας της ευρωπαϊκής ένωσης δεχθήκαμε να συνταχθούμε με το ευρωπαϊκό consensus. Αντίστροφα όμως, έχουμε την απαίτηση οι εταίροι μας να παρακολουθήσουν την ελληνική επιχειρηματολογία σε ένα θέμα, το οποίο - πιστεύουμε έχει γίνει αντιληπτό - αποτελεί μείζον εθνικό θέμα. Διότι αυτή αύτη η έννοια του consensus απαιτεί σεβασμόν προς τα ζωτικά συμφέροντα των εταίρων και ιεράρχησιν των αντικρουομένων απόψεων εις τα πλαίσια της πολιτικής συνεργασίας. Αλλώς η επίτευξις του θα απετέλει μονόδρομον αμφιβόλου αξίας. Είναι δε φυσικό ότι έλλειψη υποστηρίξεώς μας από τους εταίρους μας θα δημιουργήσει

απευκταίους προβληματισμούς της κοινής γνώμης έναντι της πορείας και της σκοπιμότητος μιας κοινής εξωτερικής πολιτικής της Κοινότητος.

ΜΗΤΣΟΤΑΚΗΣ

APPENDICES    241

# APPENDIX VIII

The flag that FYROM's Parliament adopted on 11 August 1992 and an ancient representation of the Vergina Star.

Skopje's new national flag, usurping the ancient Macedonian dynasty's emblem
(Skopje, 1992 A.D.)

*Source:* Hellenic Foundation For Defense and Foreign Policy, 1993: 11.

## APPENDIX IX

Previously unpublished letter that Greece's Foreign Minister Michalis Papaconstantinou sent to his EPC counterparts on 12 October 1992.

THE MINISTER FOR FOREIGN AFFAIRS

Athens, October 12, 1992.

Dear Colleague,

I am writing to you with some urgency to express my Prime Minister's as well as my own serious concern at the following developments today with respect to the issue of Implementary Regulation 2725/92.

We are informed that at a meeting earlier this morning of the Working Group "Mediterranean", the Commission made known to the members of the Group that Skopje have refused to accept use of the seals "F.Y.R. Macedonia", as agreed by the General Affairs Council in Luxembourg (5-6 October), unless two additional conditions that they have set are met.

Further, we are told that the representative of the Presidency, on behalf of eleven member-states of the Community, appealed to the Commission to proceed to a modification of the Implementary Regulation.

What is more disturbing however, and indeed disappointing, is that the position taken by the Presidency is tantamount to a reversal of the agreement reached by ourselves in the General Affairs Council last week.

In view of the above, and to the extent that we consider our agreement in the General Affairs Council of critical importance, I would urge you to reconsider the position adopted by the Presidency at the Working Group level and allow the Implementary Regulation to stand as adopted by the Commission and published in the Official Journal of the European Communities (JO L276/18 of 19 September 1992).

Yours Sincerely

Michael Papaconstantinou

The Rt Hon. Douglas Hurd, CBE, MP.,
Secretary of State for Foreign
and Commonwealth Affairs,
London.

## APPENDIX X

Previously unpublished speech that Greek Foreign Minister Michalis Papaconstantinou gave during the crucial meeting of New Democracy's Parliamentary Group on 21 October 1992.

Αθήνα, 20 Οκτωβρίου 1992

ΣΗΜΕΙΑ ΠΑΡΕΜΒΑΣΕΩΣ
ΕΞΕΛΙΞΕΙΣ ΣΤΟ ΘΕΜΑ ΤΩΝ ΣΚΟΠΙΩΝ

Η εκκρεμότης της αναγνωρίσεως της Δημοκρατίας των Σκοπίων δεν μπορεί να διαρκέσει ακόμη επί μακρόν. Η υπομονή των εταίρων μας δείχνει ότι κάμπτεται. Υπάρχει κίνδυνος έστω και αν στο Εδιμβούργο δεν τροποποιηθεί η απόφαση της Λισσαβώνος, ορισμένοι εταίροι να επιδιώξουν να διασπάσουν το consensus.

Και από ελληνικής πλευράς άλλωστε έχουμε επανειλημμένως υπογραμμίσει ότι είναι σκόπιμη η αναγνώριση των Σκοπίων το ταχύτερο δυνατόν. Υπό τους όρους βεβαίως που έχουν δεχθεί οι 12 στις 16 Δεκεμβρίου 1991 και στη Σύνοδο Κορυφής της Λισσαβώνος.

Πιστεύουμε ότι η αναγνώριση πρέπει να επέλθει το ταχύτερο όχι διότι διαφαίνονται κίνδυνοι πολεμικής εκρήξεως στο εσωτερικό του εδάφους αυτού ή διασπαστικές τάσεις ή ακόμα κυβερνητική αποσταθεροποίηση. Η αναγνώριση είναι αναγκαία αφενός για να παύσει αυτή η ανώμαλη κατάσταση σύμφωνα με το Διεθνές Δίκαιο και αφετέρου, κυρίως, ώστε να δοθεί η δυνατότης στο κρατίδιο αυτό να αντιμετωπίσει τις επιβολές που μεσοπρόθεσμα ή μακροπρόθεσμα επωάζονται εις βάρος του. Η Ελλάς θα πρέπει να επιδιώκει την επιβίωση και την εσωτερική σταθερότητα του κρατιδίου ώστε ν' αποτελέσει ένα υγιές κύτταρο στα Βαλκάνια.

Η Βρεταννική Προεδρία καταβάλλει προσπάθειες ώστε να βγούμε από το αδιέξοδο. Κινείται επί της ορθής βάσεως, εφαρμογής της Αποφάσεως της Λισσαβώνος. Ακόμα δεν υπάρχουν απτά στοιχεία για το τι θα αποδώσει η προσπάθεια του Πρέσβυ κ. Ο'Νηλ. Βρίσκεται σ' επαφή μαζύ μας. Του γνωστοποιούμε με επίταση τις ελληνικές θέσεις σε ό,τι αφορά την ονομασία (και την ανάγκη εφαρμογής όλων των σημείων του πακέτου Πινέιρο).

Από πλευράς του κ. HURD μετέφερε και αυτός το σωστό κλίμα της Κοινότητας στον κ. GLIGOROV. Τούτο έχει ιδιαίτερη σημασία.

Στο πρόσφατο κοινοτικό γεύμα των ΥΠΕΞ στο Μπέρμινγκαμ, όταν ο Δανός ΥΠΕΞ επανέφερε άκαιρα και άκομψα το θέμα της αναγνωρίσεως έλαβε την δέουσα απάντηση τόσο από τον Βέλγο συνάδελφό μου όσο και από τον Βρεταννό Πρόεδρο. Θέλω να πω με αυτό ότι παρά ορισμένες εντυπώσεις που δίδονται από τον Τύπο οι ελληνικές θέσεις έχουν θερμούς υποστηρικτές στο πλαίσιο των 12.

Το θέμα της χρησιμοποιήσεως των σφραγίδων σύμφωνα με τον Εκτελεστικό Κανονισμό της COMMISSION κατ'ουδένα τρόπο δεν πρέπει να θεωρηθεί ότι αποτελεί πρόκριμα για την επίλυση του θέματος της ονομασίας. Αποτελεί ένα τεχνοκρατικό πρόβλημα το οποίο σήμερα επιλύεται ικανοποιητικά για τις ελληνικές απόψεις.

Υπενθυμίζω ότι η Ελλάς αποφάσισε να αναστείλει τη ροή πετρελαίου προς τις Γιουγκοσλαβικές Δημοκρατίες όχι σαν μέτρο κατά των Σκοπίων αλλά προς εξασφάλιση ότι οι Δημοκρατίες αυτές δεν θα έσπαγαν τις κυρώσεις έναντι της νέας Γιουγκοσλαβίας. Αυτό το τελευταίο σημείο έπρεπε, κατά κύριο λόγο, να εξασφαλισθεί από την Κοινότητα.

Εχουμε επανειλημμένως δηλώσει ότι η Ελλάς, στο πλαίσιο της φιλοσοφίας που προανέφερα, ουδέποτε θέλησε να αναστείλει ανθρωπιστική, επισιτιστική ή άλλη βοήθεια προς τα Σκόπια, ακόμα και τη συνεργασία με την ΕΟΚ προς υποστήριξη της κλυδωνιζομένης οικονομίας των Σκοπίων. Ασφαλώς δεν είναι με τον οικονομικό στραγγαλισμό που θα πείσουμε την Σκοπιανή ηγεσία να ενδώσει στα δίκαια ελληνικά αιτήματα.

Θα πρέπει να σημειώσω ότι η ευρύτερη πολιτική μας έναντι των Σκοπίων έχει αρχίσει ν' αποδίδει καρπούς, ακόμα και στο εσωτερικό του κρατιδίου αυτού.

Πρέπει να συνειδητοποιήσουμε τι επιπτώσεις έχει η πολιτική μας στο εσωτερικό των Σκοπίων. Δεν πρέπει να παρα-

Βλέπουμε τις πιέσεις οι οποίες ασκούνται στην ηγεσία του κρατιδίου και την όλη ατμόσφαιρα εντόνων ζυμώσεων που σημειώνονται. Και αυτή η πτυχή έχει ιδιαίτερη σημασία την οποία δεν πρέπει να παραμερίζουμε εάν θέλουμε να έχουμε μία ολοκληρωμένη εικόνα της δυναμικής που θέλουμε να δημιουργήσουμε.

Αρκετοί κύκλοι οικονομικοί και πολιτικοί θεωρούν αναγκαία την επίλυση του ζητήματος της ονομασίας ώστε ν' αρχίσουν ομαλές οικονομικές δοσοληψίες με την Ελλάδα σε τέτοιο σημείο μάλιστα ώστε ο ίδιος ο GLIGOROV να καταγγείλει όσους προβάλλουν την ανάγκη παραχωρήσεων προς εξεύρεση λύσεως.

Συγχρόνως με την δραστήρια παρέμβαση της διπλωματικής υπηρεσίας έχει αποφευχθεί η είσοδος των Σκοπίων σε διάφορους διεθνείς Οργανισμούς. Πρόσφατα μάλιστα η ελληνική μεθόδευση είχε σαν αποτέλεσμα ο MALESKI, λεγόμενος ΥΠΕΞ των Σκοπίων, να μη γίνει δεκτός στο NATO, όπως είχε ζητήσει.

Τα Σκόπια συναισθάνονται ολο και περισσότερο την απομόνωση στην οποία τους καταδικάζουμε. Προσπαθήσαμε να εκμεταλλευθούμε, όσο μπορούμε, τα ατοπήματα της Σκοπιανής διπλωματίας. Ετσι, έχει γίνει κοινή πεποίθηση ανα την υφήλιο ότι τα Σκόπια, παρά πάσα ηθική δεοντολογία, καπηλεύθηκαν τον "Ήλιο της Βεργίνας". Στο σημείο που και αυτός ο κ. MALCOLM πού έγραψε το γνωστό άρθρο στο SPECTATOR παρεδέχθει ότι η απόφαση αυτή ήταν ανόητη και εσφαλμένη και ότι το VMRO έχει όντως διατυπώσει εδαφικές διεκδικήσεις έναντι της Ελλάδος. Βεβαίως δεν είναι δυνατόν να δεχθούμε ο "Ήλιος της Βεργίνας" να παραμείνει ως έβλημα των Σκοπίων.

Μας μένουν λιγώτερο από δύο μήνες μέχρι τη Σύνοδο Κορυφής του Εδιμβούργου. Κατ' αυτό θα πρέπει να βρεθεί λύση για το όνομα και εν συνεχεία την αναγνώριση των Σκοπίων. Σ' αυτό το μικρό διάστημα απαιτείται η πλήρης συνοχή του κόμματος αλλά και του πολιτικού φάσματος της Ελλάδος προς επίτευξη του στόχου μας. Επαναλαμβάνω ότι φοβάμαι ότι αν στο Εδιμβούργο δεν επιτύχουμε την επίλυση του ζητήματος θα αντιμετωπίσουμε πλέον την δική μας απομόνωση.

Το ΥΠΕΞ αντιμετωπίζει συγκεκριμένες και πολύπλευρες ενέργειες ώστε την ημερομηνία αυτή να έχουν δημιουργηθεί όλες οι κατάλληλες συνθήκες ώστε το θέμα να λυθεί και να λυθεί σύμφωνα με τους στόχους που έχει θέσει η Κυβέρνηση: δηλαδή την αναγνώριση των Σκοπίων ώστε η διεθνής ταυτότητά τους να μην περιέχει τον όρο Μακεδονία.

# APPENDIX XI

Previously unpublished excerpts from Antonis Samaras' speech and supporting documents that the former Greek Foreign Minister presented at the 21 October 1992 meeting of New Democracy's Parliamentary Group.

Α. ΣΑΜΑΡΑΣ: Κύριε Πρόεδρε, μιλήσατε μία ώρα και στα λόγια σας έτρεχε η δικιά μου εικόνα. Μπορώ να πω ότι είναι ένα συνεχές επί προσωπικού θέμα.. Και είναι πολύ βαρειά η εθύνηγια μένα σήμερα, αγαπητοί κύριοι συνάδελθοι. Εγώ σιώπησα και σε στιγμές που ακόμα ο καθένας θα υπεράσπιζε τον εαυτό του..Ακόμα και σε αυτή τη βάρβαρη διαδικασία, την οποία δέχθηκα για να φύγω, για να αποπευφθώ από. το υπουργείο των Εξωτερικών και σιώπησα μόνο για το καλόν του εθνικού θέματος. Μετά τη σημερινή αναφορά, τη συνεχή αναφορά σε μένα του κυρίου Πρωθπουργού σε γεγονότα του χθες, αμυνομενος όπως ειμαι· υποχρεωμένος θα πω μόνον λίγα επιλεκτικά από αυτά τα οποία σαν γεγονότα προκάλεσαν την πολυκέφαλη απόφαση του δικού μου αποκεφαλισμού.

Αναφέρομαι πρώτα στις 16.12. Στις 16.12, τρισήμισυ το πρωί ξύπνησα τον Πρωθυπουργό και του ανακοίνωσα την μεγαλύτερη επιτυχία που μπορούσε να υπάρξει. Στην πιό σκληρή ώρα, δύο το πρωί, υποχρέωσα ένδεκα συναδέλφους ενόψει των εξελίξεων της διάλυσης της Γιουγκοσλαβίας να δεχθούν ως αντιστάθμισμα του δικού μας βέτο το δικαίωμα η Ελλάδα να θέσει τους 3 όρους. Όρους κατά πολύ καλύτερους των όρων του Υπουργικού Συμβουλίου και εξηγούμαι αμέσως. Τί λέει το Υπουργικό Συμβούλιο; Νααλλάξει την ονομασία Μακεδονία η οποία έχει γεωγραφική υπόσταση. Αυτό, λέει ο Ντε Μικέλις. Ο Ντε Μικέλις είπε: Κύριε Σαμαρά,τη λέξη Μακεδονία σκέτη ως όνομα τη βγάζουμε. Μακεδονία των Σκοπίων, Μακεδονία του Βαρδάρη είναι γεωγραφική υπόσταση, πρέπει να τη δεχθείς. Τί λέει η απόφαση της 16ης Δεκεμβρίου; Να μη χρησιμοποιηθεί ονομασία που να υπονοεί εδαφικές διεκδικήσεις. Ονομασία που να υπον·οεί εδαφικές διεκδικήσεις είναι και η ονομασία με γεωγραφική έννοια. Και αυτό το ξεκαθάρισα απολύτως. Και είπα τότε στον Ντε Μικέλις, τον οποίο από έξω περίμενε ο κ. Το πουρκόφσκι των Σκοπίων, πώς είναι σήμερα το όνομα της Μακεδονίας της λεγόμενης που λέτε εσείς; Σοσιαλιστική Δημοκρατία της Μακεδονίας. Πού είναι η εδαφική διεκδίκηση; Όχι στο Σοσιαλιστική, όχι στο Δημοκρατία, στο Μακεδονία είναι η εδαφική διεκδίκηση.Και κάθε τι που έχει σχέση με Μακεδονία δημιουργεί εδαφική διεκδίκηση. Αυτά ως προς την 16η Δεκεμβρίου.

Από εκεί και πέρα θέλω να πω ότι δεν είναι ότι οι ξένοι ήταν ή δεν ήταν ενημερωμένοι. Οι ξένοι είχαν πλήρη γνώση των δικών μου θέσεων ως αρμοδίου χειριστού υπουργού των Εξωτερικών. Οι ξένοι δεν είχαν την γνώση ως προς τις θέσεις τις επίσημες κυβερνήσεως. Και το ποιός προσπάθησε και παρέμεινε να βγει η λέξη Μακεδονία από οποιαδήποτε απόφαση ονομασίας είναι άτι το οποίο μπορώ προσωπικά να το αποδείξω,και πιστεύω ότι είμαι εκείνος ο οποίος ρυμούλκησα, υποχρέωσα την κυβέρνηση τότε στην τελική θέση που πήρε και το πλήρωσα, κύριοι συνάδελφοι, και είμαι υπερήφανος που το πλήρωσα.

Από εκεί και πέρα εγώ δεν πρόκειται να αναφερθώ σε σημεία, σε στοιχεία τα οποία θα μπορούσαν να προκαλέσουν βαθύτατα τραύματα.για την παράταξη. Δεν θα ήθελα να μιλήσω για την συνάντηση της 6ης Μαρτίου.με τον κ. Πρωθυπουργό, τον·κ. Μολυβιάτη και τον κ. Τζούνη, αλλά έγινε. Δεν θα ήθελα να μιλήσω για το αν είχα ή δεν είχα εντολή στους ξένους όταν με ρωτάγανε Γκένσερ, Πινέϊρο, Μπέϊκερ, μπορείς κ. Σαμαρά να μας πεις ξεκάθαρα τη λέξη Μακεδονία ως σύνθετο όνομα τη δέχεσαι ή την απορρίπτεις; Και έλεγα εγώ.την-απορρίπτω, αλλά πρέπει να γίνει συμβούλιο αρχηγών. Και δεν θέλω να μιλήσω για ποιό λόγο τελικά έγινε συμβούλιο αρχηγών διότι είχα ήδη παραιτηθεί δια επιστολής στον Πρωθυπουργό αν δεν έκανε το Συμβούλιο αρχηγών ώστε να ξεκαθαρίσει η θέση διότι πήγαινα στο εξωτερικό και δεν είχαμε θέση για το θέμα της ονομασίας. Εγώ ειχα. Η κυβέρνηση δεν είχε. Και ζητούσα από τον Πρωθυπουργό ή συμπλεύστε μαζί μου αν έχω εγώ δίκαιο, ή διώξτε με·αν έχω εγώ άδικο. Δεν έχετε το δικαίωμα να μην έχουμε θέση και να είμαστε στον αέρα.

Και αυτό έγινε την πιό κρίσιμη περίοδο που, λυπάμαι, κύριε Λαμπρία, αλλά δεν την γνωρίζετε αυτή την περίοδο. Και δεν την γνωρίζει κανένας αυτή την περίοδο διότι δεν μίλαγα. Αυτό ως προς την πρώτη παρένθεση.

Επρόκειτο να μιλήσω στην προηγούμενη Κοινοβουλευτική Ομάδα για το θέμα της διπλής ονομασίας, στην οποία τελικά δεν μίλησα όπως γνωρίζετε. Και επειδή θεώρησα το θέμα επείγον σας πληροφορώ ότι την επομένη ημέρα της προηγούμενης Κοινοβουλευτικής, τηλεφώνησα στον Γενικό Γραμματέα,στον κ. Σημαιοφορίδη, και του είπα ότι θεωρώ χρήσιμο ενόψει των όσων λέγονται για διπλή ονομασία ο Πρωθυπουργός να κάνει, η κυβέρνηση να κάνει μιά δήλωση ότι δεν δέχεται κάτι τέτοιο. Ο κ. Σημαιοφορίδης με βεβαίωσε ότι την ίδια μέρα το μετέφερε στον Πρωθυπουργό. Βεβαίως, δεν πήρα καμμία απάντηση και είναι άλλωστε γνωστό ότι ο Πρωθυπουργός στο Μπέρμιγχαμ δεν πήρε καν εκείνη·την απόφαση υπόψη του είχαμε πάρει ως Κοινοβουλευτική Ομάδα, την τελευταία προ των διακοπών.σε ερώτηση του κ. Δήμα που έλεγε ότι αν είναι να υπάρξει μιά αλλαγή σε οτιδήποτε στη στάση μας για τα Σκόπια ή για τη διπλή ονομασία θα συνέλθει η Κ.Ο.

Δεν θα αναφερθώ εγώ στο πρωτοφανές αλαλούμ και στη σύγχυση η οποία υπήρξε ακόμη και στην κυβέρνηση μέσα με τα γεγονότα του Μπέρμιγχαμ. Θα αναφερθώ στην ουσία των όσων συνέβησαν.

Εγώ προσπαθώ να σπάσω το θαμπό τζάμι της σύγχυσης για να δούμε πώς έχει το θέμα του περίφημου Κανονισμού της ΕΟΚ το σχετικό με τις εμπορικές σχέσεις των Δώδεκα με τα Σκόπια. Ισχυρίζεται ο Πρωθυπουργός ότι δεν υποχωρήσαμε,

Ας υποθέσουμε ότι δεν τους το ζητάμε. Σημαίνει αυτό ότι πρέπει
να τους χαρίσουμε εμείς, οι θιγόμενοι από την υπόθεση αυτή, το
εσωτερικό τους όνομα εκ των προτέρων, όταν γνωρίζουμε ότι αυτό
θα είναι Μακεδονία; Γιατί το δηλώνουμε αυτό και ποιά απόφαση το
επιβάλει να το δηλώσουμε; Και γιατί τους εκχωρούμει το δεκαέπτες
δηλώσεις το δικαίωμα αυτό της δικής τους ονομασίας στο εσωτερικό
χωρίς ακόμα να έχει εφαρμοσθεί η απόφαση της Λισαβόνας; Γιατί
αυτή η βιασύνη, γιατί σπεύδει η Ελλάς, δηλαδή αυτή που έχει κάθε
συμφέρον να μην ονομασθούν τα άτομα αυτά πουθενά Μακεδόνες;
Γιατί σπεύδει η Ελλάς και διχοτομεί στην ουσία την απόφαση της
Λισαβόνας; Γιατί να τεθεί καν θέμα να τους δώσουν οι 12 αυτό που
δεν προβλέπεται από πουθενά, δηλαδή το εσωτερικό τους όνομα;
Γιατί να διαιρέσουμε εμείς στα δύο την ονομασία τους; Τί είναι
αυτός ο νέος ορισμός του δικαιώματος να αυτοαποκαλούνται
οι Σκοπιανοί στο εσωτερικό τους με κάτι το διαφορετικό; Τί θα
αυτοαποκληθούν, κύριε πρόεδρε; Σέρβοι; Μακεδόνες θα αυτοαποκαλούνται
και το γνωρίζουν. και την ώρα που εκδικάζεται αυτή τη στιγμή
μέσα σ'αυτή την ευρύτερη προσπάθεια που ασφαλώς την κάνει και το
υπουργείο Εξωτερικών, ασφαλώς την κάνει και ο πρωθυπουργός, την
ώρα που εκδικάζεται η διεθνής τοποθέτηση της χώρας,η μήνυση της
χώρας κατά του σφετερισμού του ονόματος της Μακεδονίας από τους
Σκοπιανούς, γιατί έχουμε εμείς την ανάγκη αυτή τη στιγμή να
ανακοινώσουμε την εσωτερική χρήση του ονόματος σε έναν Γκλιγκόρωφ
που περίπου μας κάνει και τον ανυποχώρητο; Στα μάτια του
Γκλιγκόρωφ γίναμε αυτόκλητοι συνήγοροι της εσωτερικής του ονομασίας. Και είμαι σίγουρος ότι θεωρεί ο Γκλιγκόρωφ ήδη ότι έχει
αποκτήσει ένα καινούργιο κέρδος. Εγώ ζητάω το δικό μας μόνιμο
κέρδος.Τι πήραμε από αυτήν την τεράστια . υποχώρηση; Υπάρχει
κάποιο άλλο αντάλλαγμα έστω να δεχθώ ότι πήραμε που να δικαιολο-
γεί αυτή τη δήλωση; Εγώ πιστεύω ότι καταστρέψαμε, δεν εδυναμώσαμε
την απόφαση της Λισαβόνας και αφαιρέσαμε από τα μάτια της Διεθούς
Κοινότητας την ουσία της ελληνικής ένστασης κατά της πειρατείας
του ονόματος. Και οι Ευρωπαίοι από δω και πέρα, και το γνωρίζω
αυτό, θα κοιτάνε με μάτι αναθεώρησης τη Λισαβόνα.
Αλλά είπατε και κάτι άλλο, πρωτοφανές, κύριε πρόεδρε, στο Ζάππειο.
Οτι μόνο προ ολίγων ημερών τέθηκε στην Ελλάδα το πρόβλημα, στην
Ελλάδα, το πώς θα αυτοαποκαλούνται οι Σκοπιανοί στο εσωτερικό τους.
Μα αυτό δεν έχουνε κάνει έργο ζωής οι Σκοπιανοί; Επί 50 χρόνια

απορρέουν για όλους τους λαούς. Και κανείς δεν μπορεί να πάει να πυροβολήσει στο στόμα κάποιο Σκοπιανό ο οποίος θα επιμένει να λέγεται Μακεδών ο ίδιος. Ποτέ δεν είπαμε αυτό. Αλλά τηδική σου θέση την προσδιορίζεις πρώτα με ένα όχι διαρκείας, με μια μόνιμη ανοιχτή ένσταση-καταγγελία στην απάτη των Σκοπιανών με τη γνώση ότι έτσι κι αλλιώς τα 2/3 από αυτούς,Βούλγαροι και Αλβανοί, επιθυμούν δικό τους όνομα, Βουλγαρία ή Αλβανία. Με την απόφαση να μη τους χαρίσουμε ποτέ με τέτοιες δηλώσεις τη νομιμοποίηση στο εξαγόμενο εσωτερικό τους ψευδώνυμο. Ιδίως τώρα που ζητάνετηη διεθνή ταυτότητα γιατί το νόμιμο κακό ψευδώνυμο θα διώξει εύκολα το καλό όνομα από τη διαδικασία του εθισμού και μέσα από τη μονόπλευρη χρήση όπως συμβαίνει και στα οικονομικά με το κακό χρήμα που διώχνει το καλό. Και εδώ είναι μεγάλη μας διαφωνία, και εδώ είναι η μεγάλη μας διαφορά. Εγώ νομίζω ότι έχει γίνει εφεύρεση του πολέμου για να σκεπαστεί σ'ένα κλίμα κιόλας ενδεχόμενου φόβου, αυτός ο συμβιβασμός διπλής ονομασίας. Εγώ σας λέω, κύριε πρόεδρε, ότι με αυτή τη διαδικασία που ακολουθήθηκε μέχρι τώρα δεν θα καταφέρετε να υπάρξει καν, τουλάχιστον στο προσεχές μέλλον, νέο όνομα απολύτως θετικό για την Ελλάδα με τα Σκόπια. Γιατί; Διότι, κυρίες και κύριοι συνάδελφοι, η απόφαση της Λισαβόνας προβλέπει ότι αν είναι να υπάρξουν βαφτίσια με νέο όνομα για τα Σκόπια,θα πρέπει αυτό το νέο όνομα να το δεχθούν και τα Σκόπια και η Ελλάδα. Και σας ρωτάω, από τη στιγμή που τους βγάλαμε από το οικονομικό άγχος, από τη στιγμή που αυτόκλητα στο εσωτερικό τους τους δώσαμε πιστοποιητικό Μακεδονικής γνησιότητας να αυτοαποκληθούν όπως εκείνοι θέλουν, αυτοί δεν θα συναινέσουν ποτέ σε νέο όνομα χωρίς ή ολόκληρο τμήμα της λέξης Μακεδονία, για να μην σας πω την χειρίστη εκδοχή, να μείνουμε τελικά με τη Μακεδονία στο εσωτερικό και το πρώην Γιουγκοσλαβική Δημοκρατία της Μακεδονίας στο δήθεν καινούργιο τους όνομα. Όλα αυτά, όμως, σημαίνουνκαι κάτι άλλο. Σημαίνουν βαρύτατη μείωση του κύρους μας στο εξωτερικό και ιδιαίτερα στα Βαλκάνια, τη στιγμή μάλιστα που συνδυασμοί δυνάμεων στη γειτονιά μας επιδιώκουν τη Μεγάλη Αλβανία και τη Μεγάλη Βουλγαρία.

Και ακόμα γράψτε και αυτό: θα έχουμε δώσει εμείς το δικαίωμα στα Σκόπια να αναθερμάνουν την προπαγάνδα τους για την ύπαρξη δήθεν Σλαβικής μειονότητας στην Ελλάδα, αφού εμείς οι ίδιοι θα έχουμε δημιουργήσει, θυμηθείτε με, Μακεδόνες του εσωτερικού και Μακεδόνες του εξωτερικού. Μιλάω, λοιπόν, για τη μείωση του εθνικού κύρους.

./.

Εχώ και μια άλλη πληροφορία. Σε τελευταία συνάντηση (και αυτή αποδεινύεται, και δεν μιλάω για τηλεγραφήματα ειδικού χειρισμού, κύριε πρόεδρε, μην πάει εκεί ο νούς σας), σε τελευταία συνάντηση που είχε ο υπουργός των Εξωτερικών, ο κ. Παπακωσταντίνου, με τον στρατηγό τον Σκόουκροφτ στην Αμερική, αναφέρθηκε επίσημα περί εσχάτης υποχωρήσεως της Ελλάδος με τη διπλή ονομασία. Όπως βλέπετε έχει ήδη γίνει θέμα διαπραγμάτευσης με τον πιό ξεκάθαρο τρόπο το θέμα της διπλής ονομασίας. Αλλά θα σας διαβάσω ένα έγγραφο παντελώς αδιαβάθμητο που μπορεί να το βρει ο πρώτος κλητήρας, το οποίο είναι ένα σημείωμα από τον Ιούλιο του κ. Τζούνη. Και λέει ο κ. Τζούνης: Με εντολή του πρωθυπουργού ζήτησε να δει τον Άγγλο πρέσβυ εδώ πέρα, για να μεταφέρει ορισμένα πράγματα στον υπουργό του. Είναι ανάγκη ο κ. Χερντ να μεταδώσει στη σκοπιανή πλευρά κατά την εκεί επίσκεψή του ότι η Ελλάδα έχει κάνει ήδη μεγάλη παραχώρηση με την αποδοχή του διπλού ονόματος. Και ως εκ τούτου ο κ. Γκλιγκόρωφ πρέπει να προβεί σε αναγκαίες παραχωρήσεις και αυτός.

Ένα σημείο ακόμα: Είπε ο πρωθυπουργός για την τελευταία σύσκεψη που είχα εγώ με τον Πινεϊρο, και το μετέφερε σωστά, 1η Απριλίου, εκεί πέρα είχαμε κερδίσει πολλά πράγματα. Πρώτη φορά αναφέρθηκε το θέμα εδώ. Εγώ δεν είχα μιλήσει ποτέ ούτε για αυτά. Αναφέρθηκε σήμερα και ευχαριστώ τον πρόεδρο. Αλλά ξέχασε να πει και ένα τέταρτο θέμα πέραν από την απόφαση της 16ης Δεκεμβρίου που κανόνισα τότε με τον Πινεϊρο, δηλαδή όλες οι βοήθειες οι κοινοτικές προς τα Σκόπια να περνάνε αποκλειστικά από την Ελλάδα. Και θα ήθελα να πληροφορηθώ, κύριε πρόεδρε, όλες αυτές οι σημαντικές κατακτήσεις, που θέλω να πιστεύω ότι υπάρχουν ακόμα, τί γίνεται αυτή τη φορά; Τί απέγιναν; Πού βρίσκονται;

Κύριε πρόεδρε, για να μην επαληθευτώ γι'αυτό που είχα πει φεύγοντας από το υπουργείο των Εξωτερικών, δηλαδή το να μη βαφτίσουμε το συμβιβασμό σε επιτυχία, για μένα άρση του συμβιβασμού και ταυτόχρονα πρότασή μου σήμερα είναι η εξής. Και εύχομαι να το κυτάξετε και αν είναι λογικό να το δεχθείτε, παρά τα όσα είπατε ότι δεν πρόκειται να κουνηθείτε ένα ιώτα από τη σημερινή σας στάση: Να γίνουν δύο δηλώσεις επίσημες και μία δέσμευση του πρωθυπουργού. Δήλωση ότι στόχο μας έχουμε την ολοκληρωμένη εφαρμογή υπέρ της χώρας μας των αποφάσεων της ΕΟΚ και της 16ης Δεκεμβρίου και βεβαίως την απόφαση της Λισαβόνας, κορυφαία, μια ολοκληρωμένη εφαρμογή αυτών των αποφάσεων ως κύριο στόχο έχουν να μην

αναφέρεται πουθενά και με οποιοδήποτε τρόπο στην ονομασία του
υπό αναγνώριση κρατιδίου η λέξη ή παράγωγο της λέξης Μακεδονία.
Σ'αυτό είμαι βέβαιος, το είπε ο πρόεδρος, δεν υπάρχει καμμία τέτοια αυτού
αντίρηση. Χρειάζεται και μια δεύτερη δήλωση, ξεκάθαρη προς την ΕΟΚ,
ότι η Ελλάδα δεν αναγνωρίζει το δικαίωμα των Σκοπίων να αυτοαποκαλούνται με όποιο όνομα εκείνοι επιθυμούν. Διότι εις την επιστολή
που την έχω ελληνικά ή αγγλικά του κ. πρωθυπουργού προς τους
11 λέει: Δύο εναλλακτικές λύσεις. Μία, η Κοινότητα μπορεί να
απλώς να δηλώσει ότι είναι έτοιμη να αναγνωρίσει τα Σκόπια κάτω
από όποιο όνομα επιλέξει αυτή η Δημοκρατία, με την προϋπόθεση
ότι δεν θα περιλαμβάνει το Μακεδονία σ'αυτό. Δύο, δεύτερη εναλ-
λακτική λύση, μπορούμε να πούμε στα Σκόπια ότι θα τα αναγνωρίσου-
με με όποιο όνομα επιλέξουν το οποίο δεν θα περιλαμβάνει το
Μακεδονία, αλλά θα έχουν την ελευθερία να αυτοαποκαλούνται με
όποιο όνομα επιθυμούν. Εγώ ζητάω μία δήλωση κ. πρόεδρε, η οποία
θε λέει ξεκάθαρα ότι η Ελλάδα δεν αναγνωρίζει το δικαίωμα των
Σκοπίων να αυτοαποκαλούνται με όποιο όνομα εκείνοι επιθυμούν
γιατί απλούστατα θα αυτοαποκληθούν Μακεδόνες, και η Ελλάδα δεν
μπορεί να αναγνωρίσει αυτό το δικαίωμα.

ΚΕΦΑΛΟΓΙΑΝΝΗΣ: . . . . .

ΣΑΜΑΡΑΣ: Κύριε Κεφαλογιάννη...

ΠΡΟΕΔΡΟΣ: Παρακαλώ, παρακαλώ, καμμία διακοπή. Μην απαντάς Αντώνη.

ΣΑΜΑΡΑΣ: Επειδή έχετε μιλήσει και εσείς συνέχεια για την 16 Δεκεμβρίου, σας ακούω, δεν έχω απαντήσει μέχρι τώρα. Δεν θα απαντήσω
εδώ.

ΠΡΟΕΔΡΟΣ: Παρακαλώ να μην ...

ΣΑΜΑΡΑΣ: ...Χρειάζεται, λοιπόν κατά την άποψή μου, να ανατρέψετε
αυτή την άποψη σε όποιους αποδέκτες την έχουν δεχθεί, όπως είναι
οι 11 υπουργοί των Εξωτερικών της ΕΟΚ.
Και, τρίτον, πιστεύω ότι θα ήταν χρήσιμο να ζητήσει ο πρωθυπουργός
στο επόμενο Συμβούλιο Κορυφής στο Εδιμβούργο, σε εφαρμογή της
απόφασης της Λισαβόνας, να υποχρεωθούν τα Σκόπια να μη χρησιμοποιούν τη λέξη Μακεδονία σε κρατικά έγγραφα, με παράλληλη δέσμευση
των χωρών-κρατών της Κοινότητας να μην αποδέχονται τέτοια έγγραφα
που θα φέρουν αυτό το όνομα. Να μην πάρει πίσω η Ευρώπη την
υπογραφή της. Και πιστεύω ότι αυτό είναι το μόνο που μπορούμε να
κάνουμε ως επίσημη διόρθωση για να παρακάμψουμε αυτά τα τελευταία
τετελεσμένα που σήμερα (ελπίζω να κάνω λάθος, ελπίζω να έχουν γίνει
κινήσεις) ολοκληρώνονται στην ψηφοφορία του Βουξελλών.

Εγώ, κύριε πρόεδρε, κυρίες και κύριοι συνάδελφοι, έκανα την πρόταση, πρόταση λογική και απλή. Δεν ξέρω αν την δέχεται ο πρόεδρος. Εγώ πάντως θεωρώ ότι η απόρριψή της θα έχει, για μένα τουλάχιστον, άμεσες πολιτικές συνέπειες. Στο θέμα συνείδησης δεν χωράει πλειοψηφία. Αν η Κοινοβουλευτική Ομάδα δεν έχει πεισθεί σ'αυτά που είπα εγώ, εάν εγώ είμαι μειοψηφία, κρατάω τη στοιχειώδη μου υποχρέωση, ανθρώπινη, ηθική, πολιτική, ευθείας γραμμής υποχρέωση, να παραιτηθώ από το αξίωμα του βουλευτή γιατί δεν μπορώ, ξεκαθαρίζω τη θέση μου, όταν έχω διατελέσει 2,5 χρόνια υπουργός Εξωτερικών να συνεργήσω σε κάτι που θεωρώ επικίνδυνο και ολέθριο. λάθος απέναντι στις νεώτερες γενιές, ούτε μπορώ να συνεργήσω όχι απλώς σε μια πολιτική, αλλά σε μια νοοτροπία όπως αυτή που ακούστηκε από τον κ. Λαμπρία, ότι η Ελλάδα σαν μικρή χώρα δεν μπορεί να έχει στέρεη άποψη, ότι θα πρέπει η ίδια να συμβιβάζεται ακόμα και με τον μικροσκοπικό Γκλιγκόρωφ, ακόμα και στο να λέει καλές λέξεις για τον κ. Πατεντέρ. Μίλησε για θέματα ασφαλείας. Και ερωτώ; Για θέματα ασφαλείας, κύριε Λαμπρία, η Ελλάδα, το άρθρο πέντε, και αν το έχασε το άρθρο πέντε της ΔΕΕ τί έκανε για να το ισοφαρίσει με το άρθρο δέκα και να βάλει μέσα την Τουρκία όπως την παρεκάλεσα την κυβέρνηση στη Βουλή στο να πηγαίνουν όλα τα θέματα των διαφωνιών της Τουρκίας με την Ελλάδα εις το Διεθνές Δικαστήριο της Χάγης για να λυθεί επιτέλους εκεί πέρα η.υφαλοκρηπίδα; θεωρητικά είναι όλα; Στην πράξη το αποδεικνύουμε; Γιατί εγώ δεν μπορώ να δεχθώ, κύριε Λαμπρία, το περί ευρωτρελών, ούτε μπορώ όμως να δεχθώ και το περί ευρωυποχωρητικών. Εγώ νομίζω ότι δεν έχουμε το δικαίωμα αυτού του συμβιβασμού της διπλής ονομασίας με το μικροσκοπικό Γκλιγκόρωφ. Και λέω δεν μπορώ να συμβιβαστώ με αυτό γιατί γνωρίζω τις φοβερές παρενέργειες που θα δημιουργήσει η εικόνα του να υποκύπτουμε στον αγνώστου ταυτότητος διεθνή απάτη Γκλιγκόρωφ όταν την ίδια ώρα αντιμετωπίζουμε πραγματικά ισχυρούς αντιπάλους όπως είναι η Τουρκία.

Κύριοι συνάδελφοι, κύριε πρόεδρε, ήταν κρίσιμες αυτές οι στιγμές για μένα, ό,τι είπα μπορώ να το αποδείξω. Και ήταν στιγμές συνείδησης. Και ήταν στιγμές που υποχρεώθηκα από την ομιλία σας να τα πω. Εγώ θα κλείσω, επιτρέψτε μου, με τον επίλογο μιας επιστολής που έστειλα στις 17/3, φέτος, ως υπουργός των Εξωτερικών στον πρωθυπουργό της χώρας. Είναι η μοίρα του κάθε εθνικού αγώνα να απαιτεί επιμονή, σταθερότητα ακόμα και θυσίες. Και πάντοτε οι αποφάσεις στον αγώνα παίρνονται από το έθνος που τον πραγματοποιεί. Στην διαδρομή μπορεί να έχουμε καθυστερήσεις, απογοη-

καλά αποτελέσματα. Όμως θα είμαστε πολιτικά και ιστορικά αδικαιολόγητοι αν δεν υποστηρίξουμε αμετακίνητα, του έγραφα, τις θέσεις μας μέχρι το τέλος. Ευχαριστώ.

(χειροκροτήματα)

ΠΡΟΕΔΡΟΣ: Κύριοι συνάδελφοι, προτού δώσω το λόγο στον κ. Παπακωσταντίνου θα κάμω δύο επισημάνσεις.
Η πρώτη αναφέρεται σε όσα είπε ο κ. Σαμαράς για την συνάντηση στις 16 Δεκεμβρίου. Είναι ανάγκη να ξεκαθαρίσει το θέμα. Η απόφαση του Υπουργικού Συμβουλίου ήταν σαφέστατη. Ζητούσε τον αποκλεισμό της λέξης Μακεδονία η οποία έχει γεωγραφική έννοια (είναι πάντοτε η μόνιμη ελληνική θέση)και όχι πολιτική έννοια και ζητούσε τον αποκλεισμό της λέξης Μακεδονία. Όταν ο κ. Σαμαράς έφευγε για την Αμερική, ήμαστε μαζί, ήταν η καλύτερη στιγμή της ελληνικής εξωτερικής πολιτικής. Είχαμε την Αμερική μαζί μας. Είχαμε τα Ηνωμένα Έθνη μαζί, είχαμε τον Σάυρους Βανς μαζί, εναντίον της διαλύσεως της Γιουγκοσλαβίας. Η πολιτική της Ελλάδος ήταν εναντίον της διαλύσεως της Γιουγκοσλαβίας.
Η Γερμανία πέρασε ως οδοστρωτήρας και πέτυχε αλλαγή της ευρωπαϊκής πολιτικής προς την διάλυση της Γιουγκοσλαβίας, η οποία έφερε και αλλαγή της αμερικανικής πολιτικής. Πέραν των αποφάσεων του Υπουργικού Συμβουλίου, που είναι γραπτές ευτυχώς, και δεν αμφισβητούνται, όταν έφευγε του είπα: "Πρόσεξε, Αντώνη, ό,τι ζητήσεις θα το πάρεις, διότι οι Γερμανοί είναι υποχρεωμένοι αυτή την ώρα να σου δώσουν ό,τι θέλεις. Και έκαμε το λάθος ή βρέθηκε σε αδυναμία να μη θέσει το θέμα του ονόματος. Διότι τα υπόλοιπα είναι σοφιστικά τα όσα λέει τί εσήμαινε. Γιατί να μην πει ευθέως, όπως το έβαλα εγώ στη Λισαβόνα, εκείνη την ώρα που ήταν σίγουρο θα το πετύχαινε, ότι η λέξη Μακεδονία δεν θα υπάρχει; — Γιατί; Δεν θέλω να προχωρήσω παραπέρα. Μου είπε κατ'ιδίαν ότι δεν το έβγαζα πέρα. Η απάντηση ήταν...

Α. ΣΑΜΑΡΑΣ: Ποτέ δεν το είπα αυτό.

ΠΡΟΕΔΡΟΣ: " Και αν δεν το είπες η απάντηση στο ενδεχόμενο να μην το έβγαζες πέρα ήταν, γιατί εκείνη την ώρα, αντί να μου τηλεφωνήσεις εκ των υστέρων δεν με πήρες ένα τηλέφωνο να με ξυπνήσεις πάλι δύο ώρες πρωτύτερα και να μου πεις, "βρίσκομαι σ'αυτή τη δυσκολία, τί να κάμω;"; Και θα σου έλεγα: "Να μην υποχωρήσεις ποτέ στη λέξη του ονόματος".
Ο Γκένσερ εκείνο το βράδυ ετηλεφώνησε δύο φορές στον Κολ, αυτό το ξέρω και από τον Αντώνη τον Σαμαρά και από τον ίδιο τον Γκένσερ. Γιατί ο υπουργός των Εξωτερικών της Ελλάδος ( νεώτερος επιτέλους του Γκένσερ, δεν είχε τη δική του εμπειρία) και έχοντας εμένα πίσω του, ο οποίος στήριξα απόλυτα την προσπάθειά του, δεν έπρεπε

ΚΥΡΙΟΣ ΥΠΟΥΡΓΟΣ ΤΟΝΙΣΕ ΟΤΙ ΔΕΝ ΕΠΙΔΙ ▓▓▓▓▓▓▓▓▓▓▓▓▓▓
ΕΚΒΑΣΗ ΝΕΟΥ ΓΥΡΟΥ ΔΙΑΒΟΥΛΕΥΣΕΩΝ ΠΡΟΣΕΧΗ ΟΚΤΩΒΡΙΟ, ΑΛΛ'ΟΤΙ ΘΕΩΡΕΙ
ΑΠΑΡΑΙΤΗΤΟ ΟΠΩΣ ΑΜΕΡΙΚΑΝΙΚΗ ΚΥΒΕΡΝΗΣΗ ΠΑΡΟΤΡΥΝΕΙ Κ.Κ. DEMIREL ΚΑΙ
CETIN, ΟΠΟΙΟΙ ΜΑΣ ΕΧΟΥΝ ΗΔΗ ΥΠΟΣΧΕΘΕΙ ΟΤΙ ΘΑ ΠΙΕΣΟΥΝ DENKTASH,
ΑΣΚΗΣΟΥΝ ΕΠΙΡΡΟΗ ΤΟΥΣ ΕΠ'ΑΥΤΟΥ, ΩΣΤΕ ΝΑ ΕΠΙΤΕΥΧΘΕΙ ΔΙΚΑΙΗ,
ΛΕΙΤΟΥΡΓΙΚΗ ΚΑΙ ΒΙΩΣΙΜΗ ΛΥΣΗ ΚΥΠΡΙΑΚΟΥ.

ΣΤΡΑΤΗΓΟΣ SCOWCROFT ΣΥΝΕΧΩΝΤΑΣ, ΠΑΡΕΤΗΡΗΣΕ ΟΤΙ ΕΙΝΑΙ ΠΑΝΤΟΤΕ
ΕΠΙΚΙΝΔΥΝΟ ΝΑ ΕΚΦΡΑΖΕΙ ΚΑΝΕΙΣ ΑΙΣΙΟΔΟΞΙΑ ΓΙΑ ΤΟ ΚΥΠΡΙΑΚΟ, ΑΛΛ'ΟΤΙ Ο
ΙΔΙΟΣ ΔΙΑΤΗΡΕΙ ΤΟΥΛΑΧΙΣΤΟΝ ''ΣΥΓΚΡΑΤΗΜΕΝΕΣ ΕΛΠΙΔΕΣ'' (CAUTIOUSLY
HOPEFUL), ΔΙΑΒΕΒΑΙΩΣΕ ΟΤΙ ADMINISTRATION ΘΑ ΚΑΤΑΒΑΛΕΙ ΚΑΘΕ
ΠΡΟΣΠΑΘΕΙΑ ΓΙΑ ΝΑ ΥΠΟΒΟΗΘΗΣΕΙ ΔΙΑΠΡΑΓΜΑΤΕΥΤΙΚΗ ΔΙΑΔΙΚΑΣΙΑ ΚΑΙ
ΕΞΕΔΗΛΩΣΕ ΙΚΑΝΟΠΟΙΗΣΗ ΓΙΑ ΤΙΣ ΕΠΑΦΕΣ ΚΑΙ ΣΥΝΑΦΕΙΣ ΠΡΟΣΠΑΘΕΙΕΣ
ΜΕΤΑΞΥ ΕΛΛΗΝΙΚΗΣ ΚΑΙ ΤΟΥΡΚΙΚΗΣ ΚΥΒΕΡΝΗΣΕΩΣ, ΥΠΟΓΡΑΜΜΙΖΟΝΤΑΣ ΟΤΙ
ΟΠΟΥ ΥΠΑΡΧΕΙ ΚΑΛΗ ΘΕΛΗΣΗ ΘΑ ΕΥΡΕΘΕΙ ΠΑΝΤΟΤΕ ΤΡΟΠΟΣ ΔΙΕΥΘΕΤΗΣΕΩΣ ΤΩΝ
ΠΡΟΒΛΗΜΑΤΩΝ.

ΣΤΗΝ ΣΥΝΕΧΕΙΑ, Κ. ΥΠΟΥΡΓΟΣ ΑΝΕΦΕΡΘΗ ΣΤΟ ΘΕΜΑ ΣΚΟΠΙΩΝ,
ΕΠΙΣΗΜΑΙΝΟΝΤΑΣ ΟΤΙ ΠΕΡΑΝ ΤΩΝ ΒΑΣΙΜΩΝ ΚΑΙ ΣΤΟΙΧΕΙΟΘΕΤΗΜΕΝΩΝ
ΙΣΤΟΡΙΚΩΝ ΛΟΓΩΝ ΚΑΘΩΣ ΚΑΙ ΤΗΣ ΣΥΝΑΙΣΘΗΜΑΤΙΚΗΣ ΑΝΤΙΔΡΑΣΕΩΣ ΟΛΟΚΛΗΡΟΥ
ΤΟΥ ΕΛΛΗΝΙΚΟΥ ΛΑΟΥ, Η ΘΕΣΗ ΤΗΣ ΕΛΛΗΝΙΚΗΣ ΚΥΒΕΡΝΗΣΕΩΣ ΚΑΘΟΡΙΖΕΤΑΙ
ΚΑΙ ΑΠΟ ΤΗΝ ΣΚΟΠΙΜΟΤΗΤΑ ΑΠΟΦΥΓΗΣ ΔΗΜΙΟΥΡΓΙΑΣ ΕΝΟΣ ΜΕΛΛΟΝΤΙΚΟΥ
ΣΗΜΕΙΟΥ ΤΡΙΒΗΣ ΚΑΙ ΑΝΑΦΛΕΞΕΩΣ ΣΤΑ ΒΑΛΚΑΝΙΑ.

ΕΙΔΙΚΩΤΕΡΑ, Κ. ΥΠΟΥΡΓΟΣ ΕΤΟΝΙΣΕ ΟΤΙ ΕΛΛΗΝΙΚΗ ΚΥΒΕΡΝΗΣΗ ΕΧΕΙ
ΕΠΙΣΗΜΑ, ΔΗΜΟΣΙΑ ΚΑΙ ΚΑΤΗΓΟΡΗΜΑΤΙΚΑ ΔΗΛΩΣΕΙ ΟΤΙ ΕΛΛΑΣ ΟΥΔΕΜΙΑ ΕΧΕΙ
ΕΔΑΦΙΚΗ ΔΙΕΚΔΙΚΗΣΗ ΕΝΑΝΤΙ ''Δ.Μ.'' ΚΑΙ ΟΤΙ ΕΙΝΑΙ ΕΤΟΙΜΗ ΝΑ ΒΟΗΘΗΣΕΙ
ΚΑΙ ΝΑ ΣΤΗΡΙΞΕΙ ΚΑΘ'ΟΙΟΝΔΗΠΟΤΕ ΤΡΟΠΟ ΤΗΝ ΝΕΑ ΔΗΜΟΚΡΑΤΙΑ, ΜΕ ΣΥΝΑΨΗ
ΠΟΙΚΙΛΩΝ ΣΥΜΦΩΝΙΩΝ, ΠΑΡΟΧΗ ΟΙΚΟΝΟΜΙΚΗΣ ΕΝΙΣΧΥΣΕΩΣ ΚΑΙ ΑΚΟΜΗ ΕΓΓΥΗΣΗ
ΤΩΝ ΣΥΝΟΡΩΝ ΤΗΣ. ΥΠΟ ΤΗΝ ΠΡΟΥΠΟΘΕΣΗ ΟΤΙ Η ΣΚΟΠΙΑΝΗ ΗΓΕΣΙΑ ΘΑ
ΣΥΜΜΟΡΦΩΘΕΙ ΠΡΟΣ ΤΟΥΣ ΟΡΟΥΣ ΤΗΣ ΓΝΩΣΤΗΣ ΚΟΙΝΟΤΙΚΗΣ ΑΠΟΦΑΣΕΩΣ
ΛΙΣΣΑΒΩΝΟΣ.

ΕΞ ΑΛΛΟΥ, ▓▓▓▓▓ ΥΠΟΥΡΓΟΣ/ΕΞΕΦΡΑΣΕ ΑΠΟΓΟΗΤΕΥΣΗ Κ. ΠΡΩΘΥΠΟΥΡΓΟΥ
ΔΙΟΤΙ ΗΠΑ ▓▓ΔΕΝ ΕΧΟΥΝ ΜΕΝ ΑΝΑΓΝΩΡΙΣΕΙ ΤΗΝ ''Δ.Μ.'', ΑΛΛΑ, ΜΕ ΤΗΝ
ΣΤΑΣΗ ΤΟ▓▓▓▓ΕΝΘΑΡΡΥΝΟΥΝ ΟΥΣΙΑΣΤΙΚΑ ΤΟΝ GLIGOROV ΝΑ ΕΙΝΑΙ
ΑΔΙΑΛΛΑΚ▓▓▓ ΚΑΙ ΖΗΤΗΣΕ ΟΠΩΣ ADMINISTRATION ΑΣΚΗΣΕΙ ΕΠ'ΑΥΤΟΥ ΟΛΗ
ΕΠΙΡΡΟΗ ΤΗΣ, ΩΣΤΕ ΕΠΙΛΕΞΕΙ ΕΝΑ ΟΝΟΜΑ ΓΙΑ ΤΗΝ ΔΙΕΘΝΗ ΥΠΟΣΤΑΣΗ ΤΗΣ
ΧΩΡΑΣ ΤΟΥ, ΤΟ ΟΠΟΙΟ ΔΕΝ ΠΡΟΚΕΙΤΑΙ, ΒΕΒΑΙΩΣ, ΝΑ ΤΟΥ ΕΠΙΒΑΛΕΙ Η
ΕΛΛΑΣ, ▓▓▓▓▓▓▓▓▓▓▓▓▓▓▓▓▓▓▓▓▓▓▓▓▓▓▓▓▓▓▓▓▓▓▓▓▓▓▓▓▓▓▓▓▓.

ΚΥΡΙΟΣ ΥΠΟΥΡΓΟΣ ΕΠΕΣΗΜΑΝΕ, ΑΚΟΜΗ, ΔΙΑΦΑΙΝΟΜΕΝΟΥΣ ΚΙΝΔΥΝΟΥΣ
ΠΕΡΙΟΧΗ ΚΟΣΣΥΦΟΠΕΔΙΟΥ ΚΑΙ ΥΠΕΓΡΑΜΜΙΣΕ ΑΠΟΨΗ ΚΑΙ ΣΚΟΠΙΜΟΤΗΤΑ
ΕΓΚΑΙΡΗΣ ΑΜΕΡΙΚΑΝΙΚΗΣ ΠΑΡΕΜΒΑΣΕΩΣ ΠΡΟΣ ΑΠΟΤΡΟΠΗ ΑΝΑΦΛΕΞΕΩΣ,
ΠΡΟΣΘΕΤΟΝΤΑΣ ΟΤΙ ΕΛΛΗΝΙΚΗ ΚΥΒΕΡΝΗΣΗ ΥΠΟΣΤΗΡΙΖΕΙ ΠΑΡΟΧΗ ΕΥΡΕΙΑΣ
ΑΥΤΟΝΟΜΙΑΣ ΣΤΟΥΣ ΚΟΣΣΟΒΑΡΟΥΣ ΑΛΛΑ ΟΧΙ ΔΙΚΑΙΩΜΑΤΟΣ ΑΥΤΟΔΙΑΘΕΣΕΩΣ ΠΟΥ
ΘΑ ΟΔΗΓΗΣΕΙ, ΑΝΑΠΟΦΕΥΚΤΑ, ΣΤΗΝ ΕΝΟΠΛΗ ΣΥΡΡΑΞΗ. ΣΤΟ ΙΔΙΟ ΠΛΑΙΣΙΟ, Κ.
ΥΠΟΥΡΓΟΣ ΕΞΕΦΡΑΣΕ ΑΠΟΨΗ ΟΤΙ PANIC ΕΜΦΑΝΙΖΕΤΑΙ ΠΙΟ ΠΡΑΓΜΑΤΙΣΤΗΣ ΚΑΙ,
ΩΣ ΕΚ ΤΟΥΤΟΥ, ΠΡΟΣΦΕΡΕΙ, ΙΣΩΣ, ΚΑΛΗ ΕΥΚΑΙΡΙΑ ΓΙΑ ΝΑ ΔΙΑΜΟΡΦΩΘΟΥΝ
ΑΝΑΛΟΓΕΣ ΣΕΡΒΙΚΕΣ ΘΕΣΕΙΣ, ΠΟΥ ΗΠΑ ΘΑ ΠΡΕΠΕΙ ΕΝΘΑΡΡΥΝΟΥΝ ΜΕ ΕΠΙΡΡΟΗ

ΣΤΡΑΤΗΓΟΣ SCOWCROFT ΑΠΗΝΤΗΣΕ ΟΤΙ ΣΥΜΦΩΝΕΙ ΓΕΝΙΚΑ ΜΕ ΑΝΩΤΕΡΩ
ΚΑΙ ΕΤΟΝΙΣΕ, ΕΙΔΙΚΩΤΕΡΑ ΩΣ ΠΡΟΣ ΟΝΟΜΑ ''ΜΑΚΕΔΟΝΙΚΟ'', ΟΤΙ ΗΠΑ
ΔΙΑΚΕΙΝΤΑΙ ΠΟΛΥ ΕΥΝΟΙΚΑ (VERY SYMPATHETIC) ΕΝΑΝΤΙ ΕΛΛΗΝΙΚΩΝ ΘΕΣΕΩΝ,
ΔΙΑ ΔΕ ΑΝΗΣΥΧΟΥΝ ΙΔΙΑΙΡΑ ΓΙΑ ΕΝΔΕΧΟ ΑΠΟΣΤΑΘΕΡΟΠΟΙΗΣΕΩΣ ΚΑΤΑΣΤΑΣΕΩΣ
ΣΤΗΝ ''Π.Δ.Μ.'' ΣΕ ΠΕΡΙΠΤΩΣΗ ΑΝΑΤΡΟΠΗΣ GLIGOROV, ΔΙΑΤΗΡΩΝΤΑΣ
ΑΜΦΙΒΟΛΙΕΣ ΚΑΤ- ΠΟΣΟ ΚΑΙ ΜΕΧΡΙ ΠΟΙΟΥ ΒΑΘΜΟΥ ΣΚΟΠΙΑΝΟΣ ΗΓΕΤΗΣ ΕΧΕΙ
ΔΥΝΑΤΟΤΗΤΕΣ ΚΑΙ ΠΕΡΙΘΩΡΙΑ ΙΚΑΝΟΠΟΙΗΣΕΩΣ ΕΛΛΗΝΙΚΗΣ ΑΠΑΙΤΗΣΕΩΣ, ΧΩΡΙΣ
ΚΙΝΔΥΝΟ ΑΝΤΙΚΑΤΑΣΤΑΣΕΩΣ ΤΟΥ ΑΠΟ ΑΚΡΩΣ ΑΚΡΑΙΑ ΚΑΙ ΡΙΖΟΣΠΑΣΤΙΚΑ
ΣΤΟΙΧΕΙΑ.

ΚΥΡΙΟΣ ΥΠΟΥΡΓΟΣ ΕΠΑΝΕΛΑΒΕ ΣΤΟΝ ΣΤΡΑΤΗΓΟ SCOWCROFT, ΟΠΟΙΟΣ
ΕΞΕΦΡΑΣΕ ΕΛΠΙΔΑ ΟΤΙ ΘΑ ΕΞΕΥΡΕΘΕΙ ΑΜΟΙΒΑΙΑ ΙΚΑΝΟΠΟΙΗΤΙΚΗ ΛΥΣΗ, ΟΤΙ
Κ. ΠΡΩΘΥΠΟΥΡΓΟΣ ΘΑ ΕΠΙΘΥΜΟΥΣΕ ΟΠΩΣ ΠΡΟΕΔΡΟΣ BUSH ΠΙΕΣΕΙ GLIGOROV
ΑΝΤΑΠΟΚΡΙΘΕΙ ΣΤΗΝ ΕΣΧΑΤΗ ΥΠΟΧΩΡΗΣΗ ΕΛΛΗΝΙΚΗΣ ΠΛΕΥΡΑΣ ΚΑΙ ΕΠΙΛΕΞΕΙ
ΟΝΟΜΑ ΧΩΡΑΣ ΤΟΥ ΠΡΟΣ ΔΙΕΘΝΗ ΧΡΗΣΗ, ΕΓΚΑΤΑΛΕΙΠΟΝΤΑΣ ΟΡΟ
''ΜΑΚΕΔΟΝΙΑ'' ΠΟΥ ΥΠΟΔΗΛΟΙ ΕΔΑΦΙΚΕΣ ΔΙΕΚΔΙΚΗΣΕΙΣ ΚΑΙ ΠΟΥ, ΑΝ
ΔΙΑΤΗΡΗΘΕΙ, ΘΑ ΑΠΟΤΕΛΕΣΕΙ ΜΟΝΙΜΟ ΣΗΜΕΙΟ ΜΕΛΛΟΝΤΙΚΗΣ ΤΡΙΒΗΣ ΚΑΙ
ΕΝΤΑΣΕΩΣ ΣΤΗΝ ΠΕΡΙΟΧΗ, ΕΝΩ ΤΥΧΟΝ ΔΙΕΥΘΕΤΗΣΗ ΠΡΟΒΛΗΜΑΤΟΣ ΘΑ
ΕΞΗΣΦΑΛΙΖΕ ΣΤΗΝ ΝΕΑ ΔΗΜΟΚΡΑΤΙΑ ΥΠΟΣΤΗΡΙΞΗ, ΣΥΜΠΑΡΑΣΤΑΣΗ ΚΑΙ ΦΙΛΙΑ
ΕΚ ΜΕΡΟΥΣ ΕΛΛΑΔΟΣ, ΑΝΑΓΝΩΡΙΣΗ ΑΠΟ ΕΟΚ, ΜΕ ΟΛΕΣ ΣΥΝΑΚΟΛΟΥΘΕΣ ΘΕΤΙΚΕΣ
ΣΥΝΕΠΕΙΕΣ ΚΑΙ ΚΑΤΟΧΥΡΩΣΗ ΕΙΡΗΝΗΣ ΚΑΙ ΣΤΑΘΕΡΟΤΗΤΟΣ.

ΤΕΛΟΣ, Κ. ΥΠΟΥΡΓΟΣ ΕΠΕΣΥΡΕ ΠΡΟΣΟΧΗ ΣΥΝΟΜΙΛΗΤΗ ΤΟΥ ΣΤΗΝ ΑΠΟΦΑΣΗ
ΕΛΛΗΝΙΚΗΣ ΚΥΒΕΡΝΗΣΕΩΣ ΓΙΑ ΠΡΟΜΗΘΕΙΑ 40 ΑΕΡΟΣΚΑΦΩΝ F-16 ΚΑΙ ΖΗΤΗΣΕ
ΑΠΟ ΣΤΡΑΤΗΓΟ SCOWCROFT ΟΠΩΣ ΑΜΕΡΙΚΑΝΙΚΗ ΚΥΒΕΡΝΗΣΗ ΔΙΑΤΗΡΗΣΕΙ ΣΤΗΝ
ΘΕΣΗ ΤΟΥ ΑΜΕΡΙΚΑΝΟ ΣΥΝΤΟΝΙΣΤΗ ΚΥΠΡΙΑΚΟΥ Κ. LEDSKY, ΜΕΧΡΙ ΚΑΙ ΤΩΝ
ΠΡΟΣΕΧΩΝ ΔΙΚΟΙΝΟΤΙΚΩΝ ΣΥΝΟΜΙΛΙΩΝ Ν.ΥΟΡΚΗ, ΛΟΓΩ ΜΑΚΡΑΣ ΕΜΠΕΙΡΙΑΣ ΤΟΥ
ΣΤΟ ΘΕΜΑ. ΣΤΡΑΤΗΓΟΣ SCOWCROFT ΑΠΗΝΤΗΣΕ ΟΤΙ ΕΧΕΙ ΗΔΗ ΑΠΟΦΑΣΙΣΘΕΙ
ΟΠΩΣ Κ. LEDSKY ΠΑΡΑΚΟΛΟΥΘΗΣΕΙ ΩΣ ΑΝΩ ΣΥΝΟΜΙΛΙΕΣ ΥΠΟ ΣΥΜΒΟΥΛΕΥΤΙΚΗ
ΙΔΙΟΤΗΤΑ.

2. ΕΞ ΑΛΛΟΥ Κ. ΥΠΕΞ ΣΥΝΑΝΤΗΘΗΚΕ, ΣΗΜΕΡΑ, ΧΩΡΙΣΤΑ ΜΕ ΠΡΟΕΔΡΟ
ΥΠΟΕΠΙΤΡΟΠΗΣ ΕΥΡΩΠΗΣ - Μ. ΑΝΑΤΟΛΗΣ, ΕΠΙΤΡΟΠΗΣ ΕΞΩΤΕΡΙΚΩΝ ΥΠΟΘΕΣΕΩΝ
ΒΟΥΛΗΣ ΑΝΤΙΠΡΟΣΩΠΩΝ, ΒΟΥΛΕΥΤΗ Κ. HAMILTON ΚΑΙ ΜΕ ΟΜΟΓΕΝΗ
ΓΕΡΟΥΣΙΑΣΤΗ Κ. SARBANES, ΜΕ ΟΠΟΙΟΥΣ ΣΥΖΗΤΗΣΕ ΟΛΑ ΤΑ ΩΣ ΑΝΩ ΖΗΤΗΜΑΤΑ
ΙΔΙΑΙΤΕΡΟΥ ΕΛΛΗΝΙΚΟΥ ΕΝΔΙΑΦΕΡΟΝΤΟΣ ΚΑΙ ΟΠΟΙΟΥΣ ΕΥΧΑΡΙΣΤΗΣΕ ΓΙΑ
ΥΠΟΣΤΗΡΙΞΗ ΠΟΥ ΕΚΑΣΤΟΤΕ ΠΑΡΕΧΟΥΝ ΣΤΙΣ ΘΕΣΕΙΣ ΜΑΣ ΚΑΙ ΠΟΥ Κ.
HAMILTON ΕΞΕΦΡΑΣΕ, ΕΚ ΝΕΟΥ, ΕΠΩΦΕΛΗΘΕΙΣ ΕΥΚΑΙΡΙΑΣ ΣΧΕΤΙΚΗΣ
ΣΥΖΗΤΗΣΕΩΣ.

ΖΑΧΑΡΑΚΙΣ/

ΝΝΝΝ

ΘΕΜΑ: Επίσκεψις στην Αθήνα Αναπληρωτού Υπουργού Ρωσίας κ.V.Churkin, 12.8.1992.-

Πρωϊνή συνάντηση στο Υπουργείο Εξωτερικών με Υφυπουργό Κυρία Β.Τσουδερού, παρουσία, μόνον, εκατέρωθεν Πρέσβεων κ.κ.Γούναρη και Nikolaenko, ώρα 10.00.

Κύριο θέμα συζητήσεως: Μακεδονικό.

Μετά συνήθεις φιλοφρονήσεις, κ.Churkin εξέθεσε τα εξής:

Εν αρχή, είπε, θα σας είπω τί δέν προτίθεται να πράξει Ρωσία τά πρόσφατη αναγνώριση Δημοκρατίας Μακεδονίας:

(α) Δέν θα επιδιώξουμε αναγνώριση Δημοκρατίας αυτής απο τρίτες χώρες, ούτε θα πυοβούμε σε οιαδήποτε ενέργεια προς κατεύθυνση αυτή. Ερωτώμενοι θα εξηγούμε απλώς λόγους ενεργείας μας, χωρίς... ωθούμε συνομιλητές μας ακολουθήσουν παράδειγμά μας.

(β) Δέν θα σπεύσουμε αποκτήσουμε διπλωματικές σχέσεις με Σκόπια Σχετικό διάταγμα Γιέλτσιν προβλέπει μέν, εκτός απο αναγνώριση, και εγκατάσταση διπλωματικών σχέσεων, χωρίς όμως να θέτει χρονικό περιθώριο γιε αυτές. Σχετικές συνεννοήσεις μπορούν να κρατήσουν πολύ καιρό και δέν προβλέπεται απολήξουν κατα το προβλεπτό μέλλον.

Στο σημείο αυτό, Κυρία Υφυπουργός ερώτησε εάν ήσαν γνωστοί
λόγοι για οποίους κ.Gligorov επισκέπτεται Σόφια "για να ανακοινώσει
κάτι σοβαρό". K.Churkin είπε οτι δέν εγνώριζε και παρετήρησε οτι
Σκοπιανοί είχαν προσκαλέσει-Γιέλτσιν τους επισκεφθεί πρό διασκέψεως
Λονδίνου.

Συνεχίζοντας ανάλυσή του, Ρώσος επίσημος διευκρίνισε οτι απόφαση
αναγνωρίσεως δέν εσήμαινε και λήψη θέσεως υπέρ μιας πλευράς, προσθέ-
τοντας οτι εάν μέρη εύρισκαν απο κοινού κάποια λύση, χώρα του θα την
απεδέχετο ευχαρίστως. Μόσχα όμως θεώρησε οτι δέν ήταν σκόπιμη παράτα-
ση εκκρεμότητος και οτι, μετά Λισσαβώνα, Σκοπιανοί είχαν περιέλθει σε
αδιέξοδο, που καθιστούσε οποιαδήποτε εποικοδομητική διαπραγμάτευση μαζί τους αδύνατη. Αναγνώριση, επομένως, σκόπευε επίσπευση λύσεως, γι'
αυτό και τους συστήσαμε διάλογο μαζί σας, οποίον αυτοί δέν απέκλεισαν
ούτε και για το όνομα.

Θα μπορούσατε, συνέχισε κ.Churkin, να δεχθήτε κάποια φόρμουλα, που
θα περιείχε το όνομα "Μακεδονία" ή ένα απο τα παράγωγά του; Αφού δέχεσθε στη "διπλή λύση" τη χρήση του όρου "Μακεδονία", τούτο σημαίνει οτι
δέν τον απορρίπτετε τελέως. Μήπως δέχεσθε κάποια φόρμουλα ως π.χ.
"Νότια Βαλκανική Δημοκρατία Μακεδονίας"; Θα μπορούσατε να αρχίσετε
διάλογο αφήνοντας προσωρινώς το όνομα κατα μέρος. Όταν ικανοποιηθούν
τα λοιπά αιτήματά σας, π.χ. απαραβίαστο συνόρων κλπ., θα μπορούσε η
Ρωσία τους επηρεάσει και προς κατεύθυνση ονόματος. Πάντως, Σκόπια δέν
δέχονται λύση Λισσαβώνος. Παρακαλώ δείξτε ελαστικότητα.

Απαντώντας, Κυρία Τσουδερού, αφού παρατήρησε οτι ελληνική πλευρά
εξεπλάγη απο αιφνίδια αναγνώριση, υπεγράμμισε εξής δύο σημεία:

1. Αναγνώριση έγινε χωρίς προειδοποίηση και χωρίς μας δοθεί ευκαιρία σας εξηγήσουμε οτι timing ήταν λάθος. Είχαμε σαφείς ενδείξεις
οτι Σκόπια εκάμπτοντο μετά απόφαση Λισσαβώνος και οτι υπήρχε ελπίς
για κάποιο συμβιβασμό. Αναγνώρισή σας ήρε πίεση και διέκοψε momentum,
γι αυτό και εξεπλάγημεν. Είναι κρίμα οτι δέν μας εδώσατε ευκαιρία σας
εξηγήσουμε όλα αυτά, διότι η παρέμβασή σας, αργότερα, θα είχε ίσως
χρησιμότητα. 2. Υπολογίζουμε στις φιλικές σας προθέσεις και επι πλέον
έχουμε κοινά συμφέροντα στα Βαλκάνια. Η Ελλάς επέδειξε ήδη μεγάλη ελα-

# APPENDIX XII

Previously unpublished letter that Greek Foreign Minister Michalis Papaconstantinou sent to his EPC counterparts on 3 November 1992.

                                        Athens, 3 November 1992

Dear Colleague,

   Following the Declaration of December 16, 1991 and the Lisbon Declaration of 27 June 1992 on the proposed recognition of the former Yugoslav Republic of Macedonia, the British presidency has undertaken to convey to Skopje the contents and the substance of the position of the "12". Ambassador O'Neill has informed me on the results of his two visits to Skopje. To this day, no apparent progress has been registered.

   On the contrary, there is a hardening of attitudes and an escalation of hostile propaganda against my country of the nature cited in the December "Declaration on Yugoslavia". More precisely, President Gligorov has publicly tried to discredit Greece by attributing to her aggressive intentions and territorial claims. In an obvious act of provocation, the Skopje Parliament passed a resolution to adopt the emblem of King Philip's ancient Greek Macedonian dynasty --a 16-ray sun found in excavations at the royal tombs of Vergina in Greek Macedonia-- as the emblem of the flag of the new Slav Republic of Skopje.

   Such acts, at a time when recognition is still pending not only undermine efforts toward good-neighbourly relations but could well inflame passions across borders.

   Various reports reaching my office attribute the intransigence of leading circles in Skopje to the belief that the Lisbon Decision is likely to be reversed in Edinburgh. They are encouraged in this stance by certain writings in major European and American journals. In addition, they appear to interpret the eagerness of European governments for humanitarian aid and interest in medium and long-term economic cooperation as support for their position on the recognition issue.

   We should not allow such gestures to be wrongly interpreted by the authorities of the former Yugoslav Republic of Macedonia. If we wish Ambassador O'Neill's mission to succeed, we should take care that no mixed signals reach Skopje.

   The Portuguese Presidency prepared a "package deal" which, in addition to the name problem, could resolve all the outstanding issues connected with recognition. This package should be part of the discussions currently being carried out by Ambassador O'Neill.

   I would urge all partners to convey to President Gligorov, in no uncertain terms, our will, as Community and as member-states, to stand firm by our December Declaration and the Lisbon Decision. And that his early compliance with it will not only prevent calamities of the nature he has repeatedly implied over the past two months, but will open the way for the safeguarding of the territorial integrity of his Republic and for peace and security in the region. Greece would be the first to join in such constructive steps.

On behalf of my Government, I would like to re-emphasize that Greece has made a serious effort toward a solution. We have discussed proposals and ideas that have already caused much concern and apprehension in important segments of the Greek public and the political parties. The parliamentary group of "New Democracy" recently approved unanimously a resolution insisting on the terms on which a viable solution of this problem should be found.

Following the official publication of Regulation No. 3031/92, Greece stands ready to resume oil supplies to the Former Yugoslav Republic of Macedonia immediately and without limit as to quantities, provided of course that the provisions of the Regulation are fully adhered to. This means that the authorities in Skopje must conform with the Regulation by, inter alia, using seals with the denomination "F.Y.R. Macedonia" for this territory as agreed in the General Affairs Council on 5 October last.

Additionally, we have said that we are prepared to send, if and when requested, aid to Skopje for humanitarian purposes, including oil for use in schools and hospitals, without any formalities whatsoever from any side. This offer of ours has never been taken up.

We have reached the "end of the rope". There are proposals on the table that if accepted will leave no one humiliated. We need and support the independence of the neighbouring Republic and we firmly believe that, through Greece, that Republic will be rendered politically and economically viable. But we cannot accept a decision, which will be a cause for constant irritation, quarrels over borders and instability in the wider Balkan region. In one word, we cannot accept to see the reopening of the "Macedonian Question" of the early decades of this century. Such an eventuality will cause terrible havoc and additional suffering in the Balkan.

I need not go over the points which speak for upholding the Lisbon Decision again. I hope you will agree that the "12" will see it advisable to communicate urgently, through any proper means, to President Gligorov our unswerving support for our common position.

Yours sincerely

Michael Papaconstantinou

## APPENDIX XIII

Previously unpublished letter that FYROM's President Kiro Gligorov sent to Greek Prime Minister Konstantinos Mitsotakis on 2 December 1992.

**PRESIDENT**
OF THE REPUBLIC OF MACEDONIA

Skopje, 2 December,1992

Dear Mr. Mitsotakis,

My intention to address you at this crucial moment for my country and people, immediately prior to the meeting of the European Community Council in Edinburgh, has been urged on by a single aim: it is the ultimate hour for the European Community to recognise the Republic of Macedonia!

All conditions for the international recognition of the Republic of Macedonia, which achieved its independance by peaceful and legitimate methods and preserved the peace thus becoming a barrier to the escalation of war in the South of the Balkans, are fulfilled.

You are familiar with the Golgotha passed by my country on the road to its constitution and international affirmation at a time of cataclisms in the area of former Yugoslavia. We are happy to have achieved preserving Macedonia from the war. The transition towards democracy has been carried by peaceful political means as well as inter-ethnic and inter-denominational tolerance. For all that we had, only through our efforts, to resolve extremely complex economic and social problems which are still seriously pressing us.

Determing our future and development as an independent, sovereign and equal member of the international community; we have built the highest principles of the United Nations Charter and the Conference on Security and Cooperation in Europe in the foundations of our state. We have chosen the European option and the policy of good-neighbourly relations and cooperation as priorities. On that base we have joined the efforts of the international community in overcomming the Yugoslav crisis. We have fully supported and met the European Community criteria for the establishment of new states, which has been confirmed by Dr. Badinter's Arbitration Commission Report.

I would take the liberty to remind you this, since there is unanimous feeling in the Republic of Macedonia that the European Community has not found strength and way for a just assessment of the elements according to which, the Republic of Macedonia should have been granted the widest international recognition so far. You are now facing yet another possibility to rectify this unjustice in a principled manner and to act preventivelly, maybe in the last moment, for preventing a new focus in the Balkans.

The flame of war is seriously threatening to expand from Bosnia Herzegovina towards the areas in which the Republic of Macedonia is located, too. The history is warning of the terrible repercussions of such an eventual war escalation over the whole Balkan area. On account of that an urgent international recognition of our country is of a decisive significance for the stability and peace in this region.

In the present conditions we are faced with great difficulties in the economic as well as other fields of life. You know of the additional difficulties our country suffers because of the impact of the international sanctions against FR Yugoslavia and because of the blockades on the supply of petrol imposed on us by neighbouring Greece. The international recognition by the European Community member-States as well as by other countries and international organisations and institutions, we are sure would represent the best way for a way out from the present unfavourable situation, for the peace in the Balkans and for the triumph of the principles on which the European Community is based.

During past eleven months we have undertaken a series of political steps aimed at assuring the European Community that we maintain a policy of good-neighbourlines and friendship, peace, cohabitation in the Balkans. Unfortunately, The Lisbon Declaration requires from us to erase the term Macedonia from the name of our country. This is a precedent in the history of nations and beyond the international standards. This request by the Republic of Greece was being followed by economic pressures and blockades on the Republic of Macedonia. In spite of all this, however, the Republic of Macedonia, facing great losses and difficulties, started a great number of initiatives for a peaceful and right solution of the international problems.

*I am calling upon you, again, on behalf of the citizens of the Republic of Macedonia, its legitimate bodies and in my own name, with an appeal for showing full understanding for arguments put forward. In the name of a good future between our countries and nations, in the name of peace and the principles the European Community is based on, I am asking you to undertake immediately the international recognition of the Republic of Macedonia by the European Community, and by your honoured country in particular.*

It would be a real expression of respect of the right of a small nation to self-determination, a support for the peace and stability in the region and a real step of a preventive activity against the threats of a new Balkan war.

Please receive Mr. Prime Minister, expressions of my highest considerations.

Kiro Gligorov<br>
President<br>
of the Republic of Macedonia

H.E. Mr. Constantin Mitsotakis
Prime Minister of the Hellenic Republic

# APPENDIX XIV

Letter that Antonis Samaras sent to Konstantinos Mitsotakis on 15 March 1993. It is published here in its entirety for the first time.

Κον Κωνσταντίνο Μητσοτάκη
Πρόεδρο της Κυβέρνησης
Μέγαρο Μαξίμου

Αθήνα, 15 Μαρτίου 1993

Κύριε Πρόεδρε,

Θα είμαι όσο το δυνατόν σύντομος.

Πράγματι η ενότητα -εάν βέβαια δεν αποτελεί ρητορική περιπλάνηση- μπορεί ασφαλώς ν' αποβεί σε αυτές τις ευαίσθητες ώρες σημαντική για τα συμφέροντα της πατρίδας μας. Αλλά και πολύτιμη για το αύριο της δικής μας παράταξης. Επομένως, εάν προσχωρήσατε -όπως τελευταία δηλώσατε- στην αξία και αναγκαιότητα αυτής της ενότητας οφείλετε, έστω και καθυστερημένα, για το καλό της χώρας και του κόμματος να κάνετε την ενότητα αυτή πράξη.

Και θα την κάνετε πράξη, όταν συμφωνήσετε ότι: οι σοβαρές διαφωνίες μας σε θέματα εξωτερικής πολιτικής, οικονομικής πρακτικής, κοινωνικής ευαισθησίας και διαχείρισης του δημοσίου χρήματος, δεν οφείλονται -όπως προπαγανδιστικά δηλώσατε- σε δήθεν δική μου "αιρετική" διάθεση, αλλά αντίθετα πηγάζουν από την ορθόδοξη θέση μου έναντι των αρχών της παράταξης και του προγράμματος του κόμματος που έχει σήμερα σχεδόν ξεχαστεί.

Επομένως, προς αντιμετώπιση των διεθνών εξελίξεων για τη χώρα μας και του εκλογικού αδιεξόδου ίσως εις την πατρίδα μας, προτείνω εγκαίρως τις εξής κρίσιμες διορθώσεις της κυβερνητικής πολιτικής:

Πρώτον, να εγκαταλειφθεί κάθε ιδέα συμβιβασμού στο Σκοπιανό. Να υλοποιηθεί η άρση όλων των ελληνικών δεσμεύσεων με τον ταυτόχρονη δήλωση ότι η Ελλάδα δεν δέχεται και δεν θα δεχθεί ποτέ μια ξένη Μακεδονία στα σύνορα της. Το εθνικό δημοψήφισμα, που έχω προτείνει, προσφέρει το νέο ισχυρό επιχείρημα τρέχοντος επανατοποθέτησης του θέματος έναντι Ε.Ο.Κ. και συμμάχων.

:ερον, ν'ακυρωθούν ή να ματαιωθούν όλες οι συμβάσεις (όπως ΑΓΕΤ, ΑΕΕ, Ε) Γιατί ο δηλητηριώδης θόρυβος και ο προβληματισμός που συν-προσ-τραυματίζουν σοβαρά την παράταξή μας. Και γιατί δεν είναι δυνατόν να προσπα μία κυβέρνηση της κάθαρσης σε ανακριτικές επιτροπές ούτε είναι δυνατόν να συνδέεται ένα υπερήφανο κόμμα, όπως το δικό μας, με τον κάθε Παντσαβόλτα.

Τρίτον, να κατευθυνθεί η οικονομία προς την ανάπτυξη και την ευαισθησία στα προβλήματα των ασθενέστερων κοινωνικών τάξεων και του Έλληνα αγρότη και να τεθεί καταληκτική ημερομηνία στη λιτότητα.

Τέλος, να περιορισθεί δραστικά και αποτελεσματικά ο υπερβολικός και καταστρεπτικός για το κόμμα "ζήλος" των ανθρώπων του περιβάλλοντός σας.

Είναι λοιπόν σαφές, κύριε Πρόεδρε, ότι το κλειδί της ενότητας βρίσκεται στην καρδιά του συνόλου αυτών των σοβαρών διαφωνιών. Να είστε επίσης βέβαιος ότι τις απόψεις αυτές συνυπογράφει η συντριπτική πλειοψηφία των οπαδών του κόμματός μας. Αν λοιπόν πιστεύετε στην ενότητα, όπως λέτε δημόσια, είναι στο χέρι σας να τολμήσετε.

Αν όμως τελικά δεν το πράξετε, τότε θα πρέπει ν'απαντηθεί από την ίδια την παράταξη, ποιός εκ των δύο -εσείς ή εγώ- είμαστε υπέρ ή κατά της Νέας Δημοκρατίας.

Με τιμή,

Αντώνης Κ. Σαμαράς

# Bibliography

Aggarwal K. Vinod. (1985), *Liberal Protectionism*, University of California Press, Berkeley.
Ahrweiller-Glikatzi Eleni, Evert Miltiades, Karamanlis Kostas, Kontogiorgis Yannis, Lambrias Tasos, Rezan Maria, Nikoloudis Elias. (1995), *Konstantinos Karamanlis the Last Great One*, Roes, Athens [in Greek].
Alexandris Alexis, Veremis Thanos, Kazakos Panos, Koufoudakis Vangelis, Rozakis A. Christos and Tsitsopoulos Yiorgos. (eds) (1991), *The Greek Turkish Relations, 1923-1987*, Gnosi, Athens [in Greek].
Allen David, Rummel Reinhardt and Wessels Wolfgang. (eds) (1982), *European Political Cooperation*, Butterworth, London.
Allen David and Smith Michael. (1991), 'Western Europe's Presence In The Contemporary International Arena', in Martin Holland. (ed), *The Future of European Political Cooperation*, Macmillan, London.
Allison T. Graham and Nicolaides Kalypso. (eds) (1997), *The Greek Paradox*, The MIT Press, Cambridge.
Anderson Benedict. (1983/1991), *Imagined Communities*, Verso, London.
Angelopoulos D. Iakovos. (1997), 'Wedding Exchanges in Culturally Mixed Agricultural Communities of Macedonia', in Vasilis K. Gounaris, Iakovos D. Michailidis and Giorgos B. Angellopoulos. (eds), *Identities in Macedonia*, Papazisi, Athens [in Greek].
Austin Robert. (1993), 'Albanian-Greek Relations: The Confrontation Continues', *RFE/RL Research Report*, vol. 2, pp. 30-5.
Averof-Tositsa Evangelos. (1996), *"Fire and Axe"*, Vivliopolion tis Estias, Athens [in Greek].
Axelrod Robert [a]. (1980), 'Effective Choice in the Prisoner's Dilemma', *Journal of Conflict Resolution*, vol. 24, pp. 3-25.
Axelrod Robert [b]. (1980), 'More Effective Choice in the Prisoner's Dilemma', *Journal of Conflict Resolution*, vol. 24, pp. 379-403.
Axelrod Robert. (1981), 'The Emergence of Cooperation Among Egoists', *The American Political Science Review*, vol. 75, pp. 306-17.
Axelrod Robert. (1984), *The Evolution of Co-Operation*, Basic Books, New York.

Axelrod Robert and Keohane O. Robert. (1993), 'Achieving Cooperation Under Anarchy: Strategies and Institutions', in David Baldwin. (ed), *Neorealism and Neoliberalism*, Columbia University Press, New York.

Baerentzen Lars, Iatrides O. John and Smith L. Ole. (eds) (1997), *Studies in the History of the Greek Civil War 1945-1949*, Museum Tusculanum Press, Copenhagen.

Baerentzen Lars. (1987), 'The "Paidomazoma" and the Queen's Camps', in Lars Baerentzen, John O. Iatrides and Ole L. Smith. (eds), *Studies in the History of the Greek Civil War 1945-1949*, Museum Tusculanum Press, Copenhagen.

Baerentzen Lars and Close H. David. (1993), 'The British Defeat of EAM, 1944-5', in David H. Close. (ed), *The Greek Civil War, 1943-1950*, Routledge, London.

Baker A. James III. (1995), *The Politics of Diplomacy*, G. P. Putnam's Sons, New York.

Baldwin David. (ed) (1993), *Neorealism and Neoliberalism*, Columbia University Press, New York.

Balwin David. (1993), 'Neoliberalism, Neorealism, and World Politics', in David Baldwin. (ed), *Neorealism and Neoliberalism*, Columbia University Press, New York.

Banac Ivo. (1984), *The National Question in Yugoslavia*, Cornell University Press, Ithaca.

Barker Elizabeth. (1950), *Macedonia Its Place in Balkan Power Politics*, Royal Institute of International Affairs, London.

Behr L. Roy. (1981), 'Nice Guys Finish Last—Sometimes', *Journal of Conflict Resolution*, vol. 25, pp. 289-300.

Beiner Ronald and Booth James William. (1993), *Kant and Political Philosophy*, Yale University Press, New Haven.

Bloed Arie and Wessel A. Ramses. (eds) (1994), *The Changing Functions of the Western European Union (WEU)*, Martinus Nijhoff Publishers, Dordrecht.

Bonvicini Gianni. (1988), 'Mechanisms and Procedures of EPC: More Than Traditional Diplomacy?', in Alfred E. Pijpers, Elfriede Regelsberger and Wolfgang Wessels. (eds), *European Political Cooperation in the 1980's*, Martinus Nijhoff Publishers, Dordrecht.

Brailsford N. Henry. (1903), 'The Macedonian Revolt', *Fortnigtly Review*, vol. 74, pp. 428-44.

Brailsford N. Henry. (1904), 'Bulgarians in Macedonia', *Fortnightly Review*, vol. 81, pp. 1049-59.

Brailsford N. Henry. (1906), *Macedonia Its Races and Their Future*, Methuen and Co, London.

Brown E. Michael, Lynn-Jones M. Sean and Miller E. Steven. (eds) (1995), *The Perils of Anarchy*, MIT Press, Cambridge.

Buchanan M. James and Tullock Gordon. (1962), *The Calculus of Consent*, University of Michigan Press, Ann Arbor.

Bulmer Simon and Scott Andrew. (eds) (1994), *Economic and Political Integration in Europe: Internal Dynamics and Global Context*, Blackwell Publishers, Oxford.

Bulmer Simon. (1991), 'Analysing EPC: The Case for Two-Tier Analysis', in Martin Holland. (ed), *The Future of European Political Cooperation*, Macmillan, London.

Busch L. Marc and Reinhardt R. Eric. (1993), 'Nice Strategies in a World of Relative Gains', *Journal of Conflict Resolution*, vol. 37, pp. 427-445.

Butterfield Herbert and Wight Martin. (eds) (1966), *Diplomatic Investigations*, George Allen and Unwin, London.

Cahen Alfred. (1989), *The Western European Union and NATO*, Brassey's, London.

Calleo P. David. (ed) (1976), *Money and the Coming World Order*, New York University Press, New York.

Calleo P. David. (1987), *Beyond American Hegemony*, Wheatsheaf Books, Brighton.

Carabott Philip. (1997), 'The Politics of Integration and Assimilation vis a vis the Slavo-Macedonian Minority of Inter-war Greece: From Parliamentary Inertia to Metaxist Repression', in Peter Mackridge and Eleni Yannakakis. (eds), *Ourselves and Others*, Berg, Oxford.

Cardoso Rita. (1987), 'The Project For a Political Community (1952-54)', in Roy Pryce. (ed), *The Dynamics of European Union*, Routledge, London.

Carnegie Endownment. (1914/1993), *The Other Balkan Wars*, Carnegie Endownment for International Peace, Washington DC.

Carr Edward Hallett. (1939/1964), *The Twenty Year's Crisis, 1919-1939*, Harper Torchbook, New York.

Chomsky Noam. (1999), *The New Military Humanism*, Common Courage Press, Monroe

Churchill S. Winston. (1948), *The Gathering Storm*, Houghton Mifflin Company, Boston.

Churchill S. Winston. (1953), *Triumph and Tragedy*, Houghton Mifflin Company, Boston.

Citizen's Movement. (1993), *Borders, Symbols, Stability*, The Citizen's Movement, Athens.

Clogg Richard. (1992), *A Concise History of Modern Greece*, Cambridge University Press, Cambridge.

Close H. David. (ed) (1993), *The Greek Civil War, 1943-1950*, Routledge, London.

Close H. David [a]. (1993), 'Introduction', in David H. Close. (ed), *The Greek Civil War, 1943-1950*, Routledge, London.

Close H. David. (1995), *The Origins of the Greek Civil War*, Longman, London.

Close H. David and Veremis Thanos. (1993), 'The Military Struggle, 1945-9', in David H. Close. (ed), *The Greek Civil War, 1943-1950*, Routledge, London.

Coase Ronald. (1960), 'The Problem of Social Cost', *The Journal of Law and Economics*, vol. 3, pp. 1-44.

Cohen J. Lenard. (1993), *Broken Bonds*, Westview Press, Boulder.

Cohen Benjamin. (1990), 'The Political Economy of Internationa Trade', *International Organization*, vol. 44, pp. 261-81.

Commission of the European Communities. (1989), *Guide to the Reform of the Community's Structural Funds*, Office for Official Publications of the European Community, Luxembourg.

Commission of the European Communities. (1992), *From the Single Act to Maastricht and Beyond. The Means to Match Our Ambitions*, Commission of the European Communities, Brussels.

Connor Walker. (1994), 'A Nation is a Nation, is a State, is an Ethnic Group, is a...', in John Hutchinson and Anthony D. Smith. (eds), *Nationalism*, Oxford University Press, Oxford.

Conybeare A. John. (1980), 'International Organization and the Theory of Property Rights', *International Organization*, vol. 34, pp. 307-34.

Costa Pereira Pedro Sancho da. (1988), 'The Use of a Secretariat', in Alfred E. Pijpers, Elfriede Regelsberger and Wolfgang Wessels. (eds), *European Political Cooperation in the 1980's*, Martinus Nijhoff Publishers, Dordrecht.

Couloumbis A. Theodore and Veremis M. Thanos. (eds) (1992), *The Southeast European Yearbook 1991*, Hellenic Foundation for Defence and Foreign Policy, Athens.

Council for Research Into South-Eastern Europe. (1993), *Macedonia and Its Relations With Greece*, Macedonian Academy of Sciences and Arts, Skopje.

Couloumbis A. Theodore. (1994), 'The Impact of EC (EU) Membership on Greece's Foreign Policy Profile', in Panos Kazakos and P. C. Ioakimidis. (eds), *Greece and EC Membership Evaluated*, Pinter Publishers, London.

Cowhey F. Peter and Long Edward. (1983), 'Testing Theories of Regime Change: Hegemonic Decline or Surplus Capacity?', *International Organization*, vol. 37, pp. 157-88.

Crampton J. R. (1987), *A Short History of Modern Bulgaria*, Cambridge University Press, Cambridge.

Crow Suzanne. (1992), 'Russia and the Macedonian Question', *RFE/RL Research Report*, vol. 1, pp. 36-9.

Crnobrnja Mihailo. (1994), *The Yugoslav Drama*, I. B. Tauris, London.

Daikin Douglas. (1966), *The Greek Struggle in Macedonia 1897-1913*, Institute for Balkan Studies, Thessaloniki.

Daikin Douglas (1972), *The Unification of Greece, 1770-1923*, St Martin's Press, New York.

Danchev Alex and Halverson Thomas. (eds) (1996). *International Perspectives on the Yugoslav Conflict*, Macmillan Press, London.
Danforth M. Loring. (1995), *The Macedonian Conflict*, Princeton University Press, Princeton.
Dangas Alexandros and Leontiadis Yiorgos. (1977), *Comintern and the Macedonian Question*, Trochalia, Thessaloniki [in Greek].
Davis Lance and North Douglass. (1971), *Institutional Change and American Economic Growth*, Cambridge: University Press, Cambridge.
Dawisha Karen and Parrott Bruce. (eds) (1977), *Power and the Struggle for Democracy in South-East Europe*, Cambridge University Press, London.
Dehousse Renaud and Weiler H. H., Joseph. (1991), 'EPC and the Single Act: From Soft Law to Hard Law?', in Martin Holland (ed), *The Future of European Political Cooperation*, Macmillan, London.
Department of Public Information. (1989), *Charter of the United Nations and Statute of the International Court of Justice*, United Nations, New York.
Deutsch W. Karl. (1968/1978), *The Analysis of International Relations*, Prentice-Hall, Engelwood Cliffs.
Deutsch W. Karl. (1979), *Tides Among Nations*, New York: The Free Press, 1979.
Diamantopoulos Thanasis. (1996), *Political Personalities of the 20th Century*, I. Sideris, Athens [in Greek].
Djilas Aleksa. (1993), 'Serbia's Milosevic: A Profile', *Foreign Affairs*, vol. 72, pp. 81-96.
Doudoumis E. Yiorgos. (1996), *Balkan Developments II*, Dodoni, Athens [in Greek].
Dougherty James and Pfaltzgraff L. Robert, Jr. (1981), *Contending Theories of International Relations*, Harper Row Publishers, New York.
Doyle W. Michael. (1986), 'Liberalism and World Politics', *American Political Science Review*, vol. 80, pp. 1151-65.
Doyle W. Michael. (1993), 'Liberalism and International Relations', in Ronald Beiner and William James Booth. (eds), *Kant and Political Philosophy*, Yale University Press, New Haven.
Doyle W. Michael. (1995), 'Liberalism and World Politics Revisited', in Charles Kegley. (ed), *Controversies in International Relations Theory*, St Martin's Press, New York.
Dragoumis Ion. (1907/1992), *Martyr's and Heroe's Blood*, Nea Thesis, Athens [in Greek].
Duff Andrew, Pinder John and Pryce Roy. (eds) (1994), *Maastricht and Beyond*, Routledge, London.
Duff Andrew. (1994), 'Ratifications', in Andrew Duff, John Pinder and Roy Pryce. (eds), *Maastricht and Beyond*, Routledge, London.

Economides Spyros. (1990), *The International Implications of the Greek Civil War: The Interaction of Domestic and External Forces, 1946-1949*, London School of Economics and Political Science, London, unpublished doctoral thesis.

Economides Spyros. (1995), 'Nationalism and Foreign Policy: Greece and the 'Macedoniam Question', *Brassey's Defence Yearbook 1995*, vol. 105, pp. 107-21.

Dunn John. (ed) (1990), *The Economic Limits To Modern Politics*, Cambridge University Press, Cambridge.

Edwards Geoffrey [a]. (1992), 'European Responses to the Yugoslav Crisis: An Interim Assessment', in Reinhardt Rummel. (ed), *Toward Political Union*, Princeton University Press, Princeton.

Edwards Geoffrey [b]. (1992), ''European Political Cooperation Put to the Test', in Alfred E. Pijpers. (ed), *The European Community at the Crossroads*, Kluwer Academic Publisher, The Hague.

Edwards Geoffrey and Spence David. (eds) (1994), *The European Commission*, Longman Current Affairs, London.

Eekelen Willem von. (1990), 'WEU and the Gulf Crisis', *Survival*, vol. 32, pp. 519-32.

El-Agraa M. Ali. (ed) (1983/1990), *The Economics of the European Community*, Philip Allan, London.

European University Institute (Florence) and the Institut fur Europaische Politic (Bonn), (eds) (1991). *European Political Cooperation Documentation Bulletin*, vol. 7.

Evrigenis Dimitris. (1961), *Ion Dragoumis and the Macedonian Struggle*, Idrima Meleton Hersonisou tou Aimou, Thessaloniki [in Greek].

Fromkin David. (1999), *Kosovo Crossing*, The Free Press, New York.

Fukuyama Francis. (1992), *The End of History and the Last Man*, Hamish Hamilton, London.

Gelner Ernest. (1983), *Nations and Nationalism*, Blackwell Publishers, Oxford.

Genscher Hans-Dietrich. (1997), *Memoirs*, Laverenthos, Athens [in Greek].

George Stephen. (1991), 'European Political Cooperation: A World Systems Perspective', in Martin Holland. (ed), *The Future of European Political Cooperation*, Macmillan, London.

Gerbet Pierre. (1987), 'In Search of Political Union: The Fouchet Plan', in Roy Pryce. (ed), *The Dynamics of European Union*, Routledge, London.

Gilbert Felix. (1970/1984), *The End of the European Era, 1890 to the Present*, W. W. Norton and Company, New York.

Gillespie Richard (ed) (1996), *Mediterranean Politics*, Pinter, London.

Gilpin Robert. (1975), *U.S. Power and the Multinational Corporation*, Basic Books, New York.

Gilpin Robert. (1977), 'Economic Interdependence and National Security in Historical Perspective', in Klaus Knorr and Frank N. Trager. (eds), *Economic Issues and*

*National Security*, National Security Education Program of New York University, Lawrence.
Gilpin Robert. (1981), *War and Change in International Politics*, Cambridge University Press, New York.
Gilpin Robert. (1989), 'The Theory of Hegemonic War', in Robert I. Rotberg and Theodore K. Rabb. (eds), *The Origin and Prevention of Major Wars*, Cambridge University Press, Cambridge.
Ginsberg H. Roy. (1989), *Foreign Policy Actions of the European Community: The Politics of Scale*, Lymme Rienner Publishers, Boulder.
Giokaris A, Dimitrakopoulos A. and Dipla X. (1994), *Points of Friction in Greek-Turkish Relations*, I. Sideris, Athens [in Greek].
Glenny Misha. (1992), *The Fall of Yugoslavia*, Penguin, London.
Glenny Misha. (1996), 'The Macedonian Question', in Alex Danchev and Thomas Halverson. (eds), *International Perspectives on the Yugoslav Conflict*, Macmillan Press, London.
Glenny Misha. (1997), 'The Temptation of Purgatory', in Graham T. Allison and Kalypso Nicolaides. (eds), *The Greek Paradox*, The MIT Press, Cambridge.
Gounaris C. Basil [a]. (1997), 'Reassessing Ninety Years of Greek Historiography on the 'Struggle for Macedonia 1904-1908', in Peter Mackridge and Eleni Yannakakis. (eds), *Ourselves and Others*, Berg, Oxford.
Gounaris C. Basil [b]. (1997), 'The Slavophones of Macedonia', in Konstantinos Tsitsikelis and Demitres Christopoulos. (eds), *The Minority Phenomenon in Greece*, Kritiki, Athens [in Greek].
Gounaris K. Vasilis, Panagiotopoulou Anna and Hotzidis Angelos. (eds) (1993), *The Events of 1903 Through the European Diplomatic Correspondence*, Mouseio Makedonikou Agona, Thessaloniki [in Greek].
Gounaris K. Vasilis, Michailidis D. Iakovos and Angellopoulos B. Giorgos. (eds) (1997), *Identities in Macedonia*, Papazisi, Athens [in Greek].
Gow James and Smith D.D. James. (1992), *Peace-Making, Peace-Keeping: European Security and the Yugoslav Wars*, London Defence Studies, London.
Gow James and Freedman Lawrence. (1992), 'Intervention in a Fragmenting State: the Case of Yugoslavia', in Nigel S. Rodley. (ed), *To Loose the Bands of Wickedness*, Brassey's, London.
Gow James. (1997), *Triumph of the Lack of Will*, Hurst and Company, London.
Gowa Joanne. (1984), 'Hegemons, IOs, and Markets: the Case of the Substitution Account', *International Organization*, vol. 38, pp. 661-83.
Gowa Joanne. (1986), 'Anarchy, Egoism, and Third Images: The Evolution Of Cooperation and International Relations', *International Organization*, vol. 40, pp. 167-86.

Gowa Joanne. (1995), 'Democratic States and International Disputes', *International Organization*, vol. 49, pp. 511-22.
Grieco Joseph. (1990), *Cooperation Among Nations*, Cornell University Press, Ithaca.
Grieco Joseph [a]. (1993), 'Anarchy and the Limits of Cooperation: A Realist Critique of the Newest Liberal Institutionalism', in David Baldwin. (ed), *Neorealism and Neoliberalism*, Columbia University Press, New York.
Grieco Joseph [b]. (1993), 'Understanding the Problem of International Cooperation: The Limits of Neoliberal Institutionalism and the Future of Realist Theory', in David Baldwin. (ed), *Neorealism and Neoliberalism*, Columbia University Press, New York.
Groom A.J.R and Taylor Paul. (eds) (1990), *Frameworks For International Cooperation*, Pinter Publishers, London.
Grunberg Isabelle. (1990), 'Exploring the "Myth" of Hegemonic Stability', *International Organization*, vol. 44, pp. 431-77.
Grunert Thomas. (1990), 'Establishing Security Policy in the European Community', in Reinhardt Rummel. (ed), *The Evolution of an International Actor*, Westview Press, Boulder.
Gulick Vose Edward. (1955), *Europe's Classical Balance of Power*, W. W. Norton and Company, New York.
Gutman Roy. (1993), *A Witness to Genocide*, Macmillan, New York.
Haas B. Ernst. (1975), 'Is There a Hole in the Whole? Knowledge, Technology, Interdependence, and the Construction of International Regimes', *International Organization*, vol. 29, pp. 827-76.
Haas B. Ernst. (1983), 'Words Can Hurt You; Or, Who Said What To Whom About Regimes', in Stephen D. Krasner. (ed), *International Regimes*, Cornell University Press, London.
Haggard Stephen and Simmons A. Beth. (1987), 'Theories of International Regimes', *International Organization*, vol. 41, pp. 491-517.
Hamlet L. Lawrence. (1992), 'The Core of Decision-Making', in Reinhardt Rummel. (ed), *Toward Political Union*, Westview Press, Boulder.
Hammond Nicholas. (1994), *Philip of Macedon*, Duckworth, London.
Hannequart Achille. (ed) (1992), *Economic and Social Cohesion in Europe*, Routledge, London.
Hannequart Achille [a]. (1992), 'Economic and Social Cohesion and the Structural Funds: An Introduction', in Achille Hannequart. (ed), *Economic and Social Cohesion in Europe*, Routledge, London.
Hanrieder F. Wolfram (1989), *Germany, America, Europe*, Yale University Press, New Haven.
Hanseclever Andreas, Mayer Peter and Rittberger Volker. (1997), *Theories of International Regimes*, Cambridge University Press, Cambridge.

Hardin Russell. (1982), *Collective Action*, The Johns Hopkins University Press, Baltimore.
Hayden M. Rober. (1992), 'Constitutional Nationalism in the Formerly Yugoslav Republics', *Slavic Review*, vol. 51, pp. 654-73.
Hellenic Foundation for Defense and Foreign Policy. (1993), *Memorandum Of Greece Concerning the Application of the Former Yugoslav Republic of Macedonia for Admission to the United Nations*, ELIAMEP, Athens.
Helsinki Watch Report. (1992), *War Crimes in Bosnia-Hercegovina*, Human Rights Watch, New York.
Hill Christopher. (ed) (1983), *National Foreign Policies and European Political Cooperation*, George Allen and Unwin, London.
Hill Christopher [a]. (1988), 'European Preoccupations With Terrorism', in Alfred E. Pijpers, Elfriede Regelsberger and Wolfgang Wessels. (eds), *European Political Cooperation in the 1980's*, Martinus Nijhoff Publishers, Dordrecht.
Hill Christopher [b]. (1988), 'Research into EPC: Tasks for The Future', in Alfred E. Pijpers, Elfriede Regelsberger and Wolfgang Wessels. (eds), *European Political Cooperation in the 1980's*, Martinus Nijhoff Publishers, Dordrecht.
Hill Christopher. (1992), 'The Foreign Policy of the European Community: Dream or Reality?', in Roy Macridis. (ed), *Foreign Policy in World Politics*, Prentice Hall International Editions, Engelwood Cliffs.
Hill Christopher. (1993), 'The Capability-Expectations Gap, or Conceptualising Europe's International Role', *Journal of Common Market Studies*, vol. 31, pp. 305-28.
Hill Christopher. (ed) (1996), *The Actors in Europe's Foreign Policy*, Routledge, London.
Hobsbawm J. Eric. (1990), *Nations and Nationalism Since 1780*, Cambridge University Press, Cambridge.
Hoffmann Stanley. (1968), *Conditions of World Order*, New York.
Hoffmann Stanley [a]. (1968), 'Obstinate or Obsolete? The Fate of the Nation State and the Case of Western Europe', in Stanley Hoffmann, *Conditions of World Order*, New York.
Hoffmann Stanley. (1982), 'Reflections on the Nation-State in Western Europe Today', *Journal of Common Market Studies*, vol. 21, pp. 21-37.
Holbrooke Richard. (1998), *To End A War*, Random House, New York.
Holland Martin. (ed) (1991), *The Future of European Political Cooperation*, Macmillan, London.
Holland Martin [a]. (1991), 'Introduction: EPC Theory and Empiricism', in Martin Holland. (ed), *The Future of European Political Cooperation*, Macmillan, London.
Holland Martin [b]. (1991), 'Sanctions as an EPC Instrument', in Martin Holland. (ed), *The Future of European Political Cooperation*, Macmillan, London.

Holland Martin. (1995), *European Union Common Foreign Policy*, St Martin's Press, London.
Hondros L. John. (1993), 'Greece and the German Occupation', in David H. Close. (ed), *The Greek Civil War, 1943-1950*, Routledge, London.
Human Rights Watch/Helsinki. (1994), *Denying Ethnic Identity*, Human Rights Watch, New York.
Huntington P. Samuel. (1993), 'The Clash of Civilizations?', *Foreign Affairs*, vol. 72, pp. 22-49.
Huntington P. Samuel. (1996), *The Clash of Civilizations and the Remaking of World Order*, Simon and Schuster, New York.
Hurd Douglas. (1994), 'Developing the Common Foreign and Security Policy', *International Affairs*, vol. 70, pp. 383-93.
Hutchinson John and Smith D. Anthony. (eds) (1994), *Nationalism*, Oxford University Press, Oxford.
Iatrides O. John. (ed) (1981), *Greece in the 1940s*, University Press of New England, Hanover.
Ifestos Panayiotis. (1987), *European Political Cooperation*, Avebury, Aldershot.
Ioakimidis P. C. (1996), 'The Role of Greece in the Development of EC Mediterranean Policy', in Richard Gillespie. (ed), *Mediterranean Politics*, Pinter, London.
Ioakimidis P. C. (1999), 'The Model of Foreign Policy-Making in Greece: Personalities Versus Institutions', in Stelios Stavridis, Theodore Couloumbis, Thanos Veremis and Neville Waites. (eds), *The Foreign Policies of the European Union's Mediterranean States and Applicant Countries in the 1990's*, Macmillan, London.
Ioannidou Alexandra. (1997), 'The Slavic Idioms in Greece', in Vasili K. Gounaris, Iakovos D. Michailidis and Giorgos B. Angellopoulos. (eds), *Identities in Macedonia*, Papazisi, Athens [in Greek].
Jacobs Francis, Corbett Richard and Shackleton Michael. (1990/1992), *The European Parliament*, Longman Current Affairs, London.
Jelavich Barbara. (1983), *History of the Balkans Twentieth Century*, Cambridge University Press, Cambridge.
Jenkins Roy. (1995), *Gladstone*, Macmillan, London.
Jervis Robert. (1976), *Perception and Misperception in International Politics*, Princeton University Press, Princeton.
Jervis Robert (1978), 'Cooperation Under the Security Dilemma', *World Politics*, vol. 30, pp. 167-214.
Jervis Robert. (1986), 'From Balance to Concert: A Study of International Security Cooperation', in Kenneth A. Oye. (ed), *Cooperation Under Anarchy*, Princeton University Press, Princeton.
Jopp Mathias, Rummel Reinhardt and Schmidt Peter. (eds) (1991), *Integration and Security in Western Europe*, Westview Press, Boulder.

Jopp Mathias. (1997), 'The Defense Dimension of the European Union: The Role and Performance of the WEU', in Elfriede Regelsberger, Phillipe de Tervarent de Schoutheete and Wolfgang Wessels. (eds), *Foreign Policy of the European Union*, Lynne Rienner Publishers, London.

Kant Immanuel. (1795/1983), *Perpetual Peace and Other Essays*, Hackett Publishing Company, Indianapolis, translated by Ted Humphrey.

Karakasidou N. Anastasia [a]. (1993), 'Politicizing Culture: Negating Ethnic Identity in Greek Macedonia', *Journal of Modern Greek Studies*, vol. 1, pp. 1-28.

Karakasidou N. Anastasia [b]. (1993), 'Fellow Travellers, Separate Roads: The KKE and the Macedonian Question', *East European Quarterly*, vol. 27, pp. 453-77.

Karakasidou N. Anastasia. (1994), 'National Ideologies, Histories and Popular Consciousness: A Response To Three Critics', *Balkan Studies*, vol. 35, pp. 113-46.

Karakasidou N. Anastasia [a]. (1997), 'Women of the Family, Women of the Nation: National Enculturation Among Slav-Speakers in North-West Greece', in Peter Mackridge and EleniYannakakis. (eds), *Ourselves and Others*, Berg, Oxford.

Karakasidou N. Anastasia [b]. (1997), *Fields of Wheat, Hills of Blood*, University of Chicago Press, Chicago.

Karavangelis Germanos (n.d), *Memoirs*, Barbounakis, Thessaloniki [in Greek].

Kartakis Elias. (n.d), *Change of Regime Karamanlis*, Roes, Athens [in Greek].

Katzenstein J. Peter, Keohane O. Robert and Krasner D. Stephen. (eds) (1999), *Exploration and Contestation in the Study of World Politics*, The MIT Press, Cambridge.

Kazakos Panos and Ioakimidis P.C. (eds) (1994), *Greece and EC Membership Evaluated*, Pinter Publishers, London.

Kedourie Elie. (1970), *Nationalism in Asia and Africa*, Frank Cass, London.

Kedourie Elie. (1960/1993), *Nationalism*, Blackwell Publishers, Oxford.

Keegan John. (1989), *The Second World War*, Viking, New York.

Kegley Charles. (1995), *Controversies in International Relations Theory*, St Martin's Press, New York.

Keohane O. Robert. (1983), 'The Demand for International Regimes', in Stephen D. Krasner. (ed), *International Regimes*, Cornell University Press, London.

Keohane O. Robert. (1984), *After Hegemony*, Princeton University Press, Princeton.

Keohane O. Robert. (ed) (1986), *Neorealism and its Critics*, Columbia University Press, New York

Keohane O. Robert [a]. (1986), 'Reciprocity in International Relations', *International Organization*, vol. 40, pp. 1-27.

Keohane O. Robert. (ed) (1989), *International Institutions and State Power*, Westview Press, Boulder.

Keohane O. Robert. [a]. (1989), 'Neoliberal Institutionalism: A Perspective on World Politics', in Robert O. Keohane. (ed), *International Institutions and State Power*, Westview Press, Boulder.

Keohane O. Robert [b]. (1989), 'Theory of World Politics: Structural Realism and Beyond', in Robert O. Keohane. (ed), *International Institutions and State Power*, Westview Press, Boulder.

Keohane O. Robert [c]. (1989), 'The Theory of Hegemonic Stability and Changes in International Economic Regimes, 1967-1977', in Robert O. Keohane. (ed), *International Institutions and State Power*, Westview Press, Boulder.

Keohane O. Robert [d]. (1989), 'International Institutions: Two Approaches', in Robert O. Keohane. (ed), *International Institutions and State Power*, Westview Press, Boulder.

Keohane O. Robert. (1990), 'International Liberalism Reconsidered', in John Dunn. (ed), *The Economic Limits To Modern Politics*, Cambridge University Press, Cambridge.

Keohane O. Robert [a]. (1993), 'The Analysis of International Regimes: Towards a European-American Research Programme', in Volker Rittberger. (ed), *Regime Theory and International Relations*, Oxford University Press, Oxford.

Keohane O. Robert [b]. (1993), 'Institutional Theory and the Realist Challenge After the Cold War', in David Baldwin. (ed), *Neorealism and Neoliberalism*, Columbia University Press, New York.

Keohane O. Robert and Nye S. Joseph. (eds) (1971), *Transnational Relations and World Politics*, Harvard University Press, Cambridge.

Keohane O. Robert and Nye S. Joseph. (1977), *Power and Interdependence*, Little Brown, Boston.

Keohane O. Robert and Nye S. Joseph. (1987), 'Power and Interdependence Revisited', *International Organization*, vol. 41, pp. 725-53.

Keohane O. Robert and Nye S. Joseph. (1989), *Power and Interdependence*, Scott Foresman and Company, Glenview (second edition).

Keohane O. Robert and Nye S. Joseph. (1993), 'Introduction', in Robert O. Keohane, Joseph S. Nye and Stanley Hoffmann. (eds), *After the Cold War*, Harvard University Press, Cambridge.

Keohane O. Robert, Nye S. Joseph and Hoffmann Stanley. (eds) (1993), *After the Cold War*, Harvard University Press, Cambridge.

Keohane O. Robert and Stanley Hoffmann. (1993), 'Conclusion: Structure, Strategy, and Institutional Roles', in Robert O. Keohane, Joseph S. Nye and Stanley Hoffmann. (eds), *After the Cold War*, Harvard University Press, Cambridge.

Keohane O. Robert and Martin L. Lisa. (1995), 'The Promise of Institutionalist Theory', *International Security*, vol. 20, pp. 39-51.

Kindleberger P. Charles. (1974), *The World in Depression, 1929-39*, University of California Press, Berkeley.
Kindleberger P. Charles. (1976), 'Systems of International Economic Organization' in David P. Calleo. (ed), *Money and the Coming World Order*, New York University Press, New York.
Kindleberger P. Charles. (1981), 'Dominance and Leadership in the International Economy', *International Studies Quarterly*, vol. 25, pp. 242-54.
Kindleberger P. Charles. (1986), 'Hierarchy Versus Inertial Cooperation', *International Organization*, vol. 40, pp. 841-47.
Kinross Patrick. (1964), *Ataturk*, Phoenix, London.
Kissinger Henry. (1982), *Years of Upheaval*, Weidenfeld and Nicholson and Michael Joseph, London.
Kitromilides M. Paschalis. (1989), '"Imagined Communities" and the Origins of the National Question in the Balkans, *European History Quarterly*, vol. 19, pp. 149-94.
Knorr Klaus and Trager N. Frank. (1977), *Economic Issues and National Security*, National Security Education Program of New York University, Lawrence.
Kofos Evangelos. (1964), *Nationalism and Communism in Macedonia*, Institute for Balkan Studies, Thessaloniki.
Kofos Evangelos. (ed) (1969), *The Macedonian Revolution During 1878*, Idrima Meleton Hersonisou tou Aimou, Thessaloniki [in Greek].
Kofos Evangelos. (1974), *Macedonia in Yugoslavian Historiography*, Etairia Makedonikon Spoudon, Thessaloniki [in Greek].
Kofos Evangelos. (1989), 'Dilemmas and Orientations of Greek Policy in Macedonia: 1878-1886', *Balkan Studies*, vol. 21, pp. 45-55.
Kofos Evangelos. (1986), 'The Macedonian Question: The Politics of Mutation', *Balkan Studies*, vol. 27, pp. 157-72.
Kofos Evangelos [a]. (1989), 'National Heritage and National Identity in Nineteenth and Twentieth Century Macedonia', *European History Quarterly*, vol. 19, pp. 229-67.
Kofos Evangelos [b]. (1989), *The Impact of the Macedonian Question on Civil Conflict in Greece (1943-1949)*, Hellenic Foundation for Defense and Foreign Policy, Athens.
Kofos Evangelos. (1992), 'The Macedonian Question From the Second World War Until Our Time', in Ioannis Koliopoulos and Ioannis Hasiotis. (eds), *Modern and Contemporary Macedonia B'*, Papazisi and Paratiritis, Thessaloniki [in Greek].
Kofos Evangelos [a]. (1994), *The Vision of "Greater Macedonia"*, The Friends of the Museum of the Macedonian Struggle, Thessaloniki.

Kofos Evangelos [b]. (1994), 'The Controversial Articles of FYROM's Constitution', in Yiannis Valinakis and Soteres Dales. (eds), *The Skopje Question*, I. Sideris, Athens [in Greek].

Kofos Evangelos [c]. (1994), 'Introduction', in Yiannis Valinakis and Soteres Dales. (eds), *The Skopje Question*, I. Sideris, Athens [in Greek].

Kofos Evangelos. (1996), *The Macedonian Issue. Assessment of Policy and Prospects*, unpublished lecture delivered at the Hellenic Centre in London on 23 February 1996 in Greek.

Kofos Evangelos. (1998), *Kosovo and Albanian Integration*, Papazese, Athens [in Greek].

Kofos Evangelos. (1999), 'Greek Policy Considerations Over FYROM Independence and Recognition', in James Pettifer. (ed), *The New Macedonian Question*, Macmillan, London.

Koliopoulos Ioannis and Hasiotis Ioannis. (eds) (1992), *Modern and Contemporary Macedonia B'*, Papazisi and Paratiritis, Thessaloniki [in Greek].

Koliopoulos S. Ioannis. (1989), 'Brigandage and Irredentism in Nineteenth-Century Greece', *European History Quarterly*, vol. 19, pp. 193-228.

Koliopoulos S. Ioannis. (1994), *Metaxas' Dictatorship and the War of '40*, Vanias, Thessaloniki [in Greek].

Koliopoulos S. Ioannis [a]. (1995), *Pillage of Beliefs A'*, Vanias, Thessaloniki [in Greek].

Koliopoulos S. Ioannis [b]. (1995), *Pillage of Beliefs B'*, Vanias, Thessaloniki [in Greek].

Koliopoulos S. Ioannis. (1997), 'The War Over the Identity and Numbers of Greece's Slav Macedonians', in Peter Mackridge and Eleni Yannakakis. (eds), *Ourselves and Others*, Berg, Oxford.

Kontis Vasilios, Kentrotis Kyriakos, Sfetas Spyros and Stephanidis D. Yiannis. (1993), *Skopje's Expansionist Policy*, Idrima Meleton Hersonisou tou Aimou, Thessaloniki [in Greek].

Kouris Leonidas. (1997), *Greece-Turkey*, A.A. Livani, Athens [in Greek].

Krasner D. Stephen. (1976), 'State Power and the Structure of International Trade', *World Politics*, vol. 38, pp. 317-43.

Krasner D. Stephen. (ed) (1983), *International Regimes*, Cornell University Press, London.

Krasner D. Stephen [a]. (1983), 'Structural Causes and Regime Consequences: Regimes as Intervening Variables', in Stephen D. Krasner. (ed), *International Regimes*, Cornell University Press, London.

Krasner D. Stephen [b]. (1983), 'Regimes and the Limits of Realism: Regimes as Autonomous Variables', in Stephen D. Krasner (ed), *International Regimes*, Cornell University Press, London.

Krasner D. Stephen, *Global Communications and National Power: Life on the Pareto Frontier*, in David Baldwin. (ed), *Neorealism and Neoliberalism*, Columbia University Press, New York.

Krasner D. Stephen. (1993), 'Sovereignty, Regimes and Human Rights', in Volker Rittberger. (ed), *Regime Theory and International Relations*, Oxford University Press, Oxford.

Krateros Ioannou. (1992), *The Issue of Skopje's Recognition*, Sakkoula, Athens [in Greek].

Kratochvil V. Friedrich. (1989), *Rules, Norms and Decisions*, Cambridge: Cambridge University Press, Cambridge.

Krause Stefan and Markotich Stan. (1996), 'Rump Yugoslavia and Macedonia Deal the Cards of Mutual Recognition', *Transition*, vol. 1, pp. 54-7.

Kydd Andrew and Snidal Duncan. (1993), 'Game-Theoretical Analysis of International Regimes', in Volker Rittberger. (ed), *Regime Theory and International Relations*, Oxford University Press, Oxford.

Kyrkos Leonidas. (1994), *The No-Exit Step of Nationalism*, Themelio, Athens [in Greek].

Lagakos Efstathios. (1996), *Populism in Our National Issues*, I. Sideris, Athens [in Greek].

Lagani Irini. (1996), *The 'Children-Gathering' and Greek-Yugoslav Relations, 1949-1953*, I. Sideris, Athens [in Greek].

Lambrias Takis. (ed) (1995), *Konstantinos Karamanlis Selected Texts*, Morphotiki Estia, Athens [in Greek].

Lak W. J. Maarten. (1992), 'The Constitutional Foundation', in Reinhardt Rummel. (ed), *Toward Political Union*, Westview Press, Boulder.

Layne Christopher. (1994), 'Kant or Cant: The Myth of the Democratic Peace', *International Security*, vol. 19, pp. 5-49.

Legg R. Keith and Roberts M. John. (1997), *Modern Greece*, Westview Press, Boulder.

Lindblom E. Charles. (1965), *The Intelligence of Democracy*, The Free Press, New York.

Lipson Charles. (1993), 'International Cooperation in Economic and Security Affairs', in David Baldwin. (ed), *Neorealism and Neoliberalism*, Columbia University Press, New York.

Lodge Juliet. (ed) (1989/1993), *The European Community and the Challenge of the Future*, Pinter Publishers, London.

Lodge Juliet [a]. (1989), 'European Political Cooperation: Towards the 1990's', in Juliet Lodge. (ed), *The European Community and the Challenge of the Future*, Pinter Publishers, London.

Lombra E. Raymond and Witte E. Willard. (1982), *Political Economy of International and Domestic Monetary Relations*, Iowa University Press, Ames.

Long David. (1995), 'The Harvard School of Liberal International Theory: A Case for Closure', *Millennium*, vol. 24, pp. 489-505.
Loulis Yiannis. (1995) *The Crisis of Politics in Greece*, I. Sideris, Athens [in Greek].
Lygeros Stavros. (1992), *Skopje, Winds of War in the Balkans*, A. A. Livani, Athens [in Greek].
Lygeros Stavros. (1996), *The Power Game*, A. A. Livani, Athens [in Greek].
McKeown J. Timothy. (1983), 'Hegemonic Stability Theory and 19th Century Tariff Levels in Europe', *International Organization*, vol. 37, pp. 73-91.
MacMillan John. (1995), 'A Kantian Protest Against the Peculiar Discourse of Inter-Liberal State Peace', *Millennium*, vol. 24, pp. 549-62.
Mackridge Peter and Yannakakis Eleni. (eds) (1997), *Ourselves and Others*, Berg, Oxford.
Macridis Roy. (ed) (1992), *Foreign Policy in World Politics*, Prentice Hall International Editions, Engelwood Cliffs.
Malcolm Noel. (1994), *Bosnia*, Macmillan, London.
Malcolm Noel, *Kosovo*, Macmillan, London.
Marks Gary (1992), 'Structural Policy in the European Union', in Alberta M. Sbagria. (ed), *Euro-Politics*, The Brookings Institution, Washington DC.
Martin L. Lisa. (1995), 'Institutions and Cooperation: Sanctions During the Falkland Islands Conflict', in Michael E. Brown, Sean M. Lynn-Jones and Steven E. Miller (eds), *The Perils of Anarchy*, MIT Press, Cambridge.
Martin L. Lisa and Simmons Beth. (1999), 'Theories and Empirical Studies of International Institutions', in Peter J. Katzenstein, Robert O. Keohane and Stephen D. Krasner. (eds), *Exploration and Contestation in the Study of World Politics*, The MIT Press, Cambridge.
Martis K. Nikolaos, *The Falsification of Macedonian History*, Athens: Evroekdotiki, 1983 [in Greek].
Mastanduno Michael. (1993), 'Do Relative Gains Matter? America's Response to Japanese Industrial Policy', in David Baldwin. (ed), *Neorealism and Neoliberalism*, Columbia University Press, New York.
Mayall James (1990), *Nationalism and International Society*, Cambridge University Press, Cambridge.
Mayne Richard. (ed) (1972), *Europe Tomorrow*, Fontana/Collins for Chatham House, London.
Mazarakis-Aenian C. J. (1992), *The Macedonian Question*, Dodoni, Athens.
Mazower Mark. (1993), *Inside Hitler's Greece*, Yale University Press, London.
Mazower Mark. (1996), 'Inroduction to the Study of Macedonia', *Journal of Modern Greek Studies*, vol. 14, pp. 229-35.

Mearsheimer John. (1995), 'The False Promise Of International Institutions, in Michael E. Brown, Sean M. Lynn-Jones and Steven E. Miller (eds), *The Perils of Anarchy*, MIT Press, Cambridge.

Mertus A. Julie. (1999), *Kosovo*, University of California Press, Berkeley.

Mela Natalia. (1964), *Pavlos Melas*, Sillogos Pros Diadosin ton Ellinikon Grammaton, Athens [in Greek].

Mertzos I. Nikos. (1992), *We the Macedonians*, I. Sideris, Athens [in Greek].

Mihailidis D. Iakovos. (1997), 'Slavophones and Refugees', in Vasilsi K. Gounaris, Iakovos D. Michailidis and Giorgos B. Angellopoulos. (eds), *Identities in Macedonia*, Papazisi, Athens [in Greek].

Milner Helen. (1992), 'International Theories of Cooperation Among Nations', *World Politics*, vol. 44, pp. 466-96.

Milner Helen. (1993), 'The Assumption of Anarchy in International Relations Theory: A Critique', in David Baldwin. (ed), *Neorealism and Neoliberalism*, Columbia University Press, New York.

Molle Willem. (1990), *The Economics of European Integration*, Dartmouth, Aldershot.

Montesquieu Charles de Secondat baron de. (1747/1989), *The Spirit of the Laws*, Cambridge University Press, Cambridge.

Moore Patrick. (1992), 'The London Conference on the Bosnian Crisis', *RFE/RL Research Report*, vol. 1, pp. 1-6.

Moravcsik Andrew, 'Preferences and Power in the European Community: A Liberal Intergovernmentalist Approach', in Simon Bulmer and Andrew Scott. (eds), *Economic and Political Integration in Europe: Internal Dynamics and Global Context*, Blackwell Publishers, Oxford.

Moravcsik Andrew. (1997), 'Taking Preferences Seriously: A Liberal Theory of International Politics', *International Organization*, vol. 51, pp. 513-53.

Mouseio Makedonikou Agona. (ed) (1997), *Greece's Counterattack in Macedonia 1905-1906*, Thessaloniki Politistiki Protevousa tis Evropes, Thessaloniki [in Greek].

Mouzelis Nikos. (1994), *Nationalism in Later Development*, Themelio, Athens [in Greek].

MRG Greece, Pettifer James and Poulton Hugh. (1994), *The Southern Balkans*, Minority Rights Group International, London.

Neumann B. Iver and Waever Ole. (ed) (1997), *The Future of International Relations*, Routledge, London.

Nuttall Simon. (1988), 'Where the European Commission Comes In', in Alfred E. Pijpers, Elfriede Regelsberger and Wolfgang Wessels. (eds), *European Political Cooperation in the 1980's*, Martinus Nijhoff Publishers, Dordrecht.

Nuttall Simon [a]. (1992), *European Political Co-operation*, Clarendon Press, Oxford.

Nuttall Simon [b]. (1992), 'The Institutional Network and the Instruments of Action', in Reinhardt Rummel. (ed), *Toward Political Union*, Westview Press, Boulder.

Nuttall Simon [a]. (1994), 'The Commission and Foreign Policy Making', in Geoffery Edwards and David Spence, (eds), *The European Commission*, Longman Current Affairs, London.

Nuttall Simon [b]. (1994), 'The EC and Yugoslavia-Deus ex Machina or Machina Sine Deo?', *Journal of Common Market Studies*, vol. 32, pp. 11-25.

O'Donnell Rory. (1992), 'Policy Requirements for Regional Balance in Economic and Monetary Union', in Achille Hannequart. (ed), *Economic and Social Cohesion in Europe*, Routledge, London.

Ohrgaard C. Jacob. (1997), '"Less than Supranational, More than Intergovernmental": European Political Cooperation and the Dynamics of Intergovernmental Integration', *Millennium*, vol. 26, pp. 1-29.

Olson Mancur. (1965/1971), *The Logic Of Collective Action*, Harvard University Press, Cambridge.

O'Meara L. Richard. (1984), 'Regimes and Their Implication for International Theory', *Millenium*, vol. 13, pp. 245-64.

O'Neil Robin. (1997), *The Macedonian Question: A Diplomatic Initiative in the 1990's*, unpublished lecture delivered for The Wydham Place Trust for Peace, World Order and the Rule of Law at the English Speaking Union Cultural Club in London on 4 November 1997.

Owen David. (1995), *Balkan Odyssey*, Victor Gollancz, London.

Owen David. (1995), *Balkan Odyssey CD-ROM*, Academic Edition: The Electric Company.

Oye A. Kenneth. (1985), 'Explaining Cooperation Under Anarchy: Hypotheses and Strategies', *World Politics*, vol. 38, pp. 1-24.

Oye A. Kenneth. (ed) (1986), *Cooperation Under Anarchy*, Princeton University Press, Princeton.

Palmer S. E. Jr and King R. R. (1971), *Yugoslav Communism and the Macedonian Question*, Archon Books, Hamden.

Pangle Thomas. (1973), *Montesquieu's Philosophy of Liberalism*, University of Chicago Press, Chicago.

Papaconstantinou Michalis. (1992), *Macedonia After the Macedonian Struggle*, Ermeias, Athens [in Greek].

Papaconstantinou Michalis. (1994), *The Diary of a Politician*, Vivliopolion tis Estias, Athens [in Greek].

Papadimitropoulos Damianos. (1994), *Greece in the Balkan Crisis*, Polis, Athens [in Greek].

Papandreou Dimitra. (1997), *10 Years and 54 Days*, A. A. Livani, Athens [in Greek].

Pavlowitch K. Stevan. (1971), *Yugoslavia*, Ernest Benn, London.

Pavlowitch K. Stevan. (1988), *The Improbable Survivor*, C. Hurst and Company, London.
Pavlowitch K. Stevan. (1992), *Tito, Yugoslavia's Great Dictator*, C. Hurst and Company, London.
Perry M. Duncan. (1988), *The Politics of Terror*, Duke University Press, Durham.
Perry M. Duncan [a]. (1992), 'Macedonia: A Balkan Problem and a European Dilemma', *RFE/RL Research Report*, vol. 1, pp. 35-45.
Perry M. Duncan [b]. (1992), 'The Republic of Macedonia and the Odds for Survival', *RFE/RL Research Report*, vol. 1, pp. 12-9.
Perry M. Duncan. (1993), 'Politics in the Republic of Macedonia: Issues and Parties', *RFE/RL Research Report*, vol. 2, pp. 31-7.
Perry M. Duncan. (1994), 'Macedonia', *RFE/RL Research Report*, vol. 3, pp. 83-6.
Perry M. Duncan. (1995), 'On the Road to Stability—Or Destruction?', *Transition*, vol. 1, pp. 40-8.
Perry M. Duncan. (1997), 'The Republic of Macedonia: Finding its Way', in Karen Dawisha Karen and Bruce Parrott. (eds), *Power, and the Struggle for Democracy in South-East Europe*, Cambridge University Press, London.
Pettifer James. (1977), *The Turkish Labyrinth*, Penguin, London.
Pettifer James. (ed) (1999), *The New Macedonian Question*, Macmillan, London.
Petkovski Mihail, Petreski Goce and Slaveski Trajko. (1993), 'Stabilization Efforts in the Republic of Macedonia', *RFE/RL Research Report*, vol. 2, pp. 34-7.
Petridis B. Pavlos. (1997), *The Politician Theodorakis*, Proskinio, Athens [in Greek].
Pijpers E. Alfred, Regelsberger Elfriede and Wessels Wolfgang. (eds) (1988), *European Political Cooperation in the 1980's*, Martinus Nijhoff Publishers, Dordrecht.
Pijpers E. Alfred. (1988), 'The Twelve Out-of-Area: A Civilian Power in an Uncivil World?', in Alfred E. Pijpers, Elfriede Regelsberger and Wolfgang Wessels. (eds), *European Political Cooperation in the 1980's*, Martinus Nijhoff Publishers, Dordrecht.
Pijpers E. Alfred. (1991), 'European Political Cooperation and the Realist Paradigm', in Martin Holland (ed), *The Future of European Political Cooperation*, Macmillan, London.
Pijpers E. Alfred. (ed) (1992), *The European Community at the Crossroads*, Kluwer Academic Publisher, The Hague.
Pollis Adamantia. (1992), 'Greek National Identity: Religious Minorities, Rights, and European Norms', *Journal of Modern Greek Studies*, vol. 10, pp. 171-91.
Poulton Hough. (1991/1993), *The Balkans*, Minority Rights Publications, London.
Poulton Hough. (1995), *Who Are the Macedonians?*, Hurst and Company, London.
Powell Robert. (1993), 'Absolute and Relative Gains in International Relations Theory', in David Baldwin. (ed), *Neorealism and Neoliberalism*, Columbia University Press, New York.

Powell Robert. (1994), 'Anarchy in International Relations Theory: The Neoralist-Neoliberal Debate', *International Organization*, vol. 48, pp. 313-44.

Pryce Roy. (ed) (1987), *The Dynamics of European Union*, Routledge, London.

Puchala Donald and Hopkins Raymond. (1983), 'International Regimes: Lessons From Inductive Analysis', in Stephen D. Krasner. (ed), *International Regimes*, Cornell University Press, London.

Putnam Robert. (1988), 'Diplomacy and Domestic Politics: The Logic of Two-Level Games', *International Organization*, vol. 42, pp. 427-60.

Rallis I. Georgios. (1995), *To Ears That Are Not Listening*, Ellinoekdotike, Athens [in Greek].

Ramet P. Sabrina. (1984/1992), *Nationalism and Federalism in Yugoslavia, 1962-1991*, Indiana University Press, Bloomington.

Regelsberger Elfriede, de Schoutheete de Tervarent Philippe and Wessels Wolfgang. (eds) (1997), *Foreign Policy of the European Union*, Lynne Rienner Publishers, London.

Regelsberger Elfriede. (1988), 'EPC in the 1980's: Reaching Another Plateau?', in Alfred E. Pijpers, Elfriede Regelsberger and Wolfgang Wessels. (eds), *European Political Cooperation in the 1980's*, Martinus Nijhoff Publishers, Dordrecht.

Regelsberger Elfriede. (1991), 'The Twelve's Dialogue with Third Countries: Progress Towards a Communaute d'Action?', in Martin Holland. (ed), *The Future of European Political Cooperation*, Macmillan, London.

Regelsberger Elfriede. (1997), *The Institutional Setup and Functioning of EPC/CFSP*, in Elfriede Regelsberger, Phillipe de Tervarent de Schoutheete and Wolfgang Wessels. (eds), *Foreign Policy of the European Union*, Lynne Rienner Publishers, London.

Republic of Macedonia Assembly of the Republic. (1991), *Constitution of the Republic of Macedonia*, Skopje.

Reuter Jens. (1999), 'Policy and Economy in Macedonia', in James Pettifer. (ed), *The New Macedonian Question*, Macmillan, London.

Ridley Jasper. (1994), *Tito*, Constable, London.

Rieff David. (1995), *Slaughterhouse*, Vintage, London.

Rittberger Volker. (ed) (1993), *Regime Theory and International Relations*, Oxford University Press, Oxford.

Rodley S. Nigel. (ed) (1992), *To Loose the Bands of Wickedness*, Brassey's. London.

Rosenau N. James. (1986), 'Before Cooperation: Hegemons, Regimes and Habit-Driven Actors in World Politics', *International Organization*, vol. 40, pp. 849-94.

Rossos Andrew. (1991), 'Document: The Macedonians of Aegean Macedonia: A British Officer's Report, 1944', *Slavonic and East European Review*, vol. 69, pp. 282-309.

Rotberg I. Robert and Rabb K. Theodore. (1989), *The Origin and Prevention of Major Wars*, Cambridge University Press, Cambridge.

Roudometof Victor. (1996), 'Nationalism and Identity Politics in the Balkans: Greece and the Macedonian Question', *Journal of Modern Greek Studies*, vol. 14, pp. 253-301.

Rousseau Jean Jacques. (1917), *A Lasting Peace Through the Federation of Europe*, Constable and Company Limited, London, translated by C. E Vaughan.

Rozakis Christos. (1996), *Political and Legal Dimensions of the New York Interim Agreement Between Greece and FYROM*, I. Sideris, Athens [in Greek].

Ruggie Gerard John and Kratochwil Friedrich. (1986), 'International Organization: A State of the Art on an Art of the State', *International Organization*, vol. 40, pp. 753-75.

Ruggie Gerard John. (1975), 'International Responses to Technology: Concepts and Trends', *International Organization*, vol. 29, pp. 557-83.

Ruggie Gerard John. (1983), 'International Regimes, Transactions, and Change: Embedded Liberalism in the Postwar Economic Order', in Stephen D. Krasner. (ed), *International Regimes*, Cornell University Press, London.

Ruggie Gerard John. (1986), 'Continuity and Transformation in the World Polity: Toward a Neorealist Synthesis', in Robert O. Koehane. (ed), *Neorealism and its Critics*, Columbia University Press, New York.

Ruggie Gerard John. (1992), 'Multilateralism: the Anatomy of an Institution', *International Organization*, vol. 46, pp. 561-98.

Ruggie Gerard John. (1995), 'At Home Abroad, Abroad at Home: International Liberalisation and Domestic Stability in the New World Economy, *Millennium*, vol. 24, pp. 507-26.

Rummel Reinhardt. (1988), 'Speaking with One Voice—and Beyond', in Alfred E. Pijpers, Elfriede Regelsberger and Wolfgang Wessels. (eds), *European Political Cooperation in the 1980's*, Martinus Nijhoff Publishers, Dordrecht.

Rummel Reinhardt. (ed) (1990), *The Evolution of an International Actor*, Westview Press, Boulder.

Rummel Reinhardt. (ed) (1992), *Toward Political Union*, Westview Press, Boulder.

Russett Bruce. (1993), *Grasping the Democratic Peace*, Princeton University Press, Princeton.

Sakellariou B. M. (ed) (1994), *Macedonia*, Ekdotiki Athinon, Athens.

Salmon C. Trevor. (1992), 'Testing Times for European Political Cooperation: The Gulf and Yugoslavia, 1990-1992', *International Affairs*, vol. 68, pp. 233-53.

Saritza Mathildi. (1996), 'FYROM's Economic Environment and Greece's Exports', in Charalambos Tsardanidis. (ed), *The Economic Relations Between Greece and the Former Yugoslav Republic of Macedonia*, I. Sideris, Athens [in Greek].

Sbagria M. Alberta. (ed) (1992), *Euro-Politics*, The Brookings Institution, Washington DC.

Schmidt Peter. (1990), 'West Germany and France: Convergent or Divergent Perspectives on European Security Cooperation?', in Reinhardt Rummel. (ed), *The Evolution of an International Actor*, Westview Press, Boulder.

Schoutheete Phillippe de. (1988), 'The Presidency and the Management of Political Cooperation', in Alfred E. Pijpers, Elfriede Regelsberger and Wolfgang Wessels. (eds), *European Political Cooperation in the 1980's*, Martinus Nijhoff Publishers, Dordrecht.

Schumpeter A. Joseph. (1995), *Imperialism and Social Classes*, Basil Blackwell, Oxford.

Scott Andrew. (1993), 'Financing the Community: The Delors II Package', in Juliet Lodge. (ed), *The European Community and the Challenge of the Future*, Pinter Publishers, London.

Seitanidis A. Diamantis. (1997), *The Causes of the Chronic Crisis in Greece's Centre-Right*, Papazisi, Athens [in Greek].

Sfetas Spyridon. (1996), 'Unwanted Allies and Uncontrolled Opponents: The Relations Between KKE and NOF During The Civil War', *Valkanika Symmeikta*, vol. 8, pp. 213-46 [in Greek].

Sfetas Spyridon and Kentrotis Kyriakos. (1994), 'Skopje In Search of Identity and International Recognition', *Balkan Studies*, vol. 35, pp. 337-77.

Silber Laura and Little Allan. (1995/1996), *The Death of Yugoslavia*, Penguin Books and BBC Books, London.

Singleton Fred. (1985), *A Short History of the Yugoslav Peoples*, Cambridge University Press, Cambridge.

Sjostedt Gunnar. (1977), *The External Role of the European Community*, Saxon House, Farnborough.

Skilakakis Thodoros. (1995), *In the Name of Macedonia*, Elleneke Evroekdotike, Athens [in Greek].

Smith D. Anthony. (1991), *National Identity*, Penguin, London.

Smith E. Michael. (1996), *The 'Europeanization' of European Political Cooperation*, Center for German and European Studies, Berkeley.

Smith L. Ole. (1993), '"The First Round"-The Civil War During the Occupation', in David H. Close. (ed), *The Greek Civil War, 1943-1950*, Routledge, London.

Smith Llewellyn Michael. (1998), *Ionian Vision*, Hurst and Company, London.

Snidal Duncan [a]. (1985), 'The Limits of Hegemonic Stability Theory', *International Organization*, vol. 39, pp. 579-614.

Snidal Duncan [b]. (1985) 'The Game THEORY of International Relations', *World Politics*, vol. 38, pp. 25-57.

Snidal Duncan [c]. (1985), 'Coordination Versus Prisoners' Dilemma: Implications for International Cooperation and Regimes', *The American Political Science Review*, vol. 79, pp. 923-42.
Snidal Duncan. (1993), 'Relative Gains and the Pattern of International Cooperation', in David Baldwin (ed), *Neorealism and Neoliberalism*, Columbia University Press, New York.
Stavridis Stelios, Couloumbis Theodore, Veremis Thanos and Waites Neville. (eds) (1999), *The Foreign Policies of the European Union's Mediterranean States and Applicant Countries in the 1990's*, Macmillan, London.
Stavrinou-Paximadopoulou Miranta. (1997), *Western Thrace in Bulgaria's Foreign Policy*, Gutenberg, Athens [in Greek].
Stavros Stephanos. (1995), 'The Legal Status of Minorities in Greece Today: The Adequacy of Their Protection in the Light of Current Human Rights Perceptions', *Journal of Modern Greek Studies*, vol. 13, pp. 1-32.
Stein Arthur. (1984), 'The Hegemon's Dilemma: Britain, the United States and the International Economic Order', *International Organisation*, vol. 38, pp. 355-86.
Stephanidis D. Ioannis. (1999), *Isle of Discord*, Hurst, London.
Strange Susan. (1983), 'Cave! Hic Dragones: A Critique of Regime Analysis', in Stephen D. Krasner. (ed), *International Regimes*, Cornell University Press, London.
Suhr Michael. (1997). 'Robert O. Keohane: A Contemporary Classic', in Iver B. Neumann and Ole Waever. (eds), *The Future of International Relations*, Routledge, London.
Svolopoulos Konstantinos. (ed) (1997), *Konstantinos Karamanlis 50 Years of Political History*, Idrima Konstantinos G. Karamanlis and Ekdotiki Athinon, 1997, Athens, [in Greek] 12 Volumes.
Tarkas Y. Alexandros. (1995), *Athens-Skopje. Behind the Closed Doors*, Laverenthos, Athens [in Greek], Volume 1.
Tarkas Y. Alexandros. (1997), *Athens-Skopje. Behind the Closed Doors*. Laverenthos, Athens, [in Greek], Volume 2.
Telloglou Tasos. (1996), *German Policy in the Yugoslav Region (1991-1995)*, Polis, Athens [in Greek].
Terme Rosa Maria Alonso. (1992), 'From the Draft Treaty of 1984 to the Intergovernmental Conferences of 1991', in Reinhardt Rummel. (ed), *Toward Political Union*, Westview Press, Boulder.
Theodoropoulos Vyron, Lagakos Evstathios, Papoulias Georgios and Tzounis Ioannis. (1995), *Thoughts and Querries for Our Foreign Policy*, I. Sideris, Athens [in Greek].
Theodoropoulos Vyron. (1988), *The Turks and We*, Fitrakis, Athens [in Greek].
Theodoropoulos Vyron. (1993), 'European Political Cooperation and Greek Diplomacy', in Loukas Tsoukalis. (ed), *Greece in the European Community*, Papazizi, Athens.

Theodoropoulos Vyron. (1966), *Review The Foreign Policy of Modern Greece*, I. Sideris, Athens [in Greek].

Thrift Nigel. (1983), 'On the Determination of Social Action in Space and Time', *Society and Space*, vol. 1, pp. 23-57.

Troebst Stefan. (1994),. 'Macedonia: Powder Keg Defused?', *RFE/RL Research Report*, vol. 3, pp. 33-41.

Tsakaloyiannis Panos. (1983), 'Greece: Old Problems', New Prospects, in Christopher Hill. (ed), *National Foreign Policies and European Political Cooperation*, George Allen and Unwin, London.

Tsakaloyiannis Panos. (1988), W*estern European Security in a Changing World*, European Institute of Public Administration, Maastricht.

Tsakaloyiannis Panos. (1991), 'The EC, EPC and the Decline of Bipolarity', in Martin Holland. (ed), *The Future of European Political Cooperation*, Macmillan, London.

Tsakaloyiannis Panos. (1996), 'Greece: The Limits to Convergence', in Christopher Hill. (ed), *The Actors in Europe's Foreign Policy*, Routledge, London.

Tsardanidis Charalambos. (ed) (1996), *The Economic Relations Between Greece and the Former Yugoslav Republic of Macedonia*, I. Sideris, Athens [in Greek].

Tsatsos Konstantinos. (1984), *The Unknown Karamanlis*, Evroekdotiki Athinon, Athens [in Greek].

Tsirkinides Harris. [1994], *Clouds in Macedonia...*, Gramma, Thessaloniki [in Greek].

Tsitsikelis Konstantinos and Christopoulos Demitres. (eds) (1997), *The Minority Phenomenon in Greece*, Kritiki, Athens [in Greek].

Tsoukalis Loukas. (ed) (1983), *The European Community*, Basil Blackwell, Oxford.

Tsoukalis Loukas. (ed) (1993), *Greece in the European Community*, Papazisi, Athens.

Tzermias N. Pavlos. (1990), *The Political Thought of Konstantinos Karamanlis*, Elliniki Evroekdotiki, Athens [in Greek].

Tziampiris Aristotle. *(1992), A Study in Failure? An Examination of the European Community's Response to the Yugoslav War*, London School of Economics and Political Science, unpublished MSc European Studies thesis.

Tzonis H. Theodoros. (1994), *Skopje's Legal and Political Regime*, I. Sideris, Athens [in Greek].

Urwin Derek. (1991), *The Community of Europe*, Longman, London.

Urzainqui Elvira and Andres de Rosario. (1992), 'The Lagging Regions of the Community', in Achille Hannequart. (ed), *Economic and Social Cohesion in Europe*, Routledge, London.

US Department of State. (1991), *Country Reports on Human Rights Practices for 1990*, US Government Printing Office, Washington DC.

Vacalopoulos E. Apostolos. (1996), *Modern Greek History 1204-1985*, Vanias, Thessaloniki [in Greek].

Vacalopoulos Konstantinos. (1989), *The Macedonian Question*, Paratiritis, Thessaloniki [in Greek].
Valden Sotiris. (1996), 'FYROM's Foreign Trade and Greece', in Charalambos Tsardanidis. (ed) *The Economic Relations Between Greece and the Former Yugoslav Republic of Macedonia*, I. Sideris, Athens [in Greek].
Valinakis Yiannis. (ed) (1992), *Yearbook of Defence and Foreign Policy '92: Greece and the World, 1990-91*, ELIAMEP, Athens [in Greek].
Valinakis Yiannis. (1993), 'Greece in European Political Cooperation: The First Ten Years', in Loukas Tsoukalis. (ed), *Greece in the European Community*, Papazizi, Athens.
Valinakis Yiannis and Dales Soteres. (eds) (1994), *The Skopje Question*, I. Sideris, Athens [in Greek].
Veremis Thanos. (1995), *Greece's Balkan Entanglement*, ELIAMEP-YALCO, Athens.
Veremis Thanos. (1997), 'The Revival of the 'Macedonian Question', 1991-1995', in Peter Mackridge and Eleni Yannakakis. (eds), *Ourselves and Others*, Berg, Oxford.
Veremis T., Couloumbis T., and Nikolakopoulos E. (eds) (1995), *The Hellenism of Albania*, I. Sideris, Athens [in Greek].
Veremis Thanos and Couloumbis Theodoros. (1997), *Greek Foreign Policy*, I. Sideris, Athens [in Greek].
Verenis Thanos and Kofos Evangelos. (eds) (1998), *Kosovo Avoiding Another Balkan War*, ELIAMEP, Athens.
Veremis Thanos and Triantaphyllou Dimitrios. (eds) (1999), *Kosovo and the Albanian Dimension in Southeastern Europe*, ELIAMEP, Athens.
Vickers Miranda. (1998), *Between Serb and Albanian*, Hurst and Company, London.
Vlasidis Vlasis and Karakostanoglou Veniamin. (1995), 'Recycling Propaganda: Remarks on Recent Reports on Greece's "Slav-Macedonian Minority"', *Balkan Studies*, vol. 36, pp. 151-70.
Vlasidis Vlasis. (1997), 'The Autonomy of Macedonia: From Theory to Action' in Vasilis K Gounaris, Iakovos D. Michailidis and Gioros B. Angellopoulos. (eds), *Identities in Macedonia*, Papazisi, Athens [in Greek].
Voutira Eftihia. (1997), 'Population Transfers and Resettlement Policies in Inter-War Europe: The Case of Asia Minor Refugees in Macedonia from an International and National Perspective', in Peter Mackridge and Eleni Yannakakis. (eds), *Ourselves and Others*, Berg, Oxford.
Vouri Sophia. (1992), *Education and Nationalism in the Balkans*, Paraskinio, Athens [in Greek].
Vulliamy Ed. (1994), *Seasons in Hell*, Simon and Schuster, London.
Wagner R. Harrison. (1983), 'The Theory of Games and the Problem of International Cooperation', *The American Political Science Review*, vol. 77, pp. 330-46.

Wallace Helen, Wallace William and Webb Carole. (eds) (1977/1983), *Policy Making in the European Community*, John Wiley and Sons, Chichester.

Wallace William [a]. (1977/1983), 'Political Cooperation: Integration Through Intergovernmentalism', in Helen Wallace, William Wallace and Carole Webb. (eds), *Policy Making in the European Community*, John Wiley and Sons, Chichester.

Wallace William [b]. (1977/1983), 'Less Than a Federation, More Than a Regime: The Community as a Political System', in Helen Wallace, William Wallace and Carole Webb. (eds), *Policy Making in the European Community*, John Wiley and Sons, Chichester.

Waltz Kenneth. (1954/1959), *Man, the State and War*, Columbia University Press, New York.

Waltz Kenneth. (1962), 'Kant, Liberalism, and War', *American Political Science Review*, vol. 56, pp. 331-40.

Waltz Kenneth. (1979), *Theory of International Politics*, McGraw Hill, Reading.

Webb Carole. (1983), 'Theoretical Perspectives and Problems', in Helen Wallace, William Wallace and Carole Webb. (eds), *Policy Making in the European Community*, John Wiley and Sons, Chichester.

Weede Erich. (1984), 'Democracy and War Involvement', *Journal of Conflict Resolution*, vol. 28, pp. 649-64.

Weiler Joseph and Wessels Wolfgang. (1988), 'EPC and the Challenge of Theory', in Alfred E. Pijpers, Elfriede Regelsberger and Wolfgang Wessels. (eds), *European Political Cooperation in the 1980's*, Martinus Nijhoff Publishers, Dordrecht.

Weller Marc. (1992), 'The International Response to the Dissolution of the Socialist Federal Republic of Yugoslavia', *American Journal of International Law*, vol. 86, pp. 569-607.

Wessels Wolfgang. (1982), 'European Political Cooperation: A New Approach to European Foreign Policy', in David Allen, Reinhardt Rummel and Wolfgang Wessels. (eds), *European Political Cooperation*, Butterworth, London.

Wessels Wolfgang. (1991), 'EPC After the Single European Act: Towards a European Foreign Policy Via Treaty Obligations?', in Martin Holland. (ed), *The Future of European Political Cooperation*, Macmillan, London.

West Richard. (1994), *Tito and the Rise and Fall of Yugoslavia*, Sinclair-Stevenson, London.

Wight Martin. (1966), 'The Balance of Power', in Herbert Butterfield and Martin Wight. (eds), *Diplomatic Investigations*, George Allen and Unwin, London.

Wight Martin (1979/1986), *Power Politics*, Penguin Books, London.

Woodhouse M. Christopher. (1976), *The Struggle For Greece, 1941-9*, Hart-Davis and MacGibbon, London edited by Hedley Bull and Carsten Holbraad.

Woodward L. Susan. (1995), *Balkan Tragedy*, The Brookings Institution, Washington DC.

Woodward L. Susan. (1997), 'Rethinking Security in the Post-Yugoslav Era', in Graham T. Allison and Kalypso Nicolaides. (eds), *The Greek Paradox*, The MIT Press, Cambridge.
Yanoulopoulos Yannis. (1999), *Our Noble Blindness*, Vivliorama, Athens [in Greek].
Young R. Oran. (1989), *International Cooperation*, Cornell University Press, Ithaca.
Young R. Oran (1994), *International Governance*, Cornell University Press, Ithaca.
Zahariadis Nikolaos. (1996), 'Greek Policy Toward the Former Yugoslav Republic of Macedonia, 1991-1995', *Journal Of Modern Greek Studies*, vol. 14, pp. 303-27.
Zimmermann Warren. (1995), 'Origins of a Catastrophe', *Foreign Affairs*, vol. 74, pp. 2-20.

**ARTICLES** from the following newspapers and magazines:
The Economist
Eleftherotypia
Ependytis
Exousia
Financial Times
The Guardian
The Independent
International Herald Tribune
E Kathimerini
Makedonia
Le Monde Diplomatique
Ta Nea
The New Republic
Newsweek
The New York Times
Oikonomikos Tachydromos
Rizospastis
Time
The Times
To Vima

**INTERVIEWS** with:
Mr Ljupco Arsovski (3 February 1997 and 11 April 1997).
Ms Maria Damanaki (30 January 1997).
Mr Viktor Dimovski (29 September 1997).
Mr Evangelos Kofos (5 January 1997).

Mr Elias Lengeris (27 August 1997).
Mr Ioannis Mertzos (18 December 1996).
Mr Konstantinos Mitsotakis (10 April 1997).
Mr Petros Moliviatis (9 January 1997).
Mr Michalis Papaconstantinou (23 December 1996, 10 January 1997 and 10 April 1997).
Mr Stelios Papathemelis (11 January 1997).
Mr Michalis Papayannakis (10 January 1997).
Mr Blaze Risteski (29 September 1997).
Mr Antonis Samaras (24 December 1996 and 3 February 1997).
Mr Theodoros Skilakakis (15 April 1997).
Mr Alexandros Tarkas (9 April 1997).
Mr Apostolos Tsohatzopoulos (3 August 1997).
Mr Ioannis Tzounis (14 April 1997).
Ms Olivera Vasileva (29 September 1997).
Mr Yiannis Vrahatis (30 August 1997).

# Index

anarchy 12
Andreotti 97
Anti-Fascist Assembly of the National Liberation of Macedonia (ASNOM) 46, 57
Arbitration Commission (AC) 64, 66, 70, 75, 92
Athens demonstration 153

Baker James 114
Balkan Communist Federation 44
Battle of the Sexes 13
Bosnia (recognition of) 126
Bosnia-Herzegovina's (recognition of) 121
boycott 112
Brioni Accord 65
Bulgarian Orthodox Church (Exarchate) 40

Cabinet meeting, 4 December 1991 70
Carrington, Lord 88, 123
Churchill Winston S. 137
Coase theorem 7
Cohesion Fund 90
Collective action (problem of) 6
Comintern 45
Commercial liberalism 11
Common foreign and security policy [CFSP] 22
Commission 28
Committee of Senior Officials (CSO) 65

Conference for Security and Cooperation in Europe (CSCE) 28, 65
  (meeting in Moscow on 27 September 1991) 67
Congress of Berlin 41
Cooperation and Trade Agreement with Yugoslavia 68
COREU 24
Council of Foreign Ministers 25

Damanaki Maria 128
Delors Jacques 64, 65, 123
Dekemvriana (December events) 57
Democratic Army of Greece (DSE) 47
Dual name formula 142, 156
Dubrovnik 68

EAM (National Liberation Front) 45, 56
ELAS (National Popular Liberation Army) 45, 46
Embargo 145
Ethnic cleansing 140
European Council 26
  meeting, Lisbon, 26 and 27 June 1992 143
  meeting, Birmingham, 11 and 12 December 1992 147
  meeting, Edinburgh, 11 December 1992 153
European Defence Community (EDC) 21

European Political Cooperation (EPC)
  decision making procedures 30
  norms 25
  organicational form 33
  principles 23
  rules 28
  scope 32
European Regional Development Fund (ERDF) 90
Exarchate 40, 42
Externalities 7

Fifth Comintern Congress 44
First Balkan War 43
First Council of the Political Leaders 109
First World War 44
Fouchet Plan 22
FYROM
  declaration of indepence 67
  irrentist propaganda against Greece 50
Functional Approach to International Regimes 4

Gaulle, Charles de 22
Genscher, Hans-Dietrich 71, 137
Gligorov, Kiro 144, 146, 152
Greek - Serbian relations 86, 155
Greek Memorandum on Yugoslav Macedonia 66
Greek oil embargo against FYROM 144
Guimaraes decision 138, 139

hegemonic stability theory 7, 17
Hellenism 42
Hurd, Douglas 138

Ilinden 42

IMRO 41, 56
Institutionalism (conditional nature) 12
Institutionalist liberalism 11
irredentist propaganda 50

JNA 68
Kalamidas (Ambassador) 74
Kant Immanuel 18
Karavangelis Germanos 54
King Boris III 45
KKE 45, 48, 71, 99, 109
KKE's Fifth Plenum 47

Lliberalism 10
Lisbon Declaration 143, 144, 146, 148, 150, 152, 154
London Conference on 26 and 27 August 1992 145

Macedonian Revolutionary Organisation (IMRO) 41
Marakis, Nikos 74
Melas, Pavlos 42, 55
Metaxas, Ioannis 56, 58
Michelis, Giannis de 72
millet system 40, 53
Milosevic, Slobodan 63, 87
Montesquieu 19
Moliviatis, Ioannis 115

National Democratic Greek League-EDES 45
National Liberation Front (NOF) 47, 57
Neoliberalism 11, 12, 19
New Democracy's MPs meeting, 21 October 1992 147

## INDEX

O'Neil, Robin (Ambassador) 147, 148
O'Neil Report 150, 155
Organisation for the Reconstruction of the KKE (OAKKE) 49

Panhellenic Socialist Movement (PASOK) 73
Papaconstantinou, Michalis 146, 147, 153
Papandreou Andreas 142
Pareto optimal 15
PD: Prisoner's Dilemma 4, 5
Petersberg Declaration 92
Pinheiro 128
Pinheiro Package 101, 117, 127
pluralistic security community 23
Political Committee 25
politics of scale 23, 24
Politiki, Anixi 147
Public goods 16

Rainbow Party 49
Rallis Georgios 73
Reciprocity 5, 9, 95, 126
Regional problems 89
Regulatory liberalism 10
Republican liberalism 10
reputational concerns 94
restrictive interpretation of the third EPC condition 73

Second Balkan War 43, 55
Second Council of the Political Leaders 122
Secretariat 33, 34
Semvouleo tis Epikrateias 92
shadow of the future 5, 9, 93, 94, 126

Slav Macedonian Popular Liberation Front (SNOF) 46, 56

Trangas, George 112
Tempo 57
Theodorakis, Mikis 71
Thessaloniki demonstration 99, 101
Third Council of the Political Leaders 141
Third Financial Protocol between the Community and Yugoslavia 64, 65
Three conditions 72
TIT FOR TAT 4
Tito (Josip Broz) 46, 47, 57, 96
Treaty of Bucharest 43, 45
Treaty of Lausanne 56
Treaty of Neuilly 44
Treaty of San Stefano 41
Troika 64
Tzounis Ioannis 121

UN Security Council Resolution 757 140

Vance, Cyrus 123
Varkiza Agreement 47
Venizelos Eleftherios 174

Western European Union (WEU) 22, 90, 92
  Article 178
  membership 91, 95

Young Turk revolution 42
Yugoslav National Army (JNA) 64

Zachariades Nikos 47, 57